T0355085

Called Beyond Our Selves

Called Beyond Our Selves

Vocation and the Common Good

Edited by

ERIN VANLANINGHAM

OXFORD
UNIVERSITY PRESS

OXFORD
UNIVERSITY PRESS

Oxford University Press is a department of the University of Oxford. It furthers
the University's objective of excellence in research, scholarship, and education
by publishing worldwide. Oxford is a registered trade mark of Oxford University
Press in the UK and certain other countries.

Published in the United States of America by Oxford University Press
198 Madison Avenue, New York, NY 10016, United States of America.

© Oxford University Press 2024

Library of Congress Cataloging-in-Publication Data
Names: VanLaningham, Erin, editor. | Hass, Marjorie, 1965– author of foreword.
Title: Called beyond our selves : vocation and the common good /
[edited by Erin VanLaningham ; foreword by Marjorie Hass].
Description: First edition. | New York : Oxford University Press, [2024] | Includes index.
Identifiers: LCCN 2023043016 (print) | LCCN 2023043017 (ebook) |
ISBN 9780197691915 (hardback) | ISBN 9780197691922 (epub) |
ISBN 9780197691939 | ISBN 9780197691946
Subjects: LCSH: Moral education (Higher) | Vocation. |
Common good—Religious aspects. | Collective settlements—Religious life.
Classification: LCC LC268 .C2416 2024 (print) | LCC LC268 (ebook) |
DDC 378/.014—dc23/eng/20231025
LC record available at https://lccn.loc.gov/2023043016
LC ebook record available at https://lccn.loc.gov/2023043017

DOI: 10.1093/oso/9780197691915.001.0001

Printed in Canada by Marquis Book Printing

Dedicated, with gratitude, to

Paul J. Wadell
voice of the virtues
champion of justice
teacher of the good
friend to all

Contents

Foreword

The appearance of a new volume in the NetVUE Scholarly Resources Project is a moment for celebration and reflection. As was the case with its three sister volumes, *Called Beyond Our Selves: Vocation and the Common Good* both reflects and shapes the intellectual ground from which vocation emerges as an object of study and practice in the undergraduate curriculum.

Earlier volumes in this series have focused on the meaning of vocation, on vocation across academic disciplines, and on the conceptual efficacy of vocations across differing religious and social traditions. Dr. VanLaningham has brought, to this current volume, the keen insight that the relationship between vocation and the common good is of special note, making this volume especially timely. She has inspired the volume's other authors to bring both scholarly insight and the practical knowledge that comes from ongoing engagement with students. Moreover, she led her contributors in a multiyear dialogue, and their mutual engagement shows in the depth of the work as well as in the emerging shared vocabulary evident in educating for vocation. The result is a book that can enjoyably be read cover to cover or that can be consulted chapter by chapter for one's own enlightenment or for use in a classroom or discussion group.

This project has been shaped by its context, and the authors wrestle with the injustices revealed by a global pandemic. These include the ways embedded inequalities continue to shape our present and our thinking about who is entitled to pursue vocation. Crucially, this book appears in the midst of a cultural reckoning about the value of higher education and about the nature of work that is almost wholly defined in terms of individual rather than collective flourishing. The public conversation about whether college matters too often devolves into a debate about what matters more: starting salary or earnings over a lifetime. Young people are encouraged to develop a personal influencer brand and to think seriously about hopping into the gig economy or the "work from anywhere" lifestyle as a means of gaining personal freedom at the expense of rootedness, relationships, or the long-term satisfaction of building a community. And most vividly, we see the tensions within even so-called effective altruism as its most visible proponent falls from grace and reveals the illusion of thinking we can do good on the side, and that a financial contribution will somehow outweigh the pillaging and scheming of our professional lives.

The authors here return us to a deeper and wider conception of what it means to succeed and to flourish. Situating vocation within an attention to the common good reminds us of the importance of considering the whole person and the whole society. In so doing, it reveals an innovative vocabulary and a set of practices for engaging students and others in the sublime effort of discernment and calling.

This volume marks an important transition in the series of which it is a part, as editorial duties are handed off from David S. Cunningham to Erin VanLaningham. David's editorial leadership shaped this series from its inception and through the first three volumes. Indeed, the centrality of the NetVUE Scholarly Resources Project to the broader NetVUE community, and increasingly to the ways that students are invited into the process of building careers and lives, is a result of the expansion of NetVUE's work under David's stewardship as the network's director.

The Network for Vocation in Undergraduate Education (NetVUE), a project of the Council of Independent Colleges (CIC), is a nationwide consortium of over three hundred colleges and universities. For more than a decade, these institutions have been committed to including reflection on vocation as an important aspect of the undergraduate experience. They have shared insights, effective practices, lessons learned, and stories of success. Touching more than a million students every year, NetVUE and its members are transforming the ways that students integrate academic study with personal conviction, religious and spiritual yearning, and engagement with the world's most pressing problems.

Along with Lynne Spoelhof and a number of additional full- and part-time staff at CIC, the NetVUE leadership has brought about a dramatic transformation at hundreds of colleges, affecting more than a million students a year. Erin has capably taken the reigns of the editorial process and we look forward to her continuing influence on theory and practice.

This work would not be possible without the financial support of Lilly Endowment Inc. and the personal commitment of Christopher L. Coble, vice president for religion at Lilly, as well as that of Jessicah Duckworth and many other Endowment staff. It is remarkable to work with funders who so fully embody the spirit and mission of giving for the common good and who themselves are clearly called to their work.

My hope is that the chapters in this volume provoke thought and motivate action. May they serve their readers as a guide for deeper reflection on vocation and an impetus toward engaging with others in acts that heal our world.

Marjorie Hass
President
Council of Independent Colleges

Preface

This book was developed as part of the Network for Vocation in Undergraduate Education (NetVUE) Scholarly Resources Project. The three previous volumes—*At This Time and In This Place: Vocation and Higher Education* (2016), *Vocation across the Academy: A New Vocabulary for Higher Education* (2017), and *Hearing Vocation Differently: Meaning, Purpose, and Identity in the Multi-Faith Academy* (2019)—were all published by Oxford University Press and edited by David S. Cunningham. The project's goal through these earlier works was to enrich, expand, and deepen the conversation around vocation within undergraduate education. These volumes provided models of pedagogical work, disciplinary approaches, and the flexibility and relevance of the concept and language of vocation as it relates to multiple faith perspectives. The series argued for the importance of vocation to today's undergraduates as they explore their identities, their purpose in the world, and what it means to live a good life.

This new volume, building upon these earlier collections, prioritizes the context of our common life when educating for vocational discernment. By exploring one's purpose in relation to contributing to the common good, the contributors believe that we can more fully understand what it means to be called beyond self, to the meeting between individual and collective flourishing. This work involves significant engagement with questions of justice and injustice, trauma and compassion. It necessitates a recognition of our connection to others in the past, present, and future. Vocation is a call to serve neighbor and to value our interdependence. We are part of an ecology of the common good, called to the commons to engage with the uncommon, to seek mutuality with others, and to care for our environment. Our volume takes up the calls of contemporary crises—the global health pandemic, bias toward the LGBTQIA+ community, antisemitism, gun violence, racial injustice, economic disparities, climate change—and seeks to provide models and practices, explorations and frameworks, for situating vocation very directly as part of the call to our communities. It is a shift in the way we talk about vocation, beginning with "we" instead of "me." The authors see higher education as uniquely situated to contribute to the common good through formation of undergraduates to engage with questions of purpose and meaning throughout their lives, helping others to do the same.

The contributors to this volume gathered over the course of a year to consider this topic, doing so with extraordinary commitment and care to the issues of the common good and questions of vocation in connection with others. The book bears witness to the deep work of the mind and heart that they bring to their classrooms and scholarship, campuses and conversations. Their willingness to engage in the exploration of purpose and meaning in a time of multiple pandemics and significant injustice in the world demonstrates their character and integrity, as well as their accomplished and nuanced thinking about what it means to teach vocation in the context of the common good. As their vocational biographies reveal, they are exemplars of how to act with courage for justice, to teach with compassion, and to walk in solidarity with others. Their chapters inspire, challenge, and imagine new pathways for all of us in higher education—I hope that you learn as much from them as I have.

On behalf of the authors, I wish to thank those who made this work possible. First, the project is supported by Lilly Endowment Inc., which we thank for continued interest in and development of the NetVUE Scholarly Resources Project. Second, I thank the Council of Independent Colleges (CIC)—in particular Rich Ekman, Hal Hartley, and Marjorie Hass—for their support of the scholarship of vocation in its many forms. Finally, the editorial staff at Oxford has been a trusted and valued partner in the work of this book.

The first three volumes in this series were edited by David Cunningham, the inaugural director of the NetVUE Scholarly Resources Project (2012–2017) and now executive director of NetVUE. He developed, alongside the many contributors to those volumes, a breadth and depth of vocation scholarship. For the foundation of this significant, inspiring work, we say thank you to David and to the contributors of the earlier volumes. Additional thanks to David for his visionary and creative spirit and his championing of the wider conversation about vocation, evidenced through his leadership and advice throughout this project. I personally thank him for extending grace, and space, as I stepped into the editor's role. Sincere thanks go to Lynne Spoelhof, director of NetVUE operations, whose commitment to our shared work nurtured each step of the project. I thank Lynne for being ever helpful, ever attentive, ever a friend. On behalf of this volume's contributors, I offer David and Lynne, and the entire NetVUE staff, our gratitude for all they have done and continue to do to make NetVUE a strong, vibrant community and organization.

Thank you to my colleagues and friends who have shown support and interest in the project, especially those who read and provided feedback on my authored parts of this manuscript: Stephanie Johnson, Geoffrey Bateman, John Barton, Deirdre Egan-Ryan, Jake Kohlhaas, Martin Lohrmann, and Jason Stevens. Thanks to my many inspiring and encouraging colleagues at Loras College, especially to the vocation seminar cohorts, the library staff, President Jim Collins, Provost Donna Heald, and conversation partners on the fifth floor of Hoffman Hall.

Those in my commons made this book project sustainable and possible, especially those gathered around the table in Harper's Ferry, at the cottage, or under the lights on our back deck. Thanks and love to my husband, Shane, a builder of beautiful dwellings whose commitment to climate action has taught me so much about how to live in and for the common good, and to my parents, Dennis and Dianne VanLaningham, who modeled how to live a good life in service to others, caring for all through ecology and hospitality. I especially thank my sons, Soren and Aidan, whose curiosity, compassion, and creativity enrich my life and contribute to the common good in wide and beautiful ways. They have shown extraordinary patience with this writing project's demands and provided comedy and sanctuary. Thank you for being my sun and moon, directing my gaze to the sky and the horizon of our shared life. Seeing you shine brightly is my greatest joy. My work on this book is dedicated to the two of you, with love beyond measure.

The contributors to this volume are extraordinary people, accomplished scholars, leaders, educators, and now friends. I thank them for their partnership and for their commitment to the project's aims and to each other. In the words of the poet David Whyte, the book is an example of "the visible/ and the invisible// working together/ in common cause,// to produce/ the miraculous."

The volume is dedicated to Paul Wadell—accomplished scholar, theologian, teacher, mentor, friend. His work echoes throughout this book, largely because he writes about the very fabric of the common good in his emphasis on social justice and friendship. One of his most significant contributions to the field of Christian ethics is his understanding of friendship, further exemplified in his own life. In his scholarship, in his teaching and mentoring, and in his care for others, he has called us to consider what it means to live a magnanimous life, to serve others before self, and to seek solidarity with neighbor. His contributions to NetVUE are many. He was an original member of the NetVUE Advisory Council for ten years until his retirement. He served on the planning committee for the NetVUE Scholarly Resources Project, contributed to the first volume of the project, directs the NetVUE Faculty Development Seminar, and is a frequent speaker at NetVUE events— national, regional, and campus based. All of these contributions are amplified through his deep, resonant voice of encouragement and his presence as a significant conversation partner on vocation and the common good.

Erin VanLaningham
Professor of English, Loras College
Director of the NetVUE Scholarly Resources Project

Vocations of the Contributors

Geoffrey W. Bateman wanted to be a teacher ever since elementary school. His younger sister can attest to his nerdy obsession, having endured endless hours of playing school in the garage of their childhood home. When he came out in high school in 1991, he still desired to teach, but given the barriers that young aspiring LGBTQIA+ teachers faced, he struggled to imagine how to realize these desires. He credits a women's literature course and its feminist professor in helping integrate sexuality and gender into his vocational exploration. She and other faculty mentors set the stage for his eventual pursuit of a PhD and teaching at the university level. His path to his current position as an associate professor of peace and justice studies at Regis University was a circuitous one—taking detours into community organizing, activism, and advocacy in the nonprofit sector, as well as his coparenting of two (now adult) children with his husband and two queer women—his vocation as a teacher has remained consistent, as has his commitment to issues facing the queer community.

It is no surprise that **Martin Holt Dotterweich** discerned a call to postsecondary education while still a young teenager, for he grew up surrounded by teachers in his immediate family: a university president, three college faculty, and two elementary teachers. They modeled a commitment to the flourishing of others, and how reading and studying could be the thing one did most of the time. This vocation was cemented in college when a revered professor asked, "Have you considered graduate school?" As a faculty member, Martin has found joyous relationships with both subject matter and students. His first department chair's advice, "cultivate eccentricity," was hardly necessary, but confirmed that he was in the right place. But the calling to teach has also brought surprises. His doctoral supervisor modeled how scholarship could be used to serve others beyond the university, and Martin's own vocation now includes community education, preaching, and directing the King (formerly Buechner) Institute for Faith and Culture. Another surprise has been parenting two children on the autism spectrum, a calling that stretches and rewards him.

As a young boy, **Jonathan Golden** aspired to be an archeologist. He later achieved that dream, ultimately earning a PhD in anthropology, participating in excavations around the world, and publishing two books. (The dream was almost derailed when his rock band was called to stages like New York City's CBGBs.) But it was his work in the Middle East, and Jerusalem in particular, that called Jonathan to a new vocation, as he became involved in grassroots efforts to build peace in the region. He began to study conflict transformation, learning from professional mediators and peacebuilders across the globe. Jonathan would go on to help establish the Center on Religion, Culture, and Conflict at Drew University, an institute dedicated to peacebuilding and conflict transformation. Involved with multiple transnational projects, including the International Rescue Committee, Jonathan engages his students directly in his own research with former combatants and victims/survivors, who become peace activists. As the situation in the United States grows increasingly volatile, Jonathan's efforts now focus on interreligious, interethnic, and intercultural peace and reconciliation initiatives nearby. His teaching revolves around one simple idea: learning cannot happen without listening.

Michelle Hayford decided that theatre making was her vocation at age thirteen while she sat rapt and tear-drenched in audience to the original Broadway cast of *Les Misérables*. She pursued this craft in high school through a transformative chosen family found in the community youth SAVE Theatre in Simi Valley, California. Michelle came to University of California Santa Cruz to major in theatre, but then added a second major in women's studies after realizing her passion for social justice theatre nurtured by independent directing and performance in feminist and queer theatre. During Michelle's senior year, in a memorable conversation underneath the redwood trees, her feminist theory professor encouraged her to pursue a PhD in performance studies, which she did at Northwestern. After writing a dissertation about performing drag with the Chicago Kings drag king troupe, Michelle landed her first gig as an interim director of a women's center, followed by employment as a theatre program director and change agent in undergraduate theatre education. Michelle shares this conviction with students: theatre can change the world and is a necessary response to our interdependence.

Christine Jeske often finds herself commenting to students, "I tried that major for a while too." She explored journalism, music education, and physics before landing with double majors in English and piano. Later she would earn an MBA in economic development and a PhD in cultural anthropology, which, she says, pretty well ties them all together, especially since she often researches and teaches about vocation. As an undergraduate she also worked as a residence hall assistant with job duties that included hanging up—and then tearing down—signs for campus events. She recalls one day "feeling sorry for the signs," prompting her to resolve to attend as many events as possible. Many of the twisting surprises in her career path—working in a halfway house, memoir writing, starting a women's crochet co-op in Nicaragua, teaching English in China, and comanaging a microfinance organization in South Africa—began by saying "yes" to opportunities in college. She now lives on a small farm and teaches anthropology at Wheaton College, where she continues to feed her insatiable curiosity.

Charles Mathewes had a peregrinatory childhood, living in seven places before he was six, and eventually attending elementary and junior high in Saudi Arabia. That mobility taught him the importance of trying to understand the world surrounding you. He inherited from his parents a curiosity about systemic connections and implications, and a fascination with individuals' idiosyncrasies, which led him to conclude that a life spent figuring stuff out was the best life for him. He intended to major in politics and international relations but before his first semester began, a computer glitch enrolled him in a class on theology. Theology, it turned out, was a discipline that let him ask questions not just about *how* the world works, but also *why* it works this way. It took him two years, three other decisive classes, and many conversations with his anxious parents to "jump ship" from his political science program into the humanities, but since then he has never looked back. He went to graduate school in Chicago and has now lived in Charlottesville, Virginia, for twenty-five years, almost as long as he lived everywhere else in his life.

David Matzko McCarthy grew up as a denizen outsider in a close-knit Québécois neighborhood, Catholic and working class, in western Massachusetts. From an early age he planned his escape, and once successful, he became wistful but could not point to why. Born on the cusp of the Boomers and Generation X, he took his contradictions into the world: individualist and community oriented, skeptical and faithful, an armchair nihilist and would-be social activist. He stuck with school, partly to avoid decisions about who he was called to be and partly to figure things out. He entered career counseling while in a PhD program and has been reading and writing, talking and teaching about vocation ever since. The contradictions remain; inquiry on vocation is the balm.

Robert J. Pampel vividly recalls his first vocational crisis during summer orientation at Valparaiso University. In what he now views as unabashed manipulation by his instructors, he read Frost's "The Road Not Taken" with future classmates. This led to intense questioning of a rather uncritical decision to study engineering, which led him to switch his major to English literature. He thought he would become a professor, but doubts crept in as the Great Recession loomed and he abandoned the path to higher education—or so he thought. After a brief stint in an entrepreneurial fellowship program in Indianapolis, Robert moved to St. Louis for graduate education in higher education and international studies. In 2014, he joined the staff of the Saint Louis University Honors Program, where he has developed a deep fascination in and appreciation for the institution's Jesuit mission and teaching, honors pedagogy, and all things vocation. He is thankful for a supportive partner and two spirited children who remind him of his vocation as a husband and father, even if he still experiences occasional vocational crises.

Meghan M. Slining can point to many forks in her vocational journey where she found herself choosing between pursuits true to her own values and ones seen by others as "cool." In early instances, her first choice was "cool": she sat with the cool kids in the seventh-grade lunchroom; she applied to the cool (but wrong) graduate program; she toiled at a very "cool" research institution when what she wanted to do was teach. Years of regular mindfulness practice helped her to see that "cool" was not her path. Trained as an epidemiologist, she has found her vocational home in the liberal arts where she balances rigorous intellectual development with the intentional cultivation of the heart. All of her courses encourage students to pause and listen, to explore and internalize their own beliefs and values, to experience belonging, and to search for a larger purpose for their lives.

Monica M. Smith attended a primarily White, Christian liberal arts institution on the East Coast, where she discovered her calling to the field of social work. As she indicates in the opening paragraph of her chapter, her undergraduate experience was not a purely positive one; still, in both its negative and positive features, it shaped her professional commitments. Monica is dedicated to education and awareness for cultural competence, social justice, peacemaking, and reconciliation with extensive experience in matters related to diversity, equity, inclusion, and justice (DEIJ). As her chapter also suggests, the call to justice in higher education is the province not only of individuals but also of institutions. Monica serves as vice president and chief diversity officer at Augustana College (Illinois), an institution that continues to strive to promote DEIJ efforts for the common good and that has gained national recognition for its efforts and outcomes. Monica is convinced that the promotion of justice for the common good is both an individual and a collective responsibility, and one that needs to be pursued relentlessly.

Before fall of 2008, **Deanna A. Thompson** was living her 95 percent ideal life. She had married her college sweetheart, had found a job at a Minnesota university, and was a busy parent of two lovely children. She taught religion to undergraduates and wrote and spoke about the ongoing relevance of Martin Luther's theology for contemporary issues like feminism and White privilege. Then cancer came along and forced her to resign from her full and wonderful life. But instead of dying she went into her first remission; she is now in remission number four. She was able to return to teaching and begin writing and speaking at the intersection of theology, cancer, trauma, and hope. In 2019, Deanna returned to her alma mater, St. Olaf College in Northfield, Minnesota, to teach religion and serve as the inaugural director of the Lutheran Center for Faith, Values, and Community. The collaboration on this volume has been a great joy in its affirmation that vocation is always about more than what's good for us; it's also, often, about the traumas that affect so many lives, and supporting ways of being in the world that enhance the flourishing of all.

David Timmerman reached a crisis of faith the summer before college and was prompted to consider what he really believed about his Catholic upbringing. After being active at a local church during college, he went to seminary and became a pastor. Through happenstance, he began teaching in the evening program at a community college close to the church he was pastoring, prompting him to complete a PhD so he could teach at the college level. He has been haunted by the questions: Why did you go to seminary in the first place? Why did you leave the ministry? Why seek a PhD at that point in your life, with two small children and a stable career? While he offers no bulletproof answers to these questions, he is thankful for each vocational decision. After many years as a professor of rhetoric and communication, he has spent the last decade as dean of the faculty at a residential liberal arts college and now as provost. Close friends have referred to him as a pastoral provost, a title he gladly, if humbly, owns.

Erin VanLaningham's love for a long, complex story began in third grade when her teacher gave her Charles Dickens's *Great Expectations*. She eventually found her way into the college classroom teaching the British novel, women's writing, and the spiritual memoir, exploring the nuance of narrative and life with students. The long story, however, reminds her of growing up on the shores of Lake Michigan and her roots as the daughter of accomplished public school teachers. After stops in England and the East Coast, Erin eventually found a home in the English department at Loras College in the "driftless region" of the Midwest. She explores the relationship between novels and vocation in her co-edited book *Cultivating Vocation in Literary Studies*. In her writing and teaching life, in raising her two sons, and in her role as director of NetVUE's Scholarly Resources Project, Erin is reminded of the great expectations that lay before us when we explore possibilities, together.

Introduction

Whose Good Life?:
Vocation and Communal Flourishing

Erin VanLaningham

Marilynne Robinson's Pulitzer Prize–winning novel *Gilead* opens with the narrator recalling a recent conversation with his son, telling him that "there are many ways to live a good life."[1] The advice seems plausible enough, and indeed most of us have been told it or shared it with others at some point. There *are* many ways to live a good life. When we consider the contours of a good life in connection to the lives of others, however, our understanding might change.

Educators ought to suggest with greater persuasion and persistence that the dominant narrative of personal success and achievement that grips so many students' pursuits be contextualized and challenged by the myriad ways to live a good life. In the context of vocation—the discovery of one's calling in contribution to community and global needs—living a good life certainly depends on how we consider obligations to and care for others and our world. While there might be many ways to live a life of meaning and purpose, talking about vocation with students can reveal how an individual's life is interdependent with the good life of not only their friends, family, coworkers, and neighbors but also of those they never meet. The good life is not only about me, but about we.[2]

Vocation is best realized when serving the common good, acknowledging our deep interconnectivity and mutual dependence. Yet, vocational exploration has often begun with individual reflection and then subsequently identified the world's needs; many have referenced Frederick Buechner's

---

[1] Marilynne Robinson, *Gilead* (New York: Farrer, Straus and Giroux, 2004), 3.
[2] Aristotle framed the good life (*eudaimonia*) as virtues in action, ultimately leading to human flourishing. For further exploration, see Meghan Sullivan and Paul Blaschko, *The Good Life Method: Reason through the Big Questions of Happiness, Faith, and Meaning* (New York: Penguin, 2022).

Erin VanLaningham, *Introduction* In: *Called Beyond Our Selves*. Edited by: Erin VanLaningham, Oxford University Press.
© Oxford University Press 2024. DOI: 10.1093/oso/9780197691915.003.0001

framing of vocation as "the place where your deep gladness and the world's deep hunger meet," in that order.[3] Vocational discernment should prioritize understanding and responding to the world's "deep hunger" as the context for discerning an individual's "deep gladness."[4] This volume reorders Buechner's framing of calling as "the kind of work a) that you need most to do and b) that the world most needs to have done."[5] What does it mean for us to ask first what needs to be done before we ask students to consider what they can, want, or need to do?

Con*vocation*: our collective calling

Buechner's definition of vocation actually begins with "the place God calls you to," where gladness and hunger "meet."[6] Vocation is a summons to a place within traditions, communities, cultures, and histories; it is not a place within oneself divorced from others. Beginning with an emphasis on the *place* of call—spiritual, familial, ecological, social, or communal—suggests that we explore what it means to be part of a shared place to arrive at a wider sense of vocation. Further, individual and collective purpose "meet" in vocation, revealing a web of connections and relationships. As we think about vocation as a place where self and world meet, we can help students discover intersections rather than singular paths.

The contributors to this volume emphasize the connections within vocation or calling, insisting that any time or space that is encouraged for vocational reflection be oriented toward a collaboration with the calls of others.[7] The volume invites vocational conversations to move away from the regular invoking of the last line of Mary Oliver's poem "The Summer Day"—"What will you do with your one wild and precious life?"—to emphasize instead the

---

[3] Parker Palmer, for example, argues, "Buechner's definition starts with the self and moves toward the needs of the world: it begins, wisely, where vocation begins—not in what the world needs (which is everything), but in the nature of the human self, in what brings the self joy, the deep joy of knowing that we are here on earth to be the gifts that God created," in *Let Your Life Speak* (San Francisco: John Wiley and Sons, 2000), 16–17.

[4] Frederick Buechner, *Wishful Thinking: A Seeker's ABC*, rev. ed. (New York: Harper Collins, 1993), 119.

[5] Buechner, *Wishful Thinking*, 119.

[6] Buechner, *Wishful Thinking*, 119.

[7] See, for example, David Cunningham's description of the ways colleges can prioritize time and space for vocational discernment in "Time and Place: Why Vocation Is Crucial," in *At This Time and In This Place: Vocation and Higher Education*, ed. David S. Cunningham (New York: Oxford University Press, 2016), 5–7.

ways that an individual's life is dependent upon the ways others have lived, can live, and should be able to live.[8] It situates the discovering of an authentic self within a deeper knowledge of and empathy for neighbor.[9] It takes the poet's observations of the natural world (the swan, the black bear, the grasshopper, and the grass) as demonstrative of "how to pay attention," a response to the call to hear, see, and attend to others.[10] Vocation, like a poem, "can only exist as a common ground between the poet and other poets and other people, living and dead. Any poem worth the name is the product of a convocation."[11] Such convocation, this collective calling, is what we seek to emphasize in this volume.

The multiple models of interdependence and community life from religious traditions help clarify how vocations reveal a meeting between self and others. Within the Christian tradition, the Jesuits' language of accompaniment or walking alongside our neighbors (not ahead of or from afar) frames a vocational journey. The Protestant reformer Martin Luther's interpretation of Paul's letters emphasizes what it means to serve others: "For thus no member of the body serves itself; nor does it seek its own welfare over that of the other. And the weaker, the sicker, the less honorable a member is, the more the other members serve it. . . . From this it is now evident how one must conduct himself with his neighbor in each situation."[12] Conducting ourselves *with* our neighbors is a way to consider vocation's relationship to the common good. In the Jewish tradition, Hillel the Elder famously says, "If I am not for myself, then who will be for me? If I am only for myself, what am I? If not now, when?" Such questions emphasize a connectedness between self and other, also echoed in the Islamic tradition: "The best of people are those who are most beneficial to others."[13] Such convergence between these multiple traditions promotes conversations about the common good that

[8] Mary Oliver, "The Summer's Day," *New and Selected Poems*, vol. 1 (Boston: Beacon Press, 1992), 94. Stephanie Johnson offers a nuanced reading of Oliver's poem, specifically the way a close reading of the complete poem challenges the final line that is so oft quoted, in her essay "Poetry's Lyric Call," in *Cultivating Vocation in Literary Studies*, ed. Stephanie L. Johnson and Erin VanLaningham (Edinburgh: Edinburgh University Press, 2022), 67–88.

[9] Charles Taylor explores the "ethics of authenticity," emphasizing how we are formed by the people, places, and experiences located outside of ourselves. See Charles Taylor, "The Ethics of Authenticity," in *Leading Lives That Matter: What We Should Do and Who We Should Be*, 2nd ed., ed. Mark R. Schwehn and Dorothy C. Bass (Grand Rapids, MI: Eerdmans, 2020), 60–64.

[10] Oliver, "The Summer's Day," 94.

[11] Wendell Berry, "The Responsibility of the Poet," in *What Are People For?* (New York: North Point Press, 1990), 88–89.

[12] Martin Luther, "Two Kinds of Righteousness," in *Luther's Works*, American ed., vol. 31, ed. Harold J. Grimm (Philadelphia: Muhlenberg Press, 1957), 302–3.

[13] Al-Mu'jam al-Awsat, Hadith No. 5937.

serve as "powerful motivations and resources for intergroup peacemaking, genuine kindness, and concern for strangers and even enemies."[14]

An ecological model provides a vision of interconnectivity within all of creation. In other words, when vocational exploration engages intentionally with our care for creation and our neighbors, it stands to reason that our vocations will bear out this accompaniment. As Kiara Jorgenson notes in *Ecology of Vocation*, "Vocation, holding space between creation and redemption respectively, speaks less about *doing* the right thing or *being* the right thing and more about *relating* in a right or appropriate fashion."[15] The relating *is* vocation—it is the meeting that we want to embody, as we move throughout our lives and make decisions in the workplace, our communities, our homes. While we certainly help students consider who to be and what to do, vocational exploration is most significantly about how our lives reveal the web of connections and relationships to friends and strangers alike. We hope, then, that this ecology of meeting and relating becomes the way we can see our vocations as part of the common good.

Extending the vocabulary of vocation

Higher education is not a stranger to responding to the call of and to the common good, most recently experienced in the COVID-19 pandemic as well as the effects of institutionalized racism, economic disparities, the struggle for LGBTQIA+ rights, gun violence, and climate justice concerns. Our contemporary public life has seen extensive political polarization as a result of historical and current conflicts. A recent study showed that a significant portion of students would not room with, date, or marry someone with a different political view.[16] The extensive effects of the multiple pandemics continue to unfold for students and educators alike on our campuses.

This volume's consideration of vocation and the common good builds upon the first three volumes in a series of scholarly work on vocation and

---

[14] John Barton, *Better Religion: A Primer for Interreligious Peacebuilding* (Waco, TX: Baylor University Press, 2022), 31. Barton further discusses the concept of "thick religion" that emphasizes the transcendent vision of a tradition, a resource for collaboration and human flourishing.

[15] Kiara A. Jorgenson, *Ecology of Vocation: Recasting Calling in a New Planetary Era* (New York: Lexington Books, 2020), 127.

[16] Mark Murray, "A New Political Divide," *NBC News*, August 18. 2022, https://www.nbcnews.com/meet-the-press/first-read/new-political-divide-nearly-half-college-students-wouldnt-room-someone-rcna43609.

higher education.[17] These collections addressed the ways in which exploring vocation with undergraduates involves attending to higher education's broader landscape, examining the contributions of different disciplines, and engaging with multiple religious traditions. We continue to believe that the vocabulary afforded by vocation can be helpful as we navigate our many roles and purposes in common life. As David Cunningham notes, the language of vocation not only is dynamic, elastic, and capacious but also can be a bridge language that applies to all through a lifelong process, envisioning a person's life as a relationship to the structures of civic life.[18] Our authors extend and enrich this vocabulary to bring forward frameworks that orient our vocational trajectories so that all may thrive. When discussing vocation, we use the language of connection, mutuality, membership, responsibility, solidarity, compassion, and empathy frequently.

Imagining the good life as a flourishing for all means that we understand success as significantly different than a common cultural narrative of prestige or achievement. Recognizing that students come to us with various levels of cynicism and brokenness, obligations to family expectations and personal hope, we seek to embed any notion of a good life within "a willingness to move beyond self-centeredness and to live for something greater than ourselves."[19] This does not mean that we ask students to abandon their dreams of career or family life, nor does it disregard the realities that many students have family and community members depending upon their pursuits. It instead focuses on how we "grow in goodness"[20] throughout our lives, practicing and living the virtues so as to restore a fuller humanity to ourselves and others.[21] This is a way of talking about vocation that emphasizes goodness, but also greatness, as we seek to live a magnanimous life so that others can as well.[22]

---

[17] See David S. Cunningham, ed., *At This Time and In This Place: Vocation and Higher Education* (New York: Oxford University Press, 2016), David S. Cunningham, ed., *Vocation across the Academy: A New Vocabulary for Higher Education* (New York: Oxford University Press, 2017), and David S. Cunningham, ed., *Hearing Vocation Differently: Meaning, Purpose, and Identity in the Multi-Faith Academy* (New York: Oxford University Press, 2019).

[18] See David S. Cunningham, "Language That Works: Vocation and the Complexity of Higher Education," in Cunningham, ed., *Vocation across the Academy*, 10–14.

[19] Paul J. Wadell, "An Itinerary of Hope: Called to a Magnanimous Way of Life," in Cunningham, ed., *At This Time*, 194–95.

[20] Wadell offers a helpful overview of Aristotle's understanding of happiness and virtue in "An Itinerary of Hope: Called to a Magnanimous Way of Life," in Cunningham, ed., *At This Time*, 193–215.

[21] See, for example, Caryn D. Riswold's "Vocational Discernment: The Pedagogy of Humanization," in Cunningham, ed., *At This Time*, 72–95.

[22] Wadell, "Itinerary," 193–215.

We acknowledge it is difficult to hear vocational calls in a world filled with so much noise. Our response in this volume is not to continue to argue for time and space apart from the world for individual vocational discernment but instead to argue for consistent engagement with neighbor and community. This engagement necessitates a nuanced understanding of reflection and noise, noting that the economic drone of the world is the backdrop for everyday life, part of the "unwanted" sounds that at times impact our quality of life. Listening to self and others means we learn to engage within and with the noise. This engagement is part of one's "noisy autonomy" that allows for "self-determination in relation to how noise (both audible and silent) affects our lives."[23] While we affirm the deep value of calling for a pause—individually or globally—from the distractions that noise represents and the deep harm it can do, we also want to encourage an integrated sense of living within and attending to the noise as part of vocational discernment. We would instead emphasize contemplation in action (in the tradition of Ignatius) so as to resist the paradigm that vocational reflection occurs apart from daily life, from the very real pressures of family and work, from our roles in economies and ecologies. The noise within us and around us can prompt a clearer vision of where a pause might be needed and afford us strategies for careful listening.

Teaching vocational exploration ought to prioritize pedagogies that heal and build, and this book offers the reasons, the approaches, and the innovations necessary to transform our classrooms and campus life. Colleges and universities, according to David Orr, ought to recognize that "the skills, aptitudes, and attitudes necessary to industrialize the earth, however, are not necessarily the same as those that will be needed to heal the earth or to build durable economies and good communities."[24] Students need tools with which they can respond to the daily crises endured individually and collectively. Educators—meaning those engaged in the life of a university—have a responsibility to teach dialogue and deliberation, reflection and action, at every juncture of our work. This is a step toward what Kathleen Fitzpatrick suggests in focusing higher education "less on what we *can* think and more on what we *need* to think about."[25]

---

[23] David Shaw, "Noisy Autonomy: The Ethics of Audible and Silent Noise," *Public Health Ethics* 14, no. 3 (2021): 289, https://doi.org/10.1093/phe/phab026.

[24] David W. Orr, *Earth in Mind: On Education, Environment and the Human Prospect*, rev. 2nd ed. (Washington, DC: Island Press, 2004), 27.

[25] Kathleen Fitzpatrick, *Generous Thinking: A Radical Approach to Saving the University* (Baltimore: Johns Hopkins University Press, 2019), 188. Fitzpatrick borrows this idea from Michael Crow and William Dunbar.

Indeed, considering vocation for the common good is also about the reframing of the calls of our institutions, disciplines, and programs. Fitzpatrick poignantly asks, "If universities were instead to focus on the development of communities, the mode of leadership they educate for might be grounded less in prestige—in individualistic markers of power—than in connection and collaboration."[26] While this positions the university as an agent of change in its role in serving the common good more directly and effectively, this line of thinking can trigger compassion fatigue for many in small colleges and universities. The work of the academy in recent years has been fraught with budget cuts, enrollment declines, the shrinking of the humanities and social sciences, and the constant adjustment of curricular and cocurricular programming to meet market demands. Marginalized faculty, staff, and students have continuously carried significant burdens of institutionalized bias and lack of support. Most would certainly agree with the aims of collaboration and connection but have yet to see the fruits of such sacrifice and little progress. We recognize both the fatigue and the need to continue to adapt to and respond to this cultural moment.

Furthermore, we see the importance of challenging utopian ideas of community and emphasize that a "call to community" needs to be analyzed for what it is a call to. If a community is a place that excludes some to the unfair benefit of others, then it is our task as individuals to resist this sort of communal call. Darby Ray reminds us that the overlap between community engagement and vocation reveals that the world is not "merely a convenient backdrop for one's personal odyssey," but when students engage "its exquisite beauty, heartbreaking suffering, and mind-boggling complexity, they often find themselves desiring not just their own flourishing, but that of the whole world."[27] These challenging vocational moments are part of the liminality of the call of the common good, part of this toggling between the world and the self that involves an unraveling so that rebuilding can happen for the benefit of all.

[26] Fitzpatrick, *Generous Thinking*, 207.
[27] Darby Kathleen Ray, "Self, World, and the Space Between: Community Engagement as Vocational Discernment," in Cunningham, ed., *At This Time*, 320.

What is common and what is good?

The language of "the common good," like the language of vocation, needs to be expanded, reclaimed, and reimagined for contemporary contexts. A place to start would be with these questions offered by Jedediah Purdy: "How do people come to be one another's problems, threats, burdens? How do we become one another's helpers, protectors, friends?"[28] By examining the multiple sides of the common good—how it obstructs and how it encourages flourishing, what prevents its achievement and what fosters it—we can better consider what we might name as the world's hungers and needs in ways that become more complex and textured. Purdy emphasizes a shift away from a zero-sum understanding in such efforts, favoring instead "the creation of new kinds of solidarity, new ways to feel that your good life is part of my good life, and an injury to you is an injury to me."[29]

Throughout this volume, you will see many iterations of "common good"—including *the* common good, *a* common good, the commons, goods, and the uncommon good. We also use language such as the flourishing of all, the good life, collective well-being, and communal wellness. The goal is to offer students of diverse identities and talents multiple models of what it means to flourish, what that looks like for communities, and what that asks each of us individually to consider as our responsibility and contribution. The common good is about breaking open the structures of oppression that have served a few and not all and have institutionalized barriers that we now seek to name and resist. The common good is about listening to others, building skills of dialogue and empathy, of valuing the uncommon as a resource for everyone. The common good is an invitation to be better about the ways we learn about the world and each other, considering the obstacles that prevent us from working toward a more just, equitable society. As Cynthia Wells suggests, vocation is an avenue "through which we can both see and seek a common good."[30] Seeing and seeking, naming and responding, acting and doing help to explore what is common and what is good.

As part of this seeing, naming, and acting, we might look to this definition from Catholic social teaching: "the basic goods and services of a society,

---

[28] Jedediah Purdy, *This Land Is Our Land: The Struggle for a New Commonwealth* (Princeton, NJ: Princeton University Press, 2019), 3.

[29] Purdy, *This Land Is Our Land*, 26.

[30] Cynthia A. Wells, "Finding the Center as Things Fly Apart: Vocation and the Common Good," in Cunningham, ed., *At This Time*, 65.

goods such as adequate food and housing, education, medical care, employment and a fair wage, and opportunities for advancement," as well as the assumption that everyone has "a right to goods that are essential for human
beings even if they are unable to contribute directly to society."[31] Vocational
exploration certainly hinges on such considerations for self and others. As
we offer models of what the common good looks like, we can offer some up
for critique, such as Thomas Hobbes's seventeenth-century idea of the body
politic and Abraham Bosse's etching of the same that shows a multitude of
faces on the body of the monarch. We can evaluate Ford Maddox Brown's
nineteenth-century painting of work that details the various kinds of labor
and privilege. We can read and respond to literature that casts our individual identities within a civic society, such as Ada Limón's "A New National
Anthem," Walt Whitman's "Song of Myself," and Langston Hughes's "I, Too."

The rich intellectual history of the common good is helpful for our
purposes, ranging from considerations of equity, democracy, diversity, and
participation in civic life.[32] Many have noted that the building of a just society involves citizens looking beyond their own private interests, and even
sacrificing for it.[33] The common good can also be defined on different planes
of existence: a common good that involves the participation in the social-
temporal life of civilization, the common good as a contemplative life that
transcends the political, and the common good of supernatural or spiritual
life to which the first two are subordinates.[34] While all of these aspects are
helpful in our understanding, we ought to consider that while it is "goods"
like clean water and free access to education that we prioritize in our everyday life, the common good is "something more profound, more concrete
and more human."[35] The common good involves the wisdom, justice, happiness, friendship, and virtues of individuals who only through a connection to
the whole "constitute the good human life of the multitude."[36]

And it is through this pursuit of the good life of "the multitude" that we
turn to the sense that our life as citizens means that we are not individuals
with unlimited freedoms but rather are bound by what James Farrell calls the

---

[31] Paul J. Wadell, *Happiness and the Christian Moral Life*, 3rd ed. (New York: Rowman and Littlefield, 2016), 242–43.

[32] Robert B. Reich, *The Common Good* (New York: Vintage, 2019).

[33] Reich, *The Common Good*, 39. Reich traces the ideas of Alex de Tocqueville, specifically of citizens looking beyond private interests to something other than themselves.

[34] Jacques Maritain, *The Person and the Common Good*, rev. ed., trans. John Fitzgerald (South Bend, IN: University of Notre Dame Press, 1994), 52–53.

[35] Maritain, *The Person and the Common Good*, 42.

[36] Maritain, *The Person and the Common Good*, 43.

"commons good,"[37] to be mindful of our environment and the obligation to care for creation and each other. This ecological citizenship is a vocation of the common good, as we participate in stewarding and contributing to our communities and common home.[38] The good life means not a good life at the expense of other people's dignity and rights, and not at the expense of our neighbors, our community, and the environment. When we prioritize the commons as the start of our consideration of what good looks like, we will significantly shift our vocational callings.

Extending the boundaries of the "common"

A significant limitation of the language of the common good is the way the term has been used to create normative notions of what a common experience can and should look like, to the exclusion and harm of many marginalized communities, including diverse racial, LGBTQIA+, religious, and disability identities. This sort of totalizing that happens when we discuss "common life" works against the just aims of a common good. As Isabel Wilkerson suggests, caste is about holding everyone in place, literally casting people into various positions of restriction or privilege, and a paradigm of a common experience in this case becomes an agent of caste.[39]

In addition, we ought to consider the threat of willed ignorance of what might constitute a different version of a common good or a denial of what binds us together. Kwame Anthony Appiah suggests that not understanding others is a privilege of the powerful, and for our concerns, it means that large portions of our communities remain unheard and misunderstood when making decisions regarding our collective well-being.[40] So too does a normative sense of the common good emerge from an insular or siloed way of thinking, so that we outright deny the things that "tie us inconveniently together"[41] to preserve our own comfort. For example, the refusal "to see how the world is deeply plural at every scale *and* that we are in it together"

---

[37] Maritain, *The Person and the Common Good*, 38.

[38] James J. Farrell, "Good Work and the Good Life: Vocation as What We Do," in *Claiming Our Callings: Towards a New Understanding of Vocation in the Liberal Arts*, ed. Kaethe Schwehn and L. DeAne Lagerquist (New York: Oxford University Press, 2014), 41.

[39] Isabel Wilkerson, *Caste: The Origins of Our Discontents* (New York: Random House, 2020), 17.

[40] Kwame Anthony Appiah, *Cosmopolitanism: Ethics in a World of Strangers* (New York: Norton, 2007), xviii.

[41] Purdy, *This Land Is Our Land*, 15.

propagates incomplete and destructive frameworks of the common good.[42] James Baldwin makes a call to confront the myths of American history and identity in "A Talk to Teachers," saying that "any citizen of this country who figures himself as responsible—and particularly those of you who deal with the minds and hearts of young people—must be prepared to 'go for broke.' "[43] Our going for broke in exploring vocation and the common good is part of what it means to challenge ourselves and our students to resist and reform at every juncture necessary.

Vocational exploration that prioritizes the common good can address these blind spots and limitations, aiming to bring reflection to action. As students discern what their gifts and talents are, we might put further emphasis on the deep plurality of the world that ties those gifts and talents to collective well-being. We might ask what it means to disrupt a system or paradigm that protects the interests of a few, and how we can better respond to the inconvenient aspects of common life so that we can achieve a good life for all. Helpful here is Danielle Allen's notion of "social connectedness," realized in "a connected society . . . in which people can enjoy the bonds of solidarity and community but are equally engaged in the 'bridging' work of bringing diverse communities into positive relations while also individually forming personally valuable relationships across boundaries of difference."[44] As we engage with others in working toward the common good, the focus is on the bridging, the work of creating relationships across "boundaries of difference." Whereas "bonds" depend on stronger, already formed connections and "links" derive from the vertical relationships such as the hierarchy in workplaces, bridges are difficult but are the most important. They involve the reforming of social structures and institutions (such as colleges and universities).[45] This is a shift within the commons to embrace the uncommon.

---

[42] Purdy, *This Land Is Our Land*, 15.

[43] James Baldwin, "A Talk to Teachers," in *Collected Essays*, Library of America no. 98 (New York: Library of America, 1998), 678. Eddie Glaude referenced Baldwin's talk in his keynote address to the NetVUE national conference in Dallas in March 2022, noting that such limitations of illusions and identities of American consciousness prohibit a seeking of a new higher self, a confrontation with the reality of our time and place.

[44] Danielle S. Allen, "Toward a Connected Society," in *Our Compelling Interests: The Value of Diversity for Democracy and a Prosperous Society*, ed. Earl Lewis and Nancy Cantor (Princeton: Princeton University Press, 2016), 90–91. See also Mark Granovetter's description of social networks in "Network Sampling: Some First Steps," *American Journal of Sociology* 81, no. 6 (May 1976): 1287–303, https://doi.org/10.1086/226224.

[45] Allen, "Toward a Connected Society," 87.

Emphasizing our social connectedness allows educators to challenge and encourage students to think about their roles as bridge builders, asking what boundaries of difference need to be crossed to expand the common good. Here, the common good is the heartbeat of vocational discernment, a radical and reformed imagining of the good life.

Significant steps toward the collective

Exploring vocation for the common good with students is a study in becoming more attuned to, aware of, and open to the needs of others. This means that we acknowledge where we might be participating in a version of the good life that limits or even damages the possibility of the good life for others. As part of breaking these destructive patterns, Ta-Nehisi Coates wishes for his son to become "a conscious citizen of this terrible and beautiful world";[46] others position such a shift as a "fundamental change in awareness"[47] or a moral "awakening from the sleep of inhumanity."[48] Education should serve as a building of awareness of the barriers to our common humanity and invite students to reorient their lives so that others can find meaning and purpose as well.

This is often a difficult and troubling pursuit, and, at times, traumatic. It involves taking on others' suffering, seeing the brokenness and struggle of others, and assessing the wrongs done to the environment and to people. There are unspeakable conversations and collective traumas that emerge. Understanding vocation's relationship to the common good means that we name and honor the persistence of systemic injustice and the ways that even work is a "disfiguring trauma" for many.[49] As John Neafsey suggests, "The vocational question, it seems, has to do with identifying *those for whom we hurt.*"[50]

When we talk with students about vocational trajectories—including their hopes and dreams for career, family life, and personal contentment—we ought to prioritize a serious consideration of what it means to live in a

---

[46] Ta Nehisi Coates, *Between the World and Me* (New York: Spiegel & Grau, 2015), 108.

[47] Wadell, *Happiness*, 258; Wadell also uses language that draws from liberation theology the concept of "conscientization."

[48] John Neafsey, *A Sacred Voice Is Calling: Personal Vocation and Social Conscience* (Maryknoll, NY: Orbis, 2006), 146.

[49] Darby Kathleen Ray, *Working* (Minneapolis, MN: Fortress Press), 109.

[50] Neafsey, *A Sacred Voice*, 86.

global capitalist society that does not promise or distribute wealth in equitable ways. Students come to us with various realities about home and food insecurity; many also come to us from significant privilege. The economic consequences of their daily work choices are vital for their understanding of and contributions to the common good. We don't have to assume that people aspire to be wealthy—indeed, we have many students who pursue professions and pathways that are decidedly not rewarded with monetary advantage. Yet, we do have a responsibility to demystify class structures and ramifications. As we present models of vocational exploration, we can provide examples that elucidate the ways our economic choices have wide-ranging impacts. This economic dimension of the common good is vital to the ways we understand not only our career path but also the sense of agency and responsibility we harness when we consider the ethical dimensions of our work.

As we educate for the common good, vocational reflection can be a bridge to becoming a conscious citizen. Part of that bridge is an invitation for students to see the common good as a question of justice, as participation in a way of life that holds individuals and societies accountable for injustices. While we hold up historical or influential figures who have made indelible marks on the world for raising awareness of the failures of societies or leaders to meet the needs of their citizens, we also ought to hold up the idea that all people have a capacity to contribute to justice in different ways. One's abilities in mind and body can be limited, but their contributions are worthy. Here, we can offer students a model of shared capacity—the idea that not everyone can do everything all the time, but that our joint efforts are part of the journey toward justice.

Colleges and universities are in a prominent position to shift the dominant narrative of freedom and rights as bound to an individual. Paul Wadell argues that social justice "especially reminds us that just societies depend on just persons, persons who see beyond their own needs, security, and comfort to the welfare of all citizens of the world, and who remember that justice is not only about personal rights but also about social responsibilities."[51] While the social responsibilities may be defined differently for individual students, it is only by asking students to draw the map of justice for their own vocational identities as part of the collective map of social justice that we might come to a better and richer understanding of what the common good is and can be.

---

[51] Wadell, *Happiness*, 245.

When colleges and universities orient practices and pedagogies toward virtue and focus on formation *in* and *for* community, our interdependence becomes more apparent. "Communal formation," Jennifer Herdt suggests, "reveals how an ethic of virtue can foster rather than frustrate the acknowledgement of dependency."[52] The rituals, habits, and practices of a community form us, and therefore, we ought to create and uphold practices that cherish such dependency. The rituals of a college campus, ranging from convocation to commencement, provide us with the opportunity to celebrate and emphasize formation within a community. A call to a community and to communal formation means that we are stepping into a practice of engaging with others to flourish, collectively and individually. Our campuses practice formation by inviting individuals into the rituals of campus life and cultivating habits that build up a capacity to respond to the needs of others.

This intentionality of habit is a step toward achieving a piece of Aristotle's practical wisdom that suggests that we must practice the virtues—not merely study them—in order to flourish. The notion of an integrated life—accounting for one's friends, work, finances, joys, and values—is best realized through such practices. Yet, there is a gap between inviting others into and seeing the application of such habits of social commitment, what the authors of the foundational text *Habits of the Heart: Individualism and Commitment in American Life* note as a frequent (and ineffective) call to "get involved."[53] The authors ask what would motivate individuals to move beyond self-interest, to "consciously link their destinies to those of their ancestors, contemporaries, and descendants?"[54] Not surprisingly, it is a "generosity of spirit" through the recognition of our interconnectedness.[55]

When we invite students into conversations about meaning and purpose, then, we might teach vocation as a building of a capacity to redistribute generosity—specifically a generosity of spirit, of thought, and of resources. This redistribution can bring us to the common good. It is a habit to practice as individuals and as communities, a habit of involvement and a habit of heart. The hope for such education that focuses on interconnectedness and social commitment is that as part of the ritualized exits and entrances of students on our campuses, and as part of the homecoming and returning of

---

[52] Jennifer A, Herdt, *Putting on Virtue: The Legacy of the Splendid Vices* (Chicago: University of Chicago Press, 2008), 350.

[53] Robert N. Bellah et al., *Habits of the Heart: Individualism and Commitment in American Life*, 2008 ed. (Berkeley: University of California Press, 2008), 167

[54] Bellah et al., *Habits of the Heart*, 167.

[55] Bellah et al., *Habits of the Heart*, 194.

alumni and friends, we build a vibrancy for the campus to serve as a locus for the common good. The college community extends to the world through its members, fostering a widening sense of interdependency.

Vocation as the meeting place

The *meeting place* of vocation within the context of the common good might best be realized through the idea of friendship and what it means to be devoted to the good of the other, not ourselves.[56] We are claimed by others, interconnected in the recognition that "we are always awash in each other's lives, and for most of us that shared life, recorded as history, will be the only artifact we leave behind."[57] Political friendship in particular demands us to consider our shared life (of economic environments, social structures, and climates) as more public than private and that our obligation is "to prove oneself trustworthy to fellow citizens."[58] We must assess what barriers exist to achieving trust as part of that friendship. This is all part of the mutual formation and dependency that we seek to elucidate in the chapters that follow.

As we explore the meeting place of mutuality, we emphasize that vocation is relational, not only between persons but also between persons and environments on every level, including home, neighborhood, community, workspace, the climate, and the universe. The call to communal well-being, serving others beyond self, means attending to the relationships we have and how our identities emerge through these connections. This is often called a realizing of an ecological self, a vocation that embraces "the integrity of being-in-the-world."[59] Such being-in-the-world is the immersion in the common good that shapes our vocations, further brought forward not only in our meeting but also within the place we are called to dwell.

Dwelling—the idea, the physical structure, and the lived practice—captures the meeting place of vocation and the common good. To build, to make a home through relationships, and to practice honoring others' dwelling are dispositions that contribute to a generative sense of dwelling in

---

[56] Paul J. Wadell, *Becoming Friends: Worship, Justice, and the Practice of Christian Friendship* (Grand Rapids, MI: Brazos Press, 2002), 49.

[57] Danielle S. Allen, *Talking to Strangers: Anxieties of Citizenship since* Brown v. Board of Education (Chicago: University of Chicago Press, 2004), xxii.

[58] Allen, *Talking to Strangers*, xxii.

[59] Bill Devall, "The Ecological Self," in *The Deep Ecology Movement: An Introductory Anthology*, ed. Alan Drengson and Yuichi Inoue (Berkeley, CA: North Atlantic Books, 1995), 121.

the world. Norman Wirzba emphasizes that our "attitude and orientation" to others and environment in the ways we build and dwell mean not imposing upon but rather honoring the many connections that intersect with our existence.[60] As we prepare students to discern their individual callings through the lens of shared purpose, inviting them to consider their identities as friends who prioritize dwelling with others, we can emphasize the shared life in this meeting place. Vocation is a call to the place we dwell together and a call to friendship that prioritizes others' well-being. It is the place where individual and collective purpose intersect. As the writer Scott Russell Sanders observes, "Strength comes, healing comes, from aligning yourself with the grain of your place and answering to its needs."[61]

The argument for vocation and the common good

This book was written by scholars from various disciplines who hold different positions within the academy, so as to draw from a range of perspectives that could orient vocation more effectively to serve the common good. The voices represented include public health, education, and social work; anthropology and peace and justice studies; rhetoric and history; performing arts and literature; and theology and religious ethics. We gathered three times over the course of a year that was marked by various pandemics that challenged the core of what it means to work toward justice and the common good. It made our work more urgent.

In what follows, we first explore the ways that our frameworks of vocation need to shift to better engage students in understanding and addressing the world's hungers. In the opening chapter, David Mazko McCarthy outlines how when we respond to the claims that others have upon us, we are better able to discern our vocations. The common good is an exercise in love, and when we situate individual freedom within a deeper understanding of justice, we can best see how our callings are a response to others. As we continue to expand the language of vocation, Deanna A. Thompson argues in chapter 2 that we have many callings that we do not choose, and that trauma of any kind is a significant part of our vocation. Making space for lament

---

[60] Norman Wirzba, *Food and Faith: A Theology of Eating* (Cambridge: Cambridge University Press, 2001), 42–43.

[61] Scott Russell Sanders, *Staying Put: Making a Home in a Restless World* (Boston: Beacon Press, 1993), 120.

and "deep sadness" is part of the way we can foster a flourishing for all and achieve a more radical hope. Christine Jeske, in chapter 3, highlights the continual shifting of our ways of thinking about vocation and the common good through the disruption of dominant strains of thought. As we work with students to challenge the narratives of merit and market that shape the way we think of the good life, we can make space for the narratives of membership and mutuality. Finally, Monica M. Smith argues in chapter 4 that the shift that many institutions and educators can make is to see that our commitment to diversity, equity, inclusion, and justice is a way we work toward collective well-being. The mission of higher education ought to prioritize serving diverse populations as part of its call to the common good.

Next, we address what it means to embrace change and action as part of our vocations for the common good. In chapter 5, Michelle Hayford argues for advocacy as a vocation, building on the idea that through confronting injustice, we help students to realize their vocations as change agents. This cultivation of a sense of activism is an important tool for students in their vocational trajectories throughout their lives. Identifying the ways the common good has excluded and discriminated against marginalized identities, Geoffrey W. Bateman in chapter 6 seeks to recover what the uncommon offers to our conception of the good life. Specifically, queer vocation challenges normative ways of knowing and being, which helps us to value the uncommon as vital for all. Jonathan Golden concludes the section in chapter 7, which brings forward the ways that sustained engagement with communities and causes that are not our own can transform our vocations. Through pedagogies of community engagement and conflict and resolution dialogues, the direct encounter with difference becomes a strategy to elucidate a common good.

Through pedagogies emphasizing compassion and dialogue, we see that the classroom is a place that can build significant skills to contribute to the common good. Here, we turn in chapter 8 to the specific need to teach discussion and deliberation. David Timmerman argues that as our students come to understand the value of listening to others and articulating multiple and nuanced perspectives, they can build a capacity to respond to difference and build spaces for reconciliation as part of their vocational callings. Many colleges and universities use common readings as a way to engage multiple segments of a campus community in fruitful discussion and reflection; in chapter 9, Erin VanLaningham argues that reading with strangers can prepare us to use interpretive and critical inquiry to work toward the common good. Reading together builds empathy for, compassion toward, and friendship with others. Finally, as we prepare students for vocations that are oriented toward serving the common good, we ought to model sustainable practices for such vocations. Throughout chapter 10, Meghan M. Slining draws on the field of public health to demonstrate that our well-being is dependent on that of another. The chapter offers ways that we can acknowledge the heavy burdens that such professional pathways can bring while also providing strategies for compassion for self and others as we address burnout.

In the final section, we return to the broader landscapes of the university, historical and personal memory, and the lifelong learning experience to see how colleges and universities are resources for the common good. Robert J. Pampel in chapter 11 shows us that the formation of the university was often prized as a common good place, and that our contemporary call to serve the common good requires reformation of the institution itself. Recovering the university as the "common (good) place," we can leverage various approaches to teaching and framing the conversation about the ways place forms us to contribute to others' well-being. As we build a capacity to understand place, exploring public monuments and the historical record through the lens of memory allows us to develop humility and a sense of possibility. In our remembering, Martin Holt Dotterweich in chapter 12 suggests, we respond to public and personal trauma and triumph, and honor those we have forgotten or will never know, which ultimately helps us to honor strangers and neighbors alike. Reflecting upon what our obligations to others may be, we return to the idea put forward in the beginning of the volume—that the claims upon us are a call, and that the freedom to pursue them is a significant part of a liberal education and vocational identity. In the final chapter, Charles Mathewes argues that the more we engage with this tension between freedom and obligation, and the more we frame higher education as a space to engage others throughout the life course, the greater clarity we can bring to our vocations. The common good of the university is realized in its contribution to public formation, reformation, and transformation.

The book concludes with an epilogue that proposes an ecology of the common good. The language of ecology—as applied to campuses, communities, systems of thoughts—emphasizes the idea of a web that needs to be built and sustained so that all can flourish. The language throughout the volume of restoring, rebuilding, overturning, and serving means that in seeking the common good, our individual work contributes to a larger ecosystem that is complex, demanding, and, indeed, precarious. Courageous conversations, deep reflection, advocacy and activism, reckoning with past traumas, and deliberate dialogue are all part of this building of the common good through vocational discernment. A call to community means a call to something and someone beyond our selves, and our response to care for and steward resources and gifts toward a greater good can mean sacrifice. Still, it can also mean mutual benefit, freedom, and friendship, as the good life becomes the common good in uncommon and wildly beautiful ways.

Our common purpose in writing this volume is to call others into the work of vocational exploration that emphasizes the importance of collective well-being. Vocation and the common good—concepts that become more radical and relevant in a fractured and vulnerable world—deserve our committed focus as we prepare students to embrace challenges and calls from their communities. As we introduce students to the many ways to live a good life, may we go for broke in our efforts.

PART ONE
VOCATION IN THE COMMONS

This opening section identifies influential frameworks of vocation and the various shifts within those frameworks needed to best identify our collective callings. The chapters show that by exploring vocation within the context of common life, we can better discover how to work for justice and respond with love to the various calls of our neighbors. Encouraging students to see individual goals as explicitly part of helping others to flourish means a redirection for vocational discernment, allowing us to address structural barriers and suffering in their many forms.

Our authors seek to redirect narratives—especially the language of individual success and gladness—to better attend to the context of the common good. The chapters emphasize distributive justice, representation of diverse and marginalized voices, and membership in communities. The discussion expands individual and collective vocation to acknowledge trauma, sadness, and institutionalized bias. The chapters also call upon colleges to better orient their mission and practices to respond to the common good. Vocation, when situated within the multiple pandemics of racism, COVID-19, economic disparities, and climate crisis, means we reimagine what living together for mutual benefit looks like. This is vocation in the commons.

We encourage readers of this section to focus on the key terms of love and justice, suffering and hope, choices and barriers, mutuality and membership, equity and inclusion. What do these terms mean in your classrooms, campus programs, strategic plans, and institutional priorities? How can expanding and reframing conventional definitions of vocation help us better realize and contribute to the common good?

The questions that follow may be used in professional development, meetings, programming, planning, and teaching. We imagine students and educators alike responding to these in discussion and in writing, in private and public settings. The goal of the questions, and of this section, is to expand the notion of vocation to engage with our collective call so that all may flourish.

What are foundational definitions of vocation and in what ways might they be limiting?

* What reframing and reimagining do educators need to do of the under-lying culturally inflected narratives and structures that shape our understanding and experiences of vocation?
* Who is "in the room" shaping the definitions and understandings of vocation and the common good that operate in our settings? What barriers prevent representation in these spaces and conversations? What can we do to be more inclusive and equitable?
* In what ways have contractual, individualist, and economic models of vocation dominated conversations of vocation?

How can we begin to think of the common good as constitutive and essential to vocation?

* How does sharing in the commons lead not just to shared burdens, but to shared hope and shared joy?
* How can we live in ways that we recognize and respond to the demands of the world upon us and others?

What kind of work is entailed in helping students to prioritize the common good in their vocational path?

* In what ways does work toward diversity, equity, inclusion, and justice support a more expansive notion of the common good?
* How can our discussions of vocation challenge educators and students alike to think beyond themselves? How can the college or university think of the institutional call as a call to contribute to the world's needs, the common good?

Consider the language of "choice" in an understanding of vocation. Who has choices and what are the limits of choice?

* What structural barriers exist at our institutions that inhibit incorporating vocation and the common good?

* In what ways do we and can we distinguish our call and make meaning of our vocations even amidst noise, or trauma, or limitations?
* In what ways is suffering a part of vocation? How does making space for deep sadness shift the idea of "choosing" a vocational path?

1

Our Call as Response

The Common Good as the Context of Vocation

David Matzko McCarthy

Vocation, according to Frederick Buechner, is "the place where your deep gladness and the world's deep hunger meet."[1] First published in *Wishful Thinking* in 1973, Buechner's definition has become a foundation of inquiry for those of us who think about and promote the concept of vocation. Buechner tapped into a common experience and hope that we can trust our desires and dreams. Christian theologians will recognize the Augustinian structure: We can look within to find our way in the world; if we struggle to know what we truly desire, we will find God guiding us along the way. We find a journey outside of ourselves. Buechner's articulation of vocation has been important and effective. Over the years, however, the inward approach has been matched by a narrow focus on the self to a degree that Buechner, it is likely, would not recognize what we have done to the search for a deep gladness. After decades of widening social fragmentation and growing distrust of basic social and political institutions, my look inward for my calling is likely to end with me.[2]

This chapter outlines a framework of vocation that does not begin with me—not with my personal journey, but with social structures and established institutional pathways.[3] The argument for starting with the world need not deny the importance and effectiveness of an internal search and discovery of one's deep desires. Rather, a framework for beginning with responsiveness to the world is necessary precisely when the commons and

---

[1] Frederick Buechner, *Wishful Thinking: A Theological ABC* (New York: Harper & Row, 1973), 95.

[2] James Mattis, "The Enemy Within," *Atlantic* 324, no. 6 (December 2019): 102–4; Erica C. Taylor, "Political Cynicism and the Black Vote," *Harvard Journal of African American Public Policy* 17 (January 2010): 3–10.

[3] See Darby Kathleen Ray, "Self, World, and the Space Between: Community Engagement as Vocational Discernment," in *At This Time and In This Place: Vocation and Higher Education*, ed. David S. Cunningham (New York: Oxford University Press, 2016), 301–20.

David Matzko McCarthy, *Our Call as Response* In: *Called Beyond Our Selves*. Edited by: Erin VanLaningham, Oxford University Press. © Oxford University Press 2024. DOI: 10.1093/oso/9780197691915.003.0002

common good are fragmented, when the personal quest is disconnected from social and common meaning-giving landscapes. While reviewing important criticisms of the common good (e.g., its use to secure dominance over others), Lisa Sowle Cahill holds that approaches to the common good "can become strategies of accountability"—especially "for the oppressors."[4] To do so, Cahill argues, we will need "a refined understanding of goods and relationships as interdependent,"[5] which draws from "the inherent sociality of human persons, the reciprocity of rights and duties among social members, [and] a responsibility to the common good that morally overrides mere assertions of power or interest."[6] In terms of vocation, a discovery of a good in and for the other is a good that we are called to share and to serve. In an age when we are expected to have our own truth, the radical turn will be outward. Others and their good call us outside of ourselves.

At the end of this inquiry, we will be in a place (I hope) where the good of persons in community is understood as a common landscape for our vocations, whether these calls are found in specific jobs or careers, family, church membership, friendship, service organizations, or other forms of engagement in neighborhood and civic life. Moving outward toward the good of others requires a sense and goal of the common good—an ecology for the flourishing of individuals—and a commons sustained by naming and attending to systemic and particular injustices. The chapter will turn first to an essay by Vincent Harding (1931–2014), historian and civil rights activist, who demonstrates through his autobiographical sketch how callings come through the needs and expectations of communities. Through these common needs and community-based expectations, Harding is able to discern a call, oriented by love and justice, to common goods. The next section sets Harding's proposal in terms of justice and a contrast between a narrow focus on oneself and an understanding of the self-in-relation. This second section will suggest a shift in emphasis from thinking about what God gives to me to how we might share in God's self-giving and love for the world. The theological point is a backdrop for the subsequent sections, which offer an extended treatment of the common good, the virtue of solidarity, and how our roles and responsiveness within institutions—within social, organized, and structured human pursuits—provide the constituent features and context for us to receive and live into our various calls. If it is possible to discern

---

[4] Lisa Sowle Cahill, "Toward Global Ethics," *Theological Studies* 62 (2002): 330.
[5] Cahill, "Toward Global Ethics," 330.
[6] Cahill, "Toward Global Ethics," 332.

a calling in terms of the common good, we will have to work through the complications and dysfunctions of doing so together, to live amid social fragmentation and to strive for justice with neighbors, coworkers, and friends who give us hope and dare to be guided by the needs of the world.

"Strange things": the adventure of response and responsibility

Vincent Harding provides a model for thinking about vocation as solidarity with others and responsiveness to the world. First published in 1974, Harding's "I Hear Them . . . Calling" is autobiographical, poetic, and subtly multivalent, and my hope in offering a short summary is that the reader will seek out Harding's own words.[7] His refrain in the piece (like a sermon or hymn) is "Callings are strange things." Harding sees the strangeness of callings because he shares deeply the struggles and aspirations of an extended community—his and other African American communities of mid-twentieth-century Harlem. James Baldwin, also a denizen of Harlem and Harding's contemporary, explains that there was "a zest and a joy and a capacity for facing and surviving disaster that are very moving and very rare . . . bound together by the nature of our oppression, the specific and peculiar complex of risks we had to run."[8] If indeed rare, that is all the more reason for us to listen carefully to the call of Harding's life.

For Harding, hearing and responding to the dictates of our situation, albeit strange, are an ever-present part of our lives—if we care to listen:

> I've heard a fair number [of callings] in my time. . . . Sometimes they proved to be nothing more than echoes bouncing off from other lives. . . . Others puzzled me and led me into ways I do not understand. . . . A few—perhaps more than I know—I have followed as far as they led; and some are still moving . . . preparing to join themselves to the sounds of the new summons, and I suspect there are yet borders to cross.[9]

---

[7] Vincent Harding, "I Hear Them . . . Calling," in *Leading Lives That Matter: What We Should Do and Who We Should Be*, 2nd ed., ed. Mark R. Schwehn and Dorothy C. Bass (Grand Rapids, MI: Eerdmans, 2020), 31–39. Harding's essay was originally published in *Callings!*, ed. James Y. Holloway and Will D. Campbell (New York: Paulist, 1974), 57–69.

[8] James Baldwin, *The Fire Next Time* (New York: Modern Library, 2021), 34.

[9] Harding, "I Hear Them . . . Calling," 32.

As a boy and then a young man, Harding responds to the expectations of his community ("He's going to be a preacher"), to social needs and struggles ("my people marching, refusing to stop"), and to the responsibilities of his place among others (in Harlem, the Bronx, and later the southside of Chicago). He even includes a calling to the army by the draft board in 1953, which he had hoped to avoid. When his service was complete, it had led him nowhere and perhaps, he reflects, that is what he needed at the time. The draft was clearly a call, and "callings are strange things."

Harding makes a point of showing the mistakes of dwelling on his own interests and aspirations. As a teenager, he aspired to be an athlete: "perhaps I simply thought that a man should be able to spend his life doing what he really liked."[10] From his interest in model airplanes, he heard "a call to be an aeronautical engineer." He continues:

> I hadn't found out that Black folks weren't supposed to be aeronautical engineers. What I did find out was that my mathematical skills weren't good enough to pass the test for the high school where all the really bright aeronautical engineer-types were supposed to attend.[11]

At City College, Harding's interest in writing turned to an emphasis on journalism and work on the campus paper, with him "eventually becoming the inevitable FIRST NEGRO editor of that ancient institution of wisdom and scandal." All capitals are used to identify his own ambitions, to stand apart rather than to stand with; the call was a temptation to make his own name in a White world of journalistic "wisdom and scandal" and, following the temptation for a time, led to "strange pathways which shut out voices I should have heard."[12] During his City College education, he was "clearly being groomed for another FIRST NEGRO position," and this expectation raised questions about the callings of his community back in Harlem and aimed to silence "the central call among the callings"—the calling to stand with and among in a shared struggle.[13]

Harding concludes the essay with the suggestion that the strange and varied calls, throughout his life and in widely different places, have been the promptings of God. These calls have come not from within him or from

---

[10] Harding, "I Hear Them ... Calling," 32.
[11] Harding, "I Hear Them ... Calling," 32–33.
[12] Harding, "I Hear Them ... Calling," 34.
[13] Harding, "I Hear Them ... Calling," 34.

his own desires to be someone or something, but from what was needed for communities and how—within community—others called him to respond.[14] As noted above, from the church of his youth, he hears a call to be a preacher, which he both accepts and resists. From their love of education and their encouragement ("encouraging my terrible poetry"), he hears a call to be a writer, which fits, for a time, with his aspiration to be a journalist. From the struggles of generations of African Americans, he hears the call to be a witness: "I hear them vowing never to give in, never to turn back, to endure, to resist, to live, to go on. I hear their calling."[15] The call of his congregation; the call to be educated, to study, and to write; and the call of slaves, former slaves, and civil rights activists coalesce as a calling to be a historian. He writes, "I am a witness, in spite of myself, beyond myself, and their voices [the voices of generations] must be heard."[16] The call of God comes not through an inner desire or aspiration; it is a collective call to an individual, a call that does not begin with a single person but within and for a community.

Before this final word about God's prompting through others, Harding concludes with his call to be a son, father, and husband—to be "hope, strength, and promise for tomorrow."[17] This conclusion is not a sentimental turn, not a shift from social change to private life, but a focus on concrete responsibilities and responsiveness to callings as a framework of life. Harding emphasizes the fact that callings are constituted by our responsiveness to the lives of others through our roles in their lives: "I hear my mother, sighing, scrubbing all the floors in all the white homes, bearing with love and pain and anxious prayer the burden that I was/am."[18] For his children, he is a connecting link, "encourager for the struggles of tomorrow, baptizer in the rivers of the past"; for his wife, he hopes to be "resting place and summons to joy in the morning."[19] By ending with his responsibilities to loved ones near, Harding makes clear that callings—particularly callings of God—do not come from grand ideas or heroic ambitions. Callings are grounded within and yet elevate ordinary life. We are called by persons and people through whom we discover our responsibilities day to day.

---

[14] Also see Margaret E. Mohrmann, "'Vocation Is Responsibility': Broader Scope, Deeper Discernment," in *Vocation across the Academy: A New Vocabulary for Higher Education*, ed. David S. Cunningham (New York: Oxford University Press, 2017), 21–43.

[15] Harding, "I Hear Them . . . Calling," 38.

[16] Harding, "I Hear Them . . . Calling," 38.

[17] Harding, "I Hear Them . . . Calling," 39.

[18] Harding, "I Hear Them . . . Calling," 39.

[19] Harding, "I Hear Them . . . Calling," 39.

Justice: finding ourselves in the claims upon us

Harding outlines an approach to vocation and personal discernment through his emphasis on finding his role and place in relation to common life. However, Harding's trust in the calls he receives in relationship to communities and institutions wanes given increasing distrust in American society, in politics and basic social institutions.[20] For my part, I wish I had read Harding's essay years ago. In teaching vocation, I have directed students to discern what they want, and it is likely that I have encouraged journeys down many dead ends. The dead ends that Harding explores aim at spending our lives doing what we really like (for Harding, airplanes and sports) and seeking to stand apart from others (to be the FIRST). In contrast, Harding invites us to look for markers that point to how we are claimed by others and the burdens we share, to sufferings and aspirations of other people and communities.[21] We find our way when someone asks us to carry a burden, to right a wrong done, and to suffer pains and celebrate joys that are not our own. With these claims upon us, we have decisions of our own to make about who we are and who we will be, but the claims and shared burdens situate us to what is good. Harding calls us to respond to the hopes and needs of others day to day, to justice as giving to others what is their due, to justice as a virtue and orientation to everyday life.

In teaching moral theology, I used to tell a story that parallels Harding's criticisms of vocation as seeking to "do what you like" and to "stand apart." My story was about my aspirations to spend my life playing professional basketball and the reality that I didn't have the athletic ability. The supposed lesson was that we find ourselves in a life not of our choosing or desiring: we are social and responsible from the beginning, and justice—as responding to the good of the other—is part of every aspect of life. As a first step, I was challenging the students' image of themselves as presocial, free-floating individuals, who determine who they are by choice. Given the conceptual weight of that last sentence, it is no surprise that it did not go well. I thought that my athletic limitations would be an uncomplicated way to talk about how we are situated. The students, however, did not accept my lack of athletic

---

[20] Lee Rainie and Andrew Perrin, "Key Findings about Americans' Declining Trust in Government and Each Other," *Pew Research Center* (July 22, 2019): https://www.pewresearch.org/fact-tank/2019/07/22/key-findings-about-americans-declining-trust-in-government-and-each-other/.

[21] For further discussion of the shared suffering and burdens in our collective vocation, see chapter 2 of this volume by Deanna A. Thompson.

ability as a barrier. Their view of the problem was that I did not dream big enough; I did not believe in myself. I could have been a professional basketball player if I wanted it enough.

I could not unseat their individualism and their commitment to self-determination by choice. As we explored the possibility that I was a quitter, I started to discover supports for their view of the unfettered self. My story contradicted a script that made sense of the students' commitment to education, to job prospects, to life—not only "believe in yourself," but also "follow your dreams" and "never say 'can't.'" It contradicted the university's admissions pitch as well as advice and encouragement given by high school teachers, guidance counselors, parents, and friends: Pursue your choices and dreams. Set yourself apart. Find a university education that provides the means to fulfill your plan for your life. This framework of an abstract, presocial individual corresponds to a minimal sense of justice as fairness, which puts individuals on a conceptual playing field where merit alone is free to win the day.[22] In this frame, justice is a currency for the deserving who stand apart and can then bestow it upon others. Some pursue careers in business or medicine, for example, while others will pursue concerns for "social justice." As far as I could tell, the students' view was that "justice" refers to abstract rules of fairness (e.g., what is deserved is based on merit), and "social justice" is concern for others that exceeds fairness. In this frame, a focus on social justice is a noble endeavor, but still very much a personal choice. Harding's landscape of community and responsiveness to various and day-to-day callings would be viewed as the same kind of personal choice.

Further, the students' path of believing in themselves fits too easily with a self-serving (that is, flawed) Christian theology. At the basic level, this self-interested theological view holds that faith is contractual and operates by means of merit: If I have faith in God, God will deliver blessings to me and those I care about. God will keep us safe from suffering—with the addendum that measures out suffering to us according to what we can handle. This framework of exchange corresponds to a deeply rooted logic of markets and meritocracy.[23] Here, I will focus on a parallel theological story that is distinctively, but not exclusively, American. If we have faith in God, God will deliver

[22] Michael J. Sandel, in *Liberalism and the Limits of Justice*, 2nd ed. (Cambridge: Cambridge University Press, 1998), critiques John Rawls's conception of the original (anonymous) position for creating rules of justice.

[23] See Christine Jeske's discussion of the ways merit and markets limit our ability to respond to communal callings in chapter 3 of this volume.

for us—as individuals and as a nation. We will stand apart as deserving and therefore blessed. One prominent and often criticized version of this theology is the prosperity gospel, which focuses on giving money (usually to other Christians) as a votive transaction. Tithing promises greater financial return. The problem with this theology is not solved if this-worldly gain is disregarded in favor of heavenly reward. If I have faith in God, God will deliver for me when it really counts: while others are cast into darkness, I will flourish in the end. This view is a distortion of the call to faith.[24]

These I- and we-directed accounts are blatant examples of a flawed theology of my blessings *in contrast to* others, but the theme is present in about half of what most Christians say with more subtlety. Sometimes we unwittingly slip from "God loves me" to "God loves me because of my faith" or "God has bestowed unmerited love upon me/us in contrast to [some yet-to-be-defined others]." Innocent gratitude on the surface often has self-centered concerns and comparisons at the root. Thank you, God, for the sunny day for our family gathering.[25] How easily we pull God into our insular plans. In contrast, the better part of biblical and Christian theology begins with faith that God's purpose is the redemption, communion, and flourishing of creation. The biblical image of the body (1 Cor 12) evokes an ecology of giving and receiving, a membership of mutual dependence and reciprocity—"ongoing giving and receiving in dependent relationships."[26] Faith does not put one in a position of benefit in contrast to or instead of other people or groups of people. Faith is not currency paid down in order to be free from suffering or risk. Rather, faith brings one into service of others and partnership with God for the sake of God's purposes—love, communion, and justice—for the world. Faith is the call of partnership.

This call to God's purposes for the world is the foundation of a theology of vocation (including, no doubt, Buechner's definition). It is the consistent message of the prophets, as in "It is too little, [God] says . . . to raise up the tribes of Jacob and restore the survivors of Israel, I will make you a light to the nations, that my salvation may reach to the ends of the earth" (Isaiah 49:2). However, the temptation to claim God as our own for our purposes is built into faith in a God who draws near and invites us into partnership—the

---

[24] The hope that all human beings and creation will be united in God's love is set deep within the tradition. See Hans Urs von Balthasar, *Dare We Hope That All Men Be Saved?* (San Francisco: Ignatius Press, 1988).

[25] See Luke 18:9–14. God promises to give us what we need *as we strive of the kingdom of God*; see, for example, Matt 6:11, 6:33, 7:11, 10:31.

[26] Jeske, "Overturning for the Common Good," this volume, 78.

temptation to think of the partnership, once accepted, in terms of our own aspirations. It is a temptation for Abraham (Gn 22:1–18), the Hebrew people liberated from Egypt (Ex 32:7–10), the kings of Israel and Judah (1 Sam 8:1–22), Jesus on the threshold of his ministry (Mt 4:1–11), the people drawn to Jesus's liberating word (Lk 4:16–29), and his disciples (Mk 9:33–37). Given the persistent tendency to make God's purposes about us (matched with the crisis of the commons in our times), it is not surprising that the emphasis of vocation tends toward "what I want" and "my delight." Given our desire to take an individualist path, Harding's emphasis on hearing and living our call through the common life and common goods is salutary.

A deeper sense of common life requires a deeper sense of justice, which sets rights and duties in relationship to human flourishing—who we are, how we are bound to others, from where we have come, and what we need to share for all persons to flourish in community. A richer sense of justice is set in terms not of abstract individuals and detached rules of engagement, but an ecology of embodied persons in relationship to a shared good.[27] Harding's ecological sense of justice and vocation, as attention and responsiveness in relationship to another, moves us toward a deeper and broader sense of community and human flourishing. On this point, Harding notes a danger that has been cited but not yet stated. Harding's desire to be an aeronautical engineer ran aground not only on his low scores in mathematics but also on systemic racism ("Black folks weren't supposed to be aeronautical engineers"). Likewise, in *The Autobiography of Malcolm X*, X recounts his time at Mason Junior High School, where he (then Malcolm Little) excels but is put in his place by his kindhearted but condescending English teacher. The teacher makes clear to X that he cannot be a lawyer, as he hopes, and should think about being a carpenter: "A lawyer—that's no realistic goal for [a Black man]. You need to think about something you can be."[28] This reference to a "realistic goal" is, ironically, a recognition of real injustices, of the reality that X has been excluded from full participation in common life and the so-called "common" good is really a set of interests of privileged White people and communities.

---

[27] See David Cloutier, "Justice," in *Redemption and Restoration: A Catholic Perspective on Restorative Justice*, ed. David Matzko McCarthy, Trudy D. Conway, and Vicki Schieber (Collegeville, MN: Liturgical Press, 2017), 5–18.

[28] Malcolm X and Alex Haley, *The Autobiography of Malcolm X*, reissue ed. (New York: Ballentine Books, 1992), 38.

The injustices of the world ought not to set the terms for human flour-ishing and the common good. The danger in allowing injustice to shape our vision is another reason that, when thinking about callings, we ought to shift emphasis, not on ourselves, but toward responsibilities to others. Malcolm X's English teacher did not hear the call in the student standing before him. He could have said, "Malcolm, being a lawyer is a good idea; there are not enough Black people in law, and I will help you." For my part, the call that I missed as a teacher telling about my short-lived basketball dream was nearly the opposite, a cultural complement from the other side of the tracks. Most of my students assumed that their college education would give and protect the privilege of setting out into a world to do whatever they want to do for themselves—to do what they like and to stand apart. We were lodged in a disagreement about my dreams, and my mistake was starting with my-self. I should have started with the ecology of giving and receiving, the reality of our lives in relation to others, with justice as responding to others day to day and the unavoidability of participating in the common good.

The common good: an exercise of love

I have suggested that Harding's responsiveness to community and to the struggles and hopes of African Americans is an example of responsiveness to the common good. To frame Harding's experience philosophically, I ap-peal to terms developed by Iris Murdoch, who shows that human fulfillment is a movement outward—often against our habituated inclinations—to the good in and for others. As Murdoch suggests, "Goodness is connected with the attempt to see the unself, to see and to respond to the real world in the light of a virtuous consciousness."[29] Virtue, for Murdoch, comes not through a focus on one's own good or the great good one can do, which is fodder for illusions of the ego, but through seeing the good of another amid the world of self-promotion, suffering, and injustice.[30] Murdoch approaches "the good" pragmatically rather than metaphysically. Goodness is transcendent insofar as it is the reality that connects us—a reality through which we transcend ourselves, albeit imperfectly, in our attentiveness to the other. We go outside of ourselves only through the concrete and particular in our lives, through a

[29] Iris Murdoch, *The Sovereignty of the Good* (London: Routledge and Kegan Paul, 1970), 93.
[30] This transition is a plotline of many of Murdoch's novels, including *The Sea, the Sea* (New York: Penguin Classics, 2001).

"just and loving gaze directed upon an individual reality."[31] What (through Harding) I have referred to as responsiveness, Murdoch refers to as attention. Attentiveness is not an occasional activity but a way of being in relation to others (the "just and loving gaze"). This "attention directed upon individuals and obedience to reality in an exercise of love . . . is the place where the concept of good lives."[32]

To this degree, the common good attends to the whole (the common) in the context of the individual good. The common good is not the individual defined or subsumed by the whole. It is not an aggregate of individual interests or a set of contractual agreements. As noted, it assumes an ecological perspective. It assumes that human beings are social by nature and are fulfilled through their contributions—as persons and in locally oriented groups—to local communities, society, and, when occasion arises, people across the globe. A standard definition can be found in *The Pastoral Constitution on the Church in the Modern World* (Vatican II, 1965).[33] The common good is constituted by "conditions of social life which allow social groups and their individual members relatively thorough and ready access to their own fulfillment," and as directed toward human fulfillment, "every social group must take account of the needs and legitimate aspirations of other groups, and even of the general welfare of the entire human family."[34] By definition, the common good is the context for each of us to receive a call that is local and specific (to me in my time and place), serves others for the good, and contributes to our own fulfillment precisely as a contribution to the good of others.

Although beginning with personal and local, the framework of the common good assumes an extension of our concerns outward to systemic questions and to distant neighbors, whom we do not see or know. This movement outward is indispensable in our interconnected world and is referred to, in Catholic social thought, as a response and responsibility of solidarity. Meghan Clark, in "Anatomy of a Social Virtue," sets solidarity in contrast to conceptions of the person and social transactions built into competing political-economic systems, such as libertarianism and corporatism, laissez-faire and state-run capitalisms, egoism and utilitarianism. Clark holds that

[31] Murdoch, *The Sovereignty of the Good*, 34.

[32] Murdoch, *The Sovereignty of the Good*, 42.

[33] *Gaudium et spes*, in *Catholic Social Thought*, ed. David J. O'Brien and Thomas A. Shannon (Maryknoll, NY: Oribis Books, 1992), 166–237.

[34] *Gaudium et spes*, no. 26.

solidarity is vitally important because economic and political institutions are not only unavoidable but also necessary for individuals and groups to attain what is needed for human life.[35] Solidarity is rooted in a "commitment to individual human dignity and the common good."[36] It invites and hopes for the participation of all, especially the vulnerable, in developing the structures and institutions of common life.[37] Clark proposes: "As an attitude, solidarity is descriptive of our feelings and awareness of interdependence. As a duty, it is a normative category rooted in the moral requirements of interdependence . . . [and] turns on the equality of all humanity."[38] Solidarity is the virtue of mutual dependence and shared life.

The mutual dependence and goods of the common good are delineated by conditions required for the flourishing of persons, groups of people, and the natural world.[39] On a requisite level, people need nutrition and a healthy life setting (e.g., clean air and water), shelter, and clothing required not just for warmth but to be participating members of a community; we need health care, healthy working conditions, and a just wage.[40] As social beings, we need "the right to [one's] good name," freedoms that enhance social interaction and discovery (free speech, inquiry, and choosing one's way of life); we need the opportunity to "share in the benefits of culture, and hence to receive a good education."[41] We are due the right to create and extend family, to gather in associations, to membership in human community (not bound by national borders), to gather to worship, to sustain ourselves through our own efforts, and to take an active role in civic life.[42] This list is not exhaustive, but hopefully sufficiently representative. Shared goods (however the list is composed) are hierarchical. Basic needs, such as matters of health, enhance the opportunities for higher goods—goods of human excellence: food is basic; the culinary art is excellent. The sharing of goods is also hierarchical; sharing can be a simple matter of allocation, or common use can be generative. Food

---

[35] Meghan J. Clark, "Anatomy of a Social Virtue: Solidarity and Corresponding Vices," *Political Theology* 15, no. 1 (2014): 29, https://doi.org/10.1179/1462317X13Z.00000000060.

[36] Clark, "Anatomy of a Social Virtue," 35.

[37] Meghan J. Clark, "Pope Francis and the Christological Dimensions of Solidarity in Catholic Social Teaching," *Theological Studies* 80, no. 1 (2019): 107, https://doi.org/10.1177/0040563918819818.

[38] Clark, "Anatomy of a Social Virtue," 27.

[39] See John XIII, *Pacem in terris*, in *Catholic Social Thought*, ed. O'Brien and Shannon, 131–62. On our relationship to the natural world, see Benedict XVI, *Caritas in Veritate: On Integral Human Development* (Vatican City: Liberia Editrice Vaticana, 2009), nos. 43–52.

[40] John XIII, *Pacem in terris*, nos. 11, 18–22.

[41] John XIII, *Pacem in terris*, nos. 12–13.

[42] John XIII, *Pacem in terris*, nos. 15–16, 23–27.

is consumed; art generates art. Education is limited in its good when the goal is individual consumption but is generative when persons are educated to be actively engaged in the goods of common life.[43]

This account of the common good draws upon a theological counterpoint to typically modern, contractual conceptions of social life, conceptions that posit as their base a presocial individual who enters social life in terms of self-interest only. The counterpoint begins with conceptions of creation as grace and of creatures, particularly human beings, as made for relationships—for the end of union with God and other creatures. For Christian theology, the self-giving of God in Christ is the ongoing and definitive activity of God in bringing creation to its fulfillment.[44] Rather than the presocial individual who justifies attachments primarily through self-interest, this alternative view sees the individual as always and from the beginning a person-in-relation who engages others through both self-interest and self-giving and who finds fulfillment when the two come together. Indeed, the coexistence and hope for a unity of self-directed and other-directed loves is Frederick Buechner's definition of vocation. This theological understanding of creation and grace and a corresponding understanding of the social self and vocation has affinity with other faith traditions (indeed, Christianity received these from Judaism) as well as other philosophical, scientific, and humanistic routes that point out that human beings are social creatures and fulfilled in relation to others.

As a concept, the common good develops through efforts—in modern Catholic social thought—to identify and cultivate a fabric of social interaction distinct from the purview of the economy and state. Early in the twentieth century, communist and fascist governments were characterized by the goal of ruling over all aspects of common life. There would be no "social" outside governmental authority. More recently, capitalist systems tend to be aggressive in relation to social relations; almost anything and all parts of life are open to becoming economic instruments. The logic of market utility works its way even into interpersonal relationships, and the notion of the social contract is understood increasingly in economic terms. To this degree, an account of the common good depends upon the existence of social life and the attainment of shared goods distinct from contractual politics and market

[43] The framework of basic goods, goods of excellence, and allocated and participatory goods is developed by Helen J. Alford and Michael J. Naughton, *Managing as if Faith Mattered: Christian Social Principles in the Modern Organization* (Notre Dame: University of Notre Dame Press, 2001), 42–67.
[44] John XIII, *Pacem in terris*, no. 38.

instrumentality, upon memberships of neighborhoods, faith communities, cooperatives, community-based businesses, and so on. It depends upon people who interact and cooperate in ways that counter structures of exclusion and injustice.

Amid the convolutions of institutional purposes, responsiveness to the common good can provide a topography—an alternative or underlying set of relationships—through which we can identify how we are called to serve, to respond to, and to participate in the good of others. One way to identify common goods is to start with the consistency of human organizations and shared practices within social life over time and work backward to the shared good that initiated the common work and concerns. Health care institutions, for example, have their *raison d'être* in health and in care for the suffering. In health care, as in other social institutions, self-interest (one's own fulfillment) often competes with common goals, market utility trumps responsiveness to the good in and for others, and institutional dysfunctions cloud over an organization's own good purposes. However, amid the dysfunction and injustice, one can hear a call to bring an institution (e.g., a hospital, bank, or university) in relationship to another's good, to extend the membership, in Murdoch's words, "to see the unself, to see and to respond to the real world in light of a virtuous consciousness." This is a way of pivoting outward through a vocational response.

For example, Vincent Harding was a historian and teacher for much of his life. He had an office and books, a salary, and perhaps his own spot in the parking lot. Surely, he struggled with the tedium of research and stillness of writing alone in his office, but he also found great delight in the creative process and in teaching. His manner of life represents the basic elements needed for historians and teachers. Many of us would take Harding's success and measure of fame as means to be set apart: teaching at prestigious universities with the best students, living in neighborhoods where neighbors don't need or bother us, and our directing efforts to individual achievements—a comfortable salary, plaques to put on the walls, and children who outpace their peers. However, Harding's call as a historian was to be a witness, to be the medium for the voices of others, especially generations past and their struggles for justice. The discipline of history and the job as a professor are set, for Harding, on a landscape of the common good. The same can be said for his responsiveness to the good in his family and roles as son, husband, and father. He describes these roles in terms of a formation of persons in community (including his own formation). No doubt, as a father he was concerned about possible careers for his children, but his call to fatherhood was to give them what they need to develop as persons and, in doing so, set their lives in relation to questions of justice and the good of others, linking generations and struggles of the past to generations in the future.

A daring venture: to be agents of institutional change, together

As developed in the previous section, Buechner's definition of vocation is based on a presumption (grounded theologically for him) that our lives and callings to serve are not in competition, that we are fulfilled as we are given the opportunity to play a role in the fulfillment of others, that we do not have to go anywhere else or be anyone different but can respond to the needs of the world where we are. The chapter began, however, with his definition fractured. After exploring vocation within the ecology of common life, we should end where we started—where sociality and shared life have already fallen apart. Institutions and common endeavors are instituted by people, sometimes intentionally and sometimes not, precisely because the goods are common and human beings flourish as persons in community. However, as often as our economic and social organizations succeed, they fail. Too often, institutions harm people (and the environment), and too often social and economic systems undermine the good to which they ought to be directed. If it is possible to discern a calling in terms of the common good, we will have to work through the complications and dysfunctions of doing so together amid social fragmentation and structural injustices.

Our universities can lead the way in prioritizing issues of justice, especially since our campuses are microcosms of wider social dynamics and conflicts.[45] The daring venture for educators—especially at the university where the classroom and research area are an individual faculty member's domain—is to give ourselves over to what students need for a common, coherent education, one that engages the whole campus in terms of human needs, goods, and excellences in all areas of life.

---

[45] See Monica M. Smith's discussion of strategies for institutions to cultivate inclusive learning experiences and align mission to the common good in chapter 4 of this volume.

For example, "Teaching what I want to research and the books I want to read" is a familiar goal among university professors, the privilege of those who teach at elite universities, and a rare delight for most of us. Perhaps we ought to give up on that goal. If one works at a liberal arts or church-related institution, it is likely that a university mission statement is already in place, which is a call and pledge to send students out with a passion and the capacity to work for a better world. Collaborative efforts to contribute to the common good may fail because of vicious self-interest, but more likely the reasons may appear benign or trivial: a sense that the mission is not relevant to what I do in my field; a commitment to departmental or disciplinary goals without or with only passing concern for how these fit with other departments, offices, and the mission; or, simply determined, exemplary focus on one's scholarly work.[46] These are paths that we can take alone; the work of institutional change is a risk of common life.

With the common good in view, we respond to the needs of others with a goal of their flourishing and, in the process, find our own. For university professors, this attention to the common good does not exclude academic specializations or research and writing. For staff, administration, and students, solidarity does not preclude personal investment in particular programs or initiatives—in student life, athletics, IT, academics, or physical plant. On the contrary, a calling to the common good means that we are willing to think ecologically, to investigate how the common good is built into our role in institutional life and not something added on, that our efforts to support the commons, however tedious, will elevate us. To shift metaphors, I may have become a physician to make money, to enjoy the benefits of a high-status profession, or because I am captivated by the science of disease. However, as a physician, my primary purpose is care for patients and their health.[47] This primary, shared (institutional) purpose sets the context for my individual purposes, which are ancillary and will fragment and diminish if made primary. I am elevated by our focus on the good of others and the institutional mission.

Attention to the common good is a focus on the good work, where we are, amid the muddle of institutions, the differences among us, systematic injustices, and barriers to participation in the goods and opportunities

---

[46] See Robert Sokolowski, "What Is Natural Law?," *The Thomist* 68, no. 4 (October 2004): 507–29, https://doi.org/10.1353/tho.2004.0000. Sokolowski surveys ways that individual purposes undermine good institutional ends (514–17).

[47] Sokolowski, "What Is Natural Law?," 513–14.

of common life. The work of public health professionals and the purpose of health care institutions, for example, are common good; the health of all is bound up with that of our neighbor. In addition to skills and virtues of public health and health care, professionals need to learn to endure frustrations, failures, and barriers to the good work. The education of health care professionals, as education for vocation, requires formation through a common vision, a vision of the good that will encourage friendship, a desire to join with others to call social institutions to strive toward collective well-being and to care for each other along the way.[48] Education for the common good is formation, not only in skills for the work, but also in its good purposes, the virtues needed for an enduring commitment to justice, and a perspective animated by love as seeking the good for another.[49]

The same model of vocation to the common good could be developed for other disciplines and professions. For example, according to the code of conduct of the American Institute of Certified Public Accountants, members pledge responsibility to the public good. When accountants "encounter conflicting pressures [of public and client interests] . . . members should act with integrity, guided by the precept that when members fulfill their responsibilities to the public, clients' and employers' interests are best served."[50] We, as educators, should ask ourselves what kind of virtues and friendships will be needed for accountants to fulfill that pledge, to work for the good of others, to face and work against injustices, and to form communities within businesses and corporations in order to develop a holistic vision of human flourishing. At least two sets of questions follow. For accounting, finance, investments, and budgets, we should ask: what is money for? Reference to the common good frames this question in relation to not only what a business, individual, or family needs and wants for itself but also what they will need to contribute to the lives of others and engage communities in a life-giving way. The question about money leads to questions about what a business or corporation, neighborhood or family is for, how it fits into an ecology of relations.[51] Another set of questions is

---

[48] For a model, see chapter 10 of this volume by Meghan M. Slining.

[49] See Charles Mathewes's discussion of education as formation for responsibility to others in chapter 13 of this volume.

[50] American Institute of Certified Public Accountants, "Code of Professional Ethics" (December 15, 2014), no. 0.300.030.03, https://pub.aicpa.org/codeofconduct/Ethics.aspx#.

[51] See David Matzko McCarthy, "Modern Economy and the Social Order," in *Heart of Catholic Social Teaching* (Grand Rapids, MI: Brazos Press, 2009), 129–40 and "Two Households," in *Sex and Love in the Home*, 2nd ed. (Eugene, OR: Wipf and Stock, 2011), 85–108.

specific to a discipline, profession, or form of life: What is our place in relation to others? How is the common good served through how we live and
what we do? Putting questions of the common good to the profession of
accounting, for example, does not attenuate one's commitment to good accounting; on the contrary, the difficult questions require more careful attention to the goods that accountants profess and the vision (how we see what
matters) of the profession, as well as ingenuity and prudence in the application of skills, principles, and procedures.[52]

Along with prudence, we will do well to cultivate and model fortitude—
both a daring inclusiveness of what is good for others and endurance in
facing injustices. If teaching management or working as manager, it may
appear to be risky to think in terms of sharing decision-making and creative job design.[53] Managers or business owners may put their own advancement or success at risk when focusing on the ecology of the workplace,
seeking to enhance individual development (including sharing in monetary success), and promoting an authentic sense of membership.[54] Similar
efforts and inventiveness in relation to the work and courage to change can
be developed in specific disciplinary ways from marketing to human resource management to criminal justice. We will learn how to contribute to
the common good as we are attentive and responsive to the good of others
amid the day-to-day challenges of the work. As Vincent Harding shows,
vocation is not a single thing but a way of responding and living into our
roles and place in relationship to others, in our work, community, neighborhood, and family.

Callings do not require us to stand apart but to stand with others and
strive for their good. To educate in this way, we will have to learn, through
our on-campus endeavors, the virtues of attentiveness, solidarity, and endurance and will have to develop friendships and form communities within our
institutions that support us in our work for the common good. University
education is under the pressure of economic forces, utilitarian logic, and individualist aspirations. Those of us at tuition-driven institutions are acutely
aware that our universities have to change how we attract students and

[52] See Ronald F. Duska and Brenda Shay Duska, *Accounting Ethics* (Hoboken, NJ: John Wiley and
Sons, 2018), 75–77.

[53] Sharon K. Parker, Daniela Andrei, and Anja Van den Broeck, "Why Managers Design Jobs to Be
More Boring Than They Need to Be," *Harvard Business Review* (June 5, 2019): 2–8. The answer is mistaken views of efficiency.

[54] Alford and Naughton, *Managing as if Faith Mattered*, 123.

cultivate our mission. These are strange times, but callings are strange things. We might hope to find a way through by educating for the common good—by beginning with the needs of the world, in recognition of our mutual dependence, solidarity, and shared life—as we discern our individual responses amid an ecology of mutual dependence.

2

Beyond Deep Gladness

Lamenting Trauma, Injustice, and Suffering in Service of the Flourishing of All

Deanna A. Thompson

Just minutes after Derek Chauvin was convicted of murdering George Floyd in April 2021, I logged in to Zoom with a small group of St. Olaf College staff and faculty. The purpose of the meeting—scheduled before anyone knew when the verdict would be announced—was to decide how the college would respond to the Chauvin verdict and the potential aftermath. Bracing for a not-guilty verdict, the college's leadership had tentatively planned to declare a "Day of Healing" for the day following the verdict.

The sense of relief was palpable from everyone on the call. Colleagues of color expressed a deep sense of shock that Chauvin, a White police officer, was actually found guilty of murdering Floyd. Even though the initial hour after the verdict was announced was calm, the decision was made that the campus needed a collective pause in the wake of the stress caused by the twin pandemics of COVID-19 and the racism on display in Floyd's murder, as well as the tension on campus and throughout Minnesota during the Chauvin trial. So, for the first time in recent memory, the college canceled all classes and most events for the coming day. "We encourage everyone to honor the intent of the day to the fullest extent possible," wrote the vice president for equity and inclusion in an email to faculty and staff. "We will have opportunities throughout the day for our community to engage as much or as little as they want in conversations, healing, and spaces of silence."[1]

Daily chapel was one of the few events to go forward as planned. Most attendees at Wednesday's chapel service of prayer were virtual, and the associate college pastor began the service with the acknowledgment that healing cannot happen in a single day. The service focused on prayers of

[1] María Pabón, email message to St. Olaf College faculty and staff, April 20, 2021.

Deanna A. Thompson, *Beyond Deep Gladness* In: *Called Beyond Our Selves.* Edited by: Erin VanLaningham, Oxford University Press. © Oxford University Press 2024. DOI: 10.1093/oso/9780197691915.003.0003

thanksgiving, lamentations of our many needs for healing, and prayers for our individual and collective hopes.

After chapel, over one hundred staff and faculty met over Zoom to talk about the verdict and the trauma of the previous year, including the relentless challenges of the pandemic and the toll it had taken across campus. We discussed the trauma—especially for Black, Brown, Asian, and Indigenous people—brought on by the murder of Floyd, the killing of other Black and Brown people at the hands of police, and the recent mass shooting of primarily Asian women in Atlanta. Staff and faculty expressed appreciation for the college's decision to create space to mourn, to breathe, to pause from this year like no other.

One impromptu space for students to gather was created by staff at the college's art museum. They invited students to channel their emotions and energy into creating a thirty-foot mural with the words "A Bouquet of Humanity" at its center, a phrase from trial attorney Jerry Blackwell referring to the many courageous witnesses who testified at the Chauvin trial and who helped bring about a conviction that held the officer responsible for the taking of George Floyd's life.

Blackwell's image also gestured toward "the more" of the moment—a glimpse into the humanity of many who refused to let Floyd's death have the last word. The mural students created embodied the paradox of the awfulness of the previous year—Floyd's murder and other forms of racism (one AAPI[2] student wove the words "I am not a virus" into the mural)—with a bold, beautiful witness to "a bouquet of humanity" that gifts us with glimpses of hope for a world that recognizes and embraces our common humanity and relatedness to one another.

The Chauvin verdict came at the close of an academic year that overflowed with challenge. In addition to countless unprecedented actions required to deal with protecting students, faculty, and staff from the ravages of COVID-19, demands that institutions renew and deepen commitments to antiracism were front and center for many colleges and universities. Like many other institutions, St. Olaf has significant work to do in becoming a more inclusive community.[3] At the same time, the college's creation of a day of healing

[2] AAPI is an acronym for Asian American/Pacific Islander.
[3] To learn more about two Black female faculty members who wrote open letters to the St. Olaf community in summer 2020 about the racism they experienced as they left the college to take positions at other institutions, see Ryan Faircloth, "Minnesota Private Colleges Reckon with Campus Racism," Star Tribune, August 21, 2020, https://www.startribune.com/minnesota-private-colleges-reckon-with-campus-racism/572171342/?refresh=true.

seemed an enactment of the common institutional vocation to which St. Olaf and other Lutheran-affiliated institutions ascribe: a calling to "serve the neighbor so that all may flourish."[4] This statement comes from *Rooted and Open*, a document penned by theologians of the twenty-six Evangelical Lutheran Church of America (ELCA)-affiliated colleges and universities that lays out a vision for twenty-first-century Lutheran higher education. The joint statement notes that our institutions equip students to "serve a common good," and they turn to the relational emphasis at the heart of Lutheran theology and employ the language of "flourishing" to spell out institutional commitments to a "good" that is common to all. The document's firm insistence that individual flourishing is inextricably bound to the flourishing of communities, families, civic spaces, and ecosystems in which all individuals are embedded undergirds this essay's reflections on vocation and the common good.[5]

What does it mean, then, to foster a climate where all may flourish amidst the ongoing pandemics of COVID-19, systemic racism, and more? This chapter argues that a necessary step toward such flourishing is to nourish vocations that make more space for sadness in our individual and collective lives. Naming and lamenting injustices and losses experienced by those within our communities and beyond increases our attentiveness to the needs of our neighbors as well as to our capacity to respond to and support specific changes that open space for a wider flourishing of all. This essay will explore what it looks like for members of colleges and universities to acknowledge and name deep sadness that stems from a variety of sufferings, including long-standing injustices. It will offer resources from trauma literature to talk about the ways trauma makes itself known in the lives and bodies of those who've been traumatized and describe how practices of lament can help those who live with suffering and trauma make more space to live alongside the sadness. In addition, the essay explores how lament also enables many of us to bear witness to the suffering and trauma of others within our community, thereby increasing our empathic muscles to be with and for those experiencing deep sadness, opening new possibilities for working together toward the flourishing of all.

---

[4] *Rooted and Open*, Network of Colleges and Universities: Evangelical Lutheran Church of America (ELCA), https://download.elca.org/ELCA%20Resource%20Repository/Rooted_and_Open.pdf, 2.
[5] *Rooted and Open*, 7.

Moving beyond deep gladness and coming to terms with vocations we don't choose

Let's begin with the need for expanding the concept of vocation beyond ways it has often been discussed at colleges and universities over the past few decades. In the 2000s, St. Olaf and many other campuses across the country were infused with grants from the Lilly Foundation to support the theological exploration of vocation.[6] One of the definitions of vocation that institutions gravitated toward comes from the writings of theologian, minister, and novelist Frederick Buechner. Buechner's approach to vocation is deeply theological. He is clear that a "calling" assumes a caller, and for Christians, Buechner observes, this caller is the living God. What makes it so difficult to hear the call, however, is that God's voice is not the only voice calling to us. The challenge is to hear God's voice amidst a cacophony of voices. "There are all different kinds of voices calling you to all different kinds of work," Buechner writes, "and the problem is to find out which is the voice of God rather than of Society, or the Superego, or Self-Interest."[7]

How can we discern God's voice amid all the others? According to Buechner, "a good rule for finding out is this: the kind of work God usually calls you to is the kind of work (a) that you need most to do and (b) that the world most needs to have done. . . . The place God calls you to is the place where your deep gladness and the world's deep hunger meet."[8] This last sentence of Buechner's definition is what has become synonymous with the word "vocation" in many institutions of higher education: our vocation is located at the intersection of our deep gladness and the world's deep hunger.

Throughout most of the 2000s I enthusiastically embraced Buechner's approach to vocation in working with students inside and outside the classroom. Being able to engage with students in vocational reflection fueled my own deep gladness. But in 2008 the world I knew and loved turned upside down when the mysterious breaking of two vertebrae in my back led to a stage IV cancer diagnosis shortly before Christmas. The year 2009 began with me resigning from nearly every aspect of my full and wonderful life. This lousy diagnosis did not relate in any way to my deep gladness. Instead of meeting

---

[6] St. Olaf College received a "Theological Exploration of Vocation" grant in the 2000s. See Tim Clydesdale's *The Purposeful Graduate: Why Colleges Must Talk to Students about Vocation* (Chicago: University of Chicago Press, 2015), for a careful study of the effects of these grants as well as a full list of institutional participants on pp. 231–32.

[7] Frederick Buechner, *Wishful Thinking: A Seeker's ABCs* (New York: HarperOne, 1993), 118.

[8] Buechner, *Wishful Thinking*, 118–19.

the world's deep need, my life became a bucket full of needs that relied on a small army to help me keep going. Any signs of flourishing vanished from my and my family's lives.

Even as I find myself in my fourth remission of living with incurable cancer and continue to appreciate the power of Buechner's vision of vocation for many, my journey with cancer has helped me realize that conversations about vocation also need to make space for the deep sadness that fills our lives. What does it mean to integrate deep sadness into our lives, even to make it part of our vocation, to figure out ways to go on?

In describing the vocation of a theologian, Willie James Jennings observes, "theologians write as fragile bodies even as we write about fragile bodies." Jennings calls on theologians to never forget that we are "fully body."[9] Since my diagnosis I have become much more aware of my own body's fragility and have tried to write and speak in ways that honestly acknowledge the bodily pain and suffering, writing and speaking to and on behalf of those who struggle to find words for similar kinds of suffering. Many days I really wish I had a different vocation—that I didn't see describing the anatomy of life with cancer as part of what I'm called to do as a theologian writing from this particular fragile body.

It has been hard work finding words to express the kind of sadness that often accompanies vocations we don't choose. Immediately after my diagnosis, words went away. Arthur Frank, whose work as a sociologist includes investigating the stories we tell one another about illness, says that seriously ill people "need to become storytellers in order to recover the voices that illness and its treatment often take away."[10] As Frank notes, the stories we tell about illness give form to lives that often inherently lack form. Frank proposes that rather than imposing a limited set of stories that often get told about illness ("He fought valiantly," "She was always so positive"), what is needed is to let our stories about living with serious illness breathe, allowing them to take a more capacious form. Those of us who work on and talk about vocation with students and one another might take a cue from Arthur Frank and create more spacious definitions of vocation and encourage more discussion, more stories about our deep sadness as well as our deep gladness and how both intersect with the world's deep need. Authoring more complex stories about

[9] Willie James Jennings, "Undone and Redone," Foreword to *Glimpsing Resurrection: Cancer, Trauma, and Ministry*, by Deanna A. Thompson (Louisville, KY: Westminster John Knox, 2018), xii.
[10] Arthur Frank, *Wounded Storyteller: Body, Illness, and Ethics* (Chicago: University of Chicago Press, 2010), 4.

the sadness embedded within our vocational journeys allows for the possibility of being more aware of how and when our students, colleagues, and neighbors are not flourishing and opens new avenues for supporting one another in the midst of some of the hardest parts of our individual and collective lives.

It's important to acknowledge that I am not the first to challenge Buechner's way of conceptualizing vocation.[11] College pastor Drew Tucker suggests that "gladness is not something that should solely define the central purposes of our lives."[12] Tucker points out that caring for the needs of the neighbor may involve more toil and suffering than it does joy or gladness. Theologian Kathryn Kleinhans also notes that the call to care for the neighbor is for the neighbor's sake rather than for the purposes of contributing to our gladness.[13] Our gladness cannot and should not be primary when it comes to the ethical dimension of the vocation of serving the neighbor in love. To actively work toward the flourishing of all at times will likely mean that one's own gladness takes a back seat to our neighbor's pain.

My own struggles with chronic illness have prompted a number of students who are on their own journeys with serious health conditions to seek me out and share some of their struggles with me. National surveys report that an estimated 7 percent of American young people live with at least one ongoing health condition that disrupts daily activities. Of particular concern, students with chronic illness tend to be grouped with students with learning disabilities or permanent physical disabilities, often despite the differences in their needs.[14] When I taught at Hamline University, students asked me to serve as faculty advisor for Advocating for Life, Illness, Visibility, and Education (ALIVE), a student organization they created for those with disabilities and chronic illnesses. It was exciting to see this group come into

---

[11] While many chapters in this volume explore Buechner's work, see especially chapter 1 by David Matzko McCarthy for a nuanced discussion of personal vocation as a response to the world as well as chapter 7 by Jonathan Golden for an exploration of what the "world's deep hunger" means.

[12] Drew Tucker, "(Re)Defining Vocation: Gladly Challenging a Vocational Giant," *Intersections*, no. 53 (August 2021): 3, https://digitalcommons.augustana.edu/intersections/vol2021/iss53/7/.

[13] Kathryn Kleinhans, "Distinctive Lutheran Contributions to the Conversation about Vocation," *Intersections*, no. 43 (August 2016): 5, https://digitalcommons.augustana.edu/intersections/vol2016/iss43/7/. See also Paul J. Wadell and Charles R. Pinches's discussion of Buechner's definition of vocation in *Living Vocationally: The Journey of the Called Life* (Eugene, OR: Cascade Books, 2021), 124–25, especially this insight: "The fact that vocational discernment must be attentive to the needs of the world indicates that our callings come from outside us as much or more than from within us" (124).

[14] Laurie Edwards, "When It Comes to Chronic Illness, College Campuses Have a Lot to Learn," WBUR online, March 5, 2014, https://www.wbur.org/cognoscenti/2014/03/05/school-and-health-laurie-edwards.

being and provide space for students dealing with postural tachycardia syndrome (PoTS),[15] epilepsy, and other chronic conditions. They gathered to help one another navigate the many challenges they encounter while being a student with a chronic condition. It was during these conversations that it became clear that any vocational talk of deep gladness alone seemed out of touch with the daily realities of many of our students. It made me question how well we support students and the real limitations they face if we emphasize "deep gladness" without making space for "deep sadness" as well.

And yet the branding of higher education accentuates the promises and possibilities of a college degree to enhance students' deep gladness in many aspects of life. St. Olaf's counseling center staff report that many students they talk with see the sadness in their lives as an obstacle to overcome in order to get on with pursuing their vocation. In many cases, however, the counselors aim to help the students (who are living with mental or physical health challenges, with the aftereffects of their parents' divorce, and beyond) become more aware that their flourishing may involve learning to live alongside the sadness rather than necessarily overcoming it.[16] This is where the language of trauma can be of help in our conversations about vocation, be they in the classroom, advising appointments, student work we supervise, or student organizations we advise.

Language of trauma as vocational language

It may seem counterintuitive that talking about trauma can make more space for people experiencing deep sadness to move toward flourishing. But using the language of trauma in the naming of injustices, losses, and sadness can be integral in addressing all of it. A number of years ago I was invited by theologian Shelly Rambo to be part of a project that eventually became *Post-Traumatic Public Theology*, a collection of essays addressing the breadth and depth of traumatic experiences we humans endure, and offering theological reflections on how we as individuals and communities might better support those living with trauma.[17] Rambo's definition of trauma is "the suffering that

---

[15] A condition where the heart rate increases on changing posture and often causes dizziness or fainting.

[16] These insights from St. Olaf's counseling center staff come from a conversation with staff on Tuesday, November 5, 2019.

[17] Stephanie Arel and Shelly Rambo, eds., *Post-Traumatic Public Theology* (New York: Palgrave Macmillan, 2016).

remains."[18] Trauma is most often caused by an event—war, forced migration, natural disaster, sexual assault, racial violence, a pandemic that has claimed millions of lives worldwide. The stress of a traumatic event is often so great "that it cannot be defended against, coped with, or managed well. The event stunts and often immobilizes. Coping skills are frozen; defense mechanisms fail. When a person experiences a traumatic event, the survival response is triggered, causing the person to fight, flee or freeze."[19]

Through my participation in the posttraumatic public theology project, I was introduced to growing numbers of studies that investigate trauma as it relates to the awful experiences of life. I learned about the ways in which traumatic experiences rob people of language to talk about what they've been through and how our bodies respond in divergent ways to traumatic events. We can feel numb, sad, depressed, exhausted. We can be combative and disagreeable, tired and disconnected. People living with trauma often try to hide these emotions, retreating from relationships in attempts to protect themselves. In sum, "trauma affects our brains, but it has a lasting effect on our bodies."[20]

One of the reasons I appreciate Rambo's definition of trauma as "the suffering that remains" is that it includes but also extends beyond the confines of posttraumatic stress disorder (PTSD). PTSD can be debilitating and life threatening, and those who suffer from it often need medical and therapeutic help to learn how to live alongside the trauma they carry. Invoking the language of trauma in conversations about vocation can provide ways for people to talk about their deep sadness and how it relates to their sense of meaning and place in the world. Trauma theorist Cathy Caruth describes the work she and others do for those living with the aftereffects of traumatic emotional wounds: "[We try] to understand the nature of the suffering without eliminating the force and truth of the reality that trauma survivors face and quite often try to transmit to us."[21] Making space for the deep sadness in our conversations and reflections on vocation, then, involves inviting those who

---

[18] Shelly Rambo, *Spirit and Trauma: A Theology of Remaining* (Louisville, KY: Westminster John Knox, 2010), 15.

[19] Beverly Wallace, "Bible Study: 'She Had to Keep Him Hidden'—Experiences of Trauma in the Lineage of Moses," *Connect Journal* (a publication of the ELCA Youth Ministry Network), June 30, 2020, https://connectjournalorg.wordpress.com/2020/06/30/bible-study-she-had-to-keep-him-hidden-experiences-of-trauma-in-the-lineage-of-moses/.

[20] Wallace, "Bible Study."

[21] Cathy Caruth, "Preface," in *Trauma: Explorations in Memory* (Baltimore: Johns Hopkins University Press, 1995), vii.

have been traumatized to begin to locate language that can help them begin to narrate stories about who they are and what they carry with them.

While the initial impetus for expanding talk of vocation to make space for deep sadness emerged both from my own experience with cancer as well as working with students with increasing mental and physical health challenges, the living through a global pandemic has upped the urgency that we make space for deep sadness in our conversations about vocation. Talk about vocations we did not choose. Many of us in academic contexts had never taught online before or run programs, departments, offices, even entire institutions largely from remote or virtual locations. While education systems across the globe pivoted and provided virtual education for students of all ages, it is crucial to acknowledge and name the losses caused by the COVID-19 pandemic. So many school events and graduations were postponed or done virtually. Countless family rituals and gatherings had to be canceled or postponed. Millions lost family members, colleagues, friends, and even students and were unable to come together to mourn and to bury our dead with the rituals and rites that give shape to our grieving.

Some experts use the language of trauma to describe what so many experienced during the pandemic. Those who study trauma and its effects note that since March 2020 "there is grief over what has been lost, and uncertainty about how to navigate daily life and concerns about what the future holds."[22] And some are now using the term "post-COVID stress disorder."[23] This talk about trauma and the pandemic gives a way to name some of the dimensions of this experience that make space for sadness.

In spring 2021 St. Olaf hosted a virtual panel of alumni talking about how their faith traditions influenced their vocational path at the college and beyond. One of the panelists spoke directly to the students, saying, "You all have a pandemic story, and whatever step you take next is going to be interested in that story—how you used this time, how the pandemic has changed you." That observation resonated with students attending the panel, as they know they've been through something where the implications have yet to be fully explored. As we practice the telling of our pandemic stories and how they relate to vocational discernment, we need to encourage space for the

---

[22] Caelan Soma, "Post-COVID Stress Disorder and Pandemic Trauma and Stress Experience," *Starr Commonwealth Newsletter*, February 19, 2021, https://starr.org/2021/post-covid-stress-disorder-and-pandemic-trauma-and-stress-experience/.

[23] Soma, "Post-COVID."

disorientation and the embodied costs of not being able to be together in person for so many life events during the pandemic.

Neighbor love and ecologies of vocation

In Kleinhans's critique of Buechner's definition of vocation, she lifts up the Lutheran insight that our individual vocations should always be understood in relationship to the neighbor, and that our vocational relationship to the neighbor is for their own sake rather than for what our neighbors might do for us. Theologian Jason Mahn draws on David Brooks's discussion of "being summoned" to expand on this insight of caring for the neighbor for their own sake. Living the summoned life, Mahn suggests, involves exercising agency in being attentive and responsive to others. He writes, "The summoned life doesn't first of all ask what the individual wants to do and then plan for how to accomplish it. It rather looks to the situation and web of relationships in which it finds itself, asking how to respond. Such lives can be incredibly meaningful, but the meaning and purpose come through a different kind of effort."[24]

One significant pandemic story for a group of dedicated St. Olaf students, faculty, and staff involved responding to a summons they experienced through working on the Hostile Terrain 94 (HT94) project to raise awareness about the suffering and trauma of so many migrants crossing the US-Mexico border. A participatory art project sponsored and organized by the Undocumented Migration Project, HT94 culminates in an exhibition of over 3,200 handwritten toe tags representing migrants who have died crossing the Sonoran Desert of Arizona. The St. Olaf HT94 group began work on the project in January 2020 with plans to install the thirty-foot map with toe tags in the fall of 2020. But the pandemic thwarted plans to offer hundreds of in-person sessions dedicated to filling out toe tags. Rather than putting the project on hold, the HT94 student members worked together to create virtual toe tag sessions so people could fill out toe tags online.

As they hosted virtual toe tag sessions throughout the summer of 2020, the group continued to refine how the sessions were conducted. Scripts for the virtual sessions provided increased guidance for participants on how to

---

[24] Jason A. Mahn, *Neighbor Love through Fearful Days: Finding Meaning and Purpose in a Time of Crisis* (Minneapolis, MN: Fortress Press, 2021), xxiii.

deal with potentially intense bodily reactions to filling out the toe tags with the precise location where the body was found, the condition of the body, whether the body had been identified with a name, and an age at the time of death.

St. Olaf's HT94's use of virtual events caught the attention of the national HT94 staff. The college began offering training sessions on how to host virtual toe tag events for HT94 teams across the country. What motivated the students to keep this project going during a pandemic? One of the student leaders, Kgomotso Magagula, emphasized the interconnectedness of the lives of those attempting to cross into the United States and those surrounding her on the Northfield, Minnesota, campus and beyond, saying, "I think that we're interested in making sure that people recognize they are not separated from these issues; we're all complicit, in some capacity, in the structural and physical violence experienced by migrants. . . . The hope is that students, and all participants of our events, take the information we provide and use it as a jumping-off point to get involved in advocacy for migrants."[25] Those who lost their lives attempting to cross the border summoned Magagula and others working with HT94 to educate the campus about border issues and ways to mitigate such suffering through advocacy work at the state and national levels.

What also is highlighted in this illustration from the HT94 project is Magagula's insistence that the suffering of those at the border is not divorced from the lives of those attending college in the Upper Midwest. Magagula's insistence leads us back to the insight that individual flourishing is always embedded within larger networks. Theologian Kiara Jorgenson builds on this point, arguing that Protestant notions of vocation take us beyond a focus on individual passions or roads to self-discovery in their emphasis on "right relation" over "right behavior." In her critical retrieval of Reformation views of vocation, she highlights the strong link in Reformation thought between creation and vocation that can be mined to focus today on the ecologies of relationships we have not just with other humans but also with the natural world.[26] When right relation becomes primary within vocational

---

[25] "Students Prepare Exhibit to Raise Awareness about Deaths on U.S. Southern Border," St. Olaf College News, November 20, 2020, https://wp.stolaf.edu/news/students-prepare-exhibit-to-raise-awareness-about-deaths-on-u-s-southern-border.

[26] Jorgenson explores how for Luther and Calvin, vocation is the "lynchpin between creation and redemption." To pursue vocation, "including one's ecological calling to live as participant of creation, is not just to honor God, nor is it primarily care for the other, but rather to do both simultaneously." See Kiara A. Jorgenson, *Ecology of Vocation: Recasting Calling in a New Planetary Era* (Minneapolis,

discernment, attending to the "ecologies of vocation" that make up our lives entails responding to the bodies and ecological systems of which we are a part. This means that our vocations are localized, embedded in particular places where each of us is summoned to be in right relationship with human and nonhuman neighbors within our midst. This ecological framing of vocation leads us back to an institutional commitment to contribute to the flourishing of *all*.

But what is evident is that all are not flourishing. How can attending to the trauma and suffering present in our ecologies of vocation help us move toward more flourishing?

Lament, protest, and inching toward flourishing

Growing awareness of trauma and its aftereffects is also being accompanied by growing interest by theologians and practitioners in practices of lament. Theologians Kathleen Billman and Daniel Migliore lift up the story in Jeremiah 31 of Rachel's cry over the loss of her children and her refusal to be consoled. She weeps for herself and the loss of her children, but Billman and Migliore also highlight the anger and resistance embedded in her lament: "She refuses to be comforted for her children, because *they* are no more."[27] Her rage is on behalf of her children and their senseless death. The figure of Rachel and her disturbing cry is revered in Judaism; she gives voice to the cries of countless Jewish mothers as well as amplifying cries of human anguish in many forms, and her refusal to be consoled "registers a powerful protest to outrageous suffering and injustice."[28]

Written in the sixth century BCE, the book of Jeremiah invokes the image of Rachel as weeping for her children exiled in Babylon. This poetic, metaphorical invocation of the Israelite matriarch, who died giving birth to her son, Benjamin (Gen. 35:16–20), is discussed by biblical interpreters as not only pointing to the suffering of Benjamin's descendants but also weeping for all of Israel, for Jews who have endured trauma passed on through

MN: Fortress Press, 2020), 63, 62. See also the epilogue of this volume for a discussion of ecology, vocation, and the common good.

[27] Kathleen Billman and Daniel Migliore, *Rachel's Cry: Prayer of Lament and Rebirth of Hope* (Eugene, OR: Wipf and Stock Publishers, 2006), 2.
[28] Billman and Migliore, *Rachel's Cry*, 2.

generations. This image of Rachel's weeping continues to be invoked even for the most traumatic of events, the Shoah. At the Yad Vashem Museum in Israel, the words from Jeremiah are displayed to commemorate countless Jewish children murdered by the Nazis: "Thus says the Eternal One, A voice heard in Ramah, lamentation and bitter weeping, Rachel weeping for her children. She refuses to be comforted for her children, because they are no more." The continued invocation of Rachel's weeping for Jewish suffering testifies to the reality of intergenerational trauma for members of the Jewish community.

Billman and Migliore note that Rachel's cry is largely overlooked in Christian circles. There is much to be said for the ongoing need for Christian recognition of Rachel's cry for Jewish trauma and suffering in particular, especially given the deep and expansive legacy of Christian anti-Judaism and anti-Semitism, a topic that deserves much more attention than can be given here.[29] After introducing the story of Rachel's cry and the central role it plays in Jewish imagination, Billman and Migliore call on Christians to follow Jewish practice in attending to Rachel's cry and its accompanying practice of lament, understanding lament as necessary and integral to religious practice and, I am proposing, to vocational reflection and practice that makes more space for deep sadness as well as deep gladness.

What is it that lament actually does for those who practice it? Lament "aims to be responsive to the realities of human experience," to honestly name the brokenness of our individual and collective lives. Theologically speaking, lament brings to God our grief, anger, and sadness over both unjust situations and the suffering that just is, and such practice affirms the integrity of people created by God and our hope in God's promised renewal of embodied life.[30]

The communal practice of lament also grants permission for people to grieve and protest.[31] On the eve of their inauguration ceremony, President Biden and Vice President Harris and their spouses stood before the Lincoln Memorial Reflecting Pool in Washington, DC. The pool was illuminated by four hundred lanterns representing the four hundred thousand US lives lost to COVID-19. Prior to this public expression of lament, there had been few ritualized opportunities at a national level for Americans to mourn the

---

[29] This topic is particularly important for Lutheran Christians to address given Luther's horrible treatise, "On the Jews and Their Lies." See an especially powerful book-length treatment of this subject by Brooks Schramm and Kirsi I. Stjerna, *Martin Luther, the Bible, and the Jewish People* (Minneapolis, MN: Fortress Press, 2012).

[30] Billman and Migliore, *Rachel's Cry*, 19–20.

[31] Billman and Migliore, *Rachel's Cry*, 109.

immense loss of life caused by the virus. Historian Micki McElya commented on the event, noting that

> sharing grief brings people together . . . like nothing else. This is a vast country of an enormous and varied population. . . . Yet it's in moments of national mourning, it's in moments of collective grief and collective honor that we come together, that we experience those bonds of nationhood and community across all of these many different lines of difference. And there can be no unity, there can be no collectivity without a shared sense of belonging, without a shared sense of community in this nation. And that's what collective grief offers.[32]

This recognition of our collective losses created space for those who lost loved ones due to the virus.[33]

Communal practices of lament also provide opportunities to enact something that cannot be done when we lament alone. As Billman and Migliore propose, the embodied experience of participating in collective lament out loud not only helps incarnate experiences of loss and grief but also offers strength to counter persistent threats of disorder, chaos, and meaninglessness. When a community embodies lament, it helps form not only individual bodies but also a corporate body to voice emotions of sadness, grief, anger, complaint, agony, and hope before God. This is how the Irish practice of keening has been described. The keen—a ritual involving "instinctive raw cries" when the Irish gather to mourn their dead—provides a powerful opportunity for cathartic release of grief as well as a linking of community members together through the grief.[34] In performing such practices, the community embodies a rebuttal to the dehumanizing effects of injustice as well as to the suffering that just is. When our sorrow and anguish are acknowledged and borne with others, we can become unstuck and able to move, as the psalmist does, toward healing and hope.

---

[32] Mary Louise Kelly, "400 Lights, for 400,000 Dead, Illuminate Lincoln Memorial Reflecting Pool," National Public Radio website, January 19, 2021, accessed December 3, 2021, https://www.npr.org/sections/coronavirus-live-updates/2021/01/19/958449203/400-lights-for-400-000-dead-to-illuminate-lincoln-memorial-reflecting-pool.

[33] A conversation with a friend about how she felt she was given permission to mourn her father's death from COVID-19 because of this Lincoln Memorial ceremony. November 19, 2021.

[34] See Mary McLaughlin, "Keening the Dead: Ancient History or a Ritual for Today?," *Religions* 10, no. 4 (March 2019): 1–11, https://doi.org/10.3390/rel10040235.

In her work on trauma and its embodied effects, womanist and pastoral care professor Beverly Wallace draws on Resmaa Menaken's powerful book, *My Grandmother's Hands: Racialized Trauma and the Pathway to Mending Our Hearts and Bodies*, and his discussion of how bodies have a form of knowledge that is different from our cognitive brains.[35] Traumatic knowledge often gets expressed as a "felt sense of constriction or expansion, pain or ease, energy or numbness. This knowledge is stored in our bodies as 'wordless stories.' These stories are about what is safe and what is dangerous. It is in the body that we have our hopes and our fears."[36] Wallace's insights increase awareness as to why silence might be the body's response to news like the Chauvin verdict.

Wallace uses the story of Moses and the characters involved in the dramatic attempt to preserve his life as an infant to reflect on the trauma she and other Black Americans experienced during the aftermath of Floyd's murder. Wallace writes:

> I write this in the midst of a pandemic, on the week anniversary of the killing of another male child. I write this as I think of an adult male child George Floyd who called for his mother, whose last breath after he told the authorities he could not breathe was to call to the one who gave him life. Since we are the children of God, then within our bodies, within our DNA are also the experiences of those who have come before us. Our very bodies house the unhealed dissonance and trauma of our ancestors— intergenerational transmission of trauma, trauma passed on in the expression of our DNA. Might we still be living with the traumatic experience of Jochebed, the mother of the liberator of God's people? Might we have within us the experiences of Moses and Miriam? Might we respond as Shiphrah and Puah with the resiliency to resist engaging in activities that are harmful to a community even though communities of people are being hurt and traumatized?[37]

Wallace's question of how we respond to traumatic situations is a question about vocation.[38] And she insists that we pay attention to the deep sadness,

---

[35] Beverly Wallace, "Bible Study," citing Resmaa Menakim, *My Grandmother's Hands: Racialized Trauma and the Pathway to Mending Our Hearts and Bodies* (Las Vegas, NV: Central Recovery Press, 2017), a critical source that investigates the power of intergenerational trauma in Black lives as well as ways to heal.

[36] Wallace, "Bible Study."

[37] Wallace, "Bible Study."

[38] See also Meghan M. Slining's discussion of trauma and vocation in chapter 10 of this volume.

to the toll that systemic injustice takes on Black bodies and spirits, and asks where we find ourselves in Moses's story, in the story of intergenerational trauma, and in cultivating resiliency amid the long legacies of raced-based violence and injustice.[39] Wallace demonstrates that stories from the biblical text and elsewhere can help give shape to the traumas we carry with us today.

It is important that Wallace's analysis does not neglect the roles of Shiprah and Puah, the midwives who refused to heed Pharoah's directive to kill the Hebrew baby boys. "When faced with a stress as great as the order to end newborn lives," Wallace notes, "the midwives chose to fight back by not following this order and doing their part to protect the lives of babies such as Moses."[40] With this description of the vocations of Shiprah and Puah, perhaps we are coming back around to Buechner's definition of vocation as God calling you to the place where your deep gladness and the world's deep need meet.

On many campuses students are leading the way in lamenting ecological damage and advocating for more sustainable practices by institutions and government officials.[41] In spring 2021 St. Olaf's student-led Climate Justice Coalition held a "Die-In" in front of the student center, protesting Line 3, a pipeline being built through Indigenous communities in Minnesota and Canada, and calling for the college's divestment in fossil fuel. Over two hundred students lay on the pavement for 1,097 seconds—just over 18 minutes—with each second representing one mile of the proposed pipeline.[42] Pipelines destroying sacred lands, wildfires raging, water sources becoming harder to access, the planet's temperatures continuing to rise—these developments embody the reality that "when the earth is in distress, humans are in distress."[43] And it is increasingly the young who are taking the lead in insisting that the flourishing of all to which we are called to be committed depends

[39] For additional work on intergenerational trauma in Black lives, see Gimel Rogers and Thema Bryant-Davis, "Historical and Contemporary Racial Trauma among Black Americans: Black Wellness Matters," in *Handbook of Interpersonal Violence and Abuse across the Lifespan*, ed. Robert Geffner et al. (Cham, Switzerland: Springer International, 2021), 165–99, https://doi.org/10.1007/978-3-319-89999-2_338, as well as Jameta Nicole Barlow, "Restoring Optimal Black Mental Health and Reversing Intergenerational Trauma in an Era of Black Lives Matter," *Biography*, 41, no. 4 (2018): 895–908, https://doi.org/10.1353/bio.2018.0084.

[40] Wallace, "Bible Study."

[41] For further examples of vocational advocacy, see Michelle Hayford's reflections in chapter 5 of this volume.

[42] Claire Strother, "CJC-Organized 'Die In' Gathers Students in Solidarity against Line 3," *St. Olaf Messenger*, March 5, 2021, https://www.theolafmessenger.com/2021/cjc-organized-die-in-gathers-students-in-solidarity-against-line-3/.

[43] Pamela R. McCarroll, "Embodying Theology: Trauma Theory, Climate Change, Pastoral and Practical Theology," *Religions* 13 (March 2022): 294, https://doi.org/10.3390/rel13040294.

on humans—especially those of us in first-world contexts like the United States—to realize that our vocations must involve inflicting less harm on the nonhuman ecologies of which we are a part.[44]

One additional word about making more space for deep sadness when we're reflecting on vocation: I'm not advocating that all of us must share our deep sadness with others, that we are required to incorporate them in public ways into our understanding of vocation, or that we should always be on the lookout for how to talk more about trauma and suffering and sadness. It could be that we simply do not have the language to talk about what we've been through. It could be that it's retraumatizing to open up about our deep sadness. The first time I returned to the classroom after my cancer diagnosis I had a little speech prepared about the diagnosis and the treatment I was undergoing and how we would try and carry on as best we could. But once I actually stood before my students on that first day of class, unsteady on my feet, I realized I couldn't talk about the cancer at all. During the early months after the diagnosis, the classroom became the one cancer-free zone of my life, and what a gift that was. Listening to colleagues and friends of color talk about the emotional labor and personal cost of rehearsing some of their own race-based trauma in the company of White people, they say, is not just exhausting but can at times feel exploitative. In addition, scholars working on the effects of the climate crisis warn that climate trauma can compound past traumas and trigger dissociation for some.[45] So this is tricky and delicate work. Still, when we name that our callings encompass sadness as well as gladness, we make space for expanded visions of vocation that relate even more profoundly to the world's deep need.

Toward hope, radical joy, and the flourishing of all

As we consider what comes after lament, it is important to lift up the fact that Rachel's cry of lament in Jeremiah 31 does not end with her refusal to be consoled: what follows is nothing less than a "startling promise" from God (Jer. 31:16–17). The text reports that God hears her cry and promises the

---

[44] Jason Mahn observes that college vocational exploration programs often do not attract student activists who view colleges and other institutions as too slow to change. He calls on educators to support the activist work of our students, suggesting we respond openly and creatively to their institutional critiques and engage them in vocational reflection as well as in the work of institutional change. See Neighbor Love through Fearful Days, 120–21.
[45] McCarroll, "Embodying Theology," 294.

return of her children, promising that justice and peace will reign,[46] that injustice and death do not have the last word.

But how are we to respond to God's promised future of justice and peace? Cultural historian Rebecca Solnit observes that we humans are not good at envisioning a time when all are flourishing when the future seems so unsettled and uncertain.[47] Solnit directs her words toward those of us who grow weary over how little progress toward justice can be detected, despite the efforts of many. "To be hopeful is to take on a different persona," Solnit writes. It's risky, taking on a persona of hope, since hope is "ultimately a form of trust, trust in the unknown and the possible."[48]

According to Solnit, hope is cultivated in no small measure by the stories we tell about ourselves. She notes that we often present the stories of history in terms of winning or losing, and this tidy framing can limit our view of what's possible in the present as well as the future. In order to take on a persona of hope, Solnit insists on moving beyond a framework of winners and losers to a trust in the possibilities of what might yet come to be. At the same time, hope is not simply focused on the future; rather, hope gets practiced and lived out, with others, in the here and now.[49]

I find Solnit's hesitancy around linking hope to a clear sense of resolution to be especially helpful and important when attending to the trauma and deep sadness many of us carry. Spending more time understanding the long-lasting effects of trauma has led me to become more aware of how Christian conversations about hope often drive toward resolution. Yes, life can contain significant suffering, but tellers of the Christian story often emphasize that resurrection is always the end of the story. While I continue to believe in resurrection, understanding trauma's effects in people's lives pushes us toward a more complicated telling of the Christian story, acknowledging that the storyline doesn't move immediately from the trauma of crucifixion to the new life of resurrection, but contains Holy Saturday, the space in between death and new life.[50] And this space in between is a space many inhabit. This is why Solnit's recommendation that hope be not simply future oriented but practiced in the now is so important.

---

[46] Billman and Migliore, *Rachel's Cry*, 2.

[47] See Rebecca Solnit, *Hope in the Dark: Untold Histories, Wild Possibilities* (New York: Nation Books, 2004), 27.

[48] Solnit, *Hope in the Dark*, 16.

[49] Solnit, *Hope in the Dark*, 23.

[50] See again Rambo's *Spirit and Trauma*, as well as Deanna A. Thompson, *Glimpsing Resurrection: Cancer, Trauma, and Ministry* (Louisville, KY: Westminster John Knox, 2018).

It is also important to affirm that living in irresolute spaces can be life giving. Black spoken word artist Joe Davis is committed to developing a new movement around practicing hope in the here and now through encouraging a "radical joy." Davis writes:

> Radical joy is more powerful than oppression—it is a joy that can't be policed. It refers to the embodiment of a deeply rooted connection to one's culture and identity, especially in times of communal grief and collective trauma caused by state-sanctioned violence, multiple mass shootings, and perpetual anti-Blackness. But that's exactly why cultivating joy is a radical act and a practice we are committed to sharing.[51]

Why radical joy amidst multiple pandemics? Davis sums it up this way: "in the midst of the 'Triple Pandemic' of racial injustice, economic inequity, and COVID-19, we need to cultivate radical joy now more than ever. We contribute to our health and well-being when we create space to authentically express our grief, anger, and joy in a system that otherwise dehumanizes us."[52] What a powerful linking of deep sadness and deep gladness and a vision that advocates for the flourishing of all.

Serious health challenges, a global pandemic, the ongoing persistence of systemic racism in our institutions and communities, growing environmental crises—we wouldn't choose any of these vocational ecologies voluntarily. In *Telling Secrets*, Frederick Buechner's memoir that chronicles his father's drinking and suicide as well as his feelings of helplessness over his daughter's anorexia, Buechner shares a vision of vocation intimately linked to not just "the world's deep need" but also to his own sadness and the sadness of those he loved most. Buechner struggled at times to accept that "God calls me to be this rather than that."[53] Our ecologies of vocation invite us to live out our callings in this time and this place, to attend to the needs of human and nonhuman neighbors, for the flourishing of all.

---

[51] Joe Davis, "What Is Radical Joy?," Facebook post, May 8, 2021, https://www.facebook.com/joe davispoetry/posts/what-is-radical-joy-radical-joy-is-more-powerful-than-oppressionit-is-a-joy-that/1683681971842745/.

[52] Davis, "What Is Radical Joy?"

[53] Frederick Buechner, *Telling Secrets* (San Francisco: Harper Collins, 1991), 91.

3

Overturning for the Common Good

Membership and Mutuality in a World of Markets and Meritocracy

Christine Jeske

A few years into my current faculty job, I designed my dream course. I poured my soul into it. I expected the title—What Is Money Good For?—would intrigue and entice students. The syllabus was packed with readings that had shaped my own path connecting vocation to the common good—accounts of modern capitalism transforming Europe, farmers growing Fair Trade coffee in Mexico, and policymakers redesigning welfare in South Africa. I imagined students' worlds overturning.

You can guess what happened. Students. In the real world. Clinging tightly to the ideas and habits that order most of this real world. They pushed back when we read that money should do more than provide individual comfort and occasional acts of charity. When I suggested that their apparent success in this high-ranked private college was due to factors of privilege beyond their earned merit alone, they checked out. They recoiled when we read that market capitalism doesn't solve all our social and ethical dilemmas, and that systemic racism mars our world. My growing sense that students were not experiencing the transformation I'd expected was confirmed in one unforgettable comment on a course feedback form: "Going into this class, I thought classes on diversity were a waste of time. I still think so."

Looking back, I see much that went wrong. I had designed the class assuming that students would already agree upon the value and meaning of seeking the common good. I underestimated what I was up against. Seeking the common good requires imagining and pursuing a reality that often gets tossed to and trampled upon at the bottom of the social concepts heap. Prioritizing that common good requires an overturning.

This word, "overturning," jumped out at me in Willie James Jennings's book *After Whiteness*. He argues that "distorted formation has been with

Christine Jeske, *Overturning for the Common Good* In: *Called Beyond Our Selves*. Edited by: Erin VanLaningham, Oxford University Press. © Oxford University Press 2024. DOI: 10.1093/oso/9780197691915.003.0004

Western education for centuries, and now we have entered a moment when we might begin to address it."[1] To address a distorted formation will take more than minor tweaks. Jennings writes that

> educational institutions . . . exist inside a revolution, the *overturning* that is the turning the world right side up by God. It is an overturning that makes possible a beautifully strange kind of building up. It is a building up inside a crumbling. We are inside the Spirit's crumbling of world orders, orders that reach all the way down to the body, claiming sovereignty over the ways we should understand ourselves.[2]

Participating in this sort of educational overturning so that we can promote practices that prioritize the common good demands that we reject many of the dominant discourses, practices, and narratives that surround us.

Much of social science and my own discipline of cultural anthropology builds on the thesis that we spend substantial portions of our lives not cognizant of the influence that our own social world has upon us. In order to participate in personal and social transformation, then, we must seek awareness of our socially and culturally ingrained patterns of thought and action. The cultural world we live in presents ways of being that become so normal that we misrecognize alternatives, seeing them as objectionable or simply unimaginable. And yet alternative social worlds always exist. Some may be better, some worse, but always society could be designed otherwise. As educators, our work involves freeing students to see, imagine, desire, and seek some better form of otherwise.

In this volume, we consider how to guide students to an "otherwise" approach to vocation—one that places priority on the common good. Presumably we (educators) are not already doing a great job of this, or we wouldn't be writing (and you reading) this book. My classroom experience shared above attests to this dilemma—in guiding students to prioritize the common good in their vocational paths, we have work to do. But what does that work entail? What is the shape of the normalcy from which we hope to free ourselves and our students?

To begin answering this question, we may do well to shift focus and acknowledge that vocational questions are not just about careers; they are

---

[1] Willie James Jennings, *After Whiteness: An Education in Belonging*, Theological Education between the Times (Grand Rapids, MI: Eerdmans, 2020), 5.

[2] Jennings, *After Whiteness*, 124, emphasis mine.

ultimately about what "the good life" entails.[3] When we talk about vocation, we tap into culturally inflected narratives that tell us how to seek good lives. When I refer to narratives, I mean not simply the ways individuals re-tell events in their own lives, but the tropes and metanarratives that our cultural setting teaches us to use to interpret and predict reality. As many social theorists have pointed out, such narratives shape our deepest understandings of what material and moral conditions constitute "good" end results, as well as what practical and ethical means we expect will take us to that good.[4] The narratives we live by are not like bedtime stories that sit on a shelf for us to flip through for entertainment—they sink into our deepest subconscious to shape our values, purpose, moralities, embodied habits, and everything about our vocational journey. We all selectively draw upon different and even opposing narratives, serially and even simultaneously. Some narratives are dominant in a society, while others are marginalized. Some have so deeply saturated our media, classrooms, parental advice, faith communities, and every blip of cultural influence that we find it hard to recognize their existence, much less welcome alternatives to their all-encompassing hegemonic normalcy.

Narratives of the good life are not neutral in their effects. Some narratives are inherently dangerous to ourselves and others. Some work to maintain oppressive power, while others navigate pathways for the survival of those whose power is sharply circumscribed. Some narratives destroy individual and social well-being, bringing loneliness, anxiety, and social disparities disguised in sham promises of happiness. To understand the core of what we're up against in teaching about vocation and the common good, then, we need to recognize narratives that present a view of the good and its pathways as something other than a common good.[5] We also need to consider what

---

[3] Studies of "the good life" trace back as far as Aristotle, who used the term "eudaimonia" to refer to a life made good through virtue rather than pleasure seeking. In recent decades, anthropologists such as Edward Fischer and Sherry Ortner have studied cultural diversity in the meanings people attach to good lives, and psychologists, philosophers, and economists have used the term to study factors contributing to subjective well-being. See Edward F. Fischer, *The Good Life: Aspiration, Dignity, and the Anthropology of Wellbeing* (Stanford, CA: Stanford University Press, 2014); Christine Jeske, *The Laziness Myth: Narratives of Work and the Good Life in South Africa* (Ithaca, NY: Cornell University Press, 2020); Lawrence J. Jost and Roger A. Shiner, *Eudaimonia and Well-Being: Ancient and Modern Conceptions* (Kelowna, BC: Academic Printing and Pub, 2003); Sherry B. Ortner, "On Key Symbols," *American Anthropologist* 75, no. 5 (1973): 1338–46, https://doi.org/10.1525/aa.1973.75.5.02a00100.

[4] See, for example, Cheryl Mattingly and Linda C. Garro, eds., *Narrative and the Cultural Construction of Illness and Healing* (Berkeley: University of California Press, 2000); Joel Robbins, "Beyond the Suffering Subject: Toward an Anthropology of the Good," *Journal of the Royal Anthropological Institute* 19, no. 3 (2013): 447–62, https://doi.org/10.1111/1467-9655.12044.

[5] See chapter 13 of this volume by Charles Mathewes for a further discussion of "what we are up against" in our conception of education as formation.

we're aiming for—the narratives that can help us envision and place ourselves within vocational journeys that seek a common good.

To recognize the power of narratives, we might begin by considering the
following statistics:

- The average household net worth of Americans identifying as White is
  eight times higher than average household net worth among Americans
  identifying as Black.[6]
- In May 2021, the U.S. Customs and Border Protection Agency
  encountered 180,034 people attempting to cross the US-Mexico border.
  Of those, the agency expelled 112,302.[7]
- A total of 619,591 abortions were reported in the United States in 2018.[8]
- Twenty-three percent of children in the United States live with only one
  parent.[9]

Each of these facts can be found at multiple reputable sources, and while
the numbers may vary slightly due to measurement methods or criteria, the
facts themselves are not where much controversy lies. And yet, anyone who
has paid attention to news in the United States will recognize that this list of
facts evokes divisions deep enough to slice apart families and communities.
Why? Because they evoke narratives. Narratives organize our bits of information, bridge gaps, make predictions, and infuse knowledge with emotion
and morality.

When we face information that doesn't fit our narratives, our minds
are wired to dismiss those facts. In reading, you may already have noticed
yourself deflecting a narrative you imagine connecting the above data with
statements of "yes, but . . ." and "what about this other thing?" In the narratives
surrounding these statistics there are headbutting differences regarding what

[6] Neil Bhutta, Andrew C. Chang, Lisa J. Dettling, and Joanne W. Hsu, "Disparities in Wealth by
Race and Ethnicity in the 2019 Survey of Consumer Finances," Federal Reserve, September 28, 2020,
https://www.federalreserve.gov/econres/notes/feds-notes/disparities-in-wealth-by-race-and-ethnic
ity-in-the-2019-survey-of-consumer-finances-20200928.htm.

[7] U.S. Customs and Border Protection, "CBP Announces May 2021 Operational Update," U.S.
Customs and Border Protection, June 9, 2021, https://www.cbp.gov/newsroom/national-media-rele
ase/cbp-announces-may-2021-operational-update.

[8] Katherine Kortsmit, Tara C. Jatlaoui, and Michelle G. Mandel, "Abortion Surveillance — United
States, 2018," MMWR, Surveillance Summaries 69 (SS-7, 2020): 1–29, https://doi.org/10.15585/
mmwr.ss6907a1.

[9] Stephanie Kramer, "U.S. Has World's Highest Rate of Children Living in Single-Parent Households,"
Pew Research Center (blog), December 12, 2019, https://www.pewresearch.org/fact-tank/2019/12/
12/u-s-children-more likely-than-children-in-other-countries-to-live-with-just-one-parent/.

the common good entails and how to get there. My point here is not to defend one of these narratives over another, but to point out two things: First, aspects of political party, religion, ethnicity, gender, race, and other social positions can incline us toward particular narratives. Second, when it comes to overturning our relationship to the common good, it's not facts that we need; it's the ability to analyze, unlearn, and relearn narratives. None of us is locked into just one narrative for life. By growing in awareness, we can exercise a degree of agency over the narratives we turn to.

A growing body of vocational literature explores ways that educators can help students discover new possible personal narratives. Shirley Showalter highlights the importance of educators telling and eliciting personal narratives in the classroom, writing, "When our stories seem 'stuck,' the answer is not to retreat but to create more and better ones."[10] Likewise Erin VanLaningham demonstrates how educators can take the narrative quality of novels as a starting point for vocational exploration as students learn to recognize alternative realities, partial points of view, differences between possible and actual events, and chaotic or unresolved forms.[11] Patrick Reyes takes this a step further, highlighting how narratives shape conceptions of vocation not merely at the personal level, but at the cultural level. He critiques the ways the "hero journey"—an arc in which an individual receives a sudden annunciation of purpose, embarks on a journey of self-discovery, and overcomes obstacles—has been used in dominant vocational literature to ignore the unequal opportunities, nonlinear paths, and ties to community and place that all inflect vocations. He writes, "Prior to even beginning the journey, many people today have been left out. . . . What if our stories are not linear or redemptive? Can they still be purpose filled?"[12] Teaching students to prioritize the common good in their vocations will require educators to join with students in recognizing and questioning the narratives we take for granted.

In this chapter, I describe four narratives, each titled with a word starting with "m." The first two are normalized dominant narratives that contribute

---

[10] Shirley Hershey Showalter, "Called to Tell Our Stories: The Narrative Structure of Vocation," in *Vocation across the Academy*, ed. David S. Cunningham (New York: Oxford University Press, 2017), 67–88. For more on narrative identities, see Dan McAdams, *The Redemptive Self: Stories Americans Live By* (New York: Oxford University Press, 2005).

[11] Erin VanLaningham, "Novels, Vocation and the Call of the Unfinished Story," in *Cultivating Vocation in Literary Studies*, ed. Stephanie L. Johnson and Erin VanLaningham (Edinburgh: Edinburgh University Press, 2022), 45–66.

[12] Patrick B. Reyes, *The Purpose Gap: Empowering Communities of Color to Find Meaning and Thrive* (Louisville, KY: Westminster John Knox Press, 2021), 34, 36.

to a distorted formation inhibiting people from seeking the common good. I call these the "markets can solve it" narrative and the "merit makes me deserve it" narrative. Both are powerfully hegemonic, by which I mean that they are so historically rooted and subtly a part of dominant discourses that they often go without question even as they sprout new Hydra-like manifestations. But people have found ways to contest them repeatedly throughout history, which demonstrates that the overturning is ongoing. I then present two alternative narratives that offer a model of vocation that prioritizes the common good. These narratives assert that we belong in a social *membership* and that we thrive not just through generosity or consumption, but when our memberships involve a *mutuality* that weaves an ecology of both giving and receiving.

It's worth noting that as educators, these narratives do not just shape our students—they shape us too. Until we recognize the ways our own lives and institutions have been malformed, we have little hope of challenging our students. Teaching students to seek the common good in their vocations is difficult for precisely this reason—we embark in overturning our own world along with theirs. But if we allow students to follow whatever narratives they or we happen to find comfortable, we fail in our own vocation as educators. We need to acknowledge together that in vocational narratives, sometimes people get it wrong. Practices of self-reflection and humility are necessary to prepare us for unlearning and overturning.

The first narrative: markets can fix it

When considering how vocation relates to the common good, we can begin by critically analyzing the taken-for-granted answers to the question: how do we meet society's needs? The answer to this question that resounds throughout much of Western society is: "markets can solve it." We live in a world in which trusting markets is central to the ways we negotiate what is good. But if we want to consider seriously how to seek the common good, we're going to have to be honest about what markets can and can't do.

A market is a system of distribution in which each good or service, be it sheet metal or a haircut, can be atomized—separated into individual goods with individual owners—and traded. Those trades occur through a process of sellers and buyers negotiating among competitive alternatives until they agree upon prices. It's a powerful system, one that allows us to efficiently distribute innumerable resources every second across our planet. But markets are more than just a distribution system. They exist because people believe narratives that make such systems make sense.[13] Throughout much of human history and in many contexts today, humans have believed other narratives, and we do well to notice what the "markets can fix it" narrative smothers.

Students—and most people in the global North—tend to assume that most exchanges happen through markets. But all exchanges, even market ones, have relational and social aspects that offer crucial insights into how to seek the common good. To teach what markets do and don't do, I sometimes begin by asking students the question, "If you get together for a shared holiday meal with extended family, how are goods exchanged?" Students recognize how absurd it would be to treat such a setting as a market, handing over cash or clicking Venmo before passing the mashed potatoes or kimchi to their grandmothers. In this setting, turning to a "market can solve it" logic for ordering behavior would leave us not only awkwardly without institutional precedents but also morally repulsed.

So too are market processes culturally reprimanded in many situations— romance, voting, asking directions, or organ donation to name a few. Anthropologists studying culture in non-Western as well as Western settings have long pointed out that exchanges involve far more than market negotiations.[14] Every exchange exists in the context of a relationship. Forms of exchange reveal and reinforce aspects of those relationships. For example, the balance of giving and receiving in an exchange can communicate status or care, as when grandparents give far more than they receive back from their grandchildren. Culture also informs how long an exchange relationship should last (a single click on Walmart.com versus an offer to reciprocate when a friend buys me coffee) and how highly valued each party is (an anonymous "made in Indonesia" clothing label versus a Fair Trade website introducing a clothing artisan). Market capitalism is never as simple as two

---

[13] Katherine Browne, "Economics and Morality: Introduction," in *Economics and Morality: Anthropological Approaches*, ed. Katherine Browne and Lynne Milgram (Lanham, MD: AltaMira Press, 2009), 1–40.

[14] See, for example, David Graeber, "On the Moral Grounds of Economic Relations: A Maussian Approach," *Journal of Classical Sociology* 14, no. 1 (2014): 65–77, https://doi.org/10.1177/14687 95x13494719; Bronislaw Malinowski, "Tribal Economics in the Trobriands," in *Tribal and Peasant Economies: Readings in Economic Anthropology,* ed. Georg Dalton (Garden City, NY: Natural History Press, 1967), 185–223; Marcel Mauss, *The Gift: The Form and Reason for Exchange in Archaic Societies,* trans. W. D. Halls (New York: W. W. Norton, 1990); Marshall David Sahlins, *Stone Age Economics* (Chicago: Aldine, 1972).

intersecting supply-and-demand curves; it's a messy affair of trust building, litigations, lobbying, financial regulation, power, boundary enforcements, and care.

In teaching students to reconceptualize what roles markets play in society, I often tell a story of my father's first astronomy course in college. He had enjoyed star gazing as a child, and when the class met to look at the night sky, he asked his instructor the name of a constellation. To his surprise, the instructor was unable to name any constellations beyond the Big Dipper. My dad never forgot the lesson: there is far more to learn about stars than the names of constellations.

Most students' knowledge of economic constellations is on par with naming just the Big Dipper, Orion, and Cassiopeia: capitalism, socialism, and communism. In this highly simplified view of economies, they make dismissive statements like "Market capitalism isn't perfect, but it's the only real option." To see the ways our vocation factors into the common good, we need to see exchanges at a whole different level, much like the level of electromagnetic fields, dark matter, and celestial coordinates in astronomy. If all we can see is individuals making morally neutral purchases and sales, and if markets are the only workable option we can imagine, we cannot formulate the questions we'll need to answer in order to find our role in the common good.

But there's something safe and comforting in believing that an invisible hand will distribute goods well enough if we just stop fussing. Naming the ways that markets fail can be threatening, not only because it interrupts a conception of the ways the world works, but also because it implies a call to more deliberate action. And yet fail markets do: a market system alone will not solve persistent inequalities, moral failures, or externalities—the costs (such as pollution) and benefits (such as educated citizens) accrued to people other than the buyer and seller.

There are a vast array of alternative forms of interaction that the market paradigm ignores. Some alternative systems for pursuing the common good, like redistribution through taxes or charities, will be familiar to students. Often the dominant "markets can fix it" narrative comfortably concedes a limited place for these systems, as if tacking on a footnote: "Markets can fix it except occasionally when we have to pay some taxes and donate some money to help people who aren't working hard enough to succeed."

A real overturning that presses students to weave a concern for the common good into the very weft of their vocational choices will have to go further than tacking on taxes and charity alone. As an example of how we

might stretch beyond "markets can fix it (except when charity is necessary),"
the anthropologist James Ferguson describes what the world could learn
from a logic of distribution prevalent in Southern Africa, which he calls "the
logic of the share."[15] By that logic, people's needs are met not solely in trade
for merit or work, but also, at times, in accordance with their belonging in
a group. It's a logic we're already familiar with because it happens in many
situations, including families: I share slices of a cantaloupe with my family
not because each member earns it, but because we belong together as a
family. My spouse could lodge complaints against me hoarding cantaloupe
not because he has something to trade for it, but because we agree that each
family member gets a fair *share*. It's a nonmarket, nonmerit logic and narrative. Ferguson points out that it also avoids the shame that often surrounds
welfare distribution—recipients are not receiving because they have failed to
be proper market participants, but because they are human, and humans deserve a living share. This logic does not need to overthrow market capitalism
altogether; rather, it operates in society concurrently with capitalism as another option already in use for making decisions about distribution.

Overturning our overreliance on market narratives and systems can begin
by seeing alternative economic logics like this "logic of the share." Vocational
paths that creatively and doggedly pursue the common good will require
exploring beyond the comfortable market logic of putting price tags on everything from cantaloupe slices to survival.

The second narrative: merit makes me deserve it

Hand in hand with the "markets can solve it" narrative comes the "merit
makes me deserve it" narrative. If the market narrative teaches us to treat
labor as just another commodity, it's only a small leap to believe that the
people getting the highest price for their labor—the highest income—are
those whose labor is most valuable. But value is slippery in a market. Value
in price doesn't necessarily mean value in skill, moral good, or benefit to society. One might just as likely receive a high salary for work that benefits the
common good as for work that does harm. Nor do high salaries necessarily

---

[15] James Ferguson, *Give a Man a Fish: Reflections on the New Politics of Distribution* (Durham,
NC: Duke University Press, 2015), 38.

correlate with working harder or longer days. The "merit makes me deserve it" narrative covers up those two big lies.

These lies—that pay correlates with moral goodness and hard work—steer us away from prioritizing the common good in at least three ways. First, when we do have resources, the narrative deters us from sharing those by assuring us that we—and not others—fairly secured all our resources. Second, when we do *not* have the resources we need, the narrative promotes shame and resentment by obscuring the deeper causes of unequal distribution. Finally, the narrative directs us toward mere personal attainment as the goal of a good life by presenting vocation as a continuous ladder of individual competitive achievements.

To delve into the merit narrative with students, I sometimes ask, "Who worked harder, a kindergartener who grew up to become a lawyer, or a kindergartener who grew up to pack items in an Amazon warehouse for $27,000 per year?" In classes of predominantly White and high-achieving students, often the majority will quickly answer "the lawyer." But then someone will raise their hand and say timidly or with frustration, "Couldn't it be the Amazon worker? What if their home didn't have enough food? Or their parents couldn't help with homework? Or they had dyslexia? Or English was their second language? In kindergarten they probably worked twice as hard as the future lawyer. By ninth grade maybe they decided school is a game they can't win. They'll keep working hard—probably harder than anyone in our classroom, because the more you fall behind, the harder life gets." Sometimes these conversations have ended with a flushed-cheeked student stating with a kind of mic-drop finality.

Hard work simply does not correlate with earnings or moral goodness. This idea is an affront to the systems and messages that have surrounded many college students all their lives, and unless we press in deep, it's an idea that will bounce off students. "Sure, but *I* worked hard to get here. *I* deserve my place, even if some don't."

Some roots of this merit narrative were famously traced by Max Weber to shifts in European Protestantism from the fifteenth through twentieth centuries. Weber suggests that in response to uncertainty of their salvation, Calvinist Protestants came to view acquisition of money as "the result and manifestation of competence and proficiency in a vocational calling."[16] As

---

[16] Max Weber, *The Protestant Ethic and the Spirit of Capitalism*, trans. Stephen Kalberg, rev. 1920 ed. (New York: Oxford University Press, 2011), 80–81.

Europe and the United States secularized, the narrative settled deeply into the moral fabric of social life and provided the ethical justification for ceaseless work upon which capitalism could thrive. Recent writers have pointed out that meritocracy today is so embedded in the United States that it dominates rhetoric across both major political parties.[17]

The "merit makes me deserve it" narrative assumes there are no real boundaries to getting what you want if you have enough perseverance. Poverty of all sorts, then, is treated as the natural comeuppance of people who presumably have the morally reprehensible quality of "laziness." The narrative thereby serves as a linchpin upholding racial hierarchy as well. Evidence of inequalities—like the statistic cited earlier that household net worth is eight times higher among White families than Black—can be neatly tucked away by invoking what I have called elsewhere "the laziness myth," a lie that says racial inequality must be merited because Black people don't work as hard.[18] To fix poverty and inequality, then, the "merit makes me deserve it" narrative prescribes training and moral redirection of the poor rather than changes in discriminatory or exclusionary social structures. For historically marginalized groups, the narrative adds insult to injury.

One way I help my students see beyond the "merit makes me deserve it" narrative is with a worksheet that walks them through a scenario of budgeting for a family with a single income-earner, a child in preschool, and a family member attending college. Students must find two actual advertisements for jobs near minimum wage and then total up the costs of living on that salary in their city. They visit and describe the apartments they choose, look up information about schools in the district, calculate transit time for public transportation, find a job option not requiring English, investigate payday loan costs, and reflect on the question, "Is it fair to expect people to escape poverty by their own initiative without assistance?"[19] In three years using the assignment, no group has yet found a way to afford childcare, tuition, rent, and food without going further into debt every month.

---

[17] Daniel Markovits, *The Meritocracy Trap: How America's Foundational Myth Feeds Inequality, Dismantles the Middle Class, and Devours the Elite*, illustrated ed. (New York: Penguin Press, 2019); Michael J. Sandel, *The Tyranny of Merit: What's Become of the Common Good?* (New York: Farrar, Straus and Giroux, 2020).

[18] Christine Jeske, *The Laziness Myth: Narratives of Work and the Good Life in South Africa* (Ithaca, NY: Cornell University Press, 2020).

[19] I got the idea to design this exercise from a similar activity mentioned in Darby Kathleen Ray's book, *Working* (Minneapolis, MN: Fortress Press, 2011).

Pay is a faulty way to judge a vocational path. If we allow our students to believe that life is one long series of "work hard, earn success, work harder, earn greater success" ad infinitum, we set them up for an existential crisis. It's a narrative that justifies hoarding and other-blaming when people succeed, shame and blame when they fail, and vocational paths with no end beyond endless climbing.

Exposing the harms done by these all-pervasive narratives is a starting point, but we also need to replace those narratives with alternatives. The final two narratives I describe offer such possibilities. They are my attempt to put words to narratives that I have seen evidenced in the lives of people who prioritize the common good in their vocations.

A first new narrative: I belong to memberships

A few weeks into an Introduction to Cultural Anthropology course, a student once spoke to me during a class break. "I'm sorry," the student said, "but you keep talking about culture and social structures, and I still don't think those things make much difference in my life. I make decisions in whatever way I want." The honesty of that student was a wakeup call that at the very basic 101 level of teaching about vocation is the lesson that society does affect each of our lives, in ways both visible and invisible. Conversely, we each affect society around us in mundane ways every day. In participating in an overturning education, we need to adopt a narrative that reminds us, "I belong already to a membership." As theologian Paul Wadell writes, "Justice does not create a bond between us and others; it recognizes and honors a bond that is already there."[20] Before we can take intentional steps toward the common good, we have to recognize that we are already part of a commons, for better or for worse.

We can help students envision our membership in society with various metaphors: an ecosystem, a machine, or in the analogy used by both the sociologist Émile Durkheim and the apostle Paul, as a body. Being a part of the body means that "If one part suffers, every part suffers with it."[21] As Martin Luther King Jr. famously put it, "Injustice anywhere is a threat to justice everywhere. We are caught in an inescapable network of mutuality,

---

[20] Paul J. Wadell, *Happiness and the Christian Moral Life: An Introduction to Christian Ethics* (New York: Rowman & Littlefield, 2016), 239.
[21] 1 Cor. 12:20, 15, 26 (NIV).

tied in a single garment of destiny. Whatever affects one directly, affects all indirectly."[22]

Recognizing how we are already members within a body of society leads to an important discovery about vocation and the common good: vocational connection to the common good is not just something we tack on to our individual lives; it's in every ripple we already make through our everyday connections. These connections can be as mundane as a smile exchanged with a classmate or as distant as a natural disaster resulting from human-induced climate change.

I recently heard vocation described as "the moment when a bell rings for me and I decide whether or not to respond." That's a ridiculous picture of vocation. Vocation is happening daily, perhaps most often when we *don't* hear a bell alerting us to the moment of decision. Vocation unfolds in a million bells, many that we're so accustomed to we no longer hear them ringing. Because we are already connected to the social body, our impact on the common good plays out constantly: in decisions whether to bike or drive, whether to "like" a social media post, and who to invite to a party. It's happening in every click and swipe, every hour wiled away in the stuff we never put on a to-do list.

A vocation for the common good could involve developing new forms of membership, but it needs to start by noticing the memberships to which we already belong. Students often assume that if they want to make a positive change in the world, they need to add some task to their life: political advocacy, protest, the purchase of ethically branded products, or the pursuit of a "service" profession like health care. By that logic, opting out of these activities simply means not having an impact on society; it's not wrong, just morally neutral. That mindset ignores the reality that our life is already incorporated into society. There is no neutral option.

The author Wendell Berry uses the word "membership" to describe a quality of life that is central to a good life. In several novels, Berry traces the changes in a community tied together by membership amidst the pressures of urbanization, modernization, and capitalism. The title character of his novel *Hannah Coulter* reflects, "One of the attractions of moving away into the life of employment, I think, is being disconnected and free, unbothered by membership. . . . The life of membership with all its cumbers is traded

---

[22] Martin Luther King Jr., "Letter from a Birmingham Jail," African Studies Center—University of Pennsylvania, April 16, 1963, https://www.africa.upenn.edu/Articles_Gen/Letter_Birmingham.html.

away for the life of employment that makes itself free by forgetting you are clean as a whistle when you are not of any more use."[23] The way to a life of meaning that Hannah discovers is membership—a weaving together of the "particular bunch" of people who happen to share life.

When Berry writes about membership, he is primarily interested in the face-to-face relationships between neighbors aware of each other's family histories. But vocation for the common good also requires recognizing our belonging in memberships that stretch beyond those we know personally, to those seemingly "other" to us whom we may never know.[24] It's one thing for me to love because a friend is similar to me or care about a cause because it affects my own life, but that sort of love is rooted in an extension of loving myself. To fully accept that someone is different, distant, and unlikely to benefit me and then still seek their good is an act of radical overturning. But loving a seemingly distant other has more in common than we might admit with loving a seemingly close family member or friend. Anyone who has tried to sustain love knows that eventually all love bumps into otherness because we are magnificently diverse humans. And we wouldn't want it any other way—difference is what makes love hard, but it is also what makes love worthwhile. Real membership, like real love, is about the joining together of people who share both sameness and difference and who value their need for both.[25]

A vocational call to membership, then, is not limited to the kind of small-town agrarian American social structures that Berry describes. Berry's writing often focuses on the ways that American life in the late twentieth century was overcome by merit- and market-driven social and cultural systems that threatened membership. But our teaching goal needs to be more than eliciting nostalgia for a bygone membership. Life in the present late-capitalist globalizing era is no less affected by memberships; if anything, our lives have become *more* entangled with others, even as we appreciate those entanglements less. We cannot attach names and faces to our sprawling memberships, but we belong to others nonetheless. What, then, does it mean to belong to such memberships?

---

[23] Wendell Berry, *Hannah Coulter* (Berkeley, CA: Shoemaker & Hoard, 2005), 133.

[24] For a discussion of how to invite students to care about causes that are not their own, see chapter 7 of this volume by Jonathan Golden.

[25] For further exploration of finding mutuality and solidarity with those who are strangers to us as part of a call to the common good, see the reflections by Geoffrey W. Bateman and Erin VanLaningham in chapters 6 and 9 of this volume, respectively.

One path toward recognizing our memberships across both sameness and difference is to first learn to discover commonalities with those who seem to be other, and from there move toward caring for others whether or not we can find the commonalities. In her book *Raise Your Voice: Why We Stay Silent and How to Speak Up,* social activist Kathy Khang describes such a progression when she attended a horrific "Pilgrim Celebration" event at her children's school.[26] Parents and staff were expected to come wearing offensive stereotyped and culturally appropriated approximations of seventeenth-century Native American clothing and face paint, sometimes accompanied by mimicked broken-English accents. She admits that while she noticed the offensiveness of the event, she said nothing. She did, though, take one small brave step at the event. Seeing a woman in a skimpy costume being leered at in "slut shaming" by other parents, Khang went to stand next to the woman and talk to her. Later she questioned why she would support a fellow mother but not challenge the racist root systems behind the event:

> I had *just* enough courage to go stand with [the scantily clad woman] because I know what it feels like to be judged by my appearance. I've been the focus of teasing, bullying, and sexualization my entire life due to my physical characteristics as a Korean American woman. I stood by the woman, not because I was Native American or had friendships with Native Americans who could've told me about the pain and danger of stereotypes, but because I had faced similar situations. . . . But now I realize that we can't wait to act until we are personally affected by something.[27]

Khang's book describes her journey since, learning that standing up for the common good in the face of injustice requires acknowledging the memberships we already have to those who seem "other." Membership is already a given, and what we do with that membership matters.

A vocation for the common good, then, involves overturning our imagined disconnection from society and beginning to recognize the memberships to which we already belong, both near and far. Merely having memberships isn't enough, though—we also need to consider what to do with those memberships.

[26] Kathy Khang, *Raise Your Voice: Why We Stay Silent and How to Speak Up* (Downer's Grove, IL: IVP Books, 2018).
[27] Khang, *Raise Your Voice,* 78–79.

A second new narrative: mutuality makes life good

Finally, to pursue a vocation for the common good requires asking, what sort of membership is good? Often, the answers seems to be a choice between two opposing options: either good membership is one where I *receive* well or good membership is where I *give* well. Will we be happiest as consumers or philanthropists? At first glance, we might assume that the second is the right answer. The mantra "it is more blessed to give and receive" instills in many people a sense of unspoken guilt and shame when we receive, whether through gifts, welfare, or a high-salaried job. We hear messages that in "good" vocations, people give interminably, perhaps as social workers, teachers, nurses, or relief workers. Not coincidentally, these careers are often high burnout, underpaid, and gendered as feminine—our society often assumes that such workers have an abundant generosity that doesn't require much in return. Meanwhile, we are surrounded by messages that while good and kindly people give, strong and successful people earn. The former get gold stars in heaven, the latter get whatever money can buy, and each supposedly gets contentment. We're left with the high-achieving wealthy philanthropist as the pinnacle of greatness.

Instead, I propose that memberships are good when we have a place for both giving *and* receiving. In other words, "mutuality makes life good." By this narrative, membership is neither a burdensome duty nor a network to exploit. Memberships sit at the very essence of what makes life good because the good life happens within mutuality—ongoing giving and receiving in dependent relationships with others. Those dependencies extend to humans, the natural world, and the spiritual realm. Margaret Mohrmann describes vocation as pursuing the virtue of responsibility—literally being "able to respond" to others.[28] Responsibility does not mean merely providing one-way service to those imagined as "having less," however.[29] Vocation for the common good is not just tacking on service for the other—it involves building a dynamic interplay between the needs and gifts of both the "inner" self and the "outer" other.[30]

[28] Margaret E. Mohrmann, " 'Vocation Is Responsibility': Broader Scope, Deeper Discernment," in Cunningham, ed., *Vocation across the Academy*, 21–43.
[29] Darby Kathleen Ray, "Self, World, and the Space Between: Community Engagement as Vocational Discernment," in *At This Time and In This Place: Vocation and Higher Education*, ed. David S. Cunningham (New York: Oxford University Press, 2015), 301–20.
[30] For more on the inner and outer aspects of calling see David S. Cunningham, "Time and Place: Why Vocation Is Crucial to Undergraduate Education Today," in Cunningham, ed., *At This Time and In This Place*, 1–24.

One starting point for envisioning a vocation centered on mutuality is to ask a strange question: why do we live in a world in which every living creature must eat? Eating is, by definition, receiving that which we cannot produce in our own bodies. And eating requires receiving life out of another's death. According to Norman Wirzba, in his book *Food and Faith*, we eat because "to eat is to be implicated in a vast, complex, interweaving set of life-and-death dramas in which we are only one character among many."[31] Eating, then, is a daily reminder of our give and take, as "every sniff, chomp, and swallow connects us to vast global trade networks, and thus to biophysical and social worlds far beyond ourselves . . . and ultimately God."[32] This is true not just for grocery shopping; it is at the heart of what makes a good vocation.

Using Wirzba's answer, vocation is to be daily reminded of our "vast, complex, interweaving life-and-death dramas." Vocation is our stewarding of the mutual ways we are both depended upon and dependent upon. To do anything less is to starve ourselves of meaning. The coffee, apple, oats, and milk I ate for breakfast were made possible through the giving of people, land, and organisms. Meanwhile my nourishment made possible the work I do to write this chapter, teach, and share time with family. Recognizing my membership with these people and land might prompt me to spend an extra dollar for shade-grown organic coffee or thank the apple farmer. Recognizing my memberships within career, family, and friendships might remind me to take sufficient breaks, walk outside, laugh with coworkers, and choose research and teaching topics that build a better society. Rather than seeing my work as a way to deserve control over resources that are mine alone, I can treat it as what anthropologist Tim Ingold calls an endless "meshwork" of giving and receiving.[33]

Making vocation about meshworks of mutuality offers a cure for some of the most prevalent pathologies we see in attempts at vocation. Mutuality rules out ableism, because we recognize that any able-bodied quality is only temporary and partial—having limited abilities is central to what it is to be a living creature. Mutuality likewise blocks the workaholic burnout tendencies of those who define success according to a never-ending quest for efficiency

---

[31] Norman Wirzba, *Food and Faith: A Theology of Eating*, 2nd ed. (Cambridge: Cambridge University Press, 2019), 40.

[32] Wirzba, *Food and Faith*, 40.

[33] Tim Ingold, *Correspondences* (Cambridge, UK: Polity Press, 2021), 11. See also Norman Wirzba, *Agrarian Spirit: Cultivating Faith, Community, and the Land* (Notre Dame, IN: University of Notre Dame Press, 2022), 38.

and accomplishment. In mutuality, rest becomes as much a part of vocation as work. Mutuality further prevents the "White savior" models of service in which the one who gives is morally superior to the seemingly helpless one who receives. Mutuality points us toward models of service as accompaniment. Finally, as I have written elsewhere, mutuality offers hope for the shame that often accompanies underemployment, because it reminds us that our value as humans is not solely in what we produce or attain, but in being a part of transformative relationships throughout our life course.[34]

Especially for the many people in working-class jobs or other all-consuming life stages like raising children, it is helpful to notice that vocation for the common good does not require vast financial donations or weekend volunteering. Barbara Ehrenreich, who spent a year exploring how people survive in minimum-wage jobs, observes that the working poor are "the major philanthropists of our society. They neglect their own children so that the children of others will be cared for; they live in substandard housing so that other homes will be shiny and perfect; they endure privation so that inflation will be low and stock prices high. To be a member of the working poor is to be an anonymous donor, a nameless benefactor, to everyone else."[35] This point turns the dominant narrative of generosity on its head. It's not the privileged and wealthy whose generous giving upholds the common good; it's those who go without—often because of social structures maintained by those who benefit from their deprivation—that keep society from cracking at the seams. Seeking the common good isn't about people of power and wealth becoming the generous benefactors of society; it's about taking steps to rebalance the unequal give and take that already exists.

I recently came to be the caretaker for two sheep who have been teaching me how mutuality can overturn our culture's dominant understandings of vocation. People often ask, "What do you plan to do with the sheep?" It's a seemingly logical market-based question. In the past, our family has raised chickens and pigs, and people generally assume that those are for utilitarian purposes: eggs and pork. But these sheep draw out a deeper reason I raise animals. They are too old to offer tasty meat, their wool is hardly worth the cost of shearing, and as castrated males they can't father a next generation. When

[34] Christine Jeske, "Are We Underthinking Underemployment?: Toward a More Inclusive Theology of Vocation," *Christian Scholar's Review* 49, no. 3 (2020): 231–48, https://christianscholars.com/are-we-underthinking-underemployment-toward-a-more-inclusive-theology-of-vocation/.

[35] Barbara Ehrenreich, *Nickel and Dimed: On (Not) Getting By in America* (New York: Metropolitan Books, 2001), 221.

people ask why I have sheep, I answer, "ecology." Ecology is a word to describe the mutual relationships between creatures. For the particular plot of land I live on, sheep work. As they nourish their bodies, their eating prevents invasive seeds from spreading, transforming so-called weeds into manure for deep rich soil. And as I care for them, I've realized they offer more than just a lawn-mowing and soil amendment—they offer me an opportunity to care. Moving their fences to welcome them into new lush pastures, filling their water pail, and scratching their wooly necks isn't just a duty; it gives me the joy of being tied up in a right relationship to place, self, others, and soul.

To choose a vocation knowing that "I belong in a membership" and "mutuality makes life good" does not preclude participating in markets or developing the necessary skills for a career. But it does require overturning much of what we assume to be true. We need to redirect our aims by defining success not by merit and markets, but according to the rightness of mutual relationships, finding our place in ecologies of dependency.

I've taught the course What Is Money Good For? several times since that first disheartening attempt. I was teaching it as I wrote this chapter, and much of what you read here found its way into the course. On the last day of class, we followed the suggestions of students to hold a combination holiday- and pajama-themed party. Students arrived in slippers and sweatshirts, carrying pillows and food contributions as reminders of our memberships and mutuality—their first attempts at homemade muffins, candy from care packages, and favorite teas. We sat in a circle on the carpet to discuss what they most wanted to remember from the class. Later, on their course feedback forms I would read the usual mix of impossible wishes—more lecture and more discussion, less homework and easier grades—but this time instead of that "waste of time" comment, I found this confirmation: "This class significantly challenged my thinking in the best ways possible." Overturning happened.

4

Diversity, Equity, Inclusion, and Justice

Institutional Mission as the Call of the Common Good

Monica M. Smith

More than thirty years ago, I was a first-generation undergraduate student at a Christian liberal arts college on the East Coast. It was a predominantly White college. One of the required first-year courses focused on vocation and common good. My experience in that class shut off any possibility that I would learn much, especially about the common good. During roll call, the professor looked up every so often to see who was responding. At one point he noted aloud, "Every year we have more nigras in these classes. We gotta let 'em in. Welcome Nigras." Since the college met the two criteria my parents set for them to fund my education—close to home and a Christian college—I had no choice but to stay. I wanted a college degree.

As it turned out, I did eventually learn a great deal about diversity, equity, inclusion, social justice, and the connections (individually and as a collective whole) between justice and the common good. But this came about through my major, which would eventually become my academic and professional discipline: social work. My views are also informed by my experience as a diversity, equity, inclusion, and justice (DEIJ) practitioner in higher education and other industries. Currently, I am the chief diversity officer at a Lutheran liberal arts college in the upper Midwest.

I am called to this writing project because of these experiences and because of my identity as an African American woman and a first-generation student who attended predominantly White colleges and universities. My identity, my experiences on these campuses, and my professional background in social work frame this chapter. However, the call to the common good is not mine alone. If these institutions are to fulfill the mission of higher education and to remain relevant to future generations of students, transformation is needed to align institutional behaviors (such as programming, processes, and policies) with mission.

Monica M. Smith, *Diversity, Equity, Inclusion, and Justice* In: *Called Beyond Our Selves*. Edited by: Erin VanLaningham, Oxford University Press. © Oxford University Press 2024. DOI: 10.1093/oso/9780197691915.003.0005

One of the chief aims of higher education—including that of my own undergraduate institution, however unevenly it pursued and achieved it—is to provide transformative educational experiences so that graduates can impact the world through service to others, ultimately contributing to the common good. For social work graduates in particular, the goal can be understood as fulfilling the command of Micah 6:8 ("What does the Lord require of you? To act justly and to love mercy and to walk humbly with your God") through competent social work practice. The commitment to justice—implicit or explicit—impacts students' development in their ability to respond with justice, mercy, and humility as they show compassion for others.

This chapter suggests that the discipline and practice of social work can provide the theoretical foundation and pragmatic steps to help colleges and universities fulfill their vocation to serve the public. When the mission of the college coalesces with DEIJ, then all students can build capacity for contributing to the common good and our collective flourishing.

Social work for the common good: the institutional call

My understanding of the common good and justice, along with the commitments to each, is rooted in my undergraduate experiences (both positive and negative) at a faith-based predominantly White college. As a social work student, I was introduced to the profession's mission: "to enhance human well-being and help meet the basic human needs of all people, with particular attention to the needs and empowerment of people who are vulnerable, oppressed, and living in poverty."[1] Populations who experience these conditions are often minoritized and marginalized. These communities and groups are disconnected from many of society's resources—access to quality education, health care, safety. They live in underresourced locales where access to social resources is limited or denied. Significant to the profession is promoting social welfare, the benefits and services to help people meet their basic needs.[2] This includes the physical and material needs and concern for personal, professional, and social relationships. Social workers perform social welfare duties—a plethora of "activities and resources designed

---

[1] "Preamble," Code of Ethics, National Association of Social Workers, 2021, https://www.social workers.org/About/Ethics/Code-of-Ethics/Code-of-Ethics-English.
[2] Philip R. Popple and Leslie Leighninger, *Social Work, Social Welfare, and American Society* (Hoboken, NJ: Pearson, 2020).

to enhance or promote the well-being of individuals, families and the larger society; and efforts to eliminate or reduce the incidence of social problems."[3] When the basic needs of people are met, the incidences of social problems are reduced. This benefits the individual contributing to society and society as a whole.

Simply put, social workers' objective in serving others is to enhance the common good. This is done by working with individuals and within any one of society's five social institutions—family and kinship, government and politics, economics, religion, and education—for the benefit of all. Each social institution serves an essential function so that communities can survive[4] and its members thrive. The social work Code of Ethics reflects the profession's core values of service, social justice, and dignity and worth of the person, among others.[5] These ideals can direct our discussion of cultivating students' vocations for the common good, prioritizing the dignity of others, and working toward justice.

Traditionally, social workers were employed in large public social service agencies focusing mostly on families. Opportunities and roles have expanded so that today social workers are found in nearly every sector of society, including governmental and educational institutions. While our primary function in educational institutions is to share knowledge and prepare the next generation for contributing to society through career pathways, an increasing number of functions have been transferred to this social institution, including the teaching of social values like civic responsibility. The scope of education has broadened to help students understand how society works along with students' role in helping it to adequately function and even thrive. This is teaching vocational exploration that centers on the common good.

Education, like social work, has expanded to meet the demands of society. Colleges have responded to social needs through creating majors, developing new programs, and shifting policies to adhere to state and federal guidelines. Since survival of this institution relies on student enrollment and completion, pivoting to meet the needs of society and the interests of students is paramount. In this vein, higher education exists to serve the public.[6] To serve the public implies working toward and for the common good. Education, as one

---

[3] J. E. Hansan, "What Is Social Welfare?," Social Welfare History Project, 2017, https://socialwelfare.library.vcu.edu/recollections/social-welfare-history/.

[4] Popple and Leighninger, Social Work, 37.

[5] "Preamble," 2021.

[6] Andrew Seligsohn, "An Observation about the Mission of Higher Education," Campus Compact, April 29, 2015, https://compact.org/an-observation-about-the-mission-of-higher-education.

of the collective social pillars, helps realize collective well-being. Colleges and universities should consider how education in relationship to the other social institutions can help us understand how our roles in and the structures of the family, government, economies, and religion manifest either barriers to or avenues toward the common good. When colleges and universities serve students by meeting their multiple needs, we also prepare them to serve society. As educators, we can disband the myth of independence by helping students understand that individual well-being is linked to the well-being of others. Individual and institutional contributions are both necessary and revealed in the many interdependent aspects of our lives.

A college's purpose to serve the public is often evident in the institutional mission statement, usually rooted in the history and formation of the college. One college may emphasize a learning environment that encourages intellectual, moral, and personal growth, while another may emphasize strengthening community through educational leadership and collaboration. In exploring the relationship between vocation and mission, David Cunningham suggests that mission focuses on what the college or university wants to do.[7] He proposes colleges move away from the language of mission, which normally focuses on internal motives established by founders and upheld by current leaders, and more readily embrace the language of vocation, which intimates purpose and relevance. Vocation pulls or "calls" institutions toward those things external to the institution. Vocation can supplement mission, Cunningham says, by linking "internal and external sources of motivation that can help [the institution] determine next steps."[8] Where mission is rooted in history, vocation is both present-day and future oriented. Colleges and universities must consider external forces that are calling and guiding the institution toward its relevant future. Vocation helps students and the institution think beyond themselves, focusing on larger issues of meaning and purpose and how they see themselves contributing to the world.[9] For example, institutional vocation is explicit at my current institution as outlined in its Five Faith Commitments,[10] one of which is social

[7] David S. Cunningham, "Colleges Have Callings, Too: Vocational Reflection at the Institutional Level," in *Vocation across the Academy*, ed. David S. Cunningham (New York: Oxford University Press), 258.

[8] Cunningham, "Colleges Have Callings, Too," 258.

[9] David S. Cunningham, "Hearing and Being Heard: Rethinking Vocation in the Multi-faith Academy," in *Hearing Vocation Differently: Meaning, Purpose, and Identity in the Multi-Faith Academy*, ed. David S. Cunningham (New York: Oxford University Press), 1–17.

[10] "The Five Faith Commitments of Augustana College," accessed October 25, 2022, https://augustana.edu/about-us/president/commitments.

justice. Thus, when we consider the ways colleges and universities contribute to the common good, we should think about our purpose as an institution as well as how we contribute to the collective purpose of our communities, being mindful especially of issues of justice.

Institutional callings: addressing bias and educating for DEIJ

Working toward the common good is mission critical for colleges and universities, and doing justice is a social imperative. Students will enter a world where injustices are commonplace, particularly those experienced by minority communities. Racism, sexism, antisemitism, homophobia, Islamophobia, hate crimes, and other forms of discrimination still exist despite laws intended to prevent these behaviors. Most recently in the United States there has been a substantial increase in hate crimes. In October 2021, the US Department of Justice reported that hate crime reports reached the highest level in twelve years. This surge of incidents primarily targeted people of color (over 60 percent of incidents), religious minorities (over 13 percent of incidents), and persons who are lesbian/gay/bisexual/queer/transgender (20 percent of incidents).[11]

Economic justice is an issue as the wealth gap continues to increase. According to the Economic Policy Institute (EPI), "Corporate boards running America's largest public firms are giving top executives outsize compensation packages that have grown much faster than the stock market and the pay of typical workers, college graduates, and even the top 0.1%."[12] In addition, the EPI reports chief executive officer (CEO) compensation increased by 1,322 percent since 1978, while employee pay increased just 11.9 percent during that same time period. In 2020 alone, CEO pay increased by 16 percent, while the average worker saw a 1.8 percent increase. On average CEOs earn 351 times more than an average employee.[13]

[11] US Department of Justice, "Hate Crime Statistics, 2020," https://www.justice.gov/hatecrimes/hate-crime-statistics.
[12] Lawrence Mishel and Jori Kandra, "CEO Pay Has Skyrocketed 1,322% since 1978," Economic Policy Institute, August 10, 2021, https://www.epi.org/publication/ceo-pay-in-2020/.
[13] Mishel and Kandra, "CEO Pay Has Skyrocketed."

Police violence and murders of Black men outpace that of any other group—even when the victim is unarmed and not violent. According to the *Proceedings of the National Academy of Sciences* in the United States:

> Police violence is a leading cause of death for young men in the United States. Over the life course, about 1 in every 1,000 black men can expect to be killed by police. Risk of being killed by police peaks between the ages of 20 y and 35 y for men and women and for all racial and ethnic groups. Black women and men and American Indian and Alaska Native women and men are significantly more likely than white women and men to be killed by police. Latino men are also more likely to be killed by police than are white men.[14]

These are only a few examples of realities external to colleges and universities. Because college campuses are a microcosm of society, incidents and relational dynamics that occur in communities external to the campus occur on campuses too. The same populations of students mentioned in the American Council on Education (ACE) report experience discrimination and marginalization on college campuses. Student demographics at historically, predominantly, and persistently White colleges and universities (HPPWCUs) are more diverse than ever before and will continue to be at those institutions that are interested in remaining relevant. The divisive political climate, our national conversations, and the social reality in communities demand that higher education recognize the experiences of students of color, LGBTQIA+ students, neurodiverse students, those with disabilities, and those with other minoritized identities. We must ask, what is salient to them in the college experience? How can we address these challenges, realities, and needs? Diversity exists, or will happen, within the student body on our campuses. Inclusion, however, is a choice and it takes work. Part of the mission and a college's inner call is to create an institutional climate and a learning environment that will ensure students experience inclusion and equity and learn how to address issues of justice.

---

[14] Frank Edwards, Hedwig Lee, and Michael Esposito, "Risk of Being Killed by Police Use of Force in the United States by Age, Race–Ethnicity, and Sex," *Proceedings of the National Academy of Sciences* 116, no. 34 (August 20, 2019): 16793–98, https://doi.org/10.1073/pnas.1821204116.

Institutional barriers to achieving the common good

In all parts of the college experience, there are common challenges that become barriers in fostering students' learning and vocational exploration. Specifically, there may be insufficient awareness of surrounding social issues and matters of equity and inclusion in academic disciplines and across the campus by administrators, faculty, and staff. Campuses may fail to acknowledge privilege and discuss the dynamics of difference and realities of minority experiences. Within higher education there are persistent incidents of identity-related bias and compensation/wage disparities connected to gender.[15] Finally, educational institutions can operate from a mistaken assumption that justice is a virtue rather than a set of rules to govern our social interactions. Such disturbing trends in higher education can be opportunities for colleges committed to the common good, allowing these institutions to address issues of bias and inequity.[16]

With the increase in diversity in the student population across higher education, institutions can respond intentionally and strategically to meet the needs of minority students and employees. This is a current and significant reality. For example, in 1996 students of color made up 29.6 percent of the undergraduate student population students, increasing to 45.2 percent in 2016.[17] Graduate students of color increased from 20.8 percent to 32.0 percent in the same time period.[18] National data relative to dropout rates shows an overwhelming disparity between students of color and non-Hispanic White students. Despite these gains, however, many areas of higher education continue to *underserve* and *underrepresent* students of color.[19]

Furthermore, over the next decade nearly half of all Americans will belong to a minority group. A recent article noted "the college-going population will drop by 15 percent between 2025 and 2029 and continue to decline by another percentage point or two thereafter."[20] Despite this impending

---

[15] Sue Clery, "The Calm before COVID: The Last Look at Faculty Stories before the Tumultuous Pandemic," *National Education Association* 39, no. 1 (2021): 1–36.

[16] See the March 2019 report released by ACE, "Racial Equity Gaps Still Plague Higher Ed," https://www.equityinhighered.org/.

[17] Lorelle L. Espinosa, Jonathan M. Turk, Morgan Taylor, and Hollie M. Chessman, *Race and Ethnicity in Higher Education: A Status Report* (Washington, DC: American Council on Education, 2019).

[18] Espinosa et al., *Race and Ethnicity in Higher Education*.

[19] Espinosa et al., *Race and Ethnicity in Higher Education*.

[20] Part of this underserving and underrepresenting is found in the racial makeup of college faculty, staff, and administrators who remain predominantly White, with nearly three-quarters of full-time faculty identifying as White. See Jill Barshay, "College Students Predicted to Fall by More Than 15%

demographic decline, known as the demographic cliff, given the Census Bureau projections, the students who will be available for college will be students of color, those who, according to the ACE report, are currently underserved and underrepresented and whose persistence and success through graduation are lower than non-Hispanic Whites. In fact, colleges and universities are likely to see increases in all populations of students whose identities are currently underrepresented.

Further, students are increasingly concerned with an institution's commitments to diversity, equity, inclusion,[21] and social justice.[22] If colleges and universities are to remain relevant (and afloat under current economic pressures), they must create a learning environment that provides the kinds of purposeful experiences students are seeking and help students develop the skill sets necessary to address social issues. Therefore, attending to issues of diversity, equity, and inclusion should be inherent in the college mission and infused throughout the student experience. Colleges and universities must also recognize student interest in social justice and integrate opportunities for learning and addressing social issues in the learning environment. In short, there is a critical need for colleges and universities to promote diversity, equity, inclusion, and social justice in all aspects of campus life. Part of a college's call and its mission is to create an institutional climate and a learning environment that will ensure students experience inclusion and equity and learn how to address issues of justice. This will ultimately help them discern vocational pathways that serve the common good.

DEIJ as a call to the common good

Diversity asks, who is in the room?

It is important to understand diversity related to group identity and affiliation since members of some groups were collectively excluded from full

---

after the Year 2025," *Hechinger Report*, September 10, 2018, https://hechingerreport.org/college-students-predicted-to-fall-by-more-than-15-after-the-year-2025/.

[21] "DEI and College Choice: Prospective Students Are Listening and It's Personal," *StudentPOLL* 14, no. 2 (November 2021), https://www.artsci.com/studentpoll-volume-14-issue-2.
[22] "Why Student Activists Care about Social Justice," Best Colleges, last modified November 18, 2021, https://www.bestcolleges.com/blog/student-activists-social-justice/.

participation in society based solely on those identities. This is essential because the history of exclusion and other discriminatory acts is the basis of current issues that education and other social institutions must address. The social issues noted above are directly related to devaluing humanity by prohibiting access to education and other resources that should have been available. Although laws have changed to no longer prohibit access and participation, the residual effects are manifested in the disparities noted in the previous section. Addressing such disparities is part of institutional vocation oriented toward flourishing for all.

Diversity is people centric. Here, diversity is defined as a range of human differences that include primary or internal dimensions such as race, ethnicity, age, sex, gender, sexual orientation, and physical and mental ability, and secondary or external dimensions such as religion, nationality, and socioeconomic status. Everyone has these characteristics. Those whose identities were not normed in society experienced exclusion and continue to experience marginalization in social institutions, of which higher education is one. Genocide in the United States, creation of and participation in slavery and subsequent Jim Crow legislation, immigration policies that limit or prohibit migration based on nationality, laws that prohibit or restrict voting, and restricted access to education and employment for LGBTQIA+ individuals all expose a social classification of difference that privileges some and disadvantages others. Individuals with these identities are considered diverse: persons of African, Asian, Latin American, and Mexican descent and Indigenous populations (commonly referred to as people of color); women; LGBTQIA+ individuals; those with physical and mental disabilities whether visible or invisible, diagnosed or undiagnosed; and Muslim, Jewish, and religious identities other than Christian. The exclusion and subsequent marginalization of these groups of people became the foothold of contemporary disparate social conditions and minoritized experiences. This is key to understanding why attention must be paid to diversity, otherwise understood as issues of minority groups. These are populations of those persons whose identities were discriminated against in the United States. These groups, previously excluded, are currently marginalized in social institutions, one of which is higher education. While discrimination is now illegal, its legacy lives on in implicit ways, most notably bias. Naming and responding with action to bias is a significant step toward orienting our institutions—and educators and students—to serve the common good.

Inclusion asks, have all voices and ideas been heard?

Whose perspectives and experiences are included in our discussions of the common good? Whose perspectives are on the margin or invisible? Inclusion is a process of creating a campus culture that recognizes, embraces, and affirms diversity.[23] It is a set of dual actions with focus on all the identities and cultures that exist at the institution and implementing processes to incorporate those that are underrepresented. It requires a process and behaviors that strengthen students' and employees' connections to the institution. Developing an inclusive culture means that the institution expresses appreciation of multifarious cultures represented by uplifting their voices and experiences and integrating cultural values into the environment. Inclusion increases a sense of belonging in minority community members through feeling valued by the institution. Inclusion also reduces marginalization that occurs when there is a power differential within the institution that results in some experiences being valued over others. In society, marginalization is evidenced by and results in disparate opportunities, resources, and outcomes. Noticing and talking about difference is productive. These are vital first steps to create momentum for effectual inclusion.

While inclusion prompts us to consider whose perspectives and experiences are included, it is important to note that inclusion *requires* diversity. Colleges and universities must consider who is in the room. Who is teaching? Who are the learners and what do they need in the learning environment? When students can engage with educators who hold similar identities as themselves, students are able to imagine the possibilities that exist for themselves. Institutions whose workforce demographic is similar to the composition of the student body normalize those students' existence and experiences. In effect, these students see themselves and engage with those who are similar to them, which affirms their identity and experiences. Far too many underrepresented students experience being the only or one of a few in the learning environment. This experience further marginalizes those students. Hiring individuals who represent those who were previously excluded from higher education and remain underrepresented in the environment spaces affirms underrepresented students' existence and belonging in the space. It offers the affirming message "You too belong here."

---

[23] See Geoffrey W. Bateman's discussion of valuing difference through queering vocation in chapter 6 of this volume.

Inclusion in higher education becomes a model for society in that we become closer to realizing the common good. Inclusive practices reflect the institution's value of diversity by investing time, talent, and resources to embrace underrepresented populations so that they will flourish.[24] Creating access and opportunities for underrepresented populations means removing institutional barriers that otherwise hinder their success. Without these barriers, underrepresented groups are able to thrive in the learning environment. Students benefit from such opportunities and contribute their knowledge, experiences, and funds to the institution. Upon graduation, these students contribute their skills to their communities and the larger society. It is a reciprocal relationship that reflects the interdependent nature of society.

Examples of strategic inclusion

Two examples of inclusion at my institution are in programs for students and the curriculum. The Offices for Student Inclusion and Diversity (OSID) and International Student and Scholar Services (OISSS) offer a variety of programs intentionally focused on students of color, LGBTQIA+ students, and international students. The PACE Multicultural Mentorship program, for example, is a year-long program for first-year students of color.[25] The goal of the program is to increase students' sense of belonging and retention by developing strong relationships within the cohort, mainly with second-through fourth-year students and with faculty and staff. PACE prepares underrepresented students for their college experience and helps them to have awareness of the dynamics of their own underrepresented identity at the college and to build a supportive community for themselves, while encouraging engagement with others across the institution. Over the last five years, participation in PACE has increased exponentially and the first-to-second-year retention rate of PACE participants is higher than other underrepresented students who do not participate in the program. PACE student retention has reached parity with nonminority students at the college. Participants have noted the positive impact the program has had in their development, sense of belonging, and success at the college.[26] In a survey,

[24] For a further exploration of how inclusive practices can orient students toward the common good, see Martin Holt Dotterweich's discussion of history and memory in chapter 12 of this volume.
[25] "PACE Multicultural Mentorship Program," Augustana College, https://www.augustana.edu/student-life/inclusion-and-diversity/mentorship. PACE is an acronym for Preparation, Awareness, Community, and Engagement.
[26] "Sense of Belonging Survey," Augustana College, 2019.

students indicated that their connections with the OSID and OISSS were significant to their success at the college.[27] These are catalytic spaces for underrepresented students.

An additional area for inclusion is the curriculum. Curriculum transformation began in the late 1960s when scholars in higher education noticed and began to respond to the dearth of women and other minority experiences, perspectives, and voices in curricular content. Over the next three decades the inclusion of minorities emerged in the literature and textbooks.[28] A core curriculum requirement at my current institution includes courses that focus on multicultural awareness and global diversity issues.[29] They are more commonly referred to as D (for diversity) and G (for global) suffix courses. The content in these courses intentionally focuses on underrepresented, minoritized, and marginalized populations that have been traditionally excluded or minimally included in curriculum content. These courses offer a "deep dive" into the cultures, experiences, and contributions of diverse populations. Diverse student identities and experiences are affirmed through the courses while students whose identities have been normed are exposed to information about these groups. All students are empowered through the curricular materials and assignments and engagement in the classroom. These courses are not standalone or additive in the curriculum. Instead, the D and G suffix courses are infused into major requirements.

Through inclusion, institutions improve the experiences and well-being of all community members. The rights and entitlements of individuals and community resources must be balanced with the needs of those who are marginalized. Such strategies develop opportunities for all involved in the life of the institution to see how our collective well-being is best achieved when inclusion is prioritized.

[27] "Sense of Belonging Survey," Augustana College.
[28] Elaine Hedges, "Curriculum Transformation: 'A Brief Overview,'" Women's Studies Quarterly 24, no. 3/4 (1996): 16–22, http://www.jstor.org/stable/40004355.
[29] Augustana College Core Requirements, https://www.augustana.edu/academics/catalog/curriculum-organization/core-requirements.

Equity responds, who is trying to get into the room but can't?

Equity is the quality of being fair and impartial, and free from bias and discrimination. Equity requires access to and the creation of opportunities for historically excluded and underrepresented populations to participate in social institutions. This includes educational programs, for example, that are capable of achieving parity in educational outcomes and experiences and require race- and other minority-conscious awareness of how identity can affect the opportunities available to an individual.[30] HPPWCUs must acknowledge their exclusionary past as discriminatory and face the challenges of creating equitable opportunities for access to a quality education for all students. This includes representation in the classroom, visibility in the curriculum, and objective discussions and critical dialogue about discrimination and its role in creating and sustaining disparities that exist in society. Where are the existing barriers that continue to hinder equitable representation, visibility, and a sense of belonging for historically excluded and currently underrepresented students?

Inclusion is an avenue toward equity. Examples in the section above help us to understand the importance and power of inclusion. Two of the six stated goals for diversity courses, for example, are to recognize (1) the extent to which a majority culture's structures and values may exploit, disenfranchise, marginalize, or alienate minority cultures and/or create or enhance privilege and power and (2) communicate an understanding of the importance of difference in shaping life experiences. To promote equity means the institution recognizes that people have different circumstances, so the institution allocates the exact resources and opportunities needed to reach an equal outcome.

Equity and inclusion are ways that institutions value personhood. Through both, institutions can create an environment that promotes a sense of belonging for those who are underrepresented. For those who are underrepresented and marginalized, equity is the threshold to ensuring fair treatment and an empowering experience. It creates conditions that advantage everyone. Equity is a just practice that allows us to better realize the common good for all.

---

[30] Association of American Colleges and Universities, *Committing to Equity and Inclusive Excellence: A Campus Guide for Self-Study and Planning* (Washington, DC: Association of American Colleges and Universities, 2015).

Justice responds, whose voice won't be heard because they are not in the majority, and whose presence in the room is under constant threat of erasure?

Diversity, inclusion, and equity always have an eye toward justice. Justice is necessary because injustice exists in society. The populations at the center of each of these efforts have experienced injustices. Injustice can be understood as misuse of power, inequitable distribution of resources, or unfair processes and procedures that result in marginalization and oppression of society members. To make things right—to do justice—society must address its wrongs. Part of our work as educators is to invite students into this effort to work for justice.[31]

Theories of justice serve as guiding principles to understand the role of justice in the path toward the common good. Specifically, three types of justice are helpful for this argument: distributive (a "fair share" in what people receive, whether goods and services or attention), procedural (fair procedures and processes), and restorative ("corrective justice" or making things right). Justice aligns with equity. The focus is to ensure that those who have been historically excluded and are currently underrepresented and marginalized have similar access to resources and opportunities to achieve as those who are more privileged in society. It results in the empowerment of those who are disempowered.

Ronald Sider, in his book *Just Generosity*, notes that justice is more than fair procedures, highlighting the restorative nature of justice.[32] Providing for the marginalized means removing barriers and empowering people through access to resources that will allow them to achieve their full capacity. Equity and inclusion are foundational in Sider's acknowledgment that we ought to distribute more to the least advantaged (those who need more) so that they may be restored to their rightful place in society. Such fair procedures and restoration are at the heart of justice. A college or university must ensure that fair processes exist in the institution so that it becomes an exemplar for justice, aligning the purpose, values, and ethical mandates with the general mission. An introspective purview and critical examination of intentionality to

---

[31] See chapter 5 of this volume for Michelle Hayford's extensive discussion of the vocation of advocacy.

[32] Ronald J. Sider, *Just Generosity: A New Vision for Overcoming Poverty in America* (Grand Rapids, MI: Baker Books, 2015), 66–68.

diversity, inclusion, and equity are necessary. Justice is the core of the institutional call to the common good.

Orienting a college's mission can be done by infusing diversity, equity, and inclusion into the strategic framework, helping the institution see its vocation in a future-oriented way. Tools such as "the inclusive excellence framework," a model for assessing campus climate used by chief diversity officers, can link vocation with mission directly.[33] There are five key areas colleges and universities need to inventory and address: access and success, training and education, organizational infrastructure, organizational climate and intergroup relations, and community engagement. In the assessment of a college's commitment to diversity and inclusion—revealing barriers and gaps that will need to be addressed—we start to see the direct ways a college can better serve the common good and orient itself to preparing students to do the same. Adopting an inclusive excellence framework requires this critical examination of the current state of the institution so it can move toward equitable practices, policies, and procedures that lead to a transformation of the institution. Outcomes that benefit marginalized community members must be the foci of these processes and communal well-being at the core of the mission.

The intersection of DEIJ and vocation

In discussions of discovering meaning and purpose in life, it is regularly noted that we can have several vocations across our lifespan.[34] For many, however, vocation is still tied to career choice. The difference is not so much the career one has chosen; instead, it is *how* one performs the tasks and responsibilities associated with that career. For example, I have been able to articulate my vocation related to career choice in the DEIJ space, even formulating a vocational statement that uses language of calling and purpose. My vocational statement is to "reconcile relationships between people, institutions, and systems by being a caring and purposeful catalyst for change."[35] It is a

[33] Association of American Colleges and Universities, *Committing to Equity and Inclusive Excellence*.

[34] Katherine Turpin, "One Life, Many Callings: Vocation across the Lifespan," *Intersections*, no. 47 (Fall 2018), 8–15, https://digitalcommons.augustana.edu/cgi/viewcontent.cgi?article=1436&context=intersections.

[35] Monica M. Smith, Vocational Statement, Lutheran Educational Conference of North America Fellows Program, 2022.

way of doing, and being, that encompasses value for humanity that impacts common good. In a recent text integrating vocation and diversity, Darrell Jodock and William Nelson note that "vocation helps inspire and guide our behavior in all areas of life."[36]

Inherent in the meaning and practice of vocation is concern for self and others and recognizing that we are intrinsically tied to one another, and concern for the world and improving life stance. Understanding our interdependence ought to lead us to a commitment to address critical social issues—injustices tied to racial, gender, religious, and other diversity. Jodock and Nelson contend that "a sense of vocation involves the realization that, as a human being I am . . . nested in a larger community and that my highest moral responsibility is to benefit . . . community and the individuals in it."[37] Each of us has benefited from the contributions of others in society—the farmer who grows food we purchase and eat, the educators who train and teach us for occupations, the mentors who have helped us develop and solve problems. An expression of our gratitude for others who have met our needs is to pay it forward to others. We offer our knowledge, influence, and expertise as a resource.

The overlap between vocation and DEIJ is a heightened awareness of the needs of others and the call to respond. Jodock and Nelson delineate several calls and responses inherent in vocation through the lens of diversity, among them treating others with dignity and respect, confronting harmful iterations of the status quo, building relationships, and imagining the world as it ought to be.[38] Our shared humanity and obligation to contribute to society are key in realizing vocations that contribute to justice and ultimately dismantle systems of injustice. Higher education can work to instill in students the call to be out of step with current social constructs that uphold racial, gender, religious, and other cultural barriers and to envision the common good. Students then can see their individual futures as embedded within collective well-being.

[36] Darrell Jodock and William C. Nelsen, *Embracing Diversity: Faith, Vocation, and the Promise of America* (Minneapolis, MN: Fortress Press, 2021), 11.
[37] Jodock and Nelsen, *Embracing Diversity*, 105.
[38] Jodock and Nelsen, *Embracing Diversity*, 105–30.

Vocation and social justice: institutional responsiveness

There are many strategic opportunities for colleges and universities to respond to the call of social justice with action. This can be done by infusing DEI into the college or university mission as well as using DEI as a lens to evaluate campus climate. Campus climate is defined as "the current attitudes, behaviors and standards of faculty, staff, administrators and students concerning the level of respect for individual needs, abilities and potential."[39] Surveys of campus climate reveal tension points and can be used to identify areas for change. Another area, as discussed above, is assessing curriculum content to determine where minority voices are underrepresented, overlooked, or silenced, and revising to include a healthy and balanced representation of diverse experiences. Campuses ought to consider other areas where students are underserved and underrepresented. While the many offices that report up through academic affairs and student affairs are the central campus hubs for the bulk of students at HPPWCUs, multicultural offices and culture houses are most often the central places underrepresented students find welcome and sanctuary. These are spaces of full acceptance and nurture. For underrepresented students these offices are both safe spaces and brave spaces.[40] Creating these spaces in other areas of the institution is necessary. Finally, strengthening relationships between the offices that serve underrepresented students and the offices that teach and promote vocational exploration can foster and improve a sense of belonging for students of color and other underrepresented groups.

As we work toward social justice across the institution, initiatives that cultivate a deep and committed sense of belonging are key to student success

[39] Jeni Hart and Jennifer Fellabaum, "Analyzing Campus Climate Studies: Seeking to Define and Understand," *Journal of Diversity in Higher Education* 1, no. 4 (2008): 222–34, https://psycnet.apa.org/doi/10.1037/a0013627.

[40] Safe spaces are areas where underrepresented students (and allies) can gather in cultural enclaves to interact with one another without the threat of being misunderstood, judged, or experiencing discrimination. Safe spaces are intended to be free of bias, conflict, criticism, or potentially threatening actions, ideas, or conversations. Culture houses are an example of safe spaces on campus. A brave space allows learners to engage with one another and have conversations about social issues with honesty, sensitivity, respect, and generosity. Classrooms can be brave spaces when the purpose is understanding various viewpoints and guidelines for discussion are established and agreed upon. Faculty can learn to facilitate these conversations that lead to the development of intercultural communication skills for the participants. Programs like sustained dialogue offer students the opportunity to identify issues on campus and encourage them to work through solutions together. Each of these provides transformative learning opportunities for college students. See Brian Arao and Kristi Clemens, "From Safe Spaces to Brave Spaces," in *The Art of Effective Facilitation: Reflections from Social Justice Educators*, ed. Lisa M. Landreman (Sterling, VA: Stylus, 2013), 135–50.

and retention and, ultimately, their flourishing on campus and beyond. Such a sense of belonging increases when a person has genuine relationships and support, inside and outside the classroom. Diversifying staff across campus allows students to see themselves reflected in those who nurture them in the various places and spaces on campus and to hear their cultural voices.[41] Further, as we seek to create vocational opportunities for all students, institutions can close the achievement gap in student success by offering research and leadership development opportunities to underrepresented students.[42] When students work alongside faculty on research, for example, the mentoring that occurs results in skill development and increases students' self-confidence. This helps foster a sense of belonging as well as create equitable access to these vocational exploration experiences.

It is important to note that equitable practices focus on access to opportunity *and* closing the achievement gaps. Many institutions create access for students in the recruitment process. Given the attrition rate of minority students, institutions should be exploring how equity is maintained throughout the college experience. Truly equitable processes include supports that assist students in achieving the end goal—the completion of a degree. Students who are unable to complete the degree often return to their home communities without enough additional knowledge and skills along with student loan debt that is hard to repay. This is an injustice. How does your institution define equity? Is there more focus on equality than equity? What do the groups that were previously excluded need? What missional obligation does the institution have to meet their needs?

Finally, institutions can respond to the call of social justice by clearly stating expectations and standards, offering regular and quality professional development, and requiring accountability for meeting the goals in the strategic frameworks and mission statements. Educators in all offices and disciplines cannot teach what they do not know or model what they do not understand. Given the connections between DEIJ and the common good, colleges and universities can best respond to the call of social justice by focusing on standards, increasing awareness and knowledge, and holding everyone in the campus community accountable to the common good. The vocation of higher education is to prepare students to value and serve their

[41] For a further discussion of the ways the campus can become a place of belonging for all, see chapter 11 by Robert J. Pampel in this volume.
[42] Association of American Colleges and Universities, *Committing to Equity and Inclusive Excellence.*

neighbor in diverse communities and environments, and such practices can bring us closer to this reality.

Is your institution ready to respond to the call of DEIJ?

Institutional change has often followed shifts in social values and culture. Since colleges and universities are indeed microcosms of society, the issues and realities in society exist within these institutions. Higher education, like other social institutions, excluded groups of people based on identity. In order to respond to the call of the common good, higher education must reconcile this past. Contemporarily, many of those previously excluded populations experience marginalization and limited upward mobility at predominantly and persistently White institutions (PPWs). Colleges and universities must make admissions about their own complicity in exclusionary practices and commit to the journey of reconciling their own offenses. This is hard work for colleges and universities.

The opportunity exists for colleges and universities to challenge and teach students to see and value collective well-being. Our campuses are communities where students engage difference and seek inclusion. Efforts to create systemic and widespread learning around DEIJ will put less pressure on underrepresented students to call out institutional deficiencies and reduce the instances of these students needing to educate the campus on the current social disparities and injustices. It would reduce the burden on these students who are often the ones pleading with administrators to transform the institution. When institutional leaders commit themselves to cross-cultural learning, we will open the space for vocational exploration for students of color in similar ways that we develop programs and processes that allow these experiences for their non-Hispanic White peers.

Students are eager to understand the realities of the society we live in and need to be prepared to contribute to the well-being of society. How students experience the college community is a precursor to how they will engage postgraduation. The opportunities for them to learn and unlearn are integral to shaping their outlook on society and their place in it and have a direct impact on their desire and ability to impact it for the common good.[43]

---

[43] For a discussion of the ways the university forms students to see their responsibility to others beyond the time and space of their college years, see chapter 13 by Charles Mathewes in this volume.

Institutional change that results from a college or university's commitment to DEIJ can impact the student experience in ways that prepare students to be catalysts for change in society. Setting the expectation that students have these experiences will equip them to do so. If they are to set this expectation with authenticity, colleges and universities must embark upon institutional change.

Vocational exploration and a commitment to justice are common to the mission of faith-based colleges and universities. As was the case for my undergraduate college and the current institution where I work, the aim is to provide transformative educational experiences so that graduates can impact the world through service to others, ultimately contributing to the common good. The commitment to justice—implicit or explicit—also impacts students' development in their ability to respond with justice, mercy, and humility as they show compassion for others.

Institutional mission statements can make explicit aspects of doing justice, seeking the common good, and valuing diversity, equity, and inclusion. Seeking the common good is implicit to the mission of higher education, and for some institutions, doing justice is explicit and embedded in the identity and mission. For example, a statement by Lutheran colleges associated with the Evangelical Lutheran Church in America (ELCA) expresses value for humanity, noting that diversity is not a barrier to unity. Further, noting a commitment to justice, the ELCA statement affirms that "we recognize and will challenge dynamics of power and privilege that create barriers to participation and equity in this church and society—for women, people of color, minority ethnic groups, people with disabilities, people who are marginalized or living in poverty, and the LGBTQ community."[44]

Augustana College, the Lutheran institution where I currently serve as the vice president of diversity, equity, and inclusion and chief diversity officer, explicitly states its commitments to education and social justice, claiming that it "is committed to offering a challenging education that develops qualities of mind, spirit and body necessary for a rewarding life of leadership and service in a diverse and changing world."[45] Explicitly inherent in this mission statement is the goal to use education as the tool to teach students to serve

[44] "Mission and Vision," Evangelical Lutheran Church in America, accessed October 25, 2022, https://www.elca.org/en/About/Mission-and-Vision?_ga=2.193246765.1692246776.1638479071-1328905386.1638479071.
[45] "Mission, Purpose and Goals," Augustana College, accessed October 25, 2022, https://www.augustana.edu/about-us/mission.

others and hence work toward and for the common good. To achieve these aims, the student's frame of reference must expand. It is our responsibility as educators to create opportunities for vocational exploration through a lens of DEIJ, connecting individual purpose with communal purpose, lifting up the "diverse and changing world" in its many dimensions.

Transformation leading to purpose

I have an unmistakable unwavering belief in the common good. I attribute a great deal of this commitment to my social work education and to experiences at historically PPWIs. Despite having attended a college where vocational exploration was not built into the framework and was an expected outcome for students, I stumbled upon and embraced this vocation later in life. My experiences and memories of those years relate more to surviving the environment and trying to thrive in it rather than exploring and embracing vocation. As a first-generation and racially underrepresented student, I did not have strong enough connections within the institution or the language to begin to understand, recognize, or pursue DEIJ as a vocation. If asked today, I can unequivocally say that DEIJ work is vocational for me. My role as a chief diversity officer is to help improve the well-being of the campus community by creating a more inclusive and equitable environment. Though I am no longer teaching in the classroom, I am helping educators across campus to give students what I did not receive in my undergraduate years.

Many of us posit that higher education is or should be a transformative experience. I argue that in order for underrepresented and marginalized students at PPWIs to embrace the academic experience and thrive, *the institution needs to transform to meet their needs*. This is the call of the common good for colleges and universities today, the vocation that accounts for the past, responds today, and looks to the future. Underrepresented students want and need to see themselves and hear the voices of those who have had similar experiences and even look like them in course content, at the front or center of the classroom, and in cocurricular leadership. They hunger for their identities to be affirmed so that they can consider their vocations, rather than merely surviving the college experience. Majority students need to see and experience similar institutional change as an exemplar for promoting DEIJ. If we want to work for the common good, we must be explicit about what stands in the way.

As I said at the beginning, this vocation is not mine alone. Higher education must embrace the salience of diversity, equity, and inclusion along with the role of the chief diversity officer as an equal partner in bringing about institutional change and transformation. Doing this work ensures that the minorities on campus have a quality experience and deep sense of belonging. It leads to increased awareness, knowledge, sensitivities, and skills that will become a strand in the academic cords with which students walk away from the institution and into the world for which we justly and adequately prepared them.

PART TWO

TRANSFORMATIONS OF THE COMMON GOOD

This section attends to the transformation and expansion of the common good to value the uncommon and the marginal as fundamental to our common well-being. The chapters emphasize the role of advocacy, social action, and community engagement as foundational to our connections to others and discovery of vocational purpose. A direct encounter with others whose experience is wholly different than our own is the place where the boundaries of the common good expand.

As we work with students to engage with the "real world," the authors in this section emphasize the various difficulties, challenges, and conflicts that students face. Attending to the ways the constructions of the common good have excluded and subsequently harmed those on the margins, the section aims to make collective well-being inclusive and far-reaching. Specifically, the authors see the vocation of caring about causes that are not ours but matter to someone else's well-being as significant in our common callings. Through the vocation of change agent and advocate, the section provides models of how we can better understand, value, and affirm the uncommon as part of the common good. The authors name queering vocation, engaging with those of differing political and religious identities, and building skills to address systemic oppression as fundamental for all to flourish.

We encourage readers of this section to focus on the terms of transformation and change, uncommon and difference, solidarity and advocacy, encounter and reflection. What do these terms mean in your classrooms, campus programs, strategic plans, and institutional priorities? How can we transform the common good so that all may live into their vocational identities?

The questions that follow may be used in professional development, meetings, programming, planning, and teaching. We imagine students and educators alike responding to these in discussion and in writing, in private and public settings. The goal of the questions, and of this section, is to expand the notion of the common good to emphasize the value of directly encountering others and working with and for those who are different than us. Communal well-being calls us to engage with diverse goods, to advocate against a "common bad," and to delight in helping others flourish.

What are the prevailing definitions and notions of the common good? How do these need to be transformed?

* What examples exist on your campus or your community that show the limits or possibilities of the concept? What norms, assumptions, and practices do we need to critique?
* What value does "uncommon" and "*a* common good" add to the discussion of the common good?
* How does the notion of the common good change when we pay attention to difference and privilege?

How does this expanded notion of the common good shape your understanding of vocation?

* How can vocational exploration engage with the common good so as to transform it?
* How can we provide opportunities for advocacy and direct encounter with those different than us as a means for vocational discernment?

What steps are available to cultivate a campus environment for the transformation of the common good?

* How can all stakeholders on campus be persuaded about the value of the common good in their individual and collective vocations?
* What are the institutional changes needed to support a common good for all?
* Where can we connect the college experience to the workplace and community for students so they can cultivate skills of advocacy and compassion for causes that are not their own?

Considering the ways we can widen the circle, queer the commons, and advocate for justice on campus and beyond:

* What practices, courses, pedagogies, and policies can be explored?
* How do you mentor and model for the common good?
* What opportunities exist for understanding, encountering, and advocating for others? How can these be better connected to vocational discernment?
* How can educators incorporate best practices of community engagement, universal design, and inclusivity as the transformation of the common good?

5

The Vocation of Advocacy

Enacting a More Just World

Michelle Hayford

Students often feel overwhelmed at the prospect that soon they will need to make their own way in the world, especially when the world is so broken and in need of their leadership. Educators know we need to attend to students' feelings of overwhelm about the state of the world in their vocational exploration. Naming our own suffering and overwhelm seems radical enough but indeed we must, and we must also make space for our students to do the same.

As a parent, colleague, educator, and administrator in higher education, I believe it is my responsibility to be a change agent and to advocate for the common good in every area of my life.[1] I believe my students should be equipped to advocate too. I instill in them a desire to contribute to a more just world by taking responsibility to create one. Change is not passive or neutral; it must be *made*. How do we form students for the vocation of advocacy? A vocation of advocacy is one that students should pursue, not only in their work, but also to discern paths taken for the rest of their lives. How do we invite students to listen to a calling that is not just an internal cue, but one that demands a response to the world? Serving the common good requires advocacy, and advocating is a common good.

At my home institution, the University of Dayton, we subscribe to the idea that "vocation involves naming desires and cultivating skills to serve others; a person perceives a need—big or small, near or far—and takes action to address it by employing his or her unique gifts," and that "vocation is formed and pursued in community, recognizing and acting on one's responsibility to assist and form mutually supportive bonds with others in pursuit of the

---

[1] My identities as Latina, queer, deviser of theatre for social justice, parent, educator, and citizen all demand that I advocate for community, my family, my colleagues, my students, and myself.

Michelle Hayford, *The Vocation of Advocacy* In: *Called Beyond Our Selves*. Edited by: Erin VanLaningham, Oxford University Press. © Oxford University Press 2024. DOI: 10.1093/oso/9780197691915.003.0006

common good."[2] The emphasis on taking action indicates that advocacy must be a part of our vocational paths. Advocacy can bring meaning to one's life, and through forging communities of purposeful mutuality we realize our collective interdependence. Vocation is about service to others by way of acting in pursuit of the common good. Therefore, advocacy is inherent to the common good, and as educators, we are called to equip students with the tools to advocate.

In the story of St. Francis in Arezzo, we learn that St. Francis can see that demons have descended on the city of Arezzo, where peasants and merchants are at war with each other. St. Francis sends Br. Sylvester to the city gates to cast the demons away, which Sylvester manages to do by praying over the city to exorcize the demons. This story could be seen as an example of a teacher, St. Francis, successfully instilling in Br. Sylvester the realization of his vocation as a man of God. When I learned this story of St. Francis and Br. Sylvester, I interpreted it from my secular educator's lens, and I imagined preparing students to take actions that would have been needed on the ground in Arezzo to prevent the civil discord in the first place. I wondered about what it means to form students for a vocation of advocacy that labors for change when miracles aren't the answer. We need to prepare students to honor both the calls that come from within to seek rest and spiritual renewal and the calls that come from outside of us to advocate on behalf of others by taking action. Systemic ills maintained by the status quo exploit the marginalized and require collective action to remedy; prayer alone will not suffice.

Those who support students in their advocacy efforts understand well that we must challenge the oppressive elements of higher education institutions. Intercultural educator Chris Arguedas suggests, "If we really want to do what's in the best interest of students, we partner with them, we show them they matter, and we actualize our shared goal of co-creating and facilitating an environment where students can become their best selves."[3] It is imperative that we partner with students and pursue shared goals for an improved campus community that fosters a sense of belonging for everyone. This is a different agenda than assuming that marginalized students alone should be burdened with the work of educating peers, faculty, and staff about their own

[2] "The Language of Vocation at the University of Dayton," February 3, 2017, https://udayton.edu/provost/ilg/_resources/res-vocation/language_of_vocation_at-ud.pdf.

[3] Chris Arguedas, "Student Activism and Belonging," interviewed by Hannah Schell, *Vocation Matters* (blog), June 24, 2020, https://vocationmatters.org/2020/06/24/student-activism-and-belonging/.

oppression. It is not the responsibility of marginalized students to advocate for change to higher education policies and infrastructure to better support their flourishing. In fact, we should model activism on campus if we expect our students to take the advocacy skills gained on campus into their vocational journeys for the whole of their lives.

How do educators begin to support student advocacy efforts? First, the recognition that our students' flourishing is a mutual goal—supporting their wholeness lifts us all into a greater sense of belonging. Darby Ray considers how we approach this kind of mutuality: "We meet others where they are on their own terms. With discipline and practice we find ourselves opening to their story, their experience, their hope for their own lives—which is to say we learn to listen."[4] And Ray states that we need to "keep listening . . . so that the relationship does not slip from partnership back into patronage, from mutuality into mastery,"[5] a point especially relevant for mentor-student relationships. When we partner with our students as advocates for change, we position ourselves as accomplices to the work of social justice, using our relative power to facilitate, mediate, and agitate in environments hostile to student advocacy efforts.[6]

When students become invested in changing their campus culture to cultivate a greater sense of belonging for those with marginalized identities, they are doing the work of advocacy within higher education.[7] Often, as Arguedas states, "many students who are activists are simultaneously learning corresponding theory in the classroom that propels their thinking forward and fuels their ambition to make change in the world."[8] Indeed, it is a credit to those educators who teach theories that compel activism when their students search for meaningful ways to put theory into practice. It helps students to understand that we too are advocates, demonstrating what motivates their mentors' own commitments to community. Students and educators alike "grapple with theory at the same time that we are living and experiencing it."[9]

---

[4] Darby Kathleen Ray, "Self, World, and the Space Between: Community Engagement as Vocational Discernment," in *At This Time and In This Place: Vocation and Higher Education,* ed. David S. Cunningham (New York: Oxford University Press, 2016), 313–14.

[5] Ray, "Self, World, and the Space Between," 314.

[6] Vulnerable contingent faculty and overburdened students cannot always publicly facilitate advocacy efforts, but their intellectual engagement and discussion and deliberation in their personal circles still serve the common good. For an extended exploration of dialogue and deliberation, see chapter 8 of this volume by David Timmerman.

[7] For further examples of student activism on campus and off campus, see this volume's chapter 2 by Deanna A. Thompson and chapter 7 by Jonathan Golden.

[8] Arguedas, "Student Activism and Belonging."

[9] Arguedas, "Student Activism and Belonging."

Yet, students' attention to injustice on their campus may not be as supported or resourced as the community service immersion trips or community-engaged efforts elsewhere. Are we modeling advocacy if we only educate our students for service off campus but not on it? Are we modeling advocacy if we don't take part in efforts to create a more just world within academia as well as outside of it?

Minoritized students often do not receive the support for advocacy efforts that their nonminoritized peers do. While nonminoritized peers' activism "is considered leadership," according to Chris Linder and colleagues, "students of Color and queer students are frequently pushed to underresourced identity-based centers (e.g., multicultural centers, women's centers, LGBT centers) to address their concerns so that administrators and educators do not have to change the ways university systems operate."[10] Many faculty and staff facilitate community-engaged collaborations and have some fluency with the mutual rewards that ethical community engagement provides. However, community engagement can still problematically be framed by notions of service for the "needy" in ways that are paternalistic, othering, and dependent on a model that assumes that students will only be engaging service work within communities where they may have more situational or systemic power than those they are serving. This outmoded and incomplete model of community engagement is not nuanced enough to account for the diverse minoritized identities of students engaging in community, nor the fact that advocacy requires challenging those with power, as well as serving the disenfranchised. How do we partner with student activists to cocreate a more just world on and off campus? We listen to understand how we need to show up, teach to improve intercultural competence, and model advocacy in our lives.

As an educator and theatre practitioner, I fulfill my vocation as a creative collaborator by facilitating spaces that perform hope by rehearsing for revolution. As an applied theatre facilitator, I direct students and community members in problem-solving together through improv and role-play to rehearse the change we want to see in the world. Performance allows a space where we can unleash our creativity to demonstrate the dismantling of oppression and imagine and celebrate a world that allows everyone to thrive. I stand on the great many shoulders of creatives who have always

[10] Chris Linder et al., "The Whole Weight of the World on My Shoulders: Power, Identity, and Student Activism," *Journal of College Student Development* 60, no. 5 (2019): 527–42, https://doi:10.1353/csd.2019.0048, 529.

done so. Alok Vaid-Menon is a performance artist and writer who is gender nonconforming and transfeminine. Their work as an artist and advocate is critical now as we see the erosion of human rights that protect bodily autonomy. Vaid-Menon shares that "advocacy is often reactionary, as an artist, I'm really interested in being proactive and imaginary."[11] Vaid-Menon has found a balance within their work as artist and advocate. I encourage my students to dissolve the barrier between artist and advocate, allowing each identity to inform the other. I create spaces for my students and the audiences we engage to consider the intersection of advocacy and imagination, so that we might practice what Vaid-Menon seeks in their artistry—a "capacity to expand."[12]

I'm invested in preparing my students to cultivate this sort of expansion, specifically to be change agents, to address the root of inequities, and to seek out systemic solutions. Glennon Doyle defines faith as "this hunch that it was all supposed to be more beautiful than this" and explains that without works that take action toward that more beautiful world, faith alone is just an "evacuation plan" to wait for heaven.[13] Advocacy, then, is the work that delivers a more beautiful world we all feel we are meant for, and a collective demonstration of our lifelong vocation in service to others.

With the Common Good Players, an undergraduate applied theatre group I direct, I lead my students in rehearsing for justice, in imagining otherwise. When we all seem to be fatigued from a world filled with so much suffering, we need to be able to pause and say, "Not this."[14] The imagination to create a better future is vital, and for all of us, the vocation of advocacy is a lifelong pursuit. In advocating for ourselves, our desires, and our curiosity to grow and evolve, the vocation of advocacy is a vocation of following the heart. Our commitment to each other demands that we also consider those same desires in others and advocate for them to pursue their own purpose. Advocacy, then, is a common good, for it allows us each to fulfill our individual purpose and our collective responsibility to honor the dignity of all.[15]

[11] Alok Vaid-Menon, "Pride 2022: Alok on How to Actively Support LGBTQ Rights Today," interviewed by Ryma Chikhoune, *Yahoo News*, June 20, 2022, https://www.yahoo.com/news/pride-2022-alok-actively-support-195945485.html.

[12] Vaid-Menon, "Pride 2022."

[13] Glennon Doyle, "Susan Cain Says Sadness Is a Superpower," in *We Can Do Hard Things*, podcast audio, April 7, 2022, https://podcasts.apple.com/us/podcast/susan-cain-says-sadness-is-a-superpower/id1564530722?i=1000556487145.

[14] See, for example, Glennon Doyle, *Untamed* (New York: Dial Press, 2020), 67.

[15] Additionally, given the necessity of advocacy to ensure the future of democracy, see Anand Giridharadas, *The Persuaders* (New York: Random House, 2022) for a critical analysis of how advocacy is a civic duty.

Liminal transformation

In my interdisciplinary field of performance studies, anthropologist Victor Turner's writing about ritual and liminality is foundational. Liminality is theorized by Turner as a state of transformation, wherein a person feels "betwixt and between" who they once were and who they will be on the other side of a transformative liminal experience.[16] College is a liminal space and time in which students are expected to be transformed by their education, and as educators, we pride ourselves on providing transformative learning. Transformation is part of the expected "why" of college, and a fundamental reason that many parents still want a college experience for their children despite rising costs. Young people are expected to discern their purpose during the college years, a time that typically precedes what most students anticipate as the known and stable structure of a career.

While the college experience may be easily understood as transformative— a student is changed by their education—a career, on the other hand, is expected by most students to be a static outcome. However, if students engage in meaningful vocational reflection, they can engage in what Tim Clydesdale calls "trajectory recalibrations," wherein they are able to "frame individual decisions within broader engagement with the world."[17] Through sustained vocational discernment, students can come to understand that one's life purpose and career paths are also sites for transformation and liminality. Students can be equipped to transform their careers and our society toward more equity and inclusion, through their exploration of vocation as a site for advocacy during their college years and throughout their lives.[18] Using theatre and performance as a model, I propose that we should provide tools for our students to be advocates. The vocation of advocacy will allow them to identify and challenge what is broken about the careers that call to them and the communities they live in, and to advocate for change in all areas of their lives, with a dedication to the common good.

Equipping our students with tools to be advocates for change begins with a confrontation of the harm embedded in the structural and institutional power dynamics of the status quo. While not all students are the

---

[16] Victor Turner, *The Ritual Process: Structure and Anti-Structure* (New York: Penguin, 1974), 232.

[17] Tim Clydesdale, *The Purposeful Graduate: Why Colleges Must Talk to Students about Vocation* (Chicago: University of Chicago Press, 2015), 90.

[18] For an extended exploration of transformative experiences through engagement with community, see chapter 7 of this volume by Jonathan Golden.

"reforming activists" of Clydesdale's typology—those already inclined to become advocates—all student types would benefit from learning how to advocate and practicing advocacy.[19] Through a curriculum that increases cultural competence, students learn about systemic inequality within society and embedded in potential career paths.[20] An effect of this learning is that students believe that there is nothing they can do to change what they perceive as entrenched. However, if we also empower students with the skills to be advocates in the world and in their work, like dramatist and actor Anna Deavere Smith,[21] then they can understand that vocation is not the passive acceptance of a life or career path already predetermined, but an active and lifelong pursuit. Some students are already aware of the inequitable practices established within the profession they wish to pursue but have few role models for pursuing the path that intrigues them because of a lack of diversity in the field. Indeed, some students decide upon a career path to break through barriers and become the representation in their field for others that they themselves never had. Education majors learn how to advocate for inclusivity in K-12 curriculum. Psychology students learn to advocate for others through a greater understanding of power dynamics. Business majors learn to advocate for the communities their business ventures serve through case study analyses of the effects of gentrification.

Additionally, vocational exploration needs to attend to our own and our students' brokenness. We cannot pretend that we are not exhausted and heartbroken by the state of the world. Trauma caused by the global pandemic, political divisiveness, legislative assaults on human rights, continued degradation of our planet, mass shootings, and police brutality, among various other contemporary tragedies, have left many of us reeling with varying degrees of trauma.[22] Using theatre and performance examples, I will highlight the need to incorporate trauma-informed pedagogical practices to hear and amplify our students' experiences with oppression and feelings of overwhelm. Out of the recognition of brokenness, after the pause of "Not this," we are able to recover a deeper longing for that elusive more beautiful world

[19] See Clydesdale's typology of students in chapter 4, where students are identified by six types: obsessive-compulsive achievers, utilitarians, minimalists, future intelligentsia, reforming activists, and rebels.
[20] For further models and discussion of curriculum that addresses systemic inequality, see chapter 4 of this volume by Monica M. Smith.
[21] "A Conversation with Anna Deavere Smith," interview by David M. Rubenstein, *American Academy of Arts and Sciences*, October 13, 2019, https://www.amacad.org/news/conversation-anna-deavere-smith.
[22] See Deanna A. Thompson's discussion of trauma in chapter 2 of this volume.

and stir our imaginations again. The vocation of advocacy arises from the heartbreak of longing for a more just world and allows us to connect to our communities again in service to one another. The liminality of the college experience is not, therefore, separate from the real world, but instead lights the path forward to create a transformed world.

Modeling advocacy

Academia itself needs more change agents. For liberal arts educators, it is really a change-or-die moment: for our own survival, academic disciplines must create sustainable practices.[23] There are many of us in academia who are done with the "way things have always been." There has never been a riper time for implementing radical change in the academy. With more resources on many campuses directed at improving diversity, inclusion, and equity, there is significant support for change in program and curriculum development.[24] We have the opportunity as educators to model advocacy for our students by being change agents in our own vocations.

Within my own discipline of theatre, the height of a reckoning came while the entire theatre industry had to take a pause during a global pandemic. The "Not this" moment allowed marginalized voices in theatre to be centered, and now academic theatre must respond. Some academic theatre programs are being forced to grapple with their oppressive practices for the first time and are beginning to introduce radical change to curriculum, policies, and procedures for production work, after being called out by harmed alumni and industry professionals during the summer of 2020.[25] Radical change in academic theatre will lay the groundwork for the advocacy and transformation

---

[23] Kim Phillips-Fein, "How the Right Learned to Loathe Higher Education," *Chronicle of Higher Education,* January 31, 2019, https://www.chronicle.com/article/how-the-right-learned-to-loathe-higher-education/; Frank Bruni, "The End of College as We Knew It?," *New York Times,* June 4, 2020, https://www.nytimes.com/2020/06/04/opinion/sunday/coronavirus-college-humanities.html.

[24] Viji Sathy, Kelly A. Hogan, and Bob Henshaw, "The More You Know about Your Students, the More Inclusive You Can Be in the Classroom," *Chronicle of Higher Education,* June 21, 2022, https://www.chronicle.com/article/the-more-you-know-about-your-students-the-more-inclusive-you-can-be-in-the-classroom; Zamudio-Suarez notes that teaching diversity courses takes a real toll on the mostly minoritized and otherwise vulnerable faculty (nontenured) who offer them. See Fernanda Zamudio-Suarez, "Race on Campus: How to Retain Diverse Faculty Members," *Chronicle of Higher Education,* May 17, 2022, https://www.chronicle.com/newsletter/race-on-campus/2022-05-17.

[25] In the wake of the Dear White American Theatre open letter penned by established industry artists, college alumni wrote open letters to academic theatre programs that had harmed them with oppressive practices. See https://www.weseeyouwat.com/.

of our graduates in their vocations in the entertainment industries. Key aspects of transformation in academic theatre include:[26]

- Eliminating racist and classist audition requirements
- Decolonizing and diversifying the curriculum, including developing community-engaged applied theatre curriculum and programming
- Providing equitable casting opportunities for all students by diversifying production seasons
- Developing trauma-informed rehearsals that provide resources and safety within the theatrical exploration of traumatic and oppressive human realities
- Giving students the tools to be content creators and not merely interpreters of others' work
- Eliminating the wearing of exhaustion and overwork as a badge of honor

The pandemic shuttered theatres and showed everyone that there are other ways to produce theatre. In response, creative solutions were invented and implemented in a virtual space that highlighted issues of access and democratization of content creation and illuminated the deep exclusionary and ableist conceits about who can "do" theatre and who can attend. With the move to accessible theatre, generous experiments emerged. We turned living rooms into stages, leveraged virtual script readings to develop new works, and danced literally when no one was watching because we were empowered to turn our Zoom cameras off and truly be in our bodies, any kind of body, for the first time in a dance class.[27]

Academic theatre is not separate from the whole of the entertainment industry, although there are some who insist it is not the "real world." The

[26] Christina Schoellkopf, "Catching Up on IATSE? What's behind Hollywood's Labor Unrest," *Los Angeles Times,* October 9, 2021, https://www.latimes.com/entertainment-arts/story/2021-10-07/iatse-hollywood-crews-strike-what-to-know. To learn about the movement for no more 10 out of 12's working hours, see https://nomore10outof12s.com/. For an open platform for disruptive voices in theatre, see https://howlround.com/; Elynmarie Kazle, "The Stage Managers' Association Creates the Council for Equity and Advocacy," *United States Institute for Theatre Technology,* October 5, 2020, https://www.usitt.org/news/stage-managers-association-creates-council-equity-and-advocacy. To read the diversity, equity, and inclusion plan for the Association for Theatre in Higher Education, see https://www.athe.org/page/deiplan.

[27] Alisa Boland, "The Challenges and Surprises of Making Theatre on Zoom," *Rescripted,* September 1, 2020, http://rescripted.org/2020/09/01/challenges-zoom-theatre/; Sho Shibata, "The Future of Inclusivity in Dance, Post-Pandemic," *Stopgap Dance,* March 16, 2021, https://www.stopgapdance.com/story/the-future-of-inclusivity-in-dance-post-pandemic-signature-blog/; https://www.infiniteflowdance.org/; and https://axisdance.org/.

"real world" versus academic theatre rhetoric in college theatre programs has historically only been used to justify exploitative and inequitable practices. Moving beyond this false notion of college not being "real" requires radical change in academic theatre, where we have the responsibility to train the transformative leaders of the future of the field. Momentum for change is underway, as theatre educators create and embed resources that protect industry practitioners' well-being by implementing change to curriculum, policy and procedures, and production work that our undergraduates and graduate students experience now.

Regardless of discipline, our responsibility as educators is to acknowledge that students are engaged in a vocation as students *now* and that their explorations during their college years are indeed vocational explorations. We also must prepare our students to challenge their respective professional fields with demands for dignity and justice and to not neglect the common good in a quest to "get ahead." Rather than thinking it best to ensure that our students can "deal with" the ways their career paths may slowly destroy them, let us prepare them to be change agents for the common good on their vocational paths by practicing advocacy and self-reflection during college.[28] This insistence that college is not the "real world" negates the fact that for our students their experience in college is indeed very real. There are educators who may disdain trauma-informed approaches as a less-than-rigorous approach to pedagogy. The false notion that our students are insulated from the harshness of the world elides the fact that educators can do real harm to students during their college experience. Instead, let's enable students to flourish as transformational leaders during their college experience.

Trauma, advocacy for the common good, and vocational discernment

When educators expect students to pursue vocational exploration as they did, similarly "paying dues" by settling for exploitative first jobs, they are trying to recreate their own outdated (potentially irrelevant) career trajectories for their students. Students do not always explicitly say "Not this" but express the sentiment through their feelings of overwhelm during advising meetings,

---

[28] For methods and models that help address burnout and cultivate sustainable vocations, see Meghan M. Slining's extensive discussion in chapter 10 of this volume.

their changing majors numerous times, their confusion about what is next after college, and their feelings of unpreparedness to connect their studies and passions with a career path. Educators of every discipline need to sit with the "Not this." We ought to take the time to name what is broken in our vocational paths and in our world so that we can devise better programs, pedagogies, and curricula that account for advocating for the common good.

We often neglect to address the oppressive practices and structures of vocational pathways due to the pressure to grow our programs and increase our numbers of majors. Self-preservation and scarcity mentality result in curricula that fail to draw attention to the darker sides of any of our disciplines in an educational model that treats the student as consumer.[29] We therefore may not provide tools for self-advocacy and leave students ill-equipped to be change agents for the common good in their vocation as students, and in future career paths as a result. A lack of attention to advocacy in matters of justice on a campus or in a career path results when educators themselves feel uncertain about their own job security or the pressures of a consumer-driven model of higher education. In a recent survey, students reported that they "experienced administrators as primarily concerned with the perception of powerful donors and board members, sometimes at the expense of students' well-being on their campuses."[30] Not this.

With the #BlackOnCampus hashtag widely used in 2015, college students posted to social media about the racism they faced at their higher education institutions. In the wake of the Black Lives Matter movement and the summer of 2020 that saw the murder of George Floyd, higher education was compelled to answer demands for greater transparency around diversity, equity, and inclusion on their campuses. Currently, we face the most aggressive political and cultural assault to date on transgender youth and trans athletes, and more students are bringing the trauma of marginalized queer identities, compounded at some institutions by silence on these issues due to religious affiliation or the perceived need to not be controversial.[31]

---

[29] Audrey Williams June, "Here's How Rising Inflation Is Affecting Higher Ed," *Chronicle of Higher Education,* April 14, 2022, https://www.chronicle.com/article/heres-how-rising-inflation-is-affecting-higher-ed.
[30] Linder et al., "The Whole Weight of the World," 539.
[31] Eric Kelderman, "The Far Right's College Crusade," *Chronicle of Higher Education,* June 28, 2021 https://www.chronicle.com/article/the-far-rights-college-crusade;   https://www.professorwatchlist.org/; Laura Pappano, "At Christian Colleges, a Collision of Gay Rights and Traditional Values," *New York Times,* June 5, 2018, https://www.nytimes.com/2018/06/05/education/learning/christian-colleges-lgbtq-social-justice.html.

We need to create space for the discernment of vocation that includes the recognition of our students' trauma and the oppressive structures of work in a capitalist society that have caused all of us pain. Our students' desire to be healed and whole—to become change agents—means that we may simply need to get out of their way and let them lead. Our students' advocacy and activism can lead them to their life's purpose, not only our "Four-Year Plans of Study." For other students whose privilege has insulated them from the trauma of oppression, our responsibility remains just as critical: in this case to awaken them to the need to advocate for another's humanity. David Cunningham points to the shortsightedness of vocational discussion with students that leans too heavily on discerning merely a unique, individual, and internal answer to a calling. He cautions that these discussions "too often send the message that 'your life is yours alone,' as though it were ultimately unrelated to that of the person sitting right next to them at the orientation session, or the pizza night, or the retreat."[32] We must ensure that vocational discernment includes students' dialectical reflection on the relative privilege and oppression experienced by themselves and others, and the fundamental truth of our vocational interdependence and responsibility to the common good. As educators we understand the value of the liminal college experience as a site of transformation, and on our best days we witness transformative discoveries as our students cross into the liminal space of reframing past experiences to incorporate new knowledge.

What might the "Not this" pause look like from a pedagogical perspective? The late bell hooks set forth her vision for a community of learners reaching toward collective freedom in *Teaching to Transgress*, wherein pedagogy serves to release us from racism, sexism, classism, and oppression.[33] When advising students, it looks like ensuring their curiosity is nurtured alongside course requirements, even if that means they pick up a minor that would diminish their capacity to contribute to your program. It looks like an insistence on professional development in diversity, equity, and inclusion in pedagogical practices. It means equipping students with the tools to make their lives and careers upon graduation more just. It means aligning curriculum with leading-edge trends in our field that problematize the way we've always done things. It means graduating change agents, agitators, and fierce

[32] David S. Cunningham, "Colleges Have Callings, Too: Vocational Reflection at the Institutional Level," in *Vocation across the Academy: A New Vocabulary for Higher Education*, ed. David S. Cunningham (New York: Oxford University Press, 2017), 266.

[33] bell hooks, *Teaching to Transgress: Education as the Practice of Freedom* (London: Routledge, 1994).

advocates for equity in the workplace and life. For example, our graduates should be concerned that the colleagues they work with in their first job are receiving equal pay for equal work and feel a sense of belonging and safety in their career and in their communities. Our graduates should demand work-life balance and no longer be told that they must "pay their dues" to oppressive structures by remaining silent and keeping their heads down at the expense of their own happiness and fulfillment. Not this.

The Common Good Players: a model for practicing advocacy for the common good

How do we get students to take responsibility for others' suffering as well as their own? We have all seen students shut down during a class discussion about society's injustices as they ask the question of "What can I do? I'm just one person." This is our cue to remind students to remember our interdependence. We can ease their feelings of overwhelm by having them practice the power of showing up for others in the micro-localities of their daily lives: in their dorms, at their jobs, on their campuses. Providing meaningful boundaries to the work of social justice and caring for the common good channels student creativity toward solving problems on a local and micro scale.[34] Such meaningful boundaries of advocacy work might look like assisting a student in their need to change their housing situation, helping them advocate for the international student at their campus job, or supporting their efforts in ethical engagement in course-based community service. Practicing advocacy as students, on behalf of other students, is a meaningful way to feel the power and effects of one's activism.

The practice of advocacy in vocational discernment is demonstrated in the work of the Common Good Players, an applied theatre troupe I direct at the University of Dayton (UD). In the broadest strokes, applied theatre is utilizing the skill sets of theatre for educational and developmental purposes. Applied theatre is an ever-expanding field in our increasingly performative world, interfacing with a broad swath of public works and projects everywhere, including museum and tourism industries, medical and social

---

[34] See Meghan M. Slining's discussion of compassionate pedagogy in chapter 10 of this volume for more examples of how to cultivate healthy boundaries and sustainable practices with students in vocational exploration.

services, and leadership training for major corporations. Most are familiar with leadership training that incorporates acting, either by the inclusion of filmed actors performing leadership scenarios that intend to spark dialogue à la "what would you do?" or the expectation of role-play in cultural sensitivity retreats. I always feel obligated to approach a facilitator at a coffee break during a leadership training to inform them that the methods they are using for their work come from a field that they typically have never heard of: applied theatre.

Theatre practitioners have figured out how to use performance, acting, improv, and role-play for liberatory ends, and theatre for social justice as a field has long relied upon these methods; therefore, leadership training facilitators ought to "consult the literature" of the applied theatre vocations.[35] I am nonetheless heartened by the dissemination of our applied theatre methods in other fields, as it is evidence of the viability, efficacy, and broad applications of applied theatre itself. On my campus, our administrative team appreciates the rich impact of applied theatre and supports the work of the Common Good Players to advocate at the institution and in our community about issues pertinent to the common good.

The students who make up the Common Good Players can practice advocacy by naming their own oppression, interrogating their own privilege, and taking seriously our interdependence to realize the common good. We accomplish this through applied theatre methods of research, creation of composite characters and scripts, and performances based on research, role-play, and tableau scenes. We also leverage Theatre of the Oppressed tactics of participatory collective creation of a scene with workshop participants that dramatizes oppression and then dramatizes the strategies to challenge that oppression. For any given project the Common Good Players take on, the appropriate applied theatre response will vary, and we choose appropriate tools from this tool kit. We launched the Common Good Players in 2018–19 with training in the methods of applied theatre and Theatre of the Oppressed, including an immersive weekend in Chicago where the Common Good Players were able to watch applied theatre performance of various kinds and receive a training in protest street theatre.[36]

---

[35] See literature on drama therapy, Theatre of the Oppressed, theatre in education, theatre in prisons, and theatre for development for insight into the scope of applied theatre.

[36] Michelle Hayford, "Performing Arts in the Service of Others: The Common Good Players and Experiential Learning in Social Justice Theatre," in *Diverse Pedagogical Approaches to Experiential Learning*, ed. Karen Lovett (New York: Springer Publishing, 2020), 207–21.

On August 4, 2019, there was a mass shooting in the entertainment district of downtown Dayton, Ohio, so near our university's campus that campus police responded. Nine people were murdered, and seventeen were injured. The Common Good Players' first project was to figure out a way to respond to this tragedy. We decided to wear large angel wings in honor of the victims, and in homage to the Angel Action wings featured in the Laramie Project.[37] Each Common Good Player prepared a performance to present at a vigil for the dead. Performances included song, dance, monologue, poem recitation, and the playing of a musical instrument. When not performing, the Common Good Players stood in a semicircle containing the vigil site like sentinels, silently holding space for the victims, with our large translucent angel wings billowing in the gentle breeze. The effect of our presence lent a gravitas and performative aspect to the vigil that captured art's capacity to illuminate the unspeakable and allowed others to mourn.[38]

Our next project was to assist in the campus-wide effort to revise faculty tenure and promotion policies to be more inclusive and equitable. Cunningham posits that "developing a good environment for the discernment of an institution's vocation will also require that more of its members are learning multiple 'languages'—including the primary forms of discourse among those groups to whom one does not belong. What would it mean for students to learn about the issues that most concern the faculty?"[39] Learning how inequitable tenure and promotion policies were negatively impacting their faculty—and by extension their own college experience—was a significant exercise in learning a new language of advocacy. It meant that UD students were given the excellent practice of advocating to change the conditions that resulted in experiences of oppression that were previously unknown to them.

The Common Good Players set out to create performances and role-play characters from our research to present in workshops on more equitable tenure and promotion policies for administrators and tenure and promotion committee members in meeting rooms on campus. Our first steps in the process included reviewing the literature about the need for more inclusive tenure and promotion policies, reading first-person accounts of the challenges faced by tenure-track faculty, and creating composite characters

---

[37] Laramie Project wings are described at http://eatromaine.com/1/laramie-angels.html.

[38] For further exploration of public lament and mourning, see Deanna A. Thompson's discussion in chapter 2 of this volume.

[39] Cunningham, "Colleges Have Callings, Too," 270.

based on our research who exemplified typical faculty facing discrimination from antiquated tenure and promotion policies.[40] Next, we created skits that situated these composite characters in dramatized scenarios that performed the oppression they were combating on the tenure track.

One skit performed the tyranny of the "publish or perish" threat, with one Common Good Player performing the tenure-track faculty member typing at her computer at her desk while the rest of the Common Good Players hover around her to perform the pressure that she is feeling, chanting, "write! write! write! write!" with increasing intensity, volume, and tempo. While frantically typing, the harried professor answers a phone call from an administrator asking her to chaperone a student retreat, which she declines, even though she had really wanted to go, because she has a writing deadline. She resumes frantically typing while the rest of the Players taunt her with their incessant "write, write, write" mantra when another Player, portraying a student, knocks on the door wanting assistance with their research. But the harried professor just slinks under her desk and pretends she's not there as the writing deadline looms and the student walks away in disappointment. The hovering Common Good Players continue to chant with frenzied pace now "WRITE, WRITE, WRITE" until, in a triumphant moment, the harried professor submits the article. But the relief is short-lived as the other Common Good Players end their enthusiastic shouts of approval to begin chanting in intense unison again, this time: "revise and resubmit! revise and resubmit! revise and resubmit!" and we see the harried professor begin to type again, this time with more exhaustion and fear.

We performed several of these kinds of skits, some including original song, all of them quite clever and finding a humorous angle that did not blunt the actual harm being performed in these scenes. Each provided a satirical exploration of oppressive tenure and promotion policies that fostered meaningful dialogue in the audience. We facilitated these workshops for administrators and faculty with Tim Eatman, a guest speaker and scholar of public scholarship and an advocate for more equitable tenure and promotion policies. We also facilitated a dialogue following the performance. After sharing our scenes, we invited participants in the workshop to role-play with a Common Good Player who was in character as a tenure-track faculty member oppressed by tenure and promotion policies. Administrators

---

[40] Julie Ellison and Timothy K. Eatman, "Scholarship in Public: Knowledge Creation and Tenure Policy in the Engaged University," *Imagining America*, 2008, 16, https://surface.syr.edu/ia/16.

and faculty were invited to role-play with the oppressed tenure-track faculty member by playing a chairperson, colleague, or member of the tenure and promotion committee, each practicing advocacy for others by naming the oppression, proposing different solutions, or encouraging change.

This was a rare opportunity for undergraduate students to be let into the most vulnerable aspects of life on the tenure track and see the dark side of academia often shielded from them.[41] To their credit, the Common Good Players immediately grasped the breadth of harm of inequitable tenure and promotion policies once they were well researched. The creation of the composite characters and scenes was affirming for me and many colleagues, in that students can see our oppression too. In the transformative and liminal space opened up by applied theatre, our students were able to advocate for change for their faculty in ways that were meaningful and moving for all those in attendance. After one workshop, a faculty member approached me in tears because he was so surprised by the empathy and understanding demonstrated by the students and the transformative experience of being in audience to the Common Good Players' earnest work on behalf of the common good. .

Engaging in applied theatre is impactful because theatre is impactful by design. Theatre is embodied and requires our presence and attention in real time and space. A shared collective experience can produce transformative effects one cannot achieve alone. As Jason Stevens asserts, "Drama gives us opportunities to reflect on both helpful and harmful political and social emotions and to clarify their roles in our collective life and our collective calling to justice."[42] When we consider that in applied theatre the audience is often called upon to play a character via role-play or improv or the creation of a tableau or movement piece, then the audience too has the opportunity to practice advocacy by performing their character's interactions with other characters. Applied theatre offers a model for vocational discernment that is less about a reflective private process and instead an embodied collective performance in everyday life that demands you show up for others.

---

[41] The Common Good Players also learned of the inequity of contingent faculty hires as a cost-saving practice, although our specific project did not take on this population. See Abbi Ross, "A Snapshot of Pandemic Life for Adjunct Faculty Members," *Chronicle of Higher Education,* February 24, 2022, https://www.chronicle.com/article/a-snapshot-of-pandemic-life-for-adjunct-faculty-members.

[42] Jason Stevens, "The Drama of Vocation," in *Cultivating Vocation in Literary Studies,* ed. Stephanie L. Johnson and Erin VanLaningham (Edinburgh: Edinburgh University Press, 2022), 107.

In the role-play and responsiveness that applied theatre demands, we practice listening and responding to one another. An actor is only as good as their ability to listen and respond. A bad actor does not listen and just waits for their scene partner to stop talking so they can say their line. Good acting requires the ability to respond to what is happening instead of a preconceived idea of what is supposed to happen. If your scene partner interprets a line in a new way but you respond as if the line was said with the intention of the last performance and not the present one, then the audience is pulled out of the reality of the scene because the actor is no longer listening and responding.

Similarly, if we consider our vocational discernment as a process informed by the collective transformative experiences that lead us toward the common good, then we might conceive of vocation too as requiring responsiveness to what is right in front of us. As a Catholic and Marianist institution, UD's educational mission is "rooted in the response of Blessed Father William Joseph Chaminade and the early Marianists to the chaos of the French Revolution. Chaminade believed that this tumultuous time required new methods of spreading the Gospel." These new methods apply to the Marianist tradition of education, in which "we strive to educate our students to be community builders with the desire to create and share a vision characterized by respect, the common good, help for the poor and a better community."[43] Applied theatre and vocational discernment require active listening, an engaged and embodied presence in the world, and a commitment to pursue the common good through advocacy. These are new methods that can foster flourishing in more dynamic, transformative ways.

To care for the common good sometimes has meant an overlooking of that which is "uncommon" in the search for solidarity.[44] For example, the early mainstream gay rights movement neglected to advocate for transgender rights even though transgender people led the Stonewall riots. At worst, efforts on behalf of the common good can be coercive, bullying, or patronizing. If humanization is a precondition for work toward the common good for all, then those who are treated as less than human, those who are denied basic human rights and dignity, should be the focus of our advocacy. We need to center the very people who are marginalized by the rhetoric

---

[43] "Common Themes in the Mission and Identity of the University of Dayton," https://udayton.edu/rector/_resources/files/common_themes_brochure.pdf.

[44] For an extensive exploration of the value and necessity of the uncommon good, see Geoffrey W. Bateman's discussion in chapter 6 of this volume.

of the common good to pursue its ends. Applied theatre gives us the tools to humanize and empathize by enabling participants to practice advocacy through actively naming oppression and rehearsing the solutions to oppression. Augusto Boal, founder of Theatre of the Oppressed, calls participants in his applied theatre method "spect-actors." Spect-actors occupy a liminal space between spectators and actors in that they are not passive like the traditional theatre spectator, but active in the rehearsing for the revolution.

For our students to be effective change agents they need to interact with people who have power in their communities. During college, students can learn to engage in advocacy efforts from a position of far less power relative to those they are challenging. Often, our minoritized students engage in advocacy within communities where their identities are marginalized. Higher education often situates work for the common good as a project of the student's encounter with service to a disenfranchised community and deploys a problematic deficit instead of an assets model in this service work. The work of the Common Good Players demonstrates how we need to provide our students with the opportunity to speak truth to power and engage with privileged community members as well as the disenfranchised. My work with the Common Good Players underscores the need to empower our students to not only advocate for the oppressed but also serve others by interrogating power in communities that have greater relative privilege than themselves.

Now this

Advocacy is for all of us in higher education. At a time when the fundamental conceits of our democracy are contested, we need to be invested in the common good. Advocacy as vocation must be taken up now by educators as a necessary response to the collective hopelessness that our current political and social climate has produced. Our responsibility to the students we mentor requires that we nurture their ambitions for activism, for change, for the world to reflect inclusivity and justice. If we nurture our students as advocates, our campuses will reap the rewards of our cocreated environments for belonging. If we mentor, model, and teach advocacy, our local communities and the communities our students will serve throughout their lives will feel the impact of our collective endeavor to pursue justice. Our student advocates will go on to lead purpose-filled lives, and our role as educators will prove to have profound value despite neoliberal pressures that would minimize such successes.

This practice of advocacy during the liminal and transformational college years will inform our students' continued advocacy for the common good in their vocational lives and as global citizens. Rather than equip students to merely survive or tolerate inhumane working conditions in their fields, unjust laws, or divisive politics, we need to provide them with advocacy skills and the opportunities to practice advocacy throughout college, so that they can be the transformational leaders for the common good that our interdependence requires. Now this.

6

Queer Vocation and the Uncommon Good

Geoffrey W. Bateman

A few years ago, in a course I teach on queer theory and social justice, a queer-identified student in the class met with a counselor in our career center to review their resume as they prepared to apply for jobs after they graduated. The counselor advised the student not to include their internship at an LGBTQIA+ advocacy organization for fear it might limit their opportunities. However well intentioned, this advice confused and frustrated the student, for they were out to their family, faculty, and peers, so they assumed they could and should be so professionally. Representing an important accomplishment, the internship had powerfully shaped their vocational discernment and represented an experience that they thought potential employers would value. Unfortunately, the counselor's advice reinforced homophobic notions about the inappropriateness of being out in the workplace, signaling that the student should remain discreet if not closeted about their queerness. In the end, this exchange thwarted the student's desire to live authentically and undermined their calling into a particular kind of professional community. How should they respond and what should they do, the student asked me and the class?

The answers we explored that day illustrated and sought to dismantle the many barriers that LGBTQIA+ students face in their vocational exploration as they attempt to live their lives in magnanimous fashion, pursue meaningful work, and engage the common good, especially in relation to how sexuality and gender structure our civic and professional worlds.[1] In many of our communities, we have made great strides against the harassment, discrimination, and violence that LGBTQIA+ people face. At the same time, we still struggle to affirm the inherent goodness of queer lives and view them not

---

[1] See Paul J. Wadell, "An Itinerary of Hope: Called to a Magnanimous Way of Life," in *At This Time and In This Place: Vocation and Higher Education*, ed. David S. Cunningham (New York: Oxford University Press, 2015), 193–215.

Geoffrey W. Bateman, *Queer Vocation and the Uncommon Good* In: *Called Beyond Our Selves.*
Edited by: Erin VanLaningham, Oxford University Press. © Oxford University Press 2024.
DOI: 10.1093/oso/9780197691915.003.0007

just as something to tolerate, but something to celebrate and value as exemplary. Further, we do not yet view queerness as a common good or consider it integral and a constitutive element of our common flourishing.

Despite the collective intent and actions of many of us in higher education, we also don't fully embrace queerness, especially at faith-based colleges and universities, even as many in recent years have made important strides in transforming our campuses into being far more inclusive of queer forms of difference, including Regis University, a Jesuit institution, where I teach.[2] As I've argued, vocation as a field, in its deep rootedness in Christianity, continues to need ongoing transformation to make available its resources to all LGBTQIA+ students.[3] And even as queer people in the United States have gained increasing political legitimacy and secured important rights that make certain common vocational choices more readily available to us—for example, marriage equality and nondiscrimination in employment—these gains remain unevenly secured across the country, depending on the state someone lives in and the intersectional nature of their identities. In certain contexts, LGBTQIA+ people remain subject to legal hostility and political eradication.[4] To complicate matters further, many of these strides, which from a mainstream political perspective seem worthy goals, reinforce a neoliberal, homonormative ideological agenda that many queer theorists and activists continue to critique. They see such gains as threatening to occlude and marginalize other forms of queerness—especially those forms of difference that intersect with other categories of identity and oppression—that are less palatable to our larger political and social imaginations.[5] Instead, these critics anchor their vision of sociality, collectivity, and futurity in more radical transformations of the White supremacist, heteronormative, settler colonialist social order, in which they anchor various forms of queer negativity, resistance, and utopian desires.

---

[2] See Alyse Knorr and Erin Winterrowd, "Fostering Jesuit Queer Inclusivity in a Charged Political Environment," *Jesuit Higher Education* 10, no. 1 (2021): 88–110, https://epublications.regis.edu/jhe/vol10/iss1/11; and Jonathan S. Coley, *Gay on God's Campus: Mobilizing for LGBT Equality at Christian Colleges and Universities* (Chapel Hill: University of North Carolina Press, 2018).

[3] See Geoffrey W. Bateman, "Queer Callings: LGBTQ Literature and Vocation," in *Dwelling in Possibility: Cultivating Vocation in Literary Studies*, ed. Stephanie L. Johnson and Erin VanLaningham (Edinburgh: Edinburgh University Press, 2022), 111–33.

[4] See Nancy J. Knauer, "The Politics of Eradication and the Future of LGBT Rights," *Georgetown Journal of Gender and Law* 22 (2020): 615–70, https://www.law.georgetown.edu/gender-journal/the-politics-of-eradication-and-the-future-of-lgbt-rights/.

[5] See Lisa Duggan, *The Twilight of Equality?: Neoliberalism, Cultural Politics, and the Attack on Democracy* (Boston: Beacon Press, 2003), 50.

Thus, queerness as a common good, or perhaps more challenging, a queer transformation of the common good, remains fiercely contested. Recent legal hostility to supporting transgender youth shows how the particularities of certain forms of queer difference still interfere with the shaping of the common good, such that the common good can function to exclude or diminish queerness.[6] In response, we need to reorient our understanding of the value of commonality and transform the common good in order to preserve more fully space for difference and particularity. Many feminist and queer scholars of color have historically engaged difference in this way, recasting our dominant social imaginary so that it sees difference not as a threat or something to neutralize and assimilate, but more as a common resource that might be valuable and good in its irreducible particularity. To better serve and support our vocational work with our queer students we might instead embrace a notion of *the uncommon good*: in the midst of either common goods (so the facilities or resources that we share in common promote our flourishing as humans) or the common good (as a feature or space or collectivity of our deliberation and discernment about the good life), we must be better attuned to the differences and particularities that, in fact, we might not share and might not even really understand but can learn to value.

These uncommon goods represent that which we might not be able to absorb or integrate into our common understanding or our common endeavors and yet ought to be considered necessary and essential for the pursuit of the good life for all. Queerness in all its many forms can and should play an important role in our collective imagination, cultures, and social, political, and economic worlds. This includes the visibility and circulation of uncommon forms of desire; sexual and gender identities that defy binary norms; bodies and all the various ways that queer people inhabit, stylize, and present them; and sex in its many unusual forms. Ultimately, the circulation and accessibility of queerness are essential for our common flourishing, for they help deconstruct stultifying and lethal forms of homogeneity that commonness can promote. Even as such queerness might be particular to minoritized identities and communities or only partially shared (if perhaps discreetly or secretively) across our population, and thus be uncommon, such uncommonness seems worth holding out for as an important good and as an

---

[6] See Knauer, "Politics of Eradication," 620–22; and Katie Glueck and Patricia Mazzei, "Red States Push L.G.B.T.Q. Restrictions as Education Battles Intensify," *New York Times*, April 12, 2022, https://www.nytimes.com/2022/04/12/us/politics/transgender-laws-us.html.

important facet of our collective well-being, so that all might live lives of dignity. As Eve Kosofsky Sedgwick observes in the first axiom of *Epistemology of the Closet*, "People are different from each other."[7] Our collective work in seeking to embed our students' vocational journeys within a vibrant and flourishing common good must affirm this fundamental fact and preserve the ability to be different in community. We must hold a space for the tension between particularity and commonality so that those whose difference cannot be assimilated can live out their lives with meaning and purpose within the context of a more just and humane world.

This chapter takes up this tension and explores the relationship between the inner call of sexuality and gender and the outer call of the common good, doing so with both deep skepticism and appreciation for the latter. It interrogates vocational models and their theological underpinnings, accounting for the importance of LGBTQIA+ identities and lived experience and integrating queer theologians' call for "erotic justice" and queer theorists' resistance to neoliberal paradigms. Queering vocation at the individual level is not sufficient though: it also depends on a transformation of the common good and the structures that make the flourishing of any given life and community possible. In the second half of the chapter, I seek to embed queer vocational discernment within a much larger concern for our collective well-being. This requires an engagement with queer dissent from normative sociality and the common good, even as it recuperates it through queer desires for a utopian future in which LGBTQIA+ people might actively participate in creating a world in which all can flourish by transforming our relationship to particular forms of queer difference. Throughout, it will include examples of how educators and colleges and universities can bring the uncommon into our common vision of human flourishing.

Queer vocation

Despite the more recent shifts in cultural attitudes and law and policy, the climate for LGBTQIA+ young people is still fraught. As Caryn Riswold observes, "Socially, politically, and even theologically, issues related to sexual orientation and gender identity are among the fastest changing in our culture.

[7] Eve Kosofsky Sedgwick, *Epistemology of the Closet* (Berkeley: University of California Press, 1990), 22.

In the meantime, dehumanizing limits continue to be imposed on those whose identities do not conform to the norm."[8] One of the barriers that our LGBTQIA+ students face as they discern their vocations is coming into right relation with their sexual and gender identities and living out these identities authentically in relationship to others. As Kathleen Talvacchia writes, "For LGBTQIA+ persons, a vocational calling is discerned most fully and clearly within the integration of their vocational journey with the process of their identification, which is deeply connected to an awareness of gender and sexuality in their lives."[9] In this way, coming out continues to be a distinct part of the vocational journey for many queer people, for it not only affirms deeply personal and evolving truths about their experiences but also works to connect them to communal and collective contexts that foster a more just and humane world. For Talvacchia, coming out is a form of "disruptive coherence" grounded in an "erotic ethical practice of truth-telling," which affirms our inner realities in the context of larger social forces.[10] This interplay allows queer students both to value the transgressive nature of their identities, desires, and embodiments and to "challenge structures of normalization that deny an authentic human freedom."[11] Such empowerment makes it possible for LGBTQIA+ individuals to imagine and pursue an ever-evolving sense of their embodied callings, reinforcing agency and self-determination without falling prey to an overly individualistic sense of vocation. In its emphasis on the intersectional and socially interconnected forces that condition a queer person's journey, coming out, then, affirms and empowers young people's evolving identity in context, helping them come out not only to themselves but also into community and larger engagement with and potential transformation of structures of oppression and injustices. Coming out facilitates an engagement with the inner truths of queer vocational experience in relation to a much broader sense of sociality, collectivity, and the common good.

For coming out to serve our students as this sort of connective, socially engaged, vocational practice though, we must continue to resist heteronormative impulses that demonize queerness and homonormative ones that would channel it only in certain respectable ways. Central to this work is a

---

[8] Caryn D. Riswold, "Vocational Discernment: A Pedagogy of Humanization," in Cunningham, ed., *At This Time and In This Place*, 93.

[9] Kathleen T. Talvacchia, "Queer Embodiment in a Vocational Journey," *Vocation Matters* (blog), November 9, 2021, https://vocationmatters.org/2021/11/09/queer-embodiment/#more-9345.

[10] Kathleen T. Talvacchia, *Embracing Disruptive Coherence: Coming Out as Erotic Embodied Practice* (Eugene, OR: Cascade Books, 2019), 5.

[11] Talvacchia, *Embracing Disruptive Coherence*, 6.

foundational theological recasting of our attitudes toward queer forms of desire and embodiment, so that LGBTQIA+ individuals, but especially young queer people, can experience them as inherently good and claim them as life affirming rather than signs of perversity, sin, sickness, or unnaturalness. As teachers and scholars, we must embrace queer theologians' transformative recasting of our beliefs about the body, desire, sexuality, and the embodiment of various forms of gender and their expression in relation to spirituality and religious faith. As they have argued, for LGBTQIA+ people to flourish fully in their humanity, queer forms of desire and embodiment must be seen as fundamentally good, God given, and worthy of organizing our lives around.[12] In their chartering of a new sexual morality, they insist that queer folks must be able to experience their erotic and sexual lives as, in Carter Heyward's words, the "most fully embodied experience of the love of God."[13] Similarly challenging Christianity's historical sex negativity and the tendency to see same-sex sexuality as inferior and immoral, Marvin Ellison proposes a sexual ethics rooted in erotic justice, which, rather than focus on the sex or gender of those people in relationship, emphasizes a "responsible use of power, including erotic power, to enhance personal well-being and strengthen community ties of mutual respect and care across social categories."[14] In other words, erotic justice protects the dignity of all individuals in relationship and by doing also strengthens the dignity and humanity of our communities. For Ellison, this ethical use of power not only "enhance[s] the dignity and well-being of persons of diverse sexual identities" but also calls everyone to use this power to foster each individual's belonging to and participation in our communities.[15] For our queer students, especially those growing up in Christian faith traditions, such transformation of sexual theology is absolutely necessary for them to come into a more integrative and affirming understanding of their own desires, identities, and embodiments as both a

---

[12] Much of this theological engagement relies on Audre Lorde, "Uses of the Erotic: The Erotic as Power," in *Sister Outsider* (Berkeley, CA: Crossing Press, 1984), 53–59. See Carter Heyward, *Touching Our Strength: The Erotic as Power and the Love of God* (San Francisco, CA: Harper & Row, 1989); Richard Cleaver, *Know My Name: A Gay Liberation Theology* (Louisville, KY: Westminster John Knox Press, 1995); Marvin M. Ellison, *Erotic Justice: A Liberating Ethic of Sexuality* (Louisville, KY: Westminster John Knox Press, 1996); Marvin M. Ellison and Sylvia Thorson-Smith, eds., *Body and Soul: Rethinking Sexuality as Justice-Love* (Cleveland, OH: Pilgrim Press, 2003); and Marvin M. Ellison, *Making Love Just: Sexual Ethics for Perplexing Times* (Minneapolis, MN: Fortress Press, 2012).

[13] Heyward, *Touching Our Strength*, 99.

[14] Ellison, *Making Love Just*, 34.

[15] Ellison, *Making Love Just*, 34.

precursor to and part of their self-actualization, as well as providing a path to connect their sexualities to larger concerns for the collective well-being.

Equally important is recognizing the role that gender identity and expression plays in vocation, both for the individual and as a force for social transformation. For Justin Sabia-Tanis, coming into awareness of and embracing the inherent goodness of his transgender identity illustrates an experience of vocational discovery and discernment. "Rather than simply being a fluke, an oddity, or a source of shame," he argues, "gender variance comes to be seen as part of our God-given identities."[16] Itself a distinct form of calling, gender identity—especially transgender identity—also serves as an entry into other facets of purpose and meaning. As Sabia-Tanis suggests, "By answering the call of our gender, we may find clarity about other vocations as well."[17] Transgender calling both empowers individuals to come into more authentic relationship with their gendered selves and circulates a powerful resistance to larger norms that demonize and pathologize transgender identities and, ultimately, constrain all of us. Such divine affirmation can be seen as yet another form of erotic, or embodied, justice that claims variable gender identities and expressions as inherently good and as having value for queer individuals on deeply theological and more practical levels. Such calling thus reveals a divine purpose to "transcend the boundaries of male and female to which our society has limited us. . . . We are called to be transformers, of both ourselves and the world around us."[18] As powerful as such a calling can be, it also carries immense burden, especially for transgender youth: even as we embrace the transformative potential of this call, the more transformative call of advocacy beckons cisgender people to shoulder as much if not more of the responsibility to make the flourishing of transgender or nonbinary lives possible.[19]

As educators, we can take such responsibility by respecting and advocating for our students' right to self-determination in how they identify and describe themselves and the relationships they find meaningful. On the first day of class, we can foster belonging by not reading names off our roster but by asking students to introduce themselves and inviting them to share the names and pronouns they use, and then using them appropriately. More

---

[16] Justin Sabia-Tanis, *Trans-Gender: Theology, Ministry, and Communities of Faith*, 2nd ed. (Cleveland, OH: Pilgrim Press, 2018), 149.

[17] Sabia-Tanis, *Trans-Gender,* 159.

[18] Sabia-Tanis, *Trans-Gender,* 159.

[19] See Michelle Hayford's rich discussion of the vocation of advocacy in chapter 5 of this volume.

structurally, we can work with our registrar's office and IT units to make sure students can change their names in our systems with ease, a process that can be far more onerous and complicated than it need be. We can also ensure that our student health services not only are trans-friendly but also address the sexual and reproductive health needs of our entire LGBTQIA+ student population.

Taking these kinds of steps illustrates how we can connect our queer students' internal callings of sexual and gender identity to larger structural transformation, starting on our own campuses. In doing so, we must not only resist the heteronormative assumptions that continue to anchor some Christian traditions but also resist forms of homonormativity that have emerged as certain members of our LGBTQIA+ communities have become more accepted and part of the cultural and political mainstream. If only thought of as an affirmation of an inner, more individualized calling—one of the larger dynamics this entire volume seeks to address—coming out can also perpetuate forms of racialized and neoliberal homonormativity: disconnecting queer vocational discernment from larger collective commitments reinforces a neoliberal, individualistic account of the good life, of purpose, and of meaning making. For Stephanie Clare, coming out has, in recent years, reflected and perpetuated its own neoliberal norms, neutralizing the radical potential for queer identities and embodiment. As she writes, "The out gay subject has become the well-adapted, neoliberal subject par excellence," one in which "norms concerning self-assertion and transparency" are "especially valued in neoliberal culture" and the lack of self-acceptance becomes the problem, rather than heteronormativity.[20] For Carlos Decena, "One comes out not to be radical or change the world but to be a 'normal' gay subject." Such desire for normalcy has disconnected coming out for some LGBTQIA+ subjects from "collective social change," reinforcing instead the values of a "neoliberal world that exalts the atomized and unmoored individual."[21] It also reinforces a particular racialized White way of experience and articulating sexual identity. "That coming out has been understood as the most emancipated way to be gay," Clare writes, "has the danger of prioritizing white subjects and dismissing how sexuality, race, gender, and class are lived intersectionally. The visibility, for instance,

---

[20] Stephanie Clare, "'Finally, She's Accepted Herself!': Coming Out in Neoliberal Times," *Social Text* 35, no. 2 (2017): 18, 17, https://doi.org/10.1215/01642472-3820533.
[21] Carlos Ulises Decena, "Tacit Subjects," *GLQ* 14, nos. 2–3 (2008): 339, 355, https://doi.org/10.1215/10642684-2007-036.

associated with being out is not necessarily freeing."[22] In this way, coming out into queer identity has its own racialized norms that play out in specific cultural contexts. As queer scholars of color have suggested, coming out— that is, embracing a visible LGBTQIA+ identity and organizing one's life primarily around it—not only reflects queer White assumptions about the closet and related norms about sexuality but also is not a practice tenable or desirable for queer people of color.[23] Even within queer communities and discourse, we must be ever vigilant to not universalize from one particular group, keeping what is deemed uncommon or different from the norm— even queer ones—at the center of our responsibility to everyone.

In our work with queer students, we must help them both come into authentic relationship with their sexualities and gender identities and expressions and articulate intersectional modes of resistance to the racialized norms embedded within homonormativity and neoliberal notions of self, vocation, and sociality. The challenge here is to continue to identify structural barriers to inclusion and integration of queerness within our collective spaces without succumbing to an overly individualistic notion of calling that fosters adaptation and assimilation into the injustices of our worlds. That is, as important as queer self-acceptance is to the affirming LGBTQIA+ vocation, it is not sufficient. We must also help our students—or any other LGBTQIA+ person trying to come out into their own sense of living a good life—connect their experiences of homophobia, transphobia, and heteronormativity to larger social, cultural, political, and economic forces and see their individual experiences of affirming their identities as deeply tied to their challenge of injustice, so that they and others can thrive in community.

Even as we must attend to the individual needs that are a part of any queer student's vocational discernment, as educators we must also model how to challenge and transform the structures that dehumanize them and other members of the LGBTQIA+ community.[24] We might start by first examining our own institution's policies and practices in relation to nondiscrimination, on-campus housing policies, bathroom accessibility, Title IX protections, and name-change procedures; or we might turn to our curriculum, in our cores and in our majors, to ensure queer issues are included and addressed.

---

[22] Clare, "Finally," 18.

[23] See Marlon B. Ross, "Beyond the Closet as Raceless Paradigm," in *Black Queer Studies*, ed. E. Patrick Johnson and Mae G. Henderson (Durham, NC: Duke University Press, 2005), 161–89.

[24] See Monica M. Smith's exploration of the ways institutions and individuals can address structural injustice in chapter 4 of this volume.

But we must do all of this without succumbing to the ever-evolving pressures of heteronormativity, homonormativity, or even neoliberal forces that seem disconnected from sexuality and gender. Ultimately, we must integrate individual discernment into the larger work of remaking the world to foster a more just and humane world, paying special attention to how the most private and intimate facets of self inform more public forms of structuring our common life together. As we do so, we must also temper homonormative impulses within LGBTQIA+ communities—impulses that center Whiteness, middle-class respectability, and civil rights—and retain the more radical tradition of coming out as a vocational strategy of resistance, one more fully attuned to the intersectional multiplicity of identities, desires, and embodiments within forms of queer subjectivity. In our work specifically on the teaching of vocation, we can include diverse queer voices in vocational narratives, providing examples and activities that invite students to reflect on their multiple and intersecting identities and how they shape their search for meaning. Perhaps most importantly, we can facilitate their questioning of the embodied assumptions inherent in our systems of purpose and meaning making.[25] To queer vocation, then, is a movement not just of inclusion, but of liberation and transformation. In the right context and under the right conditions, coming out can both affirm individual authentic queerness and connect LGBTQIA+ students to the work of the common good. Coming into clarity about their sexualities and genders, students can more fully participate in our collective work of fostering a more just and humane world.

Queering the common good

To queer vocation, then, requires a much larger rethinking and transformation of the common good. As the previous section suggests, the barriers our LGBTQIA+ students face in navigating their vocational journeys have as much to do with the structural forces that dehumanize them as it does with their own inner journeys to self-affirmation and understanding. In fact, the two are closely tied to each other, interdependent and mutually constitutive. As much as we need to see queerness in all of its forms as inherently good, we also need to see it as essential to the common good. Queerness arguably

---

[25] See Erin VanLaningham's discussion of the ways reading diverse texts with individuals who are different from us can promote collective well-being in chapter 9 of this volume.

benefits everyone, even as such benefits might resonate differently for different people: it provides a needed dissent from and important skepticism about the actual commonness of any given, historical instantiation of the common good. In this way, our collective thinking about the common good in this volume benefits from engaging queer theory's antisocial thesis, a position that rejects sociality as we know it for the ways it has and continues to threaten to erase, overwhelm, assimilate, discipline, or otherwise constrain queer difference. At the same time, queer scholars also hold out for the transformation of our collective social realities, so that we might also realize and integrate those forms of difference that have not yet been fully valued in our current social, cultural, political, and economic worlds and hold space for those forms of difference that don't even yet exist. Creative and unique forms of sex, desire, and ways of relating intimately; alternative forms of familial organization; and gender identities that open up and even subvert the rigid binaries of our gender system—what we might characterize as queerness—have the potential to serve as uncommon resources for both queer and nonqueer people alike. The circulation of these non- and antinormative ways of being and acting as uncommon goods thus serves to develop our collective life and open a more radical hospitality to difference.

To transform our understanding of the good life and embrace the inherent value of queer forms of subjectivity and desire, we must question, reimagine, and restructure the norms of the common good, which largely function to reinscribe heteronormative and cisgender sociality as the foundations not only of the good life but also of the universalized good social order. In the way the discourse of the common good aspires to represent the resources we all need to flourish across the vast range of human difference, its universalism also functions to relegate queer difference and the particular needs of LGBTQIA+ individuals to the margins or render them entirely invisible. For example, Catholic social thought defines the common good as the entirety of social conditions that allow for the fulfillment and flourishing of each person within their larger social context. In this tradition, each individual person is entitled to the conditions and goods that make flourishing possible, including food, shelter, clothing, health, work, education, culture, and the right to establish a family.[26] At first glance, the norms embedded in this elaboration of the common good might seem easily compatible with queerness and

---

[26] For a fuller discussion of the common good as defined by modern Catholic social thought, see the reflections by David Matzko McCarthy in chapter 1 of this volume.

LGBTQIA+ people, but within many if not all of these resources—clothing, health, education, culture, right to establish a family—are particularities that any social order might not have actually recognized as entitlements as a priority to secure. We might ask, do transgender or nonbinary individuals have a right to clothing and medical care that reflects and affirms their gender identity and expression? Are queer youth of any or all sexual and gender identities entitled to receive comprehensive sex education and information about relationships that express their desires and interests in organizing their intimate lives? Does law and policy support queer people's right to establish families, including the right to have and raise children, in ways that conform to traditional models of family, as well as forms of family that defy, exceed, or recast the family into very different forms, forms that might actually be unrecognizable and even antithetical to family as we currently know it?

Not to belabor the point, but it should be clear that the answer is no, or at least, not yet. Even as the LGBTQIA+ movement has secured some rights to establish a family in recent years, in many contexts, state and civil society continues to reflect a heteronormative and cisgender bent to the kinds of family that it upholds as a common good, a value that not only harms LGBTQIA+ people but also inhibits nonqueer people.[27] Our society has been and continues to be organized around policies that support and bolster traditional relationships, familial structures, and households in the name of anchoring our social and cultural worlds in a "good" that stabilizes and structures common experiences and common goodness. For many LGBTQIA+ people, having access to the kind of common good that marriage, family, and parenting represent—and to the resources, privileges, and benefits they convey, as well as the requirements and sacrifices too—is an important civil right that ought to be extended to any marginalized group. But as important as affirming gains like marriage equality has been within LGBTQIA+ social and political movements, its ascendancy has further marginalized other forms of relationality, desire, and domestic arrangements that queer people also engage in. In its emphasis on securing certain goods that most if not all of us agree are necessary for human flourishing, it leaves out the kinds of resources that any of our students might require for living a different kind of life, perhaps even what some might continue to consider as a "bad" life, a life that some might see as sinful or reflecting interests that

---

[27] See Jennifer Lane, "Anti-Heteropatriarchal Reproductive Justice," *Women's Studies* 48, no. 8 (2019): 882–99, https://doi.org/10.1080/00497878.2019.1676748.

only a minority value and whose values might in fact run counter to the mainstream or majority sense of what is "good." These issues press most immediately on our LGBTQIA+ students and colleagues, but they also raise important questions for everyone else in vocation studies invested in building a more just society. What can it mean for queer and nonqueer readers alike to question the fundamental assumptions of how we organize our intimate lives in the world we share?

This might be the most challenging problem of the "common good." For its seeming innocence and capacious generosity—for who would question the assumption that all humans have access to resources like water, clean air, or housing, seemingly disconnected from the discourses of sexuality and gender?—it maintains its own normative assumptions that can and do have pernicious effect. For some queer theorists, the goodness of our common sociality as we know it is so toxic to queer difference that the common good might be an impossible dream or a very real nightmare. As Leo Bersani provocatively asks, "Should a homosexual be a good citizen?," voicing his deep skepticism of queer integration into heteronormative sociality.[28] Bristling at the "rage of respectability so visible in gay life," Bersani questions the "compatibility of homosexuality with civic virtue."[29] His dissent from participating in the common good—vis-à-vis respectable civic activity—questions the desirability of taking a place at the proverbial table that the common good might be said to represent. Instead, Bersani articulates an alternative queer sociality, or antisociality, one rooted in homosexuality's history of refusal to conform to heterosexuality's standards. Even as major legal victories in the past decade have affirmed such compatibility, Bersani's critique continues to represent a principled aversion to promoting LGBTQIA+ assimilation into our current social order, especially given the current order's complicity in structures of violence and oppression. As Bersani argues, "In a society where oppression is structural, constitutive of society itself, only what that society throws off—its mistakes or its pariahs—can serve the future."[30] Thus, Bersani deems "society" too deeply implicated in heteronormativity's categorical exclusion of queerness and reproductive futurism to be redeemed or transformed.[31] As antagonistic as this position is in relation to our interest and investment in

[28] Leo Bersani, *Homos* (Cambridge, MA: Harvard University Press, 1995), 113.

[29] Bersani, *Homos*, 113.

[30] Bersani, *Homos*, 180.

[31] See Benjamin Kahan, "Queer Sociality after the Antisocial Thesis," *American Literary History* 30, no. 4 (2018): 811–19, https://doi.org/10.1093/alh/ajy034; and Lee Edelman, *No Future: Queer Theory and the Death Drive* (Durham, NC: Duke University Press, 2004).

the common good, this critique raises important questions about our collective endeavor in relation to the heteronormative and cisgender structures that shape our world. More pointedly, it interrogates the presumed value of shared commonness, forcing us to see the gaps, invisible investments, or hypocrisy in much of this discourse, especially those versions that emerge from religious, cultural, and political traditions that have been historically homo- and transphobic.

Other queer scholars long for a utopian and transformed realization of queer collective sociality at some unknown point in the future, even as such desire might never be fully realized. José Muñoz writes, "Queerness is always in the horizon . . . [and] must be viewed as being visible only in the horizon."[32] Locating queerness in the future provides an aspirational anchor for queer becoming and survival, a utopian fantasy that fosters queer thriving in all its multiplicity. Scholars like Muñoz reject the antisocial thesis, because it disconnects sexuality from other categories of difference and reinscribes Whiteness as the racial norm within queerness, obscuring its "relational and contingent nature."[33] Muñoz thus situates queerness within the particularities of intersecting differences to apprehend more accurately a complicated and complete picture of who is queer and to foster hope in radically refashioning our collective futures. For queer people to survive and thrive, it must be possible to imagine our future within a transformed social order, especially for those queer subjects whose multiple intersecting marginalized identities means their survival is far from guaranteed. Such utopian hope secures a more creative kind of collective sociality, one in which queers can participate and thrive because of their queer desires, not despite them. This kind of "queer sociality," Juana María Rodríguez writes, "is at its core an attempt at recognition. It is a utopian space that both performs a critique of existing social relations and enacts a commitment to the creative critical work of imagining collective possibilities."[34] Through the desire and fierce struggle for a future, queer utopian thinking remains hopeful it can challenge and transform the more pedestrian politics of gay assimilation, which depend in part on queer subjects letting go of queer difference—especially forms of queer deviance—as they enter into social institutions like marriage, the

[32] José Estaban Muñoz, *Cruising Utopia: The Then and There of Queer Futurity* (New York: New York University Press, 2009), 11.
[33] José Estaban Muñoz, "Thinking beyond Antirelationality and Antiutopianism in Queer Critique," *PLMA* 121, no. 3 (2006): 825, https://doi.org/10.1632/S0030812900165885.
[34] Juana María Rodríguez, "Queer Sociality and Other Sexual Fantasies," *GLQ* 17, nos. 2–3 (2011): 332, https://doi.org/10.1215/10642684-1163427.

military, and even parenting that make up the common good. Rather than liberate queer subjects from their deviance, queer utopianism makes space for the thriving of deviance within the fold of collective, fostering its defiant cultivation as a form of queer excellence. Ultimately, for Muñoz, "the field of utopian possibility is one in which multiple forms of belonging in difference adhere to a belonging in collectivity."[35]

In this way, we must ensure that the most uncommon of queer particularities can adhere within a framework of belonging that could become a radically transformed common good. Especially for our students, we must learn to see their forms of queerness as uncommon goods, insofar as these subjectivities and desires embody an ethos of erotic justice. We must hope to find ways to apprehend, relate to, and celebrate the particularities of queer experience such that our LGBTQIA+ students no longer face barriers to or persecution for their visible and unabashed participation in our common worlds. In the end, this kind of hope shares much with other vocation scholars who describe hope as a "bridge between the 'already' and the 'not yet'" or a "sense of the possible in difficult situations."[36] For LGBTQIA+ people, centering such hope in the particularities of our difference and our dissent is essential for our survival. The power of such paradoxical thinking—the ability to appreciate and integrate the profound ambivalence that structures queer resistance—opens up a desire for a future with a clear-eyed apprehension of the forces that seek to constrain queer vocational discernment, both at the individual and at the communal level. It allows us all to see what's wrong with the world as we recognize our dreams for ourselves in the context of our larger communities.[37]

Queer justice and the uncommon good

For many, queer theory's antisocial thesis is also insufficient because it deters us from negotiating a more reparative and constructive future path.[38] Its

[35] Muñoz, Cruising Utopia, 20.

[36] Wadell, "Magnanimity," 211; and John Neafsey, A Sacred Voice Is Calling: Personal Vocation and Social Conscience (Maryknoll, NY: Orbis, 2006), 107.

[37] See also Sharon Daloz Parks, Big Questions Worthy Dreams: Mentoring Emerging Adults in Their Search for Meaning, Purpose, and Faith (San Francisco, CA: Jossey-Bass, 2011), 146–47, 195–96, 278–79.

[38] See Eve Kosofsky Sedgwick, "Paranoid Reading and Reparative Reading; or, You're So Paranoid, You Probably Think This Introduction Is about You," in Novel Gazing: Queer Readings in Fiction, ed. Eve Kosofsky Sedgwick (Durham, NC: Duke University Press, 1997), 1–38.

fervent embrace of negativity functions best as a theoretical critique of heter-onormative and cisgender imaginaries, but it doesn't necessarily help guide ourselves or our students into a meaningful and transformative engagement with the normative constraints of the common good, which is essential for the flourishing of queer lives. In her pragmatic critique of queer theorists who maintain their antisocial dissent, Caroline Levine argues that they "foreclose" our inquiry into "whether there are better and worse orders and arrangements for collective life."[39] As she observes, "A general fact of human life is that we must live in common," which requires "humdrum routines and arrangements, such as regular distribution of food and water, norms for ad-equate shelter, smoothly running sewer systems, the maintenance of biodi-versity, mass educational and health programs, and measured distribution of labor and wealth."[40] For these arrangements to be supportive of the common good and hospitable to LGBTQIA+ people, then, we must design collective spaces that affirm queer difference in relation to the qualities of a good life that we share in common and the resources we all need to flourish. For many queer undergraduates, one such space has taken the form of a drag show, an event that has served in recent years as an important public and performative affirmation of LGBTQIA+ identities on many campuses, including my own. Through drag performances of queer identity and embodiment, students cel-ebrate particular forms of queerness and together forge a collective experi-ence of creativity and joy. To embrace the uncommon good in this way is to approach collectivity differently and maintains a critical skepticism of the ever-emerging norms that accompany any social endeavor, preserving room for singular forms of desires, embodiments, and relational arrangements. The uncommon good also facilitates the vocational discernment of those who embody such difference and those who do not, making more salient these issues of sexuality and gender within the larger social, political, and col-lective ways of organizing our world. To this end, queerness can be a shared resource, something that circulates within the public and private spheres, and a quality, disposition, or technology of the self (one that both affirms and deconstructs the self) that queers and nonqueers can access and use to inform their quest for meaning and their participation in the "common good."[41] We do so by maintaining the goodness of what is uncommon.

[39] Caroline Levine, "Model Thinking: Generalization, Political Form, and the Common Good," *New Literary History* 48, no. 4 (2017): 640, https://doi.org/10.1353/nlh.2017.0033.
[40] Levine, "Model Thinking," 640–41.
[41] See Michael Warner, *The Trouble with Normal* (Boston: Harvard University Press, 1999) and *Publics and Counterpublics* (Brooklyn, NY: Zone Books, 2005).

To secure this transformative integration of such uncommon goods—those queer differences that do not unite us—into our collective understanding, we must continue to reshape our habits of relating to the other and cultivate a cosmopolitan curiosity. Kwame Anthony Appiah encourages us to embrace this authentic interest in those who differ quite markedly from ourselves and see beyond the connections we form through shared identity and instead connect "not *through* identity but *despite* difference"[42]—or, perhaps even more queerly, to connect *because of,* or *across,* difference and value a universalism based in pluralism, much like Muñoz's vision of collectivity based in multiple forms of belonging in difference. After all, as Eve Kosofsky Sedgwick notes, "The word 'queer' means *across*" in its etymology.[43] To engage authentically across our differences provides a starting point for the transformation of the common good, especially in the context of the learning spaces on our campuses. For interfaith scholar Rachel S. Mikva, "Difference is how we learn," but as we grapple with difference and attempt to learn from it, through it, and with it, we must not simply appropriate or absorb the unique particularity of the other.[44] She cautions against reducing difference to something we can easily relate to or establish commonality within our everyday encounters. "If I merely absorb," she writes, "the otherness of a person into some similarity to self, some embodiment of society or a larger sense of 'the human,' I have erased that person's essential particularity."[45] To apprehend queerness so that our students can flourish in all their particularity, we must first acknowledge how different they might be from heteronormative and cisgender forms of identity, desire, and community without devaluing such difference. Further, we must situate the ethical vocational development of both our queer and nonqueer students within the work of building a more just and humane world; we do so, in part, by modeling the kinds of relationships that allow us and our students to "excavate our disagreements *and* cultivate our commonalities," finding purpose and meaning across and "among different lifestances."[46] To do this justly, we must be vigilant in how we view and use power responsibly, especially sexual power, as we strive to live

[42] Kwame Anthony Appiah, *Cosmopolitanism: Ethics in a World of Strangers* (New York: Norton, 2006), 135.

[43] Eve Kosofsky Sedgwick, *Tendencies* (Durham, NC: Duke University Press, 1993), xii.

[44] Rachel S. Mikva, "The Change a Difference Makes: Formation of Self in the Encounter with Diversity," in *Hearing Vocation Differently: Meaning, Purpose, and Identity in the Multi-Faith Academy,* ed. David S. Cunningham (New York: Oxford University Press, 2019), 27.

[45] Mikva, "The Change a Difference Makes," 28.

[46] Mikva, "The Change a Difference Makes," 38.

out the principles of erotic justice. We should not condemn queer identities, bodies, and desires we do not understand but focus more on evaluating the quality of their relationships and the ethics of relating they make possible in our world. If we can keep queerness on the horizon of such engagement, then we can apprehend it—learn from it and be intrigued by it—without having to appropriate, fully understand, or subsume queer difference into our frame of meaning making.

Such dialogue has the potential to reorient our sense of what is and can be good. Something doesn't have to be shareable or desirable for everyone for it to enhance collective well-being. Or, as Judith Butler writes, "we do not have to love one another to engage in meaningful solidarity."[47] We can and should certainly advocate for access to those resources that we all do need to live and flourish—clean water and air, housing, health care, education—and also ought to remember that even these resources are needed and used in particular ways, given social, cultural, and political contexts. Some humans, like transgender individuals or queer people with disabilities, might in fact need different or additional resources to thrive, and those resources and the lives they support should not be seen as somehow extra, special, or outside the scope of the common good. Paradoxically, the care they need might be the most essential component of a common good situated in and constitutive of a just and humane world for everyone.

More precisely, what does justice look like for LGBTQIA+ people? To return to the course I teach on this topic, students articulate what these uncommon goods are and what LGBTQIA+ people need in order to flourish and live magnanimous lives of dignity, purpose, and meaning. We often identify more general conditions like respect, safety, visibility, agency, and the right to language and self-determination, as well as more concrete access to knowledge about our bodies and desires, histories, and cultures. Overall, we seek an acknowledgment that our differences are paradoxically particular to our unique lives and simultaneously shared with nonqueer people across human experience. Numerically, LGBTQIA+ people are a minority and minoritized population, even as the percentages of millennials and Gen Z identifying as queer appear to be increasing.[48] We are not common, at least not yet. But that should not prevent nonqueer people from cultivating a sense of responsibility, of connected obligation to facets of humanity that they very

[47] Judith Butler, *The Force of Nonviolence: An Ethico-Political Bind* (New York: Verso, 2020), 203.

[48] Jeffrey M. Jones, "LGBT Identification Ticks Up to 7.1%," *Gallup*, February 17, 2022, https://news.gallup.com/poll/389792/lgbt-identification-ticks-up.aspx.

well might not fully understand. "Social justice," as Paul Waddell writes, moves us beyond our individual security to honor "the good of all persons," suggesting that "just societies depend on just persons, persons who see beyond their own needs, security, and comfort to the welfare of all citizens of the world, and who remember that justice is not only about personal rights but also about social responsibilities."[49] For LGBTQIA+ people to flourish, we must all grapple with any number of uncommon differences and reorient our sense of their meaning and value, see them as facets of queer welfare for which we are all responsible. Doing so is essential for the building of a more just and humane world, one in which queerness is not merely tolerated or accepted, but seen as something good in its own right.

The power of queer hope, of our utopian dreams of what might be, is that it shows us how we can value difference and use it as a rallying point for minoritized queer identities, around which to construct new ways of being and organize our collective worlds. This vision for the queer, uncommon good thus looks to the horizon to apprehend the most unique of our particularities. Doing so ignites possibilities and sustains hope in the struggle for justice, such that our common world will become radically shared by and shareable for all. To embrace the uncommon good necessitates an ongoing queer critique and resistance to the norms of the common good for the time being, but not to reject its aspirational possibility. These critical practices are certainly useful for queer survival in our current moment, but given the potential for new forms of queerness to emerge in the future, they also point us to what we will need in the future for them to thrive as they continue to evolve. One day, when through the transformation of the common good our world comes to respect the dignity of all LGBTQIA+ people and their vocations, we might not need so fiercely to defend the uncommon goods that queerness represents. But until that time, we must persist in seeing value in the uncommon good, so that queer communities might flourish fully and each and every queer person might cultivate lives of purpose and meaning within it.

[49] Paul J. Wadell, *Happiness and the Christian Moral Life: An Introduction to Christian Ethics*, 3rd ed. (Lanham, MD: Rowman & Littlefield, 2016), 245.

7

Expanding the Borders of a
Common Good

Transformational Encounters

Jonathan Golden

Institutions of higher education, at their best, are places where students have opportunities to discover their own passions and interests while formulating conceptions about the world around them. Colleges also promise the possibility to expand horizons, broaden perspectives, and engage with the world. Yet, despite the soaring rhetoric of expansion and engagement as well as recent changes that combine coursework with cocurricular activities and experiential learning programs, most students spend much of their academic learning time sitting in neatly arranged rows in a classroom with a single purveyor of knowledge at the front. We are far from fully realizing the potential for transformational learning, where students delve into vocational discernment and develop deep commitments to a common good. While students should always be encouraged to invest in their own personal growth and search for their own path, this quest should not stop with the self. Individual purpose is relational and requires meaningful engagement with others if we are ever to expand our conventional borders and categories. As philosopher Emmanuel Levinas suggests, "Responsibility for my neighbor . . . is . . . the harsh name for what we call love of one's neighbor."[1]

Rich experiential learning opportunities can create space for students to engage in discovery, but it is not a given that such experiences on their own lead to transformation. Experiential learning, to be truly transformational,

---

[1] Emmanuel Levinas, *Of God Who Comes to Mind*, trans. Bettina Bergo (Redwood City, CA: Stanford University Press, 1998), 103.

Jonathan Golden, *Expanding the Borders of a Common Good* In: *Called Beyond Our Selves*. Edited by: Erin VanLaningham, Oxford University Press. © Oxford University Press 2024. DOI: 10.1093/oso/9780197691915.003.0008

requires thoughtfully structured reflection around those experiences, where students can connect what is learned outside the classroom with knowledge acquired inside the classroom. Students can glean the greatest amount of transformative power and wisdom from immersive experiences when they invest the time in meaningful reflection, both on their own and with others. The active feedback cycle of classroom learning, experiential learning, and deep reflection can open doors for students to locate themselves in the broader world and thus make vocational discernment discoveries while arriving at a fuller understanding of a common good.

In this chapter, we will examine a range of questions pertaining to transformational learning as a means for students to explore the space where individual fulfillment intersects with contribution to a common good. We will also probe the concept of epistemic transformation, which argues that novel experiences teach us something we could not have learned without that particular experience.[2] How can educators create opportunities for epistemic transformation that fosters vocational discernment? What types of transformative experiences develop a sense of a common good, allowing us to see beyond narrowly defined self-interest? How can students expand their vision into the interconnected and interdependent nature of our world? How can we motivate and inspire young people to act more generously and responsibly, pushing people toward a broader definition of *common* when imagining a common good? How do we define the borders of responsibility to others, and under what conditions can those borders expand?

In an effort to address these questions, I explore a shift from *the* common good to *a* common good. This exploration involves an examination of how we typically delineate categories and parameters like us/them and here/there and an exposure of the narrow zero-sum worldview that too often traps us in stingy ways of thinking about our world and others. Ultimately, the chapter imagines the possibilities for transforming and expanding our conventional boundaries of interconnection through various forms of experiential learning.

---

[2] L. A. Paul, *Transformative Experience* (New York: Oxford University Press, 2014); David Lewis, "What Experience Teaches Us," in *Mind and Cognition,* ed. William G. Lycan (Cambridge, MA: Blackwell, 1990), 29–57.

A common good instead of *the* common good

It might be useful to speak of *a* common good rather than *the* common good. Fixing on the singular common good has two drawbacks. First, there is the problem of who gets to define what is common. In the search for the universal in the common, we have a propensity to see the world through what is common in our *own* experience. Too often, we neglect significant cultural differences. Second, our understanding of what is good is deeply influenced by our own privileges, priorities, and preconceptions about the world and what we may think the world needs. Community-based learning (CBL), without deep partnerships with the community, can backfire and reinforce preconceptions; for example, students who don't really engage with the beneficiaries of their efforts may remain stuck in a "victim-savior" mentality, inhibiting true transformation. Thus, centering on *a* common good is more helpful in localized contexts.

The "solidarity dividend" as a common good

I direct Drew University's Center on Religion, Culture, and Conflict, an interdisciplinary center whose mission is to educate the next generation of leaders in interfaith and intercultural understanding and peace. The center regularly hosts dialogue programs involving people around the world, in the community, and on campus. During a left-right dialogue program at the center, participants from a range of backgrounds talked about their experiences with housing insecurity. Conservative participants generally believed that people in these situations had gotten there through indolence, poor choices, or some combination of the two. But upon listening to the firsthand stories of people they had come to know and admire—people who had been knocked down and gotten up over and over again—perspectives began to change. The participants were now asking questions about why some people had to work harder just to get to the same place as others, and why some folks seemed to have bad breaks and little luck, considering that maybe it had nothing to do with breaks or luck. But above all, their ability to even entertain these questions was a direct result of these face-to-face encounters. They were beginning to grasp the value of the "solidarity dividend."

The solidarity dividend, as discussed by Heather McGhee, responds to the zero-sum mentality in which people tend to view another's gain as entailing some cost to themselves, and the irony that denying something to others is where the true cost occurs.[3] She cites the example of a mostly White town that preferred to close a community pool altogether rather than integrate. As an alternative, McGhee proposes the solidarity dividend, through which people appreciate the value of mutually beneficial policies. An interesting twist to this model is that it does not require one to be particularly selfless or magnanimous. It simply recognizes that often people's interests are not in competition but coincide. While there will always be an us-and-them, the ratio can be more inclusive (*more* us and *less* them) and them/they/other need not be labeled enemies. Excessive allegiance to identity and clinging to beliefs about social status are what drive people to perceive competition and conflict. The solidarity dividend helps us to imagine a world where there is less competition and more cooperation, but this requires a broader conception about who and what constitutes our community. On a practical level, McGhee's solidarity dividend applies to the left-right dialogue program in that people could see that the cost of needless competition is a bottom-line question: practices that entrap people in perpetual cycles of poverty cost us, while greater cooperation pays a dividend. On a more qualitative level, through regular interactions (even those of a transactional, economic nature) people can build relationships beyond conventional lines of division.

Even if there was a singular, universal common good, our quest to find it would likely lead us to a lowest common denominator, something feel-good or anodyne, but nothing particularly rich or inspiring. And if we acknowledge that the notion of "good" is relative and situational, it becomes clear that to have an authentic understanding of good, we must have the encounter or meeting. An opportunity to see all people in their full humanity is the true solidarity dividend.

The summoning of a common good

When people, communities, identity groups, and nations become increasingly insular and isolated, they tend to view others' interests and their own as mutually exclusive. Moving people away from a zero-sum, win-lose mentality toward more of a win-win mentality is a key part of any conflict

---

[3] Heather C. McGhee, *The Sum of Us: What Racism Costs Everyone and How We Can Prosper Together* (New York: One World, 2021), xxii.

resolution process. It is typical that people in conflict tend to separate and self-segregate, further reducing opportunities for encounters and inter-action. Rabbi Aryeh Cohen, in *Justice in the City*, applies the ideas of phi-losopher Emmanuel Levinas to his own Talmudic interpretations to pose questions about how we understand, define, and act on our obligations to others. "At the heart of a community of obligation," writes Cohen, "is the web of relationships that engenders obligations between residents who are other-wise anonymous to each other."[4] What we learn from conflict resolution and peacebuilding practices—dialogue, collective problem-solving, the search for deep emotional needs—can help us to build up and build upon these webs of relationships.

Frederick Buechner speaks of vocation as the place where one's "deep glad-ness and the world's deep hunger meet."[5] Jeff Brown, however, asks if we are sometimes too quick to substitute the word "needs" for "hunger," recalling our earlier question about the difference between what *we* think the world needs and allowing the world to show us its hunger through face-to-face encounters. Hunger, argues Brown, is more personal and intimate than needs, and "points to something that no one individual is capable of dis-cerning or articulating without the help of others."[6] Accordingly, we must have direct interaction with others if we are to move toward a true common good that is inclusive, representative, and responsive.

In a powerful *New York Times* op-ed entitled "The Summoned Self," David Brooks lays out the idea of a life where one is summoned, where one reckons meaning in their own life as called forth by others.[7] In guiding and advising our students, we often emphasize things like self-authorship along with individual mapping and pursuit of one's own self-determined goals. Brooks's conception of the summoned life, however, imagines people finding fulfillment when they conceive of meaning in their lives as embedded within relationships. This recalls Levinas's notion of knowing oneself in order to truly know others.[8] Jason Mahn applies Brooks's idea to higher

[4] Aryeh Cohen, *Justice in the City: An Argument from the Sources of Rabbinic Judaism*, New Perspectives in Post-Rabbinic Judaism (Boston: Academic Studies Press, 2012), 136.

[5] Frederick Buechner, *Wishful Thinking: A Seeker's ABCs* (New York: HarperOne, 1993), 119.

[6] Jeff R. Brown, "Unplugging the GPS: Rethinking Undergraduate Professional Degree Programs," in *Vocation across the Academy: A New Vocabulary for Higher Education*, ed. David S. Cunningham (New York: Oxford University Press, 2016), 208.

[7] David Brooks, "The Summoned Self," *New York Times*, August 2, 2010, https://www.nytimes.com/2010/08/03/opinion/03brooks.html.

[8] Emmanuel Levinas, *Totality and Infinity: An Essay on Exteriority*, trans. Alphonso Lingis (Chicago: Duquesne University Press, 1969), 36–40.

education, pointing out that colleges today tend to value employability and career readiness as the highest priorities, while underestimating the value of relationships. To be clear, the summoned life leans outward toward others but in no way implies a lack of direction or intentionality. While the student's experience is still deliberate and introspective, it also involves listening to others with one's heart. It is seeing oneself as part of a bigger story that makes one "response-able," what Margaret Mohrmann describes as our ability to respond "to other people, to situations, to the world."[9] It is also important to acknowledge the tension students face in striking a balance between attending to our own needs and interests and the claims that others make upon one's life.[10] Mahn builds on Brooks's view of the summoned life by arguing that one can follow their own heart but should stay "open to the pleas, gifts, needs, interruptions, and summons of others."[11] Below, we will see how this conception can be put into play though experiences like CBL. The path of the summoned life is also more likely to lead one to the discovery of a common good because it envisions vocation as responding to multiple voices and not just one's own.

Caring for those we will likely never meet

How and where we draw our lines of commitment to others is not easy. One can imagine a typical fall-off pattern, where one cares first about themselves, much about their family, and somewhat about the people we deem to constitute our community, while ultimately shrugging at people on the other side of the globe who we will likely never meet. In an assignment that addresses this pattern, Hannah Schell discusses commitment mapping in which students are asked to make a diagram of their commitments in the form of concentric circles and then to work in reverse, asking, "Who claims you?"[12] This raises a key question about the intersection of vocation and a common good: how do

---

[9] Margaret E. Mohrmann, "'Vocation Is Responsibility': Broader Scope, Deeper Discernment," in Cunningham, ed., *Vocation across the Academy*, 23; Jason A. Mahn, *Neighbor Love through Fearful Days: Finding Purpose & Meaning in a Time of Crisis* (Minneapolis, MN: Fortress Press, 2021), 40–41.

[10] Hannah Schell, "Commitment and Community: The Virtue of Loyalty and Vocational Discernment," in *At This Time and In This Place: Vocation and Higher Education*, ed. David S. Cunningham (New York: Oxford University Press, 2016), 238.

[11] Mahn, *Neighbor Love*, xxiii.

[12] Schell, "Commitment and Community," 238.

we motivate students to care about problems that do not, or do not seem to, directly impact them?

Darby Ray talks about this relationship in terms of self-work and world work.[13] Self-work refers to "efforts to discover and cultivate one's authentic self, as well as everything that brings it alive," while world work represents "efforts to understand and transform the systems of thought and practice that contest and undermine the world's goodness and integrity."[14] Thich Nhat Hanh reminds us to be in touch with ourselves first, and to discard what we think we know if we wish to learn and understand others.[15] Conversely, one of the main ideas proposed here is that it is through our interactions with others, outside of our conventional scope of experience, that we discover new parts of ourselves. As such, we should try to imagine the process of transformation as an ongoing cycle of input and feedback.

This brings us to the critical question of how we determine our commitments and where we draw the boundaries. How do we implement world work and an authentic turn outward? One challenge is that college students are often adrift in terms of understanding their own social location. Yet, as students seek to formulate new relationships with the broader world, it helps when they are able to articulate who they see as their own community. Schell suggests, "If vocation is understood both in terms of discerning a call but also in terms of forming and acting upon commitments, our students need help in identifying and sorting through the communities of which they are a part and the commitments they may hold."[16] In other words, to whom do we hold commitments, and how can educators inspire students to think more generously about those commitments?[17] Such emphasis on loyalty allows us to treat ideals as a compass for life and "encourages and even challenges young adults to set about the task of vocational discernment by starting from where they are: from the current relationships, communities, and commitments that are the substance of their lives and their identities."[18] Vocational exploration and discernment can be a means of encouraging

[13] Darby Kathleen Ray, "Self, World, and the Space Between: Community Engagement as Vocational Discernment," in Cunningham, ed., *At This Time and In This Place*, 301–20.

[14] Ray, "Self, World, and the Space Between," 301.

[15] Thich Nhat Hanh, *Being Peace*, 2nd ed. (Berkeley, CA: Parallax Press, 2005).

[16] Schell, "Commitment and Community," 249.

[17] Schell, "Commitment and Community," 254; see also Kathleen Fitzpatrick's *Generous Thinking: A Radical Approach to Saving the University* (Baltimore, MD: Johns Hopkins University Press, 2021).

[18] Schell, "Commitment and Community," 254.

students to understand themselves and their place in the world, as part of exploring boundaries and turning outward.

I have written elsewhere about my conversations with people who push these boundaries of commitment and responsibility about as far as they can go, namely individuals who have either lost, caused loss, or both and are now engaging directly with their ostensible enemies.[19] Rami Elhannan and Bassam Aramin today are codirectors of the Parents Circle Family Forum, an organization dedicated to fomenting dialogue between bereaved parents in the Israeli-Palestinian conflict. Rami and Bassam are, respectively, an Israeli Jew and a Palestinian Muslim, both of whom have endured the greatest of losses: as a direct result of the conflict between their peoples, both men had to bury a young daughter. One might be tempted to assume that they view each other as enemies, that anger and hatred would push them to thirst for revenge. But this shared experience, at the deepest human emotional level, constitutes a space where they could come together to start a conversation, one that years later has evolved into the closest of friendships and their tireless work with the Parents Circle.

In Northern Ireland, I have introduced my students to people who regularly cross identity borders in ongoing efforts to maintain the hard-won peace outlined in the Good Friday Agreement. As a young man, Martin Snodden was a combatant for the Ulster Volunteer Force (UVF) in Belfast. When a bomb intended for an Irish Republican Army (IRA) meeting went off prematurely in a bar, killing one of the Republican militia's mothers, Snodden was nearly beaten to death on the spot. He would ultimately spend over a decade in the notorious Maze prison, where this sectarian conflict carried over and even intensified. Oddly enough, Snodden's closest friend in that prison would be a member of the IRA, and even before his release, Snodden would begin a new life as an ambassador for peace and reconciliation, focused on warning teens about the human costs of sectarian conflict.

These examples demonstrate how we can engage students in drawing forward their commitments, interests, and loyalties while also broadening their notions of what they can, even should, care about as a common good. I do not mean to paint images of peacemaking and caring for others beyond our worldview as always easily achieved. In a visit to Belfast, my students took a tour of Belfast led by Reverend Harold Goode, who guided the precarious process of weapons decommissioning during the Good Friday process. Rev.

---

[19] The manuscript is tentatively titled *Turning Point*.

Goode had brought us to a mural commemorating the site of a particularly grim incident where children had been killed. Most of the students were deeply moved by this story, and the Rev. Goode's gentle, soft-spoken manner elicited tears. At the same time, a small group of students were distracted by a passerby, their laughter sounding rather obtuse in what was a very different moment for the rest of the group. Clearly, not everyone experiences immersion in precisely the same way, even when standing side by side. This sort of dissonance demonstrates the importance of conducting group reflection on a regular basis, always pushing at the borders of our worldviews and our commitment to others, even strangers.

The power of the direct encounter

What types of educational experiences present the most fertile ground for encouraging students to contemplate their callings and cultivate commitments to an ever-broader community and, ultimately, a common good? How can we maximize the potential of such experiences?

The power of the direct encounter with others and its potential for transformation is central to the work of Emmanuel Levinas, especially his influential work, *Totality and Infinity*. For Levinas, encountering "the face of the other" causes disruption and compels a person to act; "the face presents itself, and demands justice."[20] Levinas sees human existence as embodied and interpersonal, situated within relationships. He emphasizes encounters with the other as the space where we envision the opening to responsibility. It is these encounters that speak directly to an individual, imploring or commanding them, and in responding to these calls, one can discover responsibility to others.[21] This can also help advance how we understand the intertwining of vocational discernment and a common good. Most people are happy to invest in doing good, even to the point of great inconvenience to themselves, when the beneficiary is someone close to them. Whether this act is out of genuine concern for a loved one or is simply transactional, our suspension of self-interest typically does not extend beyond a delimited social circle. How can we reimagine an expansion of these boundaries?

---

[20] Levinas, *Totality and Infinity*, 294.

[21] For extended discussions of our responsibility to others as significant for our vocations, see reflections by David Mazko McCarthy in chapter 1 and Charles Mathewes in chapter 13 of this volume.

Encounters with alterity, especially with others whose experiences range far from our own, have multiple benefits. For one, they push us out of the normal confines of our experience, forcing us to question our embedded perspectives and assumptions. Second, if these interactions succeed in cultivating empathy, that empathy likely also extends to people beyond our normal social circle. We have learned that empathy for one group can lead to the cultivation of empathy more generally.[22] Identity is formed through an understanding of one's environment and one's place within it through interaction with others.[23] To quote a beautiful hymn, first written by Gordon Light and arranged by my colleague Marc Miller, we need to draw the circle wide. In the best of circumstances, that caring can even extend to people we perceive as adversaries, or even enemies: "Draw the circle wide. Draw it wider still."[24]

As we consider the widening of our circle, we might return to how we define love for neighbor and community. While we are "fiercely focused on the communities to which we belong," Mahn asserts, "love needs to be summoned and stretched through unbidden encounters with the alien, the stranger, the one deemed enemy."[25] Learning by engaging with those with whom we disagree, even adversaries, may seem like an entirely foreign concept in our current world, but it need not be. Relationships are not fixed organizational charts; they live in a perpetual state of evolution and realignment. We can reframe the ways we think about meeting others who differ from us, who contradict us, who challenge us. But the more we stay in the same old classroom, particularly when class composition mirrors certain conventional demographics, the more we do our students a disservice. This model does little to dissolve our traditional borders, and it more likely functions to harden those lines. Therefore, various forms of experiential learning are critical.

---

[22] Daniel H. Bowen and Brian Kisida, "Never Again: The Impact of Learning about the Holocaust on Civic Outcomes," *Journal of Research on Educational Effectiveness* 13, no. 1 (2020): 67–91, https://doi.org/10.1080/19345747.2019.1652712.

[23] Sandra Jarvis-Selinger, Daniel D. Pratt, and Glenn Regehr, "Competency Is Not Enough: Integrating Identity Formation into the Medical Education Discourse," *Academic Medicine* 87, no. 9 (2012): 1185–90, https://doi.org/10.1097/ACM.0b013e3182604968.

[24] Gordon Light and Mark A. Miller, *Draw the Circle Wide (SATB) Sheet Music* (Winona, MN: Abingdon Press, 1994).

[25] Mahn, *Neighbor Love*, 5

Pedagogies of "epistemic transformation"

Academic programs should urge students to explore their own thoughts, feelings, and ideas about the world's many deep hungers. Many of us say we want to teach our students *how* to think, not *what* to think; thus, we need to expand students' experience beyond the campus and classroom and the instructor's lens. If we truly aspire to raise student awareness of and concern for the world around them, we need to offer direct encounters and epistemic experiences.

As we consider what types of experiences are most likely to lead to growth, we can turn to Robert Kegan's model of constructive development theory, which explores how a person's consciousness and meaning making continue to evolve well into adulthood.[26] Evolution toward what Kegan describes as a developing consciousness occurs most often, according to Kuhnert and Eigel, when we have "experiences that challenge and contradict our current ways of understanding ourselves, others, and our situations."[27] This coincides with Levinas's emphasis on the notion of exteriority and on face-to-face meetings with others.[28] All of this points to the importance of learning through the firsthand encounter.

L. A. Paul, building on the work of David Lewis, employs the term "epistemic transformation" to describe the type of novel experience that teaches one something they could not have learned without having that kind of experience.[29] Paul claims that "stories, testimony, and theories aren't enough to teach you what it is like to have truly new types of experiences—you learn what it is like by actually having experience of that type."[30] Through direct experience, our knowledge and therefore our subjective point of view can change. With any such epistemic transformation, "the degree of epistemic change depends on how much the person already knows and on the type of experience that is involved."[31] Encounters teach us about the other while challenging us to think about our own identities and commitments.

---

[26] Robert Kegan, *In Over Our Heads* (Cambridge, MA: Harvard University Press, 1994) and *The Evolving Self* (Cambridge, MA: Harvard University Press, 1982).

[27] Keith M. Eigel and Karl W. Kuhnert, "Authentic Development: Leadership Development Level and Executive Effectiveness," in *Authentic Leadership Theory and Practice,* ed. W. L. Gardner, B. J. Avolio, and F. O. Walumbwa (London: Elsevier, 2005), 357–85.

[28] Levinas, *Totality and Infinity,* 194–95.

[29] Paul, *Transformative Experience,* 13.

[30] Paul, *Transformative Experience,* 13.

[31] Paul, *Transformative Experience,* 11.

Students discover these other voices and the world's hungers through opportunities both inside and outside the classroom. Examples include CBL classes, immersive experiences such as internships and research assistantships, and domestic and international study programs. CBL, also known as service learning,[32] is a form of education based on the notion that certain subjects, ideas, and/or practices are best learned when students engage directly with the outside world. Such learning opportunities can be precisely the type of epistemic experience we are discussing here. In order for transformation to occur, however, CBL courses must also involve deep reflection in ways that ask students to make connections between their community activities and course content, offer fuller appreciation of the discipline, and instill a greater sense of civic responsibility.[33]

CBL can contribute to building a sense of a common good precisely because it involves deep engagement with members of the community served.[34] Similarly, community-based research is collaborative and change oriented, searching for its initial research questions in the needs of communities.[35] Done properly, CBL experiences can cultivate empathy and a sense of civic duty in students. Scholars have attempted to assess the impact of CBL on students and how their understanding of social change can be influenced by these experiences.[36] These studies indicate that participating in CBL immersion trips can help promote compassion and community spirit in college students.

[32] CBL is a term that stresses the importance of consulting with community stakeholders in designing and implementing projects intended to benefit that community. This term acknowledges the fact that in many instances, students and universities benefit as much as, if not more than, the communities they serve. Finally, the term "CBL" is used to reflect the importance of community engagement and relationship building, while the term "service" suggests one could simply provide a service, usually as a volunteer, without necessarily engaging with community members. For direct exploration of CBL and vocation, see Ray, "Self, World, and the Space Between: Community Engagement as Vocational Discernment," in Cunningham, ed., *At This Time and In This Place*, 301–20.

[33] For more on this subject see Robert G. Bringle and Julie A. Hatcher, "A Service-Learning Curriculum for Faculty," *Michigan Journal of Community Service Learning* 2 (1995): 112–22, http://hdl.handle.net/2027/spo.3239521.0002.111; Emily E. Straus and Dawn M. Eckenrode, "Engaging Past and Present: Service-Learning in the College History Classroom," *History Teacher* 47, no. 2 (2014): 253–66; Thomas G. Plante, Katy Lackey, and Jeong Yeon Hwang, "The Impact of Immersion Trips on Development of Compassion among College Students," *Journal of Experiential Education* 32, no. 1 (2009): 28–43, https://doi.org/10.5193/JEE.32.1.28

[34] Straus and Eckenrode, "Engaging Past and Present," 253–54.

[35] Kerry J. Strand, Nicholas Cutforth, Randy Stoecker, Sam Marullo, and Patrick Donohue, *Community-Based Research and Higher Education: Principles and Practices* (Hoboken, NJ: John Wiley & Sons, 2003).

[36] Bet S. Catlett and Amira Proweller, "College Students' Negotiation of Privilege in a Community-Based Violence Prevention Project," *Michigan Journal of Community Service Learning*, 18, no. 1 (2011): 34–48; Plante et al., "The Impact of Immersion Trips."

Students can also learn these sensibilities when we teach conflict transformation. The latter is distinct from conflict resolution or conflict management in that the overarching goal is to transform the very conditions that
contribute to the conflict in the first place. To achieve this, we must uncover what lies deep beneath the surface, the root causes that drive conflict.
Too often our investigation of a problem remains at the level of the stated
positions one presents on the surface, often called proximate causes, the immediate or short-run triggers. Sometimes people even adopt "prefabricated"
positions without careful consideration or do so through blind loyalty.[37]
When we probe a problem, we may uncover the more personal interests or
stakes that people have in each issue. Going deeper still, we may encounter
people's foundational needs, including emotional needs, identities, what we
deem sacred, and the things we will fight to protect at all costs.[38] Accordingly,
this is where possibilities to transform conflict are discovered, at the level
of significant human need, and where, despite our many differences, there
is tremendous overlap and affinity. Understanding that all people have certain emotional and foundational needs is an important first step toward
discovering the world's deep hunger.

The local and the global classroom

In my teaching, I have had myriad opportunities to create "classrooms" outside the classroom, creating immersive learning environments involving
encounters with people ranging from underserved communities of the
greater New York City metro area to cultures in conflict around the globe.
Multiple trips to the Republic of Ireland and Northern Ireland, focused on
the history of civil rights and the Troubles, have included visits to landmark
sites where students speak with survivors of the conflict and learn directly
from people involved with the peace process. In most cases, this program
culminated with an academic conference in Bundoran where our students
presented alongside academics, community organizers, and politicians.

As my work in this global classroom evolved, I came to realize that not
all immersive experiences are created equal, and that the deep, transformative learning does not necessarily happen just because we have placed our

---

[37] Schell, "Commitment and Community," 243.

[38] Daniel Shapiro, *Negotiating the Nonnegotiable: How to Resolve Your Most Emotionally Charged Conflicts* (New York: Penguin Books, 2016).

students in that environment, even when our project was as ambitious as building a school block for orphans in Uganda. There needed to be more developed framing, contextualizing, and creating of opportunities for students to process what they were doing and learning. I began developing classes that involved a constant interplay between teaching relevant skills in the classroom, implementing these strategies while working in the community, and then debriefing with students about the community activities when we next gathered in the classroom. I've learned (the hard way) that while we know the importance of having community partners guide the work we do, this framework has its own challenges. The world's deep hunger doesn't come laid out in a glossy prospectus with a list of projected needs. Finding out what people need, while gaining their trust and buy-in, is often a complex process.

In 2019, the Center on Religion, Culture, and Conflict at Drew University joined the Center for Civic Engagement to launch the Drew Action Scholars program. Built on the latter's record of over ten years of supporting CBL courses and community service opportunities, the new program includes global engagement and technology/design/innovation in addition to civic engagement. Our objective was to create a program that merges curricular and cocurricular activities with a set of specific courses and experiential learning opportunities. The courses are designed to impart to students the skills necessary for success as community organizers, social entrepreneurs, and changemakers, while the experiential learning opportunities put those skills into play. For example, we teach students to draw stakeholder maps for their projects and then to engage those who are doing and are impacted by the work. We make heavy use of the logic model, which allows students (1) to see how well a planned intervention aligns with their short- and long-term goals, (2) to take stock of all the inputs needed to initiate and sustain a project, (3) to recognize the difference between outputs and outcomes, and (4) to measure success. Transformation can happen despite an experience going awry (or even especially when an experience goes awry). Working in the field of conflict resolution and peacebuilding, I urge students to see problems from multiple perspectives, acknowledging that while all perspectives on a conflict are not necessarily equal, students ought to be aware of the complexities associated with terms like "justice" and "good." This is an extremely difficult task, but one that is easier to achieve when students can see and hear for themselves the very people who are forced to live with the reality of conflict.

Some years ago, a colleague and I led a group of students on a three-week international study trip to Israel-Palestine that was focused on peace and coexistence. The trip was preceded by a semester-long course in which we studied the history of the conflict and efforts to make peace, with a focus on the work of grassroots organizations, not-for-profits, and nongovernmental organizations engaged in peacebuilding through fields ranging from environmental conservation and justice, theatre and the arts, and education and child development to interfaith dialogue. This meant that most of the students were able to connect the peace work with some other area they were studying in college. In the region, we visited roughly a dozen of these organizations, sometimes two per day, in some cases spending several days working with one organization. Every evening, with a few exceptions, we held a circle discussion to reflect upon what we learned that day and what we saw, thought, and felt. We would all draw connections between what we had learned in the classroom and what we experienced firsthand. The tensions in and around the Old City of Jerusalem—that feeling that real violence could break out at any time—contrasted sharply with the peaceful coexistence of Haifa, which differed from the genuine shared living on Neve Shalom/Wahat es-Salaam. The stress of the border crossings to the West Bank contrasted markedly with the integrated living and study at the Arava Institute, whose motto is "Nature knows no borders." As it were, Arava's own story mirrors one of the lessons we are discussing here. Initially, when first establishing the institute and its educational programs, their belief was that getting the Israeli, Jordanian, and Palestinian students into the same room would be sufficient for them to build relationships across their divides without additional intervention. About one year in, they realized that this was not happening on its own, and so they added the Peace and Environmental Leadership Seminar, which was designed to facilitate dialogue.

My students had read about the Israeli-Palestinian conflict, seen hundreds of photos, and screened multiple videos during the predeparture course, but it was completely different when they experienced it firsthand. They experienced emotions ranging from genuine fear to joy and hope. Their predeparture preparation and nightly processing of these encounters during the trip allowed them to compare their direct experience with their academic study and discuss and process the emotions they felt. For at least one student, it became a step in her own vocational discernment journey.

Melissa[39] had graduated between the time of the course and the overseas program. She had studied political science and international relations and

---

[39] I have changed all student names in this chapter for privacy.

was excited to break into the peacebuilding field, treating each visit as a networking opportunity. Before we even left the country, she'd been offered a position with an organization that focused on bringing kids from Israel and Palestine together. Within a few months she was directing their fundraising efforts, which soon led to the position of director of fundraising for one of the biggest organizations operating in the field of peacebuilding and a five-year sojourn in Tel Aviv. By the time Melissa came back to the United States she had landed a job with one of the biggest antihate organizations in North America, with a top position in their largest regional office, focusing on interfaith affairs and community outreach.

Another example involves a young woman who took my CBL class, Refugees and Resettlement. The idea for this project grew out of the same principles of the epistemic experience. As war in Syria and the concomitant refugee situation reached crisis levels c. 2015, an "over there" problem had become a "right here" problem, as hundreds of refugees from Syria and elsewhere resettled in the northern New Jersey region. Recognizing an immediate need here in our own communities, we quickly formed a partnership with the local office of the International Rescue Committee (IRC) and, in turn, the Elizabeth School District, where our students could supplement the educational services offered to youth arriving in New Jersey. It began as a relatively informal tutoring program at a church in Elizabeth. I recall sitting in my car one morning, watching some fifteen students exit the student center and climb into a van heading an hour away, dedicating a large chunk of their weekend to volunteer for neither pay nor credit. It was clear that both sides were benefiting, but the work itself was extremely difficult and, for some, emotionally exhausting. Most of our clients spoke virtually no English and the cultural differences were stark. By year two, however, it became apparent that to increase the learning for both our clients and the Drew students, we needed to convert this program into a formal CBL course.

The CBL course meets on Tuesdays in the classroom, without our clients, where we debrief from the week before and prep for our upcoming session with the clients. There is a conventional academic content component, where students learn about the root causes of forced migration and the formal resettlement process, knowledge that complements their hands-on experience. On Thursdays we travel to Elizabeth to meet with the students at the offices of the IRC. In most cases, we make use of the van ride to and from Elizabeth for instant self-assessment. We develop our own culture of checking in on each other on a regular basis. My students even check in on me.

One student story from this program stands out. For Sunita, the course was a venture into a whole new world. In the final semester of her senior year, Sunita (a psychology major) had taken the course largely because she needed to fulfill an immersive experience, general education requirement to graduate. She reached out to me in advance of the class to ask what would be involved; she was unsure where she would fit. On our first day of class, she was nervous, but also optimistic and open-minded.

In the second class, we took stock of the various languages spoken by the college students and the clients. We discovered that the first language of one client was Tamil, one of several languages Sunita spoke. She had always found joy in speaking Tamil at family, communal, and religious gatherings back home, but after nearly four years living in the United States, she had come to regard the language as a sentimental treasure, not something that could ever be practical here in the United States. Something clicked and everything changed when she realized she, and she alone, possessed a critical skill and cultural knowledge that was central to our mission.

By the end of the semester, Sunita confided in me that prior to taking this class she had absolutely no idea what she wanted to do with her life. Her postgraduation job search began with a call to her local IRC office. She also began exploring work in childhood education. In this course, she discovered skills and talents she was either unaware she possessed or had never imagined she could put to good use. Stumbling into new content areas and getting in touch with her own strengths were now driving Sunita's career decisions. Sunita now wanted to make her next step in life about working with underserved people; she had been summoned, drafted into the world's vast web of interrelationship.

Expanding the borders

Most people yearn for some form of fulfillment, often realized through joy, but also found in sadness if it imparts a deep sense of meaning.[40] Holocaust survivor Viktor Frankl, in *Man's Search for Meaning*, claims that this search for meaning is the primary force driving humanity.[41] For many, it is not easy

---

[40] Deanna A. Thompson, in chapter 2 of this volume, explores the ways sadness calls us to vocations that we do not choose.

[41] Viktor E. Frankl, *Man's Search for Meaning*, trans. Helen Pisano and Ilse Lasch (Boston: Beacon Press, 2014).

to articulate what it is they are yearning for. This may be particularly true of college students, many of whom are just beginning to ponder these things. Nonetheless, people experience a deep hunger for fulfillment. (Conversely, it could be a lack of fulfillment that drives so many to act in hate and anger, for example, young men who perceive of limited opportunities open to them and join violent movements).

If colleges and universities are to offer experiences that are truly transformational, there are several key steps we can take. As argued already, the experience itself, no matter how rich, is not alone sufficient, and we must help create space where students can engage in deep reflection. We must infuse this space with a spirit of critical thinking and questioning if students are to convert the experience into an opportunity for transformation. Students cannot expand the borders that delineate their conventional sphere of concern if they don't first question what it is that determines those boundaries in the first place. If we are to instill in students not only a sense of a common good but also the drive to fulfill it, we must ask students to explore the range and scope of their own commitments. It is not enough to expose students to different people with different ideas; we must push students to engage with and truly entertain ideas, opinions, and experiences that challenge their thinking about who will be impacted by their actions, both negatively and positively. An urban development plan may look stunning on paper, in terms of both a beautified neighborhood and a robust bottom line. What if students also saw the faces of the people— young families with children, elderly people in rent-controlled apartments— who were displaced?

This latter point, concerning encounters with alterity, may be more important today than at any time in recent decades. There is a widespread sense that our society is highly polarized, a perception that is certainly represented, if not openly encouraged, by the media's typical framing, where either people are offered just one point of view or opposing views are presented as hostile and mutually exclusive. We need an overall reframing of the ways we think of meeting or encountering others. The binary thinking so pervasive today implies that meeting up with the "other side" means a confrontation, potentially volatile or even violent. We can begin to reframe these interactions through training for all students, active listening, civil dialogue, and mediation—all skills that will be of tremendous value to our students, no matter what path they opt to pursue.[42]

---

[42] See David Timmerman's exploration of discussion and deliberation as ways to cultivate vocation for the common good in chapter 8 of this volume.

We need to generate sustained opportunities where students have genuine encounters and exchanges with people whose lives, experiences, and perspectives are distinctly different than their own. Too often, in both domestic and international learning experiences, students see and hear the locals but do not have enough opportunity to interact with them. This is a perennial problem that is not easily overcome. Person-to-person exchanges contradict and challenge our own ways of thinking and can prompt a reexamination of even the most deeply held beliefs. Perhaps students will hold onto those beliefs pursuant to an encounter that tests their values; still, they will be the better for it since they have gained a greater understanding of why they hold those beliefs in relation to other people. It may not close the circle, but the student's deep gladness and the world's deep hunger begin to come into view.

Deep gladness and deep hunger don't bump into each other by accident. Thus, our investment in thoughtful reflection, debriefing, and group processing is necessary. Many people go a lifetime without truly grasping what fulfills them because they don't take the time to engage in intentional reflection and active listening. Nor can we count on "aha" moments. When discovery is construed in this manner, we may inadvertently create false or superficial discoveries and miss the quiet moments where the plodding yet profound change occurs. Educators need to recognize that no single experience, no matter how deep or spectacular, is likely to result in transformation.[43]

Group reflection is also vital. Understanding how classmates respond differently to the same stimuli provides space to value a broad range of perspectives. Group reflection exercises require that students organize and present their thoughts on their community work to each other while inviting them to respond to one another in meaningful ways. These interactive reflections yield richer, more relational interpretations of experience. Levinas employs the term "infinity" to convey the idea of an individual person's uniqueness, urging us to avoid the common mistake of assimilating others to us and our own way of knowing.[44] In Cohen's words, Levinas exposes a core problem in the Western philosophical tradition, where we tend to "'know' the world by describing it with categories that originate with the knower."[45]

---

[43] Jason A. Mahn, "The Conflicts in Our Callings: The Anguish (and Joy) of Willing Several Things," in Cunningham, ed., *Vocation across the Academy,* 50–51.

[44] Levinas, *Totality and Infinity,* 212.

[45] Cohen, *Justice in the City,* 81.

Finally, we must search for ways to connect the classroom and experiential learning whenever possible. Students can be introduced to the strategies and tools for building change in the conventional classroom setting. Still, developing the skills to effectively wield those tools, knowing which to employ and when, must be learned through action. Few lessons are more powerful than failure and making mistakes. It's not that we should actively encourage the latter, but they are bound to happen, and when students are able to see what went wrong, assess why, and understand the implications, they are likely to do much better going forward. Mistakes and failures, experienced by students and educators alike, yield a better process in the end.

The most important thing I have learned is that the space where an individual's deep gladness and the world's deep hunger converge is not some fixed destination we arrive at; rather, it is a path we pursue. With open minds and hearts, we discover new forms of gladness and hunger. If students are to have transformational experiences where vocational discernment occurs and where new horizons for a common good are explored, we must do more than provide the venue. We must engage students in ongoing processes of personal reflection, discovery, and genuine exchange with people from all places and walks of life. Only then do we see the transformation of ourselves in the world, extending the boundaries to reach beyond what we knew was possible.

PART THREE
PEDAGOGIES AND PRACTICES FOR THE COMMON GOOD

While this section focuses on pedagogies and practices, these are not only for the classroom. The chapters invite faculty across disciplines and administrators and staff across the college to consider how their interactions with students as advisors and mentors, educators and leaders invite changes in perspective about our serving others beyond self.

Our authors present the various ways that learning in communities—on campus and off campus—builds significant skills that contribute to the common good. The section argues that teaching discussion and deliberation and reading with and responding to others and diverse texts contribute to communal well-being. Further, as we practice and value the "pause" in our classrooms and common life, recognizing burnout and emotional exhaustion, we can help students build sustainable vocations. Such pedagogies as reading with strangers, deliberating with those whose views are different from our own, and caring for self and others prepare students for vocations that serve the common good.

We encourage readers of this section to focus on the terms discussion and deliberation, compassion and accompaniment, sustainability and responsibility, friend and stranger. What do these terms mean in your classrooms, campus programs, strategic plans, and institutional priorities? How can we teach and model the skills needed to contribute to the common good?

The questions that follow may be used in professional development, meetings, programming, planning, and teaching. We imagine students and educators alike responding to these in discussion and in writing, in private and public settings. The goal of the questions, and of this section, is to provide examples of practices of compassionate caring for self and others and foster dialogue across difference as we help students see their own purpose as connected to others' flourishing.

How does an emphasis on deliberation, discussion, and reading together, offer models for contributing to the common good?

* What pieces of the curriculum, or offices and programs on your campus, cultivate skills of dialogue and deliberation? Where could that be embedded or extended?
* Does your campus use common texts, and to what end? Can pedagogies, texts, and classroom structures be revised to better cultivate discussion across diverse groups?
* What issues most need to be addressed through discussion and deliberation on your campus? How can the pedagogies and practices presented in these chapters facilitate next steps?

How do we teach toward difficulty and toward courageous conversation?

* How do we work to confront polarization of viewpoints, through difficult and traumatic experiences, and through the various burdens of history?
* How can our practices and pedagogies cultivate sustainability in our vocations so that we might repeatedly confront difficulty, suffering, and injustice?
* How can we use the examples of the COVID-19 pandemic, institutional racism, and gun violence to bring forward the idea that we must address systems that erode the common good?

What is the role of compassion in the classroom, across campus, and within public life? How do we teach self-compassion and cultivate compassion for others?

* What experiences—inside and outside the classroom—develop students' ability to respond to others with compassion and empathy? Are there particular practices that you have found useful and effective?
* What are the barriers or limitations on your campus to this work?
* How do you teach students, colleagues, and yourself to engage with the heart?
* How does the language of accompaniment help us teach for the common good?

Think about the power of the pause and the power of listening.

* How are you finding pause as an educator? How do you facilitate pause in students?
* How is listening productively modeled across campus?
* What practices allow students and educators to create space for the care of self and others, for pausing, and for listening?

8

A Too Uncommon Common Good

The Role of Discussion and Deliberation in Vocational Discernment

David Timmerman

There are two kinds of nations in the world today, only two: those who in crises want to shoot it out, and those who have learned to talk it out.[1] The quotation is from scholar of rhetoric W. Norwood Brigance in an essay published in 1946 at the conclusion of World War II.[2] I have used this quotation often in my teaching, but typically with the suspicion that students find it a bit overwrought. No more. Place names such as Uvalde, Texas; Buffalo, New York; and in any given week, Anywhere, USA, have become horrific verbal markers for mass shootings. It can appear as if there is a randomness to the location and victims, but we cannot deny, even if we cannot fully understand, that the motivations are not random. We know that there is a sense of powerlessness, hopelessness, despair, and alienation among a significant portion of the population, and dramatic political polarization across the whole. News stations and other media outlets cater to pre-existing positions, and we find fewer and fewer forums in which Americans with differing views can converse with one another, or worse, simply understand each other. Additionally, we must acknowledge that regarding demographic categories, the victims of the shootings are not evenly distributed across our population, with students and minoritized groups targeted at higher rates.

My own community of Kenosha, Wisconsin, is still trying to find a path forward after the tragedies of 2020. On August 23, 2020, Kenosha resident

---

[1] W. Norwood Brigance, "1946: Year of Decision," *Quarterly Journal of Speech* 33 (1947): 131, https://doi.org/10.1080/00335634709381279. This is a paraphrase of a section where Brigance is contrasting totalitarian and democratic nations.

[2] W. Norwood Brigance was a top scholar in the field of what was then referred to as speech communication in the middle of the twentieth century. He had served in World War I and taught through World War II at Wabash College in Crawfordsville, Indiana. Given the prolific and highly regarded scholarship Brigance had produced, my colleagues and I often drew from his writing in our teaching.

David Timmerman, *A Too Uncommon Common Good* In: *Called Beyond Our Selves*. Edited by: Erin VanLaningham, Oxford University Press. © Oxford University Press 2024. DOI: 10.1093/oso/9780197691915.003.0009

Jacob Blake, a 29-year-old Black male, was shot seven times by Kenosha Police Department (KPD) officer Rustin Chesky as Blake was trying to get into his vehicle. No charges were filed against Chesky, and Blake remains paralyzed. Protests in Kenosha included broken windows, looted businesses, and fires. Governor Tony Evers called in the National Guard while protests and destruction continued for several days. Then, on Tuesday, August 25, as the National Guard and police officers were trying to stop the damage, Anthony Huber and Joseph Rosenbaum were killed and Gaige Grosskreutz injured when Kyle Rittenhouse, a 17-year-old White male, shot them with an automatic rifle he had brought to downtown Kenosha that night. Rittenhouse stated that he brought the gun and was present to help protect businesses and property. Rittenhouse was charged with homicide but was found innocent due to acting in self-defense.

In a reflective essay published one year later, Rex Davenport, a *Kenosha News* editorialist, wrote:

> Like it or not, Kenosha became famous for all the wrong reasons. Most of us heard from out-of-town friends and relatives during that week. First, they would typically ask about our own safety. Then, they would implore us to explain what was going on in our beautiful lakefront community. The bad news was that many of us had no good answer to give them. We just had a horrible gut-wrenching fear that the situation could get worse.[3]

Following the events of the summer of 2020, the Kenosha community entered a season of searching for how to move forward. Churches and community organizations held vigils, gatherings, and panel discussions. These efforts helped, but many still puzzled over how to organize for constructive action for the future in response to the destructive actions of the past. This was hard. It remains hard. Over two years later, Kenosha residents and city leaders have not been able to make progress on a shared plan for positive change in the city. Rather, this has largely fallen into the same polarization and paralysis as many other significant political issues across the county.

[3] Rex Davenport, "A Year after the Jacob Blake Shooting, Where Do We Stand?," *Kenosha News*, August 22, 2021, https://www.kenoshanews.com/opinion/editorial/kenosha-news-editorial-a-year-after-the-jacob-blake-shooting-where-do-we-stand/article_d01f544f-9104-5ada-a141-5a500b1c0472.html.

A November 2021 draft plan by the city rehearses opening steps in addressing well-known problems, but without a shared will for action. Even the title of the plan was changed to take out the word "action."[4] As for the county, a great deal of public effort was directed toward establishing a racial equity commission. Sadly, it is hard to see how sufficient energy and will can push this forward to constructive, collective change. As we know, supporting students in their vocational exploration necessitates supporting them as they engage the profoundest junctures in our society and world. Stunningly, these difficult events that began the 2020–21 school year for Carthage College were book-ended by a triple homicide at a bar less than a mile from campus in an outdoor area where a good number of Carthage students were present, gathered to celebrate their impending graduation. Many were graduating nursing majors who helped the wounded on the spot.

Responding constructively to events and realities such as these is a tall task for all of us, but especially for our students. Recently, theologian and civic engagement scholar Darby Ray asked the question this way:

> How do we (as individuals or as institutions) meet students where they are in this time of global pandemic, entrenched inequity, climate emergency, and imperiled democracy—with the anxiety, despair, denial, disconnection, and other signs of existential threat these realities produce for so many of them?[5]

And then how do we guide and support these same students to engage in and impact the too large world with its far too great problems? Our current social and political context has made productive discussion and deliberation nearly impossible. This chapter charts a course to reverse this trend, offering some directives toward more productive discussion and deliberation, which have become uncommon common goods.

Models for productive deliberation are hard to find for America's next generation of democratic participants and leaders. Yet so much of what we provide for students at our institutions has training for civic engagement

---

[4] Kenosha mayor John Antaramian convened a group of leaders of faith-based organizations to develop a plan of action. After a year, they gave a public presentation: "Kenosha Action Roadmap to Inclusion, Equity and Equality," PowerPoint presentation, Kenosha, WI, November 2021, https://www.kenosha.org/images/mayor_admin/KAR_Nov_2021.pdf.

[5] Ray was a keynote speaker at the Regional NetVUE Gathering held at St. Norbert College, June 1–3, 2022. The gathering focused on engaging faculty members in the work of vocation.

at its core. Educating for vocation with its unshakeable focus beyond self and toward others directs us toward such engagement. Thankfully, we have a rich past to draw from that possesses worthy, if by no means perfected, exemplars. As democracy took hold in ancient Greece in the fourth century BCE, so too did early forms of education by the group known as the sophists. While those they educated were exclusively male, only of the upper portion of the economic ladder, and nonforeigners, still it was a dramatic broadening from prior forms of education focused solely on the nobility. Likely the first of these teachers to teach a stable group of students for a year or more was the sophist Isocrates, who began his career as a speechwriter for others. Isocrates described the power of public speech:

> But since we have the ability to persuade one another and to make clear to ourselves what we want, not only do we avoid living like animals, but we have come together, built cities, made laws, and invented arts. Speech (logos) is responsible for nearly all our inventions. It legislated in matters of justice and injustice and beauty and baseness, and without these laws, we could not live with one another. . . . If one must summarize the power of discourse, we will discover that nothing done prudently occurs without speech (logos), that speech is the leader of all thoughts and actions, and that the most intelligent people use it most of all.[6]

Isocrates highlights the power of words to alter and shape and hold together our society and world.

As we seek to best prepare students for a life of service beyond self, the critical role played by discussion and deliberation is indispensable as these are the skills needed to be engaged purposefully with others. This chapter develops this contention in three sections. First, it describes the divided and disconnected context in which we and our students presently reside; second, it explains the powerful role discussion plays in students' learning and their lives; lastly, it portrays the transformative role that public deliberation both in the classroom and beyond can have in student lives and their developing sense of vocation.

---

[6] *Isocrates I*, trans. David Mirhady and Yun Lee Too (Austin: University of Texas Press, 2000), 251–52.

The context: divided and disconnected

Presently, the quality of public deliberation upon matters of shared importance is quite poor. It is not simply political commentators who decry the
decrepit state of our public discourse today. In fact, the assessment that our
public discourse is broken is a sentiment shared across party and partisan
lines. This is not only true at the public level; the political polarization we face
extends to the level of our families. Many of us have had experiences with
family members that have been quite difficult in the last few years. Many find
it best to not discuss matters of shared concern, and more regrettably, some
families have stopped talking to each other at all due to the strain. Will we
allow this to get worse without having the courage to respond?

Greater than this specific component of deliberation in our collective lives,
many worry that an understanding of and commitment to public, common
goods at the societal or organizational level is nearly a thing of the past. As
Robert Reich puts it: "Yet the common good is no longer a fashionable idea.
The phrase is rarely uttered today, not even by commencement speakers
and politicians. It feels slightly corny and antiquated if not irrelevant."[7] Paul
Wadell echoes Reich on this point, noting that the end result is defeating not
only at the societal level but also at the personal level:

> We live in a society that teaches us to put ourselves and our needs before
> the needs and well-being of others. Even our moral vocabulary reflects this.
> Gone is the language of the common good. In its place is the language of in-
> dividual rights, personal choice, and privacy. . . . This is foolish. The irony of
> individualism is that while it promises happiness and success, it dead ends
> in a very lonely, empty life.[8]

We are well into a communication era in which staying connected can easily
be achieved without interacting with others who hold dissimilar views from
our own. The use of social media and other forms of digital communication
also means fewer requirements or expectations to engage in the give and take
of in-person conversation.

---

[7] Robert B. Reich, *The Common Good* (New York: Vintage, 2019), 14.
[8] Paul J. Wadell, *Becoming Friends: Worship, Justice, and the Practice of Christian Friendship* (Grand
Rapids, MI: Brazos Press, 2002), 44.

While we could easily despair, self-first is not the only passion alive among us. There are those who focus on developing thoughtful and coordinated responses to the significant challenges facing us, from mass shootings to extreme and damaging weather events. The efforts arrange on a continuum as to their political and ideological approaches and positions, but their ubiquity and strength belie the fact that a commitment to the common good is not truly dead. John Neafsey lays out this reality:

> It's not right! is the natural response of a sound heart to injustice and inhumanity. The unsettling emotional responses evoked in us by social suffering usually consist of some combination of compassion and indignation. Such feelings, I think, are the emotional reverberations of social conscience within us. The experiences that stir such feelings are wake-up calls. . . . They remind us of the common humanity we share with the sufferers and of our social responsibility to do as much as we possibly can to relieve their sufferings.[9]

Today many of our students capture this sentiment by expressing, affirming, and acting on their growing commitment to social justice. Students stage protest marches on our campuses in support of the extension of the Deferred Action for Childhood Arrivals (DACA) program. Students participate in holding space conversations and public forums on campus or vigils and town hall meetings in our host communities in response to police shootings of Black males and other forms of discrimination and harassment. Fine arts students produce artwork and stage performances that portray the marginalization, harassment, and discrimination experienced by too many in America and around the world. Students attend debates of congressional candidates held on their campuses and speak up during the question time. This commitment to good beyond self is expressed in variegated ways and forms on our campuses but (thankfully) it is present.[10]

Respectful and frank discussion and deliberation is the desperately needed and only genuine hope for community progress. I do not mean to downplay the level of difficulty of this effort, but neither am I willing to downplay the need. We have a deep responsibility to prepare students to meet this need.

---

[9] John Neafsey, *A Sacred Voice Is Calling: Personal Vocation and Social Conscience* (Maryknoll, NY: Orbis Books, 2006), 146.

[10] For further explorations of student activism and vocational commitments, see reflections by Deanna A. Thompson in chapter 2 and Michelle Hayford in chapter 5 of this volume.

This is the current reality of America and our campuses, which makes the pursuit of respectful yet authentic discussion and deliberation so vitally important and so extremely difficult. While this chapter focuses primarily on discussion and deliberation in the classroom setting, I am convinced easy entry and lower-stakes forms of discussion and deliberation can be made available to students through other campus engagements as well. The responsibility for and benefits of the work of discussion and deliberation on matters of shared concern are common goods and part of the common good in a democracy. We can both help our students understand their values and commitments more deeply and form practical and productive paths for acting upon them in and through discussion and deliberation. What is more, we can learn and find new and better paths for action ourselves.

This "It's not right!" reaction reveals a developed and closely held commitment to realities and dimensions well beyond personal freedom. Historically speaking, this is not surprising. Reich characterizes early American democracy as exhibiting just these impulses:

> It was through governing themselves that Americans learned to put public responsibility over selfish interest. . . . The public spiritedness of New Englanders was replicated across America in barn-raisings and quilting bees. It can still be observed in neighbors who volunteer as firefighters or help one another during natural disasters, whose generosity erects the local hospital and propels high school achievers to college, and who send their young men and women off to fight wars for the good of all. It is found in America's tradition of civic improvement, philanthropy, and local boosterism. Popular culture once echoed these sentiments without sounding corny or inauthentic.[11]

While we presently operate in an extremely divided national context, we can look to methods that have aided us in the past, revise and update them, and nourish new forms, including new means of communication such as social media. These democratic practices and inclinations—when adjusted to each contemporary moment—can serve us well in the present and future on our work with students on our campuses. I don't mean to suggest that the college classroom, lab, studio, recreation center, or residence hall is the only place in America where this can happen well. But it is one such.

---

[11] Reich, *The Common Good*, 39.

We can also gain both inspiration and grounding on how to foster and forge deepened commitment to and understanding of the common good from the earliest versions of democracy in ancient Greece and, in particular, the meetings of the Athenian assembly. Josiah Ober claims that the important obligation of democratic participants is to speak and listen, fully:

> The practice of democracy assumed that citizens had a capacity to reason together, in public (as well as in private), via frank speech, and that the results of those deliberations would (in general and over time) conduce to the common good. Deliberation meant listening as well as speaking; accepting good arguments as well as making them.[12]

In this way, we can talk our way to a growing, shared understanding of the common good and a growing and shared understanding about how to best pursue it. This is not to say we can talk our way to complete agreement or full harmony. It is the practice of moving forward in discussion, including open-hearted and active listening and respectful speaking, that provides the first step to more meaningful progress. Experience and skill development for our students in both discussion and deliberation provide the necessary tools they need to move from self to engagement with the larger society and world around them. These are the same skills needed for an authentic engagement of vocation, finding one's purpose and meaning as we consider others, our collective well-being, and the calls that the world has for us.

Discussion in the classroom, and beyond

The college classroom can be a place for students to engage, authentically if not always comfortably, the deepest and most troubling issues of the day and to hear and consider the ideas and positions of their classmates. This common good is collectively created through discussion and shared understanding. Brigance highlights the importance of this work:

> To keep a free society free. To settle differences by talk instead of force. To alter and promote thought. To water and cultivate ideas, hopes, sentiments,

---

[12] Josiah Ober, *Athenian Legacies: Essays on the Politics of Going on Together* (Princeton, NJ: Princeton University Press, 2005), 130.

and enthusiasms in a way and to a degree that cannot be done while we are separated from one another.[13]

Our individual and collective views and values are fed by many streams including religious beliefs and traditions, past experiences, organizational affiliations and commitments, and familial and personal identities. The expression of these streams in our lives is not fixed, but one of our many living and growing parts. The college classroom has long served the role as a space for expression and opportunity to listen to others and ourselves and be transformed through it. The act of verbal and public expression of one's ideas with others clarifies our beliefs, values, and thoughts. Ultimately, this growing and deepening sense of ourselves—through participation in the common good of classroom discussion—pulls us beyond self and toward a more complete understanding of our place in the world and our call to shape it.[14]

At the same time, we must be vigilant in recognizing and responding to the ways in which discussion can be hurtful and seek to foster an environment in which productive responses are modeled for them and open for students to practice listening and responding effectively. One approach is to pause the discussion and allow students to consider how they are feeling at a certain point in the discussion and then express that in some way, either as a verbal response shared with others in the class or as a response that they write for reflection and show to no one. Importantly, there can be things spoken in such discussions that are best named by the professor as outside the bounds of the agreed-upon rules for class discussion. Thankfully, examples of discussion guidelines for college classrooms are ubiquitous, as are descriptions of how to work with a class of students to involve them in generating them.[15] These moments present an opportunity to return to these ground rules and simply say, "Our discussion moved beyond our rules in my

[13] William Norwood Brigance, *Speech: Its Techniques and Disciplines in a Free Society* (New York: Appleton-Century-Crofts, 1952), 66.

[14] In chapter 9 of this volume, Erin VanLaningham makes a parallel argument about the power of reading with those different than us to cultivate a broader and deeper sense of the common good.

[15] For example, see "Sample Guidelines for Classroom Discussion Agreements," Brown University, https://www.brown.edu/sheridan/sites/sheridan/files/docs/sample-guidelines-classroom-discussion-agreements.pdf; and "Guidelines for Engaging in Respectful and Productive Dialogue," University of Maryland, https://cidlis.umd.edu/accessibility/guidelines-for-engaging-in-respectful-productive-dialogue/. Many faculty members find it productive to allow students in individual classes to help generate and establish the list of guidelines. For example, see "Getting Started with Establishing Ground Rules," Cornell University, https://teaching.cornell.edu/resource/getting-started-establishing-ground-rules.

estimation." Mostly, though, shy of such a breach, the professor can acknowledge and name tensions and difficult moments, allowing time for students to
process them.

I use both terms—discussion and deliberation—purposely. Discussion
refers to the many ways educators engage student minds and hearts by providing the opportunity for them to talk with each other and with us at public
lectures, readings, and performances as well as in our offices, at student organization meetings, and at chapel. Through multiple means including
writing assignments, research and project topic selections, and even the
choice of which courses to take, college students are prompted to consider
their values, commitments, and political orientation. Classroom discussion
is a productive means for this development. Beyond this, our offices and all
the spaces where we meet students daily become formative sites for the work
of vocation through discussion.[16]

Recognizing the power of discussion reaffirms educators' agency and
deepens their fulfillment in their interactions with students. We have all, of
course, experienced the question-and-answer session or discussion period
gone awry. A particularly adamant participant puts a stranglehold on the
focus, or one or more participants resort to yelling or biting sarcasm. Such
experiences only affirm the need to set guidelines and consider ways to best
manage such situations before they occur. Depending on the group and content of the discussion, management techniques include asking participants
to write down questions on cards and turn them in, having more than one
moderator, and setting time limits for topics to keep things moving forward.
Through the leadership of the educator, discussions can be guided in productive paths for all participants. We ought not let our own anxieties about
difficult moments hinder this important work.

It is important to recognize and name that these discussions are real but
not final or finished. These spaces and opportunities have a real but also a
proto quality to them, and as such they can be safe, challenging, and supportive. Rosa Eberly uses the term "protopublic" to describe our classrooms,
contending they are "real world" interaction and discussion, "practiced
within and for real groups of people who need their discourses," namely,
their classmates and instructor.[17] Within the space and experiences, we must

---

[16] For further exploration of the ways the various spaces on our campuses can foster collective
well-being, see Robert J. Pampel's discussion in chapter 11 of this volume.

[17] Rosa A. Eberly, "From Writers, Audiences, and Communities to Publics: Writing Classrooms
as Protopublic Spaces," *Rhetoric Review* 18 (1999): 165–77, https://doi.org/10.1080/0735019990
9359262.

be attuned to when and how they may veer in less helpful and potentially harmful directions. Still, simply avoiding the most deeply held or serious matters facing our world today or steering clear of all matters about which participants disagree is not a good option either. Leading such discussions is a learnable skill, one that we can improve on throughout our lives.

Additionally, discussions can serve the function of creating "third spaces" for participants. The idea comes from the fields of architecture and city planning and refers to physical spaces where people can meet for conversation and interaction.[18] The first two spaces—home and work or school—do not typically allow for the same type of interaction. Examples of such third spaces include parks, recreation centers, gyms, churches, hair salons, and coffee shops. Good discussions in these different places make new ways of thinking and experiencing others and their ideas possible.[19]

For example, consider a class discussion about climate change or racial justice in which students enter a liminal space to consider these important matters and hear how others are thinking about them. When well led by a faculty member, a staff member, or a student who has been prepared to do so, such discussions have an open-ended and expansive character to them. The discussion more than likely ends with participants having more questions and wonderment about the topic than before the discussion began, having learned from the perspectives of others. Along these lines, good discussions create their own sense of time and space outside or alongside actual time and space; this makes the experience generative and productive. Students approach it with various degrees of engagement, knowing that once each class session is over, they will return to their interior selves. In this way, while not necessarily always being comfortable, our classrooms can be safe in the sense that those involved in the discussion need not fear judgment, embarrassment, or coercion of any type.

Relatedly, educators can model inquisitiveness and "not knowing" to help overcome the myth that a person ought to have their views solidly nailed down prior to speaking. Far from it. Anthony Weston suggests that

---

[18] Stuart M. Butler and Cameron Diaz, "'Third Places' as Community Builders," *Brookings* (blog), September 14, 2016, https://www.brookings.edu/blog/up-front/2016/09/14/third-places-as-community-builders/; "Third Space Theory," *Oxford Reference*, https://www.oxfordreference.com/view/10.1093/oi/authority.20110803103943995.

[19] For further considerations of how we can engage with complex topics in the public sphere and how these can prompt us toward further relationship with others across history and contemporary life, see Martin Holt Dotterweich's reflections in chapter 12 of this volume.

when it comes to moral values we sometimes hear a different story. Here, all too often, we're supposed to know what we think already, and we're supposed to stick to it, come what may. To talk about moral complexity or compromise, or to be curious about other moral views, makes you sound (to some people) spineless, "wishy—washy," practically immoral already.[20]

Class discussions encourage multiple goods for our students. We can normalize the behavior of considering new ideas, deepening understanding, and, when appropriate, adjusting one's views as a result.[21] Seeking to understand others' views should not be seen as agreeing because conflating the two negatively impacts authentic discussion and learning. A response such as "Tell me more and help me understand better what you are saying" or "Thank you, I'm going to give that some more thought" or "I hadn't thought about it in that way before" can go a long, long way.

Admittedly, some disciplines have made discussion a prominent pedagogical practice while others less so. Nevertheless, no matter our discipline, we all bear the burden of promoting authentic and respectful discussion as an effective pedagogical practice and common good. Case studies in professional studies courses readily provide the opportunity to get our students discussing in small and large group format. Presenting data, graphs, and research results in social science courses and asking students to draw conclusions from them also lends itself to discussion. Fostering open questioning and discussion of natural science course content can enhance student learning, helping the instructor to know more deeply what students do and do not yet understand.

A very common and rational reason many educators refrain from raising difficult issues and topics in their classrooms for discussion is that they surmise, correctly, that doing so entails raising the possibility of students saying things that offend their classmates. Yet, this possibility of difficult discussions taking place is precisely why they are such vital means for moving us toward a sense of collective understanding and purpose. How can we best respond to and prepare for emotionally tense moments that arise in such discussions? An important first step when tensions rise is to name the discomfort or the offensive and hurtful statement that has been made. Educators can pause a

[20] Anthony Weston, *A 21st Century Ethical Toolbox* (New York: Oxford University Press, 2001), 9.

[21] Resources on leading discussions in the college classroom are plentiful. See, for example, Stephen D. Brookfield and Stephen Preskill, *Discussion as a Way of Teaching: Tools and Techniques for Democratic Classrooms* (San Francisco: Jossey-Bass, 2005); Jay R. Howard, *Discussion in the College Classroom: Getting Your Students Engaged in Participating in Person and Online* (San Francisco: Jossey-Bass, 2015).

discussion to allow students to speak or write, and then share or not share. Acknowledging these moments helps students make sense of their experience. For example, depending on the specifics, an instructor might say, "Discussing the role race plays in this matter can feel difficult because we are not as used to doing so together as we should be," or "Yes, it is true that in our country or on campus individuals hold different viewpoints on sexual orientation and gender expression, which makes it important for us to discuss them and seek to understand these differing views on their own terms." Further, if the mood in the class has shifted to being tense or students appear constrained or reticent to speak and you are not sure precisely how to name it, pause.[22] You then offer a brief observation such as "We seem less able to discuss this topic" or "We seem to be struggling to collect and express our thoughts on this." Doing this organizes and normalizes these difficult moments in discussion and helps students process them. The simple step of naming can be very productive.

While our goal should be to orchestrate these moments to create and maintain a safe environment for students, at the same time, safe does not mean comfortable. We must also attend to the many ways that the participants in discussions do not come to them or participate on equal footing. As described in other chapters in this volume, our experiences and identities are met with differential treatments and inequities and therefore we must be cognizant of the ways discussion can activate and play into these structural inequalities.[23] We should seek to name these power differentials for students. Then, we can collectively seek their diminishment to enable productive discussion in the classroom and beyond. Relatedly, we need to labor to foster and protect freedom of expression as part of building trust and learning. Regrettably, sometimes students fear "blowback" for their views from fellow students.[24]

One of my mentors[25] had a well-honed strategy I saw him use many times when a particularly harmful or offensive statement was made by a student in a discussion about race and ethnicity, typically in one of the community conversations that took place after a bias incident on the campus where we

---

[22] For more examples of the power of the pause in helping students navigate challenging conversations, see Meghan M. Slining's discussion in chapter 10 of this volume.

[23] See this volume's chapter 4 by Monica M. Smith and chapter 6 by Geoffrey W. Bateman.

[24] Timothy J. Ryan, Andrew M. Engelhardt, Jennifer Larson, and Mark McNeilly, "Moving Past Free Expression Theater," *Insider Higher Education*, June 14, 2022, https://www.insidehighered.com/views/2022/06/14/promote-free-speech-build-trust-among-students-opinion.

[25] Peter Frederick was a professor of history at Wabash College from 1969 through 2004.

both taught. Immediately after a student made a problematic statement of one type or another, he would repeat a key phrase or portion of it back to the student or the whole group or class and put a question mark at the end of it and then wait for a response. For example, "It's not significant that the security staff immediately and first approached the minority students in this situation, leaving the larger group of majority students be?" or "We no longer need a multicultural concerns committee because of all the progress that has been made?" This mostly leads to students picking up on the question and responding to it. Or, if none do, the instructor may simply use it as a marker before proceeding. The range of issues where these moves can be helpful is wide, including LGBTQIA+ matters, immigration and legal residency status concerns, the legal status of abortion, and, as previously mentioned, gun violence.

When discussion takes place with transparency and authenticity, it is to some degree inevitably frightening. Educators can help our students face this fear together, which is of course the best way to face any of our fears in life. Kathleen Fitzpatrick explains:

> Focusing on conversation . . . points to the things we owe one another, the things we owe our colleagues, and also the things we owe those publics whom we hope to engage. Conversation imposes an obligation that cannot be easily concluded, that asks me to open myself again and again to what is taking place between us. Conversation thus demands not that we become more giving, but instead that we become more *receptive*. It requires us to participate, to be part of an exchange that is multidimensional. It disallows any tendency to declare our work concluded, or to disclaim further responsibility toward the other participants in the exchange. It asks us to inhabit a role that is not just about speaking but also about listening, taking in and considering what our conversational partners have to say, reflecting on the merits of their ideas and working toward a shared understanding that is something more than what each of us bears alone.[26]

Fitzpatrick's insights are a reminder that full and open discussion requires and teaches significant skills—to be present, to listen actively, to be reflective,

[26] Kathleen Fitzpatrick, *Generous Thinking: A Radical Approach to Saving the University* (Baltimore: Johns Hopkins University Press, 2019), 54–55.

and to share genuine thoughts and ourselves. These are the goods—the ideals—toward which we strive.

Deliberation, productive and unproductive

The discussions students engage in are the rhythmic heartbeat of their learning. Deliberation is a more specific form of discussion, fitted for democracy, that combines three principal elements. First, deliberation involves matters of significant public and shared concern. Ready examples include global warming, racism, wealth inequality, and issues on university campuses such as student mental health and wellness, curricular change, and the operation of public safety officers. Second, deliberation includes multiple perspectives on the topics considered, their advantages and disadvantages weighed, and their competing values named. Third, deliberation includes how individuals, working alone or collectively, can best respond to these challenges and opportunities materially, politically, and socially.

Deliberation offers a critically important vocational step and path for participants in a democracy. Historical antecedents of these organizations include the Athenian Assembly as previously noted, but also, in our own country, New England townhall meetings in the eighteenth century, the Lyceum movement in the early nineteenth century, and the late nineteenth-century Chautauqua movement, which has had a resurgence in recent decades. All gathered citizens and residents to learn, discuss, and build community and civic relations.

The rhetorical tradition began parallel to the birth of democracy in ancient Greece and the need for citizens and leaders to make arguments before their fellow citizens in the assembly and courts, to evaluate the arguments of others, and to determine a path forward collectively, most typically through the vote. This tradition was part of the foundation for a public speaking course colleagues and I at Wabash College constructed that included students learning to lead and participate in public deliberation. Our method drew upon a pattern utilized by the National Issues Forum, an arm of the Kettering Foundation.[27] National Issues Forums

---

[27] The National Issues Forum website is rich with resources for deliberations, including an explanation of what they mean by deliberation as well as a list of network partners, resources for moderators, and free National Issues Forum Issues Guides for use by communities of all types, including classrooms: https://www.nifi.org/en/deliberation.

typically have five steps. The first is the personal stakes stage, in which participants identify and name their personal connection to the issue. In steps two, three, and four the group considers three different approaches to the issue. The fifth stage is the reflection stage, during which each participant reflects on what they have heard. During this last stage the group identifies common ground or clarifies the tensions present. Finally, there may be action steps identified or a pathway identified for a next deliberation about the matter.

We adapted this format to an assignment for students in the public speaking course. First, students were asked to select and define fairly a public problem or issue, identify multiple perspectives and the trade-offs for each approach, and finally name and weigh competing values among them. Working in pairs, they constructed and delivered a presentation designed to prepare their classmates for a deliberation on the topic. These presentations shared the pertinent information to establish a common baseline of understanding for the group gathered for the deliberation.

This basic pattern can be adopted and utilized in a range of courses throughout the curriculum. Students taking policy classes can lead deliberative discussions on any issue alive in our society today, from homelessness to renewable energy to taxation. Students in science courses can lead deliberations on climate change, the Human Genome Project, and public health policy. As every discipline contributes to our understanding and ability to address these issues, each can also support classroom deliberation and community deliberation about them. To be clear—these practices and the collective good created for student learning and vocation should be part of all our courses, no matter the discipline, and all our interactions with students, within and beyond the curriculum.

When deliberation is productive, it affirms all participants and it deepens understanding for all. While differing ideas, values, and political positions are shared, none of the people doing the sharing feel shut down or devalued in the process. Alternatively, when such deliberations in class or in the hallway or in our communities go poorly, they can leave participants feeling frustrated, angry, and hurt. For this reason, many seek to avoid it. Yet, considering that the benefits can be significant for our common well-being and purpose, we ought to continue to learn how to best teach and utilize structured deliberation.

Qualities and Characteristics of Productive Deliberation

- *Commonality:* Emphasizes what people share rather than what divides them including interests, values, and goals[28]
- *Deliberation:* Engages the arguments and positions rather than the people themselves, seeing multiple solutions rather than needing a sin-gular outcome
- *Inclusiveness:* Seeks dissenting voices and demonstrates awareness of the many ways voices are silenced in communities and in conversation
- *Provisionality:* Recognizes that conclusions are never final because ideas, insights, and possibilities evolve within the process of public discussion
- *Listening:* Attempts to hear and understand alternative perspectives and to incorporate those perspectives into the whole
- *Learning:* Seeks to better understand the issues, multiple perspectives, and people involved, with an openness to make accommodations or shift prior thinking
- *Lateral communication:* Circulates among community members rather than between leaders and is multidirectional discourse rather than one-way communication
- *Imagination:* Explores creative ways of approaching and rethinking the issues at hand
- *Empowerment:* Enables people to *do* something positive and effective for the community—productive discourse is not an end in itself

Qualities and Characteristics of Unproductive Deliberation

- *Division:* Highlights and accentuates differences among participants and their positions
- *Dichotomous thinking:* Features debate between two extreme positions instead of exploring additional perspectives or middle ground

---

[28] The list of qualities and characteristics of productive deliberation are adapted from Benjamin R. Barber, "Civility and Civilizing Discourse," in *A Place for Us: How to Make Society Civil and Democracy Strong* (New York: Hill and Wang, 1998), 114–23. The list of the qualities and character-istics of unproductive deliberation are from Jennifer Abbott, Todd McDorman, David Timmerman, and Jill Lamberton, *Public Speaking and Democratic Participation: Speech, Deliberation, and Analysis in the Civic Realm* (New York: Oxford University Press, 2016), 23–24.

- *Combativeness:* Utilizes aggressive behavior toward other participants and alternative perspectives, such as repeated interrupting, emotionally charged labels and terms, yelling, and personal attacks
- *Certainty:* Exhibits sureness about a position without recognizing its weaknesses or drawbacks
- *Lack of listening:* Listens exclusively to an alternative perspective to find weaknesses in it; uses questions as veiled arguments ("Isn't it true that . . . ?") or as attempts to humiliate other participants
- *Winning:* Uses any means necessary to win, such as false or misleading illusions, quoting statements out of context, and misstating or exaggerating the facts
- *Distrust:* Suspects other participants' motives or goals, presuming they have a hidden agenda, and thus lacks faith in the honesty or authenticity of what they say
- *Hierarchical communication:* Encourages communication from the "top" decision makers, which subjugates ordinary individuals' preferences and insights
- *Dogmatism:* Features familiar and even predictable talking points as well as entrenched, predetermined positions

My colleagues and I found that discussing these characteristics—both the productive and unproductive—had a positive effect on class deliberations. The lists help move students beyond a sense that discussion is whatever happens to take place or "anything goes." Rather, they can have agency in these experiences and build their critical thinking skills in analyzing both *how* a discussion is going and in what ways they can help it to be productive. Students can learn that there is a reasonable way to distinguish good from poor discussion, evaluating the productive and unproductive qualities of the deliberation, either verbally as a group or as a follow-up written assignment. The instructor can also connect the experience with the larger world and our collective role in building and maintaining a democracy, especially during the most difficult of times. When we engage students in the exploration of issues that affect our shared life—such as equity and inclusion, our degrading environment, a global pandemic, the growing wealth gap—we engage them in practices that cultivate vocational reflection.

Once students have learned how to lead a deliberative discussion in the classroom, they can, with coaching and support, be prepared to lead them in our communities. Such experiences can be powerful for both the students and the community members.[29] In a required course on citizenship for senior students, I had the opportunity to see this firsthand. The local Kiwanis group was meeting for their once-a-month lunch session. The group had agreed to allow college students to prepare a document on deepening the college and city connections through enhanced tax incentives to local businesses for this purpose. The students prepared a brief document outlining several positive city-college collaborations in the recent past and suggesting a few possible new ones. They also sought to fairly present the lost tax revenue from those tax incentives. The conversation during the deliberation ranged from the current status of the college-city relationship to the future potential and mutual benefit of both. Residents made good comments and wrestled with the costs and the benefits of tax breaks for this purpose. However, there was one resident, a middle-aged man whose family was well known in the city, who became disruptive by dominating the speaking time. He raised various objections and essentially took the position that the college was more of a liability to the city than an asset. He worried about homes the college had purchased in the last decade that had gone off the tax rolls and the cost of fire department runs to the college due to false alarms. At a particular moment, when one of the students was making a good response to a tough question from this individual, he interrupted the student before he could finish his response. I was about to step in when, to my delight, the other senior did so and successfully shifted the energy and the focus back to the rest of the participants.

Our car ride to that meeting was quiet, as the two students were nervous about the task before them. On the way home—as soon as we shut the car doors—they began talking excitedly, recounting how it had gone. They were clearly feeling proud of how they had been able to present their material and lead the deliberation. This included managing the difficult participant who was more than twice their age. And they got a much more nuanced understanding of the give and take of town-and-gown relations than they had before the session.

There were ten groups in that class that led similar community deliberations. Other community deliberations focused on a proposed law to block windmills too close to town, the problematic application of a new

---

[29] For further examples of the role of direct encounter with community members and the role of dialogue and deliberation in conflict resolution, see Jonathan Golden's reflections in chapter 7 of this volume.

dilapidated housing rule, and whether or not the local public school should teach courses in Spanish to new immigrants while they learned English. Through such experiences, students were learning, as Reich expressed, the means by which they can put public responsibility above self-interest.

Speaking and listening, together

It would be understandable if the current generation of college students finds the challenges we collectively face—mass shootings; racial, economic, sexual, and gender injustice; the impacts of climate change; and ineffective local and national political practices and structures—so daunting as to be debilitating. Learning the skills to participate in productive deliberation and dialogue positions them to have a different and more empowering response and to work toward the common good. And in working toward this good, which is collectively created and owned, they can deepen and expand their sense of vocation and living beyond self. In addition, in the practice of discussion and deliberation we implicitly and explicitly communicate to our students that their thoughts and words truly matter. They see that we trust their ability to think for themselves and to consider radically different ideas. We invite them into responding to issues of our common life. I believe students are hungry for this difficult engagement. Bill Placher, speaking from his own religious tradition and about Christian churches, offers these words, which I believe are equally applicable to our students and our colleges:

> I have long suspected that most young Christians are more willing to be challenged than their churches are to challenge them. We are so concerned to make Christianity seem easy that we fail to notice that maybe young people are not looking for an easy Christianity.[30]

Our work as educators ought to make deliberation and discussion a common experience, however difficult. We should serve them no weak tea.

The deep challenges of contemporary society have made the ability to discuss and deliberate uncommon, to the detriment of us all. In a recent article in *The Atlantic*, social psychologist Jonathan Haidt argues that the last decade

---

[30] William C. Placher, *Callings: Twenty Centuries of Christian Wisdom on Vocation* (Grand Rapids, MI: Eerdmans, 2005), 10–11.

has left America in the functional equivalent position of the people in the Tower of Babel story in the book of Genesis in the Hebrew Bible. He writes:

> The story of Babel is the best metaphor I have found for what happened in America in the 2010s, and for the fractured country we now inhabit. Something went terribly wrong, very suddenly. We are disoriented, unable to speak the same language or recognize the same truth. We are cut off from one another and from the past.[31]

When the very basis of our ability to work collectively together for goods we all share is so broken, how can we not seek to repair it, no matter how difficult? Our society, and our world, is indeed deeply challenged in seeing and valuing what we hold in common; yet, through teaching the skills of authentic and respectful discussion and productive deliberation, we can prepare our students to effectively meet the challenge of building the common good in their generation.

---

[31] Jonathan Haidt, "After Babel: How Social Media Dissolved the Mortar of Society and Made America Stupid," *The Atlantic*, May 2022, 56.

9

Reading with Strangers

Our Collective Vocation

Erin VanLaningham

Can reading together, as a group of strangers gathered in a college class-room, prompt us to act and think differently about ourselves and others? Can reading be a catalyst for considering and contributing to collective well-being? In the search for meaning and identity, reading diverse texts, with people we might not otherwise know or meet, can direct vocational explo-ration toward a communal context. Such reading reveals how environments, perspectives, and people unfamiliar to us can enrich and expand our sense of purpose as we better orient our lives toward the common good. As Adam Newton suggests in *Narrative Ethics*, "The very act of reading, in other words, like prayer or casual looking, permits things to happen."[1] Reading with strangers invites us into new identities, new ideas, and new relationships. It practices critical inquiry of and reflection upon what makes us strangers—our varied life experiences, privileges, and beliefs. The strange—in the ways that it helps us see ourselves and others anew—can prompt a deeper val-uing of difference while also cultivating connectedness. Reading together moves us toward un-becoming strangers and a deepening of bonds—even friendship—with others.

The argument here is that students might integrate individual voca-tion with the concerns of others as they discuss and analyze texts, together. Reading—especially the reading of fiction and nonfiction that represents imagined "others" and allows for an exploration of the complex realities of human experience—requires consideration of people, places, and ideas that may be foreign, uncomfortable, and, in many students' minds, unrelatable or irrelevant. Such engagement is the practice of building a capacity that prioritizes others' needs and insights while challenging our own. Common

[1] Adam Zachary Newton, *Narrative Ethics* (Boston: Harvard University Press, 1995), 23.

Erin VanLaningham, *Reading with Strangers* In: *Called Beyond Our Selves*. Edited by: Erin VanLaningham,
Oxford University Press. © Oxford University Press 2024. DOI: 10.1093/oso/9780197691915.003.0010

reading can be a locus point for discussing social ills and solutions to them, practicing empathy for neighbors we do not know, and considering diverse viewpoints. Thus, reading with strangers is perhaps one of the strongest ways college educators can hone students' intellectual and moral capacities to focus not on self-development but on the development of our common civic life.

As I and others have argued elsewhere, reading literature can be an avenue toward vocational discernment, sharpening interpretive and analytic skills that can aid in reflecting on one's purpose and place in the world.[2] In this chapter, I make a broader claim that reading together can mirror collective discussion in communities and workplaces, allowing students to probe difficult concepts, work with new people, and offer up responses to significant problems and realities. These habits are the habits that foster the common good—access to and realization of well-being for all—but also happen to be habits that are taught through reading texts together, most often with peers they do not know in deep or meaningful ways.

This work involves a commitment to each other. While students may not recognize this positioning initially, it is our responsibility to point out that reading binds us together whether we like it or not. Adam Newton explains that "textual interpretation comprises both private responsibilities incurred in each singular act of reading and public responsibilities that follow from discussing and teaching."[3] Students and educators alike confront the private responsibility of dedicating ourselves to engaging with the material and the public responsibilities of listening and responding to texts and to each other. Of specific import are Newton's questions about responsibility: "Responsibility for what exactly? For simply opening the book? For reading it? For responding to it? For putting it back?"[4]

When we situate collective reading as collective responsibility, students can see their present vocations *as students* clearly—their call to read is a call to self and others. Some students may feel the calling of reading, but many do not. Most students do, however, understand what it means to accompany others or build in common cause with others—which are also pieces of this reading experience. If we think about reading as constructing meaning together—and that this process is only as rich and layered as the voices

---

[2] See Stephanie L. Johnson and Erin VanLaningham, eds., *Cultivating Vocation in Literary Studies* (Edinburgh: Edinburgh University Press, 2022).

[3] Newton, *Narrative Ethics*, 19.

[4] Newton, *Narrative Ethics*, 19.

who are allowed to and take seriously their obligation to contribute—then students might be better able to hear the call of that interpretive and analytic work. They can better see that if a person chooses to put the book back, grossly misread it, or ignore it, we all bear the consequences in class and beyond. It is not too much of a mental leap to see that the skills cultivated by reading with strangers in college may then have important consequences of reading with strangers in life.

This chapter explores how our encounters with the strangeness of those we do not know might allow us to become less strange to each other. As we help students see their calls to be readers as the call to serve neighbor, we can better demonstrate that reading together can contribute to the common good. Pedagogies that address the difficulties of and barriers to the reading experience can provide models for fostering a more nuanced sense of how to value the stranger and strangeness. Ultimately, through our reading together, we un-become strangers to each other, making possible mutual flourishing. "Things happen"[5] when we enter a classroom, interpret a text, and listen and respond to the collection of voices. We negotiate and make meaning together in those happenings, allowing us to act and live in ways that honor the strange, the new, and the unfamiliar beyond classroom and text.

In the company of strangers: our responsibilities

This chapter draws from the tradition of narrative ethics, including what Wayne Booth calls "the ethics *of* readers—their responsibilities *to* stories."[6] Booth notes in *The Company We Keep: An Ethics of Fiction* that ethical criticism encompasses the aesthetic, political, ideological, and philosophical aspects of literature and literary criticism, explaining that the aim of most ethical criticism is to improve self and society.[7] He focuses on the experience as we read, on the "many relations we are asked to build . . . with the various authors we encounter," describing it as a "conversation," even a "good conversation."[8] Here, in this notion of "people meeting" through reading, we find

[5] Newton, *Narrative Ethics*, 19.
[6] Wayne C. Booth, *The Company We Keep: An Ethics of Fiction* (Berkeley: University of California Press, 1988), 9.
[7] Booth, *The Company We Keep*, 11–12.
[8] Booth, *The Company We Keep*, 169.

the possibility of "the types of friendship or companionship a book provides *as* it is read."[9]

Booth's concept of "people meeting" is a helpful steppingstone to my argument. It is not just the meeting between reader and author, or reader and character (although those are always present), but also the kinds of experiences we can foster in the literal meetings in the classroom and in the various public spaces where reading happens. Booth's project purposefully focuses on the "obligation inward" as he explores a reader's individual ethics;[10] the addition of exploring vocation through reading—discovering one's responsibility to others in so doing—is the ethical shift outward emphasized in this chapter. Our humanity resides in trust and affection for others in a reciprocal relationship, and it is in this social bond that reading with strangers can build a capacity for contributing to the common good.[11] Booth uses the language of friendship as a metaphor, suggesting that authors and their stories offer an invitation of companionship to the reader. For our purposes, I suggest that texts and our reading of them individually and collectively can foster relationships that are more real than metaphorical—being "full friends" (to use Booth's term) in reciprocal care for another's well-being.[12]

Our responsiveness to others is the turn toward the collective in vocational exploration. Margaret Mohrmann suggests that in cultivating such responsibility, we experience "human mutuality" with all of its potential and dangers, a reminder that "the nature of human flourishing is complex and communal."[13] In addition, when we consider our responsibility to people "beyond those we are sharing a life with" and cultivating an interest in others' beliefs and well-being, we are committed more seriously in our vocations to those whom Kwame Anthony Appiah calls "imaginary strangers."[14] Vocation as responsibility informs students' call to the classroom, campus, and communities to which they belong. Reading in the company of strangers is part of the membership in the class but also a membership in the world.[15]

---

[9] Booth, *The Company We Keep*, 170.

[10] Booth, *The Company We Keep*, 167.

[11] Booth draws from Aristotle in his exploration of trust between individuals in the various levels of friendship (173).

[12] Booth, *The Company We Keep*, 174.

[13] Margaret E. Mohrmann, "'Vocation Is Responsibility': Broader Scope, Deeper Discernment," in *Vocation across the Academy: A New Vocabulary for Higher Education*, ed. David S. Cunningham (New York: Oxford University Press, 2017), 25.

[14] Kwame Anthony Appiah, *Cosmopolitanism: Ethics in a World of Strangers* (New York: Norton, 2007), xv.

[15] For an exploration of membership as a helpful narrative to teach vocation and the common good, see Christine Jeske's reflections in chapter 3 of this volume.

Reading as responsibility, then, is very much about the context of "people meeting" to discuss, listen, and explore together. This engenders exploration of vocation connected to others' perspectives and experiences and recognizes our embeddedness in the ecology of common life.

Reading with strangers

A unique aspect of classroom life is that the roll of the dice each semester means a different collection of learners gathered in a common space. Especially in the context of first-year seminars and general education courses, the group is bound to have some people we have never or barely met, or who are wholly "other" to us. Their strangeness, and indeed our strangeness to them, means that we need to have a way of honoring the unique gifts of our neighbor and learning from them. As sociologist Georg Simmel suggests, the stranger does not just pass through, but is "a person who comes today and stays tomorrow," who is not necessarily familiar to us but "connect[s] a great many people.[16] Being with people we generally don't know, or are new to us, but feeling close to them because of some shared features (we are all students in this class, we all picked this college), we can see what Simmel describes as "many possibilities of commonness" between us. That potential for common ground is found in our strangeness, identifying the connections between diverse individuals within the ecology of our shared life.

The value of connecting with strangers is to challenge dominant group identities and the ways such groups keep us from actively understanding or participating in outside groups (those who are strangers to us). Yet, once those in the "out-group" become people with whom we work and learn, it becomes more difficult to dismiss their needs and dreams as not part of our own.[17] While there may be a few "in-groups" embedded in the classroom, students still gather with others from outside of their friend circles, teams, and majors in these spaces. These out-groups can slowly erode through a shared reading experience as they together embrace the strange and unfamiliar—in challenging and diverse texts as well as in the room. Students'

---

[16] Georg Simmel, "The Stranger," in *The Sociology of Georg Simmel*, trans. Kurt Wolff (New York: Free Press, 1950), 402–8.

[17] Kwame Anthony Appiah, *Cosmopolitanism: Ethics in a World of Strangers* (New York: Norton, 2006), 98.

un-become strangers to each other and at the same time might become less familiar to themselves.

When we approach reading as a platform to explore our responsibilities to others, our pedagogy should highlight, in the words of theologian Willie James Jennings, the ways that "education that aims at the good" is transformed through the gathering of strangers.[18] Jennings describes the crowd gathered to hear Jesus teach, a crowd that includes "people who would not under normal circumstances ever want to be near each other, never ever touching flesh to flesh. . . . The crowd is the beginning of a joining that was intended to do deep pedagogical work."[19] If we consider our classrooms as inspired spaces for "deep pedagogical work," the crowds of strangers who might never be gathered together otherwise are cause for an intentional pedagogy of transformation that educates for the "good." An education that orients us toward mutuality accounts for the strangers seated beside us as well as those beyond our immediate reach.

The call to the classroom, and the collective act of reading together, is an invitation to act justly to each other. Theologian Paul Wadell writes that "justice does not create a bond between us and others; it recognizes and honors a bond that is already there."[20] If we think of reading with strangers as part honoring a bond between us, then we can focus on two key aspects of justice: "an abiding quality of character and a principle of action."[21] Teaching students that their collective readings can foster a more just relationship to each other—one that already exists but can be made explicit—positions reading as a gateway for response to the world. Introducing reading as an avenue to understand, support, and contribute to our common flourishing might be the way students start to see such work as relevant but also necessary.

Reading is strange: barriers

When we invite students to read any text at all, we are inviting them into what is often a strange and confusing experience. Many students in contemporary

---

[18] Willie James Jennings, *After Whiteness: An Education in Belonging*, Theological Education between the Times (Grand Rapids, MI: William Eerdmans, 2020), 13.

[19] Jennings, *After Whiteness*, 13.

[20] Paul J. Wadell, *Becoming Friends: Worship, Justice, and the Practice of Christian Friendship* (Grand Rapids, MI: Brazos Press), 239.

[21] Wadell, *Becoming Friends*, 240.

classrooms have had very little exposure to reading extended narratives and annotating texts, to say nothing of handling the physical object of the book.[22] Furthermore, the skills we often ask for in the reading experience are demanding and difficult, expecting students to practice careful analysis alongside reflection and critical thinking.

There are also significant barriers to student engagement with common reading, namely a time famine due to obligations to family or support networks, increasing work hours, or general "busyness." We know well the ways that the classroom and the text can be exhausting and alienating—because of various life circumstances, learning differences, interests, and even space and time. Thus, it is necessary to name the real challenges posed both by reading with strangers and by reading texts that seem strange to us. It is important that educators lead conversations that recognize the varied ways that students feel alienated by the text, feel set apart from the group in discussion, and experience self-doubt about one's beliefs or identity through the reading experience.

Notably, the ways reading and interpretation have been presented as particular cultural capital, part of what Pierre Bourdieu would describe as a person's "habitus," remind us that reading has historically been associated with elitism and specialized knowledge.[23] "Reading" (a term used interchangeably for "education" and then in turn for "civilization") signifies status, leisure, and intellectual work, which have not been accessible or valued in many people's worldviews.[24] Establishing common ground between readers in the classroom means a willingness on the part of educators to bridge the divide between amateur and scholarly ways of reading, starting from a position not of "correcting" but of "listening."[25] We certainly want to invite students into the depth and breadth of disciplinary knowledge and interpretive modes, as well as explore the power of negotiating and creating

[22] Joanne E. Myers writes beautifully of how her students decenter themselves when they handle archival materials and the physical object of the book, understanding their purpose as readers and thinkers through new lenses in "Encountering the Archive," in Johnson and VanLaningham, eds., *Cultivating Vocation through Literary Studies*, 215–32.

[23] Pierre Bourdieu, *Distinction* (Cambridge, MA: Harvard University Press, 1984). See also John Guillory's *Cultural Capital: The Problem of Literary Canon Formation* (Chicago: University of Chicago Press, 1993).

[24] Michael Bérubé, Hester Blum, Christopher Castiglia, and Julia Spicher Kasdorf write of the elitism of the "reading class" in "Community Reading and Social Imagination," *PMLA* 125, no. 2 (March 2010): 421, https://doi.org/10.1632/pmla.2010.125.2.418.

[25] Kathleen Fitzpatrick, *Generous Thinking: A Radical Approach to Saving the University* (Baltimore: Johns Hopkins University Press, 2019), 102.

meaning together through a common text.[26] Yet, we also ought to note that students are experiencing defamiliarizing moments in the process—seeing the self in a new (strange) way while potentially coming to see the stranger as more familiar than before. The shared reading experience lays bare all sorts of values and preconceptions for students to navigate, difficulties that can be addressed as part of the vocational reflection of what it means to be a student called to read.

In addition, we must recognize that the reality of who identifies as a stranger in college classrooms, and in the public sphere, is certainly marked by the dominant White, heteronormative, patriarchal systems of thought and systems of learning. Accommodating varied experiences and viewpoints is certainly more emotionally, mentally, and physically taxing for some than others. As Jennings notes:

> Many students of color arrive at our institutions friendship-fatigued and rightly suspicious of an educational journey that promises more burden. They aim for friendship, but they are skeptical of the depth it can reach, not because of time or space but because of a habit of mind born of the plantation that centers the feelings and needs of white bodies and turns such students of color into service providers in a search of shared knowledge.[27]

The "habit of mind born of the plantation" can replicate its systemic effects in the classroom dynamics, interpretive approaches, and ways of understanding what is "common" and what is "good." We need to challenge pedagogies that assume students will find common ground without first understanding what creates the experiences that separate and alienate them. Instead, approaching reading together by challenging plantation mindsets—as we encounter them in the texts as well as in class discussion—is a fundamental step in our classrooms. Furthermore, acknowledging the fatigue and traumas repeatedly endured by some students, and the institutional and ideological structures that preserve such disparities, is our collective reading responsibility.

All aspects of reading across a college campus—in the texts, in discussions, in assignments, in public dialogue—should not seek to achieve a homogeneous or self-affirming sense of the world but listen to and understand a

---

[26] See Charles Mathewes's discussion of formation through the study of and the experience of the disciplines in chapter 13 of this volume.

[27] Jennings, *After Whiteness*, 13.

broader range of people with whom we share life. Our choices of texts and pedagogies ought to attend to destructive structures that alienate and dehumanize, the complex realities that unfairly promote one group's flourishing on the shoulders of others. Reading together has the paradoxical capacity to fracture a sense of belonging and knowing while also providing the tools to build new approaches to meaning and purpose. Through this common work, students build a capacity to understand the stranger beside them and create a ritual of thinking about problems together. Students not only practice interpretation but also negotiate competing interpretations, arriving at shared understandings and even solutions and actions.[28]

Educators know too well how hard it is to watch students refuse to read. We see them come to class unprepared, stalwart in ambivalence, unconvinced of the relevance of the material or the work of interpretation. The continued devaluing of the humanities and the liberal arts has suggested that reading is insignificant to success in a market economy and many students see it as either irrelevant or difficult. They may carry embarrassment of not understanding the assignment and lack the emotional or reasoning capacity to respond as we might hope. Part of our task as educators, then, is to rewrite this script. This may involve emphasizing the ways texts can help us appreciate suffering and ambiguity, or how narrative form illustrates the ways our stories are always bound by the stories of others.[29] It may involve moving toward a greater acceptance of the various emotional responses to reading (and resisting what digital humanities scholar Kathleen Fitzpatrick names as an overtly masculinist casting of "objective" readings as "strong").[30] It also means that we share very candidly with students a belief that reading has the possibility to transform us. I do not wish to suggest that naïve or unchallenged reading be a goal but rather that if we aim to cultivate a community consciousness through reading, then we ought to start by showing students how reading with strangers is a way to participate in that process. Making the process as accessible and equitable as possible is part of our responsibility in realizing that reading is difficult for all sorts of reasons while continuing to assign difficult texts and challenge students to read with a critical eye.

I recently experienced a sequence of class sessions in which students were underprepared, neither reading the texts nor bringing the books to class.

---

[28] See David Timmerman's reflections on discussion and deliberation in chapter 9 of this volume.
[29] See *Cultivating Vocation in Literary Studies*, ed. Johnson and VanLaningham, for the various approaches literary studies as a field offers to explore vocation with students.
[30] Fitzpatrick, *Generous Thinking*, 107.

Eventually, I pivoted to asking them to read *in* class, choosing one quote from the assigned reading (they could share the books that were brought to class) and then pairing it with a short additional reading that I distributed. As a next step, I asked them to prepare a slide for presentation, working in small groups. This allowed students to practice their vocations as responsible to others in the class setting: closely reading the assigned text, connecting it to another set of ideas in the short excerpts, and then creating a "reading" of the two for presentation to others. I saw students un-learn patterns of disengagement and attempt to apply and practice new forms of being, as students, in the classroom. When these practices are applied to significant literary texts (such as Alice Walker's "Everyday Use" or Virginia Woolf's *A Room of One's Own*) or similarly important topics such as reparations or immigration reform, it becomes clearer to students why their reading matters and what it takes to be responsible to others through that interpretive work.

As Marge Piercy says in her poem "To Be of Use:" "The work of the world is common as mud."[31] And so too is the work of reading with students, consistently creating the opportunities to embrace the vocation of reader. Even a class reading of Piercy's poem can help students understand that common and collaborative work matters, creating "the common rhythm" for "the thing worth doing."[32] When we embody this in the classroom, we are preparing students— those who read and those who won't—for shared life with others.

Reading "with and against"

Reading together creates a "point of entry" for connection building.[33] The point of entry leads to other locus points, what student development theorist George Kuh calls "pathways to engagement,"[34] for students to learn the strategies of reading together. The skills regularly attributed to common reading programs on college campuses—analysis and inquiry, appreciating diverse viewpoints, and applying the material to life—make reading the exact

---

[31] Marge Piercy, "To Be of Use," in *Circle on the Water* (New York: Knopf, 1982).

[32] Piercy, "To Be of Use."

[33] Appiah, *Cosmopolitism*, 97.

[34] Quoted in Jodi Levine Laufgraben, *Common Reading Programs: Going Beyond the Book*, Monograph No. 44 (Columbia: University of South Carolina, National Resource Center for the First Year Experience and Students in Transition, 2006), 6.

point of entry for considering what one's responsibilities are to the strangers in the seats next to us and to those we meet along the way.[35]

The interpretive work of reading—considering various viewpoints and experiences—invites us to complicate the stranger and move beyond stereotype, caricature, and assumption. Teaching students to do this work is imperative if we want to see the acts of reading writ large in other spheres of experience. David Bartholomae and Anthony Petrosky emphasized such possibilities in their groundbreaking composition text *Ways of Reading*,[36] which directs students to read "with the grain" and "against the grain" of difficult and provocative texts. The theory of reading advanced in this approach positions students with the authority to respond to texts that are considered influential in public spheres while also remaining in a position of humility as a reader.[37] Emboldening students to read this way involves first cultivating a readerly identity of an observer and even friend. Reading with the grain means to sympathize with the writer's aim, to attempt to trace the nuance of argument and example, even if we only understand fragments of it. As part of this strategy of reading, we might introduce the notion of what it means to accompany the strangers in the text, what it means to see ourselves alongside them. A colleague shared scripts for students to use when beginning discussions of challenging texts, scripts that ask students to say first that the author is "right because . . . ," which is certainly necessary in classrooms where marginalized and/or nonnormative voices are studied by majority students.[38] In this way, students learn to vocalize viewpoints that may be new or challenging to their worldviews. Petrosky and Bartholomae describe it as reading "generously."[39]

Equally necessary is teaching critical inquiry, an active role that challenges and questions, as significant to our responsibility to others. This is a moment of assuming agency as a reader, reading against the grain. For Bartholomae and Petrosky, this means to "refine it, to extend it, to put it to the test."[40]

---

[35] For an extended overview of the various goals of common reading and community reading programs, see Laufgraben's *Common Reading Programs.*

[36] See David Bartholomae and Anthony Petrosky, *Ways of Reading: An Anthology for Writers* (Boston: Bedford/St. Martins). Initially published in 2002, it is now in its twelfth edition (2019). For a similar argument for a reading approach "of openness, of learning, of listening" see Fitzpatrick's *Generous Thinking,* 87.

[37] Readings have included works by Michel Foucault, Gloria Anzaldúa, Paulo Friere, Mary Louise Pratt, and Edward Said, among others.

[38] Deanna Thompson shared this in a conversation in January 2021, in which she explained that in a course on Contemporary African American Religious Thought, she uses these phrases: "Malcolm is right because . . . , Howard Thurman is right because. . . ."

[39] Bartholomae and Petrosky, *Ways of Reading,* 9.

[40] Bartholomae and Petrosky, *Ways of Reading,* 10.

Putting ideas to the test is exactly what we do in our civic, political, spiritual, and intellectual lives, attempts to see ourselves enmeshed in causes and communities. It also accentuates alienation, the disenfranchised, and difference. Reading against the grain, individually and collectively, reckons with reality and makes possible a shifting of our sense of purpose and meaning. Leveraging the language of reading both "with and against" is helpful when we work with students to cultivate a common good. We are not preparing for lives of simply being with *or* positioned against others; we are preparing for lives that ask us to be with so as to understand, and to test structures and experiences so that we can collectively flourish.

Common readings

What we read matters in the sense that the range of voices offers a window to the world beyond the college experience. Investigating what gets to be a common read—a part of a canon of texts, be they scriptural, literary, or any other disciplinary category—brings forward important considerations. In the history of literary studies, for example, the canon was once the protected field of the classics, literature that certainly has aesthetic and even moral significance but is largely the province of White, educated men. For decades, scholars have tried to expand, reframe, and revise the canon, a process of democratizing and diversifying the texts published, anthologized, and taught. This is significant. Yet, literary critic John Guillory points to the ways educators put too much emphasis on common readings on a course syllabus, warning us that "changing the syllabus" does not mean "in any *immediate* sense changing the world; what is required now is an analysis of the institutional location and mediation of such imaginary structures as the canon."[41]

We should then think about how to investigate the root causes and the larger structures that produced the most recent versions of the canon in the first place. As part of this analysis, we can consider our own institutional canons. A college's canon might include historical and social documents—readings that range from the founders' intentions for the school or documents related to the cultural or spiritual traditions of the place. Naming the canon of the place would involve naming Indigenous stories and land

---

[41] John Guillory, *Cultural Capital: The Problem of Literary Canon Formation* (Chicago: University of Chicago Press, 1993), 37.

acknowledgments or reckoning with the role the institution has played in a slave-owning past. Thus, when we introduce students to "common readings," we might ask how it builds upon and necessarily challenges the notion of what counts as common and canonized in our culture and on our campuses.

Further, common digital and social media spaces have the capacity to build empathy but also to polarize. As we know from recent national and global events, news narratives and information frameworks can advance dangerous ideologies that threaten collective well-being. Part of the reader's responsibility is to consider how to respond to the wide availability of information from media platforms, purposefully diversifying the sources that shape us while being critically mindful of the origins of such sources. This is where we guide students from syllabus to institution, from institutions to the world.

As we continue to imagine different canons and common texts, we can look to oral cultural traditions that "conceptualize and verbalize all their knowledge with more or less close reference to the human lifeworld, assimilating the alien, objective world to the more immediate, familiar interaction of human beings."[42] The sharing of, and listening to, oral knowledge and stories emphasizes the goals of the common reading, including building empathy and relating material to the lived experience. Further, it can be a bridge to the wisdom and education of our families, communities, and networks, which offer different texts for consideration. Bridging the gaps between familial stories and a text for a first-year seminar, between cultural traditions and the canon of a discipline, means that we might start to see how reading a common text together helps students work toward a more integrated understanding of vocational identity.[43]

Finally, as we consider the composition of syllabi, curricula, and campus common texts, we ought to weigh our work within the cultural threat of silencing, restriction, and censure. Late in the nineteenth century, the editor at *Harper's* told novelist Thomas Hardy that the magazine would include "nothing which could not be read aloud in any family circle."[44] In response,

[42] Walter Ong, *Orality and Literacy: The Technologizing of the Word* (New York: Routledge 1982), 42.

[43] See, for example, Richard Rodriguez's *The Hunger of Memory: The Education of Richard Rodriguez* (New York: Bantam, 1983), in which he articulates the gulf between him and his family as a result of his education. Patrick Reyes highlights the ways that the knowledge in homes and communities could be better leveraged to help "generate new knowledges" in *The Purpose Gap: Empowering Communities of Color to Find Meaning and Thrive* (Louisville, KY: Westminster John Knox, 2021), 129.

[44] Linda K. Hughes and Michael Lund, *The Victorian Serial* (Charlottesville: University of Virginia Press, 1991), 231.

Hardy and many other authors had to abridge or alter manuscripts according to social norms.[45] A century later, in her Nobel lecture, writer Toni Morrison poses the question: "But who does not know of literature banned because it is interrogative; discredited because it is critical; erased because alternate? And how many are outraged by the thought of a self-ravaged tongue?"[46] Given the recent surge in banning of books and intervention in school curricula, asking students to consider what is available and why that is, followed by inquiry into how it affects the way they live their lives and will live in the future, is a vital step to claiming responsibility for the common good.[47]

Reading as response

As part of identifying the complexities that reading calls us to, we can also examine how "narrative situations create an immediacy and force, framing relations of provocation, call, and response."[48] Such language of reciprocity frames reading as a tie that links the reader to the multiple points of view and experience, enacted within the narrative and outside of it. How does this "narrative situation" cultivate a reader's identity, and how does that identity relate to a student's vocational identity? How can the relationship between the "provocation, call, and response" of reading encourage students to best hear the call to another's well-being?

Take, for example, what students might learn in a class in which we study the definition of monstrosity (and various iterations of the stranger), largely through an examination of Mary Shelley's *Frankenstein*. When placed next to Victor LaVelle's graphic novel *Destroyer*, a response to Shelley's novel that imagines the scientist as a Black woman and her life experience—inclusive of sexist and racist barriers that inhibit her career as well as her teenage son being killed in an act of police violence—we can invite students to name the

---

[45] Hughes and Lund, *The Victorian Serial*, 231–32.

[46] Toni Morrison, "Nobel Lecture," December 7, 1993, https://www.nobelprize.org/prizes/literat ure/1993/morrison/lecture/.

[47] While banning books and various forms of censorship of course texts is not a new issue or debate in American education, it has seen a recent surge in response to critical race theory and sexual identity politics. See, for example, Elizabeth A. Harris and Alexandra Alter, "Book Ban Efforts Spread across U.S.," *New York Times*, January 30, 2022, https://www.nytimes.com/2022/01/30/books/book-ban-us-schools.html, and Josh Moody, "How K-12 Book Bans Affect Higher Education," *Inside Higher Ed*, February 10, 2022, https://www.insidehighered.com/news/2022/02/10/how-k-12-book-bans-affect-higher-education?v2.

[48] Newton, *Ways of Reading*, 13.

responsibilities that Shelley and LaVelle ask us to consider. Specifically, we are asked to work against institutional structures that destroy, literally, the possibility of collective flourishing. We grapple with applications of science and artificial intelligence, with the dangers of human power, and with understanding those whom we despise. We see ourselves in the characters, and in our classmates' responses, wrestling with what the narrative situations ask of us. The various student responses illuminate the vocational work of reading together, moving the conversation from literary content to concern for others. The texts provoke and call students to respond to significant and complex experiences—of the strangers represented in the texts but also to those sharing in the class discussion.

Moreover, the textual voices can invite sympathy from the reader at various points. In Amanda Anderson's reading of Charles Dickens's *Bleak House*, she notes that when we read about the young street sweeper character Jo, "the passage thus works to insist on common humanity even as it shows extreme social marginality."[49] Anderson continues:

> It is also worth noting that the narrator is asking the reader, through language, to consider the situation of those who cannot read the very book he is writing, a book that includes a complex linguistic representation of the illiterate condition. The narrator is thus asking the reader to recognize the great gulf between those who can read and those who cannot, and the even greater gulf between those who can read a complex narrative like *Bleak House* and those who cannot read at all.[50]

Anderson's argument emphasizes the ethical consequences of reading, noting how the novel invites the reader to consider the experiences of others across the notable "great gulf." Reading assumes we are bound to the others within narrative but also to those around us, and therefore, we must reckon with such a wide gap. This passage, Anderson remarks, "forces the reader to break out of the comfort of being moved by represented scenes of sympathy between characters in the novel and instead to contemplate the effects of reading about the lives of those who are profoundly socially marginalized."[51] Such effects are what Newton would describe as "blurred boundaries between reading people and reading plots, between the separate domains of

[49] Amanda Anderson, *Bleak Liberalism* (Chicago: University of Chicago Press, 2016), 55.
[50] Anderson, *Bleak Liberalism*, 55.
[51] Anderson, *Bleak Liberalism*, 55.

life and story."[52] As ethical readers, we pause to consider the actions required of us by this blurring—what does it mean to read (with) strangers if we only sympathize but do nothing to mitigate the situations we encounter through reading?

At this point in a course, we can ask students to identify the ties that bind us to others, starting with the text and classroom but certainly looking beyond it. We can design assignments that directly address that "gulf" and move us not only to sympathy but also to action. I invite students' honest responses to the textual conflicts: the character's choice to leave their family, the silencing of certain voices, the tearing down of a social institution. Would you have done it? What is hard about it? Why should we care about it? Such questions can sometimes allow students to identify as the stranger or feel less like the stranger. As students address injustice, extend compassion, or stand in solidarity through the reading experience, they are also stepping forward to share the responsibility of reading. Responding to the textual "gulfs" allows them repeatedly to return to the complex topics, to the pain and beauty within the text, to the human capacity for growth and transformation in the fractures of lived experience. That is the kind of reading that can build a capacity to contribute to the common good.

Reading communities

The bridge between campus and community here is significant, as we have noted that the skills of reading with strangers are those that connect our vocations to other collaborative, shared spaces and experiences of common life. Reading with others is a membership in a class, digital environments, or public space. True membership, however, means that we not only feel a sense of belonging and empowerment to contribute but also enable others to thrive. Reading can foster this sort of participation as part of vocational identity in its many intersecting communities.[53]

Entry into the university is often synonymous with the "common read," which gathers students, normally in the first year, to study and discuss a text. Sometimes there are cocurricular programs involving the entire campus;

---

[52] Anderson, *Bleak Liberalism*, 14.
[53] For an example of how the practice of reading can be used to facilitate calling in community life, see Christopher C. Smith's *Reading for the Common Good: How Books Help Our Churches and Neighborhoods Flourish* (Downers Grove, IL: IVP Press, 2016).

often the goal is to build a common language around an important topic. Community programs—hosted by public libraries or "big read" initiatives programs—also promote the gathering of citizens for discussion and idea exchange.[54] Sometimes the two programs intersect, bringing town and gown together.[55]

The practice of reading also creates what cultural theorist Benedict Anderson describes as an "imagined community," contributing to the development of shared, communal identities (such as national identities), which he describes "as a deep, horizontal comradeship."[56] Anderson's theory of imagined community is based, in part, on the rise of the newspaper and its mass consumption. The ritual of reading daily news is akin to a religious ritual—confident in millions of others doing the same—whose identities remain unknown to us.[57] The common text, and reading in concert with strangers, leads to an affirmation of communal identity even if it is "community in anonymity."[58]

The ritual of reading to build this sort of invented community and new forms of selfhood has only expanded in our digital, multitextual world in which we connect with others through digitized platforms and programs, building up "followers" and "friends" who connect via shared textual content. Literacy scholar Maryanne Wolf posits that the uninterrupted access to digital information, when coupled with a lack of significant formation in careful, deep-reading skills, also means that while we are reading together, what and how we read can render all of us vulnerable to false notions of authentic community and friendship.[59]

To facilitate participation in community through reading, I regularly employ "roundtable" days in which we move desks to simulate a boardroom-style table around which we all sit in close proximity. The roundtable idea draws from the seminar, which William Clark suggests "is a curious institution, outward-looking and inward-focused, private and public, formal and

[54] See for example the "Big Read" initiative of the National Endowment for the Arts at https://www.arts.gov/initiatives/nea-big-read or the University of Wisconsin's "Go Big Read" program, which engages "the campus community and beyond in a shared, academically focused reading experience," at https://gobigread.wisc.edu/archive/.

[55] See Bérubé et al., "Community Reading and Social Imagination."

[56] Benedict Anderson, *Imagined Communities: Reflections on the Origin and Spread of Nationalism*, rev. and extended ed. (New York: Verso, 1991), 7.

[57] Anderson, *Imagined Communities*, 35.

[58] Anderson, *Imagined Communities*, 36.

[59] Maryanne Wolf, *Reader, Come Home: The Reading Brain in a Digital World* (New York: Harper, 2018), 105–27.

informal."[60] Student discussion leaders propose passages to discuss, offer initial interpretations, and invite additional responses. On other roundtable days, students prepare short examples (written) to share how the text relates to a piece of contemporary life. We also collectively interpret objects or images or media that students bring that relate to our course texts. The physical form of the roundtable invites students into the embodiment of a collective. The aim is accessible participation and contribution. As literary scholar Caroline Levine suggests, when "organized around thought-provoking questions, the seminar room affords acts of collective, open-ended thinking that then have the potential to unsettle conventional, rigid social and conceptual forms."[61]

Finally, in various literature courses, I use serialized reading over the course of the semester to build a classroom community around a common narrative thread. Every Friday throughout the semester, for example, we discuss an installment from a serialized novel, an experience that the students find familiar from their digital streaming platforms but also strange—in the "waiting" to read the next "episode" until the following week.[62] The reading of the serial and the sitting at the roundtable become symbols of and avenues toward a shared experience. The strangers in the text and around the table become less strange to everyone as the course progresses.

These patterns of collective reading help students intervene in their individual ponderings and to puzzle out together what might be a better reading, an alternative reading, a thicker reading. Our students see themselves embedded in various groups, ranging from teams to clubs to workplaces to families, but likely don't have the tools to move outside of these groups readily. As we show them how to be both generous and skeptical readers, we can offer new iterations of how reading together can inspire movement toward others, an encounter with strangers in various communities. Through reading, Fitzpatrick suggests, "scholars, students, book club members, and casual readers—have the potential to come into a more generous relationship

---

[60] William Clark, "On the Dialectical Origins of the Research Seminar," *History of Science* 27, no. 2 (June 1989): 111–54, https://doi.org/10.1177/007327538902700201. While beyond the scope of this chapter, Clark's positioning of the seminar as dialectical also offers a sense of how the common good can be discovered through the exchange and tension between self and community.

[61] Caroline Levine, *Forms: Whole, Rhythm, Hierarchy, Network* (Princeton, NJ: Princeton University Press, 2015), 47.

[62] Hughes and Lund discuss the ways that serialized reading "allows modern students to recover the excitement, suspense, and involvement that characterized so much of the nineteenth-century literary experience" and that such reading together cultivates a "sense of community" in *The Victorian Serial*, 276. I have also used this format to teach contemporary novels with similar results.

with the world."[63] Indeed, our hope as educators is that reading with strangers helps students approach the uncommon, the different, and the strange as significant and vital to the common good.[64]

From strangers to friends: *why* we read

At the end of the semester, and certainly after a sequence of semesters, we might say that we are all no longer strangers, having spent enough time with common readings, in common spaces, collectively learning. How do we help students see that this experience, in all of its failures and highlights, can help them with the next piece of engagement and purpose?

One way is to consistently suggest that reading with strangers is also a process of befriending, to share pieces of our lives, however vulnerable or broken those may be. This is an affirmation of what it means to honor others, to seek justice on their behalf, to cherish connectivity. It is about being responsible to strangers throughout our life.[65] It continues to value the other's difference. It is a way of un-becoming strangers while still prizing the strange.

When it comes to thinking about ourselves in relation to others, political scientist Danielle Allen, in her book *Talking to Strangers*, frames our connections through the lens of friendship, which is "not an emotion, but a practice, a set of hard-won, complicated habits that are used to bridge trouble, difficulty, and differences of personality, experience, and aspiration."[66] So too with the ways we teach and approach reading common texts together, through the practices and habits that help us bridge differences. She continues: "Friends have a *shared* life—not a common nor an identical life—only one with common events, climates, built-environments, fixation of the imagination, and social structures."[67] We would do well to emphasize the shared life of a college classroom and campus as not common or identical, but a life that is a web of interdependence.

---

[63] Fitzpatrick, *Generous Thinking*, 90.

[64] See chapter 6 by Geoffrey W. Bateman for a discussion of the uncommon as valuable for collective well-being.

[65] See Martin Holt Dotterweich's reflections about how we remember others as part of our call to the common good in chapter 12 of this volume.

[66] Danielle S. Allen, *Talking to Strangers: Anxieties of Citizenship since* Brown v. Board of Education (Chicago: University of Chicago Press, 2004), xxi.

[67] Allen, *Talking to Strangers*, xxi–xxii.

Sometimes it is about allowing the text to both show and tell how we can build a common good. One such avenue to talk about collective well-being is Anne Lamott's spiritual memoir *Travelling Mercies: Some Thoughts on Faith*, specifically the chapter entitled "Barn Raising." Teaching the chapter in the upper Midwest, where barn raisings are still part of many communities, is recognizable to some of my students but completely foreign to others. As we discuss the chapter, we cover all aspects of barn raising: building construction, community support, rural and urban experience, people coming together for a common cause. Lamott's own barn raising—surrounding dear friends whose child has a terminal illness with practical, emotional, and spiritual support—becomes a metaphor all of the students can understand and adopt.[68] When students air these observations with strangers in class, inevitably the demarcations of in-groups and out-groups within the classroom will shift if for no other reason than they now share a common identity (readers of *Travelling Mercies*) and a common purpose (to understand what it means for strangers to show up for each other in the book, in the classroom, and in our communities).

Our vocation as readers is to care about the ideas of the other, to value the different, and to honor the bonds between us. This practice of reading with strangers enriches the potential of "people meeting" through encounters with texts and each other. As students realize their call to the task of interpretive work, they begin to see that they are connected to strangers and communities beyond their immediate circles. It is in this connectivity that they become less strange to each other, so that they might raise barns or build communities, become neighbors or even friends, and be advocates of the strange and for the stranger, in our common life.

---

[68] Anne Lamott, *Travelling Mercies: Some Thoughts on Faith* (New York: Pantheon, 1999).

10

A Case for Compassionate Pedagogy

Caring for the Public's Health, Cultivating Sustainable Vocations

Meghan M. Slining

In a class session with senior public health students, a generally quiet student asked a piercing question: "Knowing everything you know about the suffering in the world, how do you keep going? When I learned about climate change and realized how far gone we are and how little we can really do, I became hopeless." Through watery eyes and a shaky voice, the student continued, "How do you remain hopeful?" Others nodded in agreement while another fervently shot their hand into the air. "Yes. I *need* you to answer this. I am already getting cynical and the overwhelm I feel is *debilitating*." I took a deep breath and invited the class to do the same. Following a long pause, I said, "Thank you for your questions. I care deeply about your inquiry and I appreciate your vulnerability in sharing and asking. I will attempt to respond with comparable vulnerability." In my response, I tried to articulate and model compassion in action. I shared some of my crucible moments where I sat with the suffering of others and understood our interdependence. I shared the importance of acknowledging and becoming intimately familiar with my own suffering, in order to know how to act skillfully to alleviate others' suffering and to attend to our communal responsibilities. And I shared how I deliberately work to stay grounded and to keep my heart open. I attempted to model compassionate pedagogy.

College and university educators know that we need people caring for and protecting the common good. Many of our students feel called to do so, through work such as medicine, public health, ministry, social work, or education. Significant to note is that those working for the common good have some of the highest rates of burnout of all professions. Therefore, we must ask, how can we equip and prepare students to live their vocations sustainably as they care for the common good?

Meghan M. Slining, *A Case for Compassionate Pedagogy* In: *Called Beyond Our Selves*. Edited by: Erin VanLaningham, Oxford University Press. © Oxford University Press 2024. DOI: 10.1093/oso/9780197691915.003.0011

In this chapter, I explore how those who find meaning and purpose in caring for the common good often feel a pronounced sense of responsibility to their work and experience some of the highest rates of burnout among professions. I highlight how public health broadens our understanding of the common good, acknowledging and providing empirical evidence of interdependence. I extend the lessons of interdependence from public health to provide a counterpoint to the dominant paradigms of individualism and meritocracy and increasing commoditization of higher education. I argue that discerning a call to care for the common good needs to be tended mindfully and that educators have an important role to play in preparing students (and ourselves) to do so. In offering a case study of compassionate pedagogy, I show how such an approach can mutually transform educators and students, preparing both for sustainable vocational responsiveness.

Public health and the common good

Public health is the science and art of protecting and improving the health of all people and their communities.[1] The field is dedicated to caring for and protecting the common good. Public health broadens our understanding of the common good, highlighting *interdependence*. As core public health values, interdependence and solidarity acknowledge that "the health of every individual is linked to the health of every other individual within the human community, to other living creatures, and to the integrity and functioning of environmental ecosystems."[2]

Public health is dedicated to protecting the health of *all*, with special attention to those who have been marginalized. Social justice is at the heart of public health[3] and "requires us to recognize the specific disadvantages that face members of social groups who are subject to systematic discrimination and reduced power."[4] Decades of research demonstrate differences in health

---

[1] "What Is Public Health?," Centers for Disease Control Foundation, accessed October 30, 2022, https://www.cdcfoundation.org/what-public-health.

[2] American Public Health Association, "Public Health Code of Ethics," Issue Brief 2019, https://www.apha.org/-/media/files/pdf/membergroups/ethics/code_of_ethics.ashx, 5.

[3] See, for example, R. R. Faden and M. Powers, "Health Inequities and Social Justice: The Moral Foundations of Public Health," *Bundesgesundheitsblatt Gesundheitsforschung Gesundheitsschutz* 51, no. 2 (2008): 151–57, https://doi.org/10.1007/s00103-008-0443-7; D. E. Beauchamp, "Public Health as Social Justice," *Inquiry* 13, no. 1 (1976): 3–14.

[4] Francoise Baylis, Nuala Kenny, and Susan Sherwin, "A Relational Account of Public Health Ethics," *Public Health Ethics* 1, no. 3 (2008): 204, https://doi.org/10.1093/phe/phn025.

status between groups, arising from social conditions.[5] A public health approach to the common good acknowledges how hierarchies of power have created disparities in health outcomes and set out to take action to ensure that *all* can be safe and healthy.

Public health extends concern beyond individuals to communities and populations. Bioethicist Francoise Baylis and colleagues highlight the problem of focusing on the rights and interests of individuals, citing Wendy Rogers's assertion that it "allows researchers and politicians alike to ignore the social and political context, leading to increased risks of ill health."[6] In contrast to market justice, which emphasizes individual responsibility and minimal collective obligation, public health, rooted in social justice, is fundamentally about community and "shared human interests in survival, safety, and security (the common good)."[7] Drawing upon insights from feminist relational theory, Baylis and colleagues describe a view of public health ethics with an orientation that is relational rather than individualistic: "Public health joins a few other key public goods (e.g., universal education, prevention of further contributions to climate change, avoidance of nuclear war) in helping us to appreciate the reality of our mutual interest in survival, safety and security on one hand, and our mutual vulnerability to disease, violence and death on the other."[8] Promoting our shared interests in health and minimizing our shared vulnerabilities to disease requires a communal approach.[9] Whether we like to acknowledge it or not, we are all interconnected.

Much discussion throughout the COVID-19 pandemic positioned individual and collective interests as oppositional or contradictory, undermining the ability to acknowledge the significance of interdependence. Arthur Kleinman, psychiatrist and medical anthropologist, writes:

> Perhaps it's useful to remain oblivious to this caring ethic in order to cling to the idealized image of the individual in society as a self-interested, autonomous agent. To recognize the centrality of care would be to shatter so many politically useful fictions: the self-made man, the self-sufficient

---

[5] Rachel Thornton, Crystal Glover, Crystal Cené, Deborah Glik, Jeffrey Henderson, and David Williams, "Evaluating Strategies for Reducing Health Disparities by Addressing the Social Determinants of Health," *Health Affairs* 35, no. 8 (2016): 1416–23, https://doi.org/10.1377/hlth aff.2015.1357.

[6] Baylis et al., "A Relational Account," 204.

[7] Baylis et al., "A Relational Account," 204.

[8] Baylis et al., "A Relational Account," 206.

[9] For an extended discussion of our connections through mutuality and membership, see chapter 3 of this volume by Christine Jeske.

pioneer, the rebel innovator, the superhero, the free agent unfettered by government, none of whom would actually exist outside the context of human interdependence.[10]

While the nature of public health requires an approach that is "public" rather than individualistic,[11] Kleinman highlights the significant challenge of recognizing that our individual flourishing is conditional on collective well-being.

Epidemiology provides empirical evidence that the health of strangers is inextricably linked. While the spread of infectious disease is a clear example of interdependence, strangers are also linked in their shared exposure to environmental and social conditions that harm health. The water crisis in Flint, Michigan, demonstrated how the health of strangers was similarly impacted by exposure to lead in their water and how the most severe impacts of public health problems are often felt by marginalized populations.[12] One of the biggest threats to public health today is climate change. Epidemiologic evidence demonstrates how rising temperatures, extreme weather, air quality, and increased vector-borne diseases all impact health and exacerbate health inequities.[13]

One tool that illustrates interdependence is the social-ecological model (SEM), a framework widely utilized in the design and implementation of public health interventions. The SEM highlights connectivity and the complex interplay between intrapersonal, interpersonal, community, and societal factors. Composed of concentric circles, the SEM illuminates the complex role played by context in the development of health problems as well as in the success or failure of attempts to address these problems. Public health professionals use this framework to identify factors at different levels that contribute to well-being and to develop corresponding approaches to disease prevention and health promotion at each level.

Public health broadens our understanding of the common good, acknowledging and providing empirical evidence of interdependence. As

---

[10] Arthur Kleinman, *The Soul of Care: The Moral Education of a Husband and a Doctor* (New York: Penguin Random House, 2020), 240.

[11] Baylis et al., "A Relational Account," 206.

[12] See Mona Hanna-Attisha, *What the Eyes Don't See: A Story of Crisis, Resistance, and Hope in an American City* (New York: One World, 2018).

[13] Linda Rudolph, Catherine Harrison, Laura Buckley, and Savannah North, *Climate Change, Health, and Equity: A Guide for Local Health Departments* (Oakland, CA, and Washington DC: Public Health Institute and American Public Health Association, 2018).

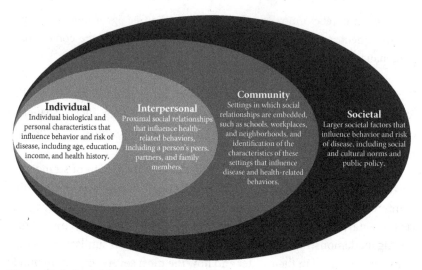

Figure 10.1 Social-Ecological Model (SEM)
Source: Adapted from the World Health Organization World Report on Violence and Health, 2002.

shown in Figure 10.1, individuals are embedded in, and influenced by, systems that are developed and sustained by others. The idealized image of the individual in society as a self-interested, autonomous agent is false. In recent years, the public health, medical, and animal health communities together have further expanded our understanding of interdependence with the concept of "One Health," recognizing the connection between the health of people, animals, and the environment.[14] Recognizing inequity in health and acting to protect and promote the health of all, public health is compassion in action.

Finding vocation in caring for the common good

Interdependence also shapes our understanding of vocation. As psychologist John Neafsey highlights, "Vocation is not only about 'me' and my personal fulfillment, but about 'us' and the common good."[15] Those called to care for

---

[14] "One Health," Centers for Disease Control, last modified October 19, 2022, https://www.cdc.gov/onehealth/index.html.
[15] John Neafsey, *A Sacred Voice Is Calling: Personal Vocation and Social Conscience* (Maryknoll, NY: Orbis Books, 2006), 1.

the common good are often called in response to circumstances they view as unjust; many students select a major seeking skills and knowledge to address such problems. Familiar examples include public health students eager to address health inequities, environmental science students motivated to have a positive impact on climate change, and education students moved to address growing education inequity. These vocational callings are not independent, individualistic drives but rather are commonly influenced and inspired by current context. Importantly, as students explore their aspirations to serve the common good, educators have an opportunity to support identity development and critical self-reflection.[16] For example, exploring the White savior complex could help to highlight self-interested and altruistic motivations that may actually be harmful or hinder effectiveness.[17] Acknowledging the complex and challenging work of effectively serving the common good, Keith Edwards's conceptual model of ally identity development is one helpful tool that educators can use to support critical self-reflection.[18]

Psychologists Bryan Dik and Ryan Duffy highlight that "living out a calling is not a solitary endeavor; it is inherently relational."[19] In addition to circumstances of time and place, relationships influence vocation, prompting students to consider pathways because a mentor noticed a particular strength or interest. Theologian William Cavanaugh states, "The call is mediated by professors and pastors and friends who let individuals know their lives belong, in some significant way, to others who expect and need the individual to give his or her talents in a particular way."[20] Duffy and Dik agree, calling attention to research that supports the importance and effectiveness of social support and modeling in helping people make good decisions about their careers.[21] Cavanaugh recognizes the powerful

---

[16] Keith Edwards, "Aspiring Social Justice Ally Identity Development: A Conceptual Model," *NASPA Journal* 43, no. 4 (2006): 39–60, https://doi.org/10.2202/1949-6605.1722; also see Keith Edwards, "Toolkit for 'Anatomy of an Ally,'" *Teaching Tolerance Magazine*, no. 53 (Summer 2016), https://www.learningforjustice.org/magazine/summer-2016/toolkit-for-anatomy-of-an-ally.

[17] Lilly Wilcox, "Reforming the Unreformable: The Peace Corps, Neocolonialism, and the White Savior Complex," *Undergraduate Journal of Global Citizenship* 4, no. 1 (2021), https://digitalcomm ons.fairfield.edu/jogc/vol4/iss1/5.

[18] Edwards, "Aspiring Social Justice Ally."

[19] Bryan Dik and Ryan Duffy, *Make Your Job a Calling: How the Psychology of Vocation Can Change Your Life at Work* (West Conshohocken, PA: Templeton Press, 2012), 195.

[20] William Cavanaugh, "Actually, You Can't Be Anything You Want (and It's a Good Thing, Too)," in *At This Place and In This Time: Vocation and Higher Education*, ed. David S. Cunningham (New York: Oxford University Press, 2016), 44.

[21] Dik and Duffy, *Make Your Job a Calling*, 193.

opportunity that universities provide for students to enter into community and to draw upon the wisdom and affirmation of others to respond to a call to care for the common good.[22]

Dik and Duffy, in their analysis of what characterizes a work calling, emphasize the importance of whether one's work "contributes (directly or indirectly) in some positive ways to 'the common good' or well-being of a society."[23] Other components of a work calling include the degree to which one's approach to work aligns with their broader framework of meaning and purpose in life, and the extent to which an individual perceives their motivation to come from an external source (whether a higher power, the needs of a society, or any other force external to the individual). They highlight consistent links between perceiving a calling and higher levels of career maturity, career commitment, work meaning, job satisfaction, life meaning, and life satisfaction.[24]

Yet having a calling can also be a stressful experience. In a recent article entitled "Called to Do Meaningful Work: A Blessing or a Curse?," Mark van Vuuren illustrates how the goals pursued by someone with a sense of calling are often hard to accomplish.[25] Deeply meaningful work can become a double-edged sword. A strong sense of calling can lead to broader meaning in work and life, but those with a strong sense of calling were also more likely to see their work as a moral duty, to sacrifice pay, personal time, and comfort for their work.[26] Those who find their vocation in caring for the common good often feel a responsibility to the importance of the work and care deeply. It is critical to consider the actual cost of one's calling. For those who feel called to care for the common good, vocational discernment needs to be tended to carefully.

---

[22] For further reflection on the university as a place for fostering the common good, and for formation during the college years and beyond, see this volume's chapter 11 by Robert J. Pampel and chapter 13 by Charles Mathewes, respectively.

[23] Ryan Duffy and Bryan Dik, "Research on Calling: What Have We Learned and Where Are We Going?," *Journal of Vocational Behavior* 83, no. 3 (2013): 429, https://doi.org/10.1016/j.jvb.2013.06.006.

[24] Duffy and Dik, "Research on Calling," 429.

[25] Mark van Vuuren, "Called to Do Meaningful Work: A Blessing or a Curse?," *Christian Higher Education* 16, nos. 1–2 (2017): 47–54, https://doi.org/10.1080/15363759.2017.1251245.

[26] J. Stuart Bunderson and Jeffery Thompson, "The Call of the Wild: Zookeepers, Callings, and the Double-Edged Sword of Deeply Meaningful Work," *Administrative Science Quarterly* 54, no. 1 (2009): 32–57, https://doi.org/10.2189/asqu.2009.54.1.32.

Caring for the common good and burnout

Because caring for the common good can have costs such as burnout, educators must consider burnout as we prepare students (and ourselves) for sustainable vocational responsiveness. Burnout was first described by psychologist Herbert Freudenberger in 1974 as "exhaustion resulting from excessive demands on energy, strength, or resources in the workplace, characterizing it by a set of symptoms including malaise, fatigue, frustration, cynicism, and inefficiency."[27] Initially discussed in reference to professions caring for the common good (health care, social work, and law enforcement), Freudenberger noted that burnout occurred primarily among "the dedicated and committed."[28] Psychologist Christina Maslach and colleagues complemented Freudenberger's work identifying three key dimensions of burnout: emotional exhaustion, depersonalization, and a diminished sense of personal accomplishment.[29] Burnout research portrayed an experience in which people lost both their energy and their sense of the value of their job. The loss of meaning was particularly distressing for those dedicated to serving others and the common good.[30]

The roots of burnout are complex and embedded within social, cultural, and economic developments in the 1960s and 1970s. The origins of the concept have been connected to the cohort of idealistic young people working to eradicate poverty who became frustrated by the systemic factors perpetuating poverty. Frustrated idealism became a defining quality of the burnout experience as service providers were discouraged by their diminished capacity to perform or to show compassion toward their recipients. Wilmar Schaufeli and colleagues importantly note:

> The experience of burnout was not merely an inconvenience or occupational hazard, but a devastating attack on their professional identity. They had chosen a career path of service, forsaking other options in the vibrant American economy of the era. Exhaustion on its own would not be so

[27] Thomas Reith, "Burnout in United States Healthcare Professionals: A Narrative Review," *Cureus* 10, no. 12 (2018): e3681, https://doi.org/10.7759/cureus.3681.

[28] Herbert Freudenberger, "Staff Burn-Out," *Journal of Social Issues* 30, no. 1 (1974): 159–65, https://doi.org/10.1111/j.1540-4560.1974.tb00706.x.

[29] Christina Maslach and Susan Jackson, "The Measurement of Experienced Burnout," *Journal of Organizational Behavior* 2, no. 2 (1981): 99–113, https://doi.org/10.1002/job.4030020205.

[30] Wilmar Shaufeli, Michael Leiter, and Christina Maslach, "Burnout: 35 Years of Research and Practice," *Career Development International* 14, no. 3 (2009): 204–20, https://doi.org/10.1108/136204 30910966406.

compelling: dedicated people may even derive fulfillment from exhausting themselves through exerting extraordinary effort for a deeply valued cause. The lack of compassion and diminished effectiveness implicit in the full burnout experience had a much more devastating impact on their identity.[31]

Jonathan Malesic expands our understanding of burnout, defining it as "the experience of being pulled between expectations and reality at work."[32] We burn out, Malesic suggests, because we believe work is the sure path to social, moral, and spiritual flourishing. Work cannot deliver what we want and therefore "the gap between our ideals and our on-the-job reality leads us to exhaustion, cynicism, and despair."[33]

Burnout in professions dedicated to caring for the common good has been on the rise for decades. Health care worker burnout in the United States is a public health crisis, with over 50 percent of physicians and 44 to 78 percent of medical students and residents experiencing burnout.[34] The COVID-19 pandemic brought acute attention to burnout, with an exodus of more than five hundred top health officials leaving their jobs in the nineteen months spanning March 2020 to September 2021,[35] and over 50 percent of K-12 educators reporting feeling burnout in a May 2021 survey.[36] In contrast, Cherniss and Kranz observed that burnout was nearly absent in monasteries and religious care centers. They argued that a "sense of collective identity" helps curb burnout because of "social commitment, a sense of communion, contact with the collective whole and shared strong values."[37] A logical extension of this study is that if we are unable to learn to think in collective ways, burnout will worsen.

Anthropologist and Buddhist teacher Roshi Joan Halifax emphasizes the important role of compassion in both preventing and responding to burnout. Halifax recounts her own experiences as well as those of caregivers, activists,

[31] Schaufeli et al., "Burnout," 204–20.

[32] Jonathan Malesic, *The End of Burnout: Why Work Drains Us and How to Build Better Lives* (Oakland: University of California Press, 2022), 2.

[33] Malesic, *The End of Burnout*, 3.

[34] Reith, "Burnout," e3681.

[35] Mike Baker and Danielle Ivory, "Why Public Health Faces a Crisis across the U.S.," *New York Times*, November 24, 2021, https://www.nytimes.com/2021/10/18/us/coronavirus-public-health.html.

[36] Rivka Liss-Levinson, *K-12 Public School Employee Views on Finances, Employment Outlook, and Safety Concerns Due to COVID-19* (Washington, DC: MissionSquare Research Institute, 2021), https://www.slge.org/wp-content/uploads/2021/09/k-12surveyfindings_sept21.pdf.

[37] Schaufeli et al., "Burnout," 207.

teachers, clinicians, and others serving the common good, responding to the question, "How is it that some people don't get beaten down by the world but are animated by the deep desire to serve?" She foregrounds the crucial role of compassion in understanding vocational identity and responding to burnout: "When we're at the edge, in danger of falling over the precipice into suffering, compassion is the most powerful means I know for keeping our feet firmly planted on the earth and our hearts wide open."[38]

Living one's vocation caring for the common good is a recognition of communal responsibilities. The weight of responsibility and structural realities can lead to overwhelm and burnout.[39] Training in compassion may facilitate sustainable care for the common good.

Compassion as vocation

While there are many definitions of compassion, psychologist Jennifer Goetz's definition, "the feeling that arises in witnessing another's suffering and that motivates a subsequent desire to help," is widely accepted.[40] Compassion is an action-oriented state that goes beyond empathy to include the impulse to *relieve* the suffering. Buddhist scholar Thupten Jinpa highlights that "compassion is a response to the inevitable reality of our human condition—our experiences of pain and sorrow . . . and offers the possibility of responding with understanding, patience and kindness."[41]

Part of vocational calling for those in helping professions is compassion—a recognition of suffering and a desire to help alleviate that suffering. Compassion can nurture the sense of commitment to care for another or the common good. In caring for the health of strangers, public health and medicine are expressions of compassionate action.

Unfortunately, the seeds of burnout are often sown before careers even begin. Jinpa highlights that "sometimes in the process of becoming

---

[38] Joan Halifax, *Standing at the Edge: Finding Freedom Where Fear and Courage Meet* (New York: Flatiron Books, 2018), 205.

[39] In chapter 2 of this volume, Deanna A. Thompson reflects on the importance of recognizing sadness and the effects of trauma and injustice in vocational discernment.

[40] Jennifer Goetz, Dacher Keltner, and Emiliana Simon-Thomas, "Compassion: An Evolutionary Analysis and Empirical Review," *Psychological Bulletin* 136, no. 3 (2010): 351, https://doi.org/10.1037/a0018807.

[41] Thupten Jinpa, *A Fearless Heart: How the Courage to Be Compassionate Can Transform Our Lives* (New York: Penguin Random House, 2015), xxiii.

'educated,' we slide into cynicism and lose touch with our caring heart."[42] Kleinman describes the negative impact that much of medical education has on the "calling to care," noting that training of doctors "undermines their social and existential skills at the same time that their technical knowledge and competencies are advancing."[43] Undergraduate education is an important opportunity to equip students with an understanding and appreciation of compassion as well as the skills for compassionate caring for self and others.

While compassion is a core feature of most spiritual and religious traditions and philosophers have examined the meaning and nature of compassion for millennia,[44] compassion is only recently an emerging focus of scientific research.[45] Research shows strong positive associations between compassion and mental health and emotional regulation[46] as well as associations with positive interpersonal and social relationships.[47] Compassion is also widely recognized as a hallmark of quality health care, appearing in the American Medical Association Code of Ethics.[48] The World Health Organization (WHO) also recognizes compassion as essential for quality health care and works with several ministries of health to develop compassionate health systems.[49] *Compassionomics* authors Stephen Trzeciak and Anthony Mazzarelli conclude that compassionate care enhances healing and immune function, leads to better clinical outcomes, and provides measurable benefits to patients, health care workers, and health systems.[50]

---

[42] Jinpa, *A Fearless Heart*, 115.

[43] Kleinman, *The Soul of Care*, 38.

[44] See Martha Nussbaum's *Upheavals of Thought: The Intelligence of Emotions* (Cambridge: Cambridge University Press, 2003) for a comprehensive review of ancient and modern Western philosophers' work on compassion.

[45] Goetz et al., "Compassion." See also Jason Kirby, Cassandra Tellegen, and Stanley Steindl, "A Meta-Analysis of Compassion-Based Interventions: Current State of Knowledge and Future Directions," *Behavior Therapy* 48, no. 6 (2017): 78–92, https://doi.org/10.1016/j.beth.2017.06.003; Shane Sinclair, Jill Norris, Shelagh McConnell, Harvey Chochinov, Thomas Hack, Neil Hagen, et al., "Compassion: A Scoping Review of the Healthcare Literature," *BMC Palliative Care* 15, no. 1 (2016): 6, https://doi.org/10.1186/s12904-016-0080-0.

[46] Angus MacBeth and Andrew Gumley, "Exploring Compassion: A Meta-Analysis of the Association between Self-Compassion and Psychopathology," *Clinical Psychology Review* 32, no. 6 (2012): 545–52, https://doi.org/10.1016/j.cpr.2012.06.003.

[47] Lisa Yarnell and Kristin Neff, "Self-Compassion, Interpersonal Conflict Resolutions, and Well-Being," *Self and Identity* 12, no. 2 (2013): 146–59, https://doi.org/10.1080/15298868.2011.649545.

[48] The first principle of the American Medical Association Code of Ethics states, "A physician shall be dedicated to providing competent medical care, with compassion and respect for human dignity and rights." https://www.ama-assn.org/about/publications-newsletters/ama-principles-medical-ethics.

[49] WHO, "Quality Health Services 2020," https://www.who.int/news-room/fact-sheets/detail/quality-health-services.

[50] Stephen Trzeciak and Anthony Mazzarelli, *Compassionomics* (Pensacola, FL: Stunder Group, 2019).

Higher education can draw from the growing body of research that compassion can be taught and cultivated.[51] At least six distinct compassion-based interventions[52] have been tested using randomized controlled trials (RCTs), considered the gold standard of quality in experimental research. A recent meta-analysis synthesized the impacts of these compassion-based interventions tested in 21 RCTs conducted across the globe, identifying statistically significant, moderate effects on compassion, self-compassion, mindfulness, depression, anxiety, psychological distress, and well-being.[53] Furthermore, evidence indicates a negative correlation between compassion and burnout in social work, nursing, pediatrics, palliative care, and chaplaincy,[54] suggesting that the cultivation of compassion may be protective against burnout. Additionally, emerging research suggests that training in compassion can prevent or lessen burnout among health care professionals and chaplains.[55] Given that compassion can be cultivated, it is critical that we equip students and ourselves with the skills of compassion. Drawing upon a framework from the field of public health, the remainder of this chapter proposes strategies for educators to support vocational sustainability through the lens of compassion.

[51] Jinpa, *A Fearless Heart*. See also Jennifer Mascaro, Sean Kelley, Alana Darcher, Lobsang Negi, Carol Worthman, Andrew Miller, et al., "Meditation Buffers Medical Student Compassion from the Deleterious Effects of Depression," *Journal of Positive Psychology* 13, no. 2 (2018): 133–42, https://doi.org/10.1080/17439760.2016.1233348.

[52] Compassion-Focused Therapy (CFT), Mindful Self-Compassion (MSC), Compassion Cultivation Training (CCT), Cognitively Based Compassion Training (CBCT), and Lovingkindness (LKM) and Compassion Meditations (CM).

[53] Kirby et al., "A Meta-Analysis of Compassion-Based Interventions."

[54] See, for example, Caroline Cummings, Jonathan Singer, Ryan Hisaka, and Lorraine Benuto, "Compassion Satisfaction to Combat Work-Related Burnout, Vicarious Trauma, and Secondary Traumatic Stress," *Journal of Interpersonal Violence* 36, nos. 9–10 (2021): NP5304–NP5319, https://doi.org/10.1177/0886260518799502; Suzanne Slocum-Gori, David Hemsworth, Winnie Chan, Aanna Carson, and Arminee Kazanjian, "Understanding Compassion Satisfaction, Compassion Fatigue and Burnout: A Survey of the Hospice Palliative Care Workforce," *Palliative Medicine* 27, no. 2 (2013): 172–78, https://doi.org/10.1177/0269216311431311; Ying-ying Zhang, Cheng Zhang, Xiao-Rong Han, Wei Li, and Ying-lei Wang, "Determinants of Compassion Satisfaction, Compassion Fatigue and Burn Out in Nursing: A Correlative Meta-Analysis," *Medicine (Baltimore)* 97, no. 26 (2018): e11086, https://doi.org/10.1097/md.0000000000011086; Jason Hotchkiss and Ruth Lesher, "Factors Predicting Burnout among Chaplains: Compassion Satisfaction, Organizational Factors, and the Mediators of Mindful Self-Care and Secondary Traumatic Stress," *Journal of Pastoral Care Counsel* 72, no. 2 (2018): 86–98, https://doi.org/10.1177/1542305018780655.

[55] See Marcia Ash, Elizabeth Walker, Ralph DiClemente, Marianne Florian, Patricia Palmer, Kathryn Wehrmeyer, et al., "Compassion Meditation Training for Hospital Chaplain Residents: A Pilot Study," *Journal of Health Care Chaplaincy* 27, no. 4 (2021): 191–206, https://doi.org/10.1080/08854726.2020.1723189; Kristin Neff, Marissa Knox, Phoebe Long, and Krista Gregory, "Caring for Others without Losing Yourself: An Adaptation of the Mindful Self-Compassion Program for Healthcare Communities," *Clinical Psychology* 76, no. 9 (2020): 1543–62, https://doi.org/10.1002/jclp.23007.

Promoting sustainable vocational responsiveness—a public health approach

Caring for the common good involves caring over the long haul. Across professions, burnout is more prevalent among those early in their career.[56] Margaret Mohrmann emphasizes the important role that educators play in preparing students for sustainable vocational responsiveness: "Because responsibility requires a total response of the whole person, it is something for which students need equipping, encouragement, direction, and even formation."[57]

Utilizing the social-ecological model from public health, we can better understand and address the complex interplay of the components of burnout: exhaustion (at the individual level), depersonalization or cynicism (at the interpersonal level), and feelings of infectiveness (at the systems level). Educators can implement strategies to cultivate compassion and support sustainable vocational responsiveness, addressing each level of the components of burnout through the lens of the social-ecological model. Consciously facilitating learning in ways that support the whole person, acknowledge interdependence, and foster belonging in community, educators can model compassionate pedagogy.

Promoting replenishment and preventing exhaustion

Exhaustion is the most thoroughly analyzed component of burnout. Exhaustion represents the basic individual stress dimension of burnout, referring to feelings of being overextended and depleted of one's emotional and physical resources.[58] As educators, we have opportunities to model and support strategies that may reduce exhaustion (both for our students and for ourselves) and thus support sustainable caring for the common good.

Ask nearly anyone on a college campus how they are doing and you will likely hear, "I'm so busy." Time famine is the feeling of having too much to do and not enough time to do it.[59] Educators have important opportunities

---

[56] Malesic, The End of Burnout, 105.

[57] Margaret M. Mohrmann, "'Vocation Is Responsibility': Broader Scope, Deeper Discernment," in Vocation across the Academy: A New Vocabulary for Higher Education, ed. David S. Cunningham (New York: Oxford University Press, 2016), 22.

[58] Christina Maslach, Wilmar Schaufeli, and Michael Leiter, "Job Burnout," Annual Review of Psychology 52, no. 1 (2001): 397–422, https://doi.org/10.1146/annurev.psych.52.1.397.

[59] Leslie Perlow, "The Time Famine: Toward a Sociology of Work Time," Administrative Science Quarterly 44, no. 1 (1999): 57–58, https://doi.org/10.2307/2667031

to be intentional with time in our courses, providing more space for reflection. Both within the structure of a class period and with outside assignments, we can prioritize and create space for purposeful reflection. Inspired by Mary Rose O'Reilley, I have adapted reflective writing practices at the beginning and end of class periods.[60] At the beginning of each class period, students have five minutes for quiet reflection on a quote or short passage related to the topic of the day. I invite students to pause, read the passage at least twice, and then write freely, connecting the passage and topic to their own lives. At the end of class, I create space for students to gather their thoughts and come to an experience of closure. Following five minutes of free writing, the floor is open for anyone to share concluding thoughts. The assignments we develop are another way to demonstrate prioritization of slowing down. In a senior capstone course, students complete a series of reflections to explore their own commitments, abilities, values, and purpose. Students regularly report that these assignments are transformative, providing permission and incentive to slow down and take a wider view.

We can also demonstrate the significance and importance of slowing down by modeling the pause when we teach.[61] While I have certainly felt pressure to cover more material, I know that rushing through a class period models time famine and perpetuates cursory engagement. Throughout a class period, I pause. Whether following a poignant share from a student or a slide with disturbing statistics on the scale of global undernutrition, I pause. In the beginning of the semester, I am transparent about the pause. I tell students that I pause to notice the impact on me and I invite them to notice any effects on them as well, whether in body, mind, or heart. As the semester evolves, students understand that they have agency to pause and resource however is best for them in any given moment—whether sitting in silence to breathe, pray, or journal or even taking a silent walk down the hall to integrate challenging material.

Finally, a fundamental way we interact with students is through the reading we assign. In our efforts to share our love of a subject, spark inspiration, or cover the material, we often assign so much reading that our students do not have time to engage carefully. In choosing to assign fewer texts, we

---

[60] Perlow, "Time Famine," 57–81.
[61] See chapter 8 of this volume by David Timmerman for other examples of pausing during class discussion, specifically to provide space to frame and process challenging conversations.

allow for slow and careful reading. We can also use exercises that compel students to slow down and carefully attend to their reading. As described in *Contemplative Practices in Higher Education*:

> Contemplative reading in the classroom is radically different. It slows down the reading. . . . It is a process of quiet reflection, which requires mindful attentiveness . . . to be fully in the moment with the text. It requires patient receptivity . . . allowing a more profound experience and understanding. It often involves repeated reading of one passage. Students read and advance, then return and read again. Each time they may hear something new, leading to more connection with the material.[62]

Choosing to assign fewer readings and teaching contemplative reading have the potential to deepen student engagement and reduce exhaustion.

Promoting connection, preventing depersonalization

Caring for the common good requires an acknowledgment of interdependence. In contrast, depersonalization attempts to put distance between oneself and others.[63] Researchers demonstrate consistent links between exhaustion and depersonalization,[64] theorizing that actions to distance oneself emotionally and cognitively from one's work may be ways to cope with work overload.

Some of the most important work we can do in educational settings is to support resilience against depersonalization. Palliative medicine physician Sunita Puri highlights that compassion begins with recognizing suffering: "The prelude to compassion is the willingness to see."[65] Our choice of texts, our transparency in motivation for selection of texts, and our facilitation of student engagement with those texts have the potential to increase students' awareness of suffering as well as strengthen their capacity to be with suffering. Tess Maginess and Alison MacKenzie highlight the opportunity to

---

[62] Daniel Barbezat and Mirabai Bush, *Contemplative Practices in Higher Education* (San Francisco, CA: Jossey-Bass, 2014), 113.

[63] Maslach et al., "Burnout," 403.

[64] Maslach et al., "Burnout," 403.

[65] Sunita Puri, "We Must Learn to Look at Grief, Even When We Want to Run Away," *New York Times*, February 23, 2022, https://www.nytimes.com/2022/02/23/opinion/death-grief-covid.html.

cultivate compassion through literature, noting, "At best literature enables us to imagine not just ourselves but the 'other.' And so, sometimes, literature can encourage us to [re]imagine or [re]conceive our own beliefs or attitudes, can allow us to explore our hidden selves and also the experience of characters in situations different from our own, and whose point of view or angle of vision is vastly different from our own."[66] Rhetoric scholar Robert Hariman describes how photojournalism provides a forum for "compassionate seeing," explaining that when we look at a "mediated image" that "reproduces the form of interpersonal interaction while lowering the costs, it allows viewers to take risks at self-extension that might be more difficult in person. By placing strangers into the silent visual space of face-to-face interaction, it activates the imagination to extend oneself into the world of the other."[67] Christopher Wade and colleagues further demonstrate how the use of film in undergraduate public health education facilitates emotional connection to efforts that address health-related challenges.[68] Such strategies that cultivate connection among students and nurture engagement with suffering can support resilience against depersonalization and further contribute to sustainable vocational responsiveness.

In *The Pedagogy of Compassion at the Heart of Higher Education*, Michalinos Zembylas describes unhelpful possible student reactions when recognizing histories of injustice and oppression, including compassion fatigue, desensitization, and self-victimization.[69] He argues for critical and strategic pedagogies of compassion that consider these student responses, supporting student understanding of interdependence, mutual vulnerability, social justice, and common humanity.[70]

[66] Tess Maginess and Alison MacKenzie, "Achieving Moralised Compassion in Higher Education," *Journal of Perspectives in Applied Academic Practice* 6, no. 3 (2018): 45–46, https://doi.org/10.14297/jpaap.v6i3.370. See also Erin VanLaningham's discussion in chapter 9 of this volume about the ways reading with strangers fosters the common good.

[67] Robert Hariman, "Cultivating Compassion as a Way of Seeing," *Communication and Critical/Cultural Studies* 6, no. 2 (2009): 202, https://doi.org/10.1080/14791420902867971.

[68] C. Wade, T. Barrientos, M. Macarulay, W. Alderson, P. Shibale, and C. Le, "Student and Faculty Perspectives on the Use of Movies in Public Health Pedagogy," *Pedagogy in Health Promotion: The Scholarship of Teaching and Learning* 4, no. 2 (2018): 131–39, https://doi.org/10.1177/2373379917715055.

[69] See Martin Holt Dotterweich's reflections in chapter 12 of this volume for an extended examination of the role of history and memory in cultivating a sense of hospitality and grace toward others.

[70] M. Zembylas, "In Search of Critical and Strategic Pedagogies of Compassion: Interrogating Pity and Sentimentality in Higher Education," in *The Pedagogy of Compassion at the Heart of Higher Education*, ed. P. Gibbs (London: Springer, 2017), 173–87.

Promoting perspective, preventing feelings of ineffectiveness

The final component of burnout—feelings of ineffectiveness—may be the most challenging to address. Systems-level interventions are necessary to reduce burnout and take time. While working toward systemic change, my aspiration is to fuel compassionate caring and a belief that students can make a difference, while introducing enough of the long view that they are not too shocked by realities they will encounter.

Providing a broader sense of perspective can help our students to meet the challenges of sustaining their work in the face of systemic and structural barriers. The arc of a typical class may support the impression that complex issues can be understood and even "resolved" over a semester. To emphasize the vast view, educators can incorporate voices of those who have spent their careers working to address problems that may not be solved in their lifetime. Thus, we can explore and nuance questions such as the following: How does one feel a call to a problem that seems unsolvable? What strategies do those who feel such a call use to sustain their calling over the long haul?

In the medical school classroom, Arthur Kleinman directly addresses structural influences, connecting the bureaucratization of health care to a serious loss of caring among health care professionals: "Perhaps—armed with this appreciation of why their professional care is subverted by frustrating bureaucratic tasks that contribute to disillusionment—medical students and young doctors can defend themselves against burnout."[71]

Global public health: a case study in compassionate pedagogy

Knowing that many undergraduate students enroll in a Global Public Health course with aspirations of a career in global health, I sought to design a course that would provide space for such vocational exploration while also supporting the development of skills and perspectives to care for the common good sustainably. Inspired by others working in the intersection of

[71] Kleinman, *The Soul of Care*, 114.

health care and compassionate care,[72] I brought compassion to the center of the course.

Framing: Global Public Health is a writing- and research-intensive course that explores the unequal distribution of health and disease and introduces some of the major achievements in public health across the globe. In addition to developing the foundational public health knowledge and skills to think, feel, and act like global health scholars, I emphasize to students that the course is also designed to cultivate the heart. I carefully frame our attention to compassion through reflection on the following passage:

> The university is well-practiced at educating the mind for critical reasoning, critical writing and critical speaking as well as for scientific and quantitative analysis. But is this sufficient? In a world beset with conflicts, internal as well as external, isn't it of equal if not greater importance to balance the sharpening of our intellects with the systematic cultivation of your hearts?[73]

Given the individualistic competitive culture in universities, we also spend time discussing collaborative learning and compassionate group work.

Finally, we discuss global health scholar Paul Farmer's description of "accompaniment," not only as an important approach to public health and medicine but also as a guiding principle animating my approach as an instructor. Farmer describes accompaniment as "going with you and supporting you on your journey where it leads." He emphasizes mystery and trust as the *accompagnateur* "share[s] your fate for a while . . . sticking with the task until it's deemed completed—not by the *accompagnateur*, but by the person being accompanied."[74] Committing to an open-ended partnership with students from the beginning of the course, I model compassionate pedagogy.

Course structure/process: Most class sessions begin in silent reflection, directly joining the day's text and topic with students' experiences and inner observations. Students maintain a journal throughout the semester that captures their emotional connections to the course material. These

[72] See Focus Area for Compassion and Ethics, a Program of the Task Force for Global Health: https://www.taskforce.org/face/; Hillebrand Center for Compassionate Care in Medicine: https://compassionatecare.nd.edu/.

[73] Arthur Zajonc, quoted in Daniel Barbezat and Mirabai Bush, *Contemplative Practices in Higher Education,* xii.

[74] Paul Farmer, *To Repair the World: Paul Farmer Speaks to the Next Generation,* ed. Jonathan Weigel (Oakland: University of California Press, 2013), xxv.

reflections then become data for a final self-evaluation in which students as-sess the evolution of their cognitive and affective learning and any vocational insights across the arc of the semester.

When asking students to engage their hearts, pedagogical flexibility is es-sential. I often pause and invite students to capture their responses in their reflective journal. After reading the room, we may move into paired sharing, a large discussion, or an opportunity for physical movement.

As students assess the magnitude of various global health problems, they utilize epidemiologic methods to interpret global health data. While interpreting quantitative data, we also discuss the importance of "seeing the faces" of people whose health we are working to protect. We discuss how considering health at the global level, it is too easy to see only "num-bers." We continually refocus our attention on the ethical and compas-sionate dimensions of global health, incorporating first-person accounts of the people behind health statistics. We also read portions of memoirs from professionals working in global health, attending to the authors' descriptions of seeing and being with suffering, their process of discerning wise action to alleviate suffering, and any attention to their understanding of vocation.

At the end of the semester, we examine the potential negative impacts of feeling responsibility for the health of others. After reading Courtney Martin's "The Reductive Seduction of Other People's Problems," we examine how our seemingly altruistic acts to relieve suffering can actually cause harm to ourselves or those whom we are trying to serve.[75] We also discuss em-pathic distress and the potential for taking on too much suffering of another, identifying too intensely with it, and becoming unable to act.[76] We then re-turn to our exploration of vocation, acknowledging that while engagement in working for the common good can give a sense of purpose and meaning to our lives, the magnitude of the challenge and the sense of responsibility can lead to burnout.

[75] Courtney Martin, "The Reductive Seduction of Other People's Problems," *Bright Magazine*, January 11, 2016, https://brightthemag.com/the-reductive-seduction-of-other-people-s-problems-3c07b307732d.
[76] Halifax, *Standing at the Edge*, 68–78.

Promoting flourishing and preventing burnout
among faculty

If we are to hope that our students sustainably live their vocations caring for the common good, we must provide a model. College educators face a culture of productivity and scarcity, with increasing expectations for advising, teaching, research, and service, in addition to institutional financial pressures. The temptation to establish emotional distance from students and colleagues is understandable. Yet, when we do, we also distance ourselves from the source of meaning and purpose in our work.

Prior to the COVID-19 pandemic, more than a third of faculty members reported suffering from burnout, with women experiencing higher levels than men.[77] COVID-19 brought increased burnout in higher education, with more than two-thirds of faculty respondents to an October 2020 survey reporting that they felt "very" or "extremely" stressed or fatigued in the past month.[78]

To sustainably care for the common good, we must *survive*. As the poet and activist Audre Lorde suggests, "Caring for myself is not self-indulgence, it is self-preservation, and that is an act of political warfare."[79] Lorde and others practicing radical self-care explain that in cultivating the capacity to create a just and loving world, we must make choices that reduce our own exhaustion.[80] Setting aside time to reflect on our initial motivations and the evolution of our meaning and purpose, we are better equipped to prioritize the components of our professional lives that provide renewal and resourcing.

While educators may cope with exhaustion and feelings of ineffectiveness through cognitive distancing, thus developing an indifference or cynical attitude toward students, research points to the centrality of compassion in the pedagogic relationship. Faculty responses describing their experiences of kindness and collegiality in their careers were "infused with language of

[77] Priscila Castro Alves, Aurea de Fatima Oliveira, and Helena Borges Martins da Silva Paro, "Quality of Life and Burnout among Faculty Members: How Much Does the Field of Knowledge Matter?," *PLoS ONE* 14, no. 3 (2019): e0214217, https://doi.org/10.1371/journal.pone.0214217.

[78] Beth McMurtie, "The Pandemic Is Dragging On. Professors Are Burning Out," *Chronicle of Higher Education*, November 5, 2020, https://www.chronicle.com/article/the-pandemic-is-dragging-on-professors-are-burning-out.

[79] Audre Lorde, *A Burst of Light: And Other Essays* (New York: Broadside Press, 1988), 131.

[80] Courtney Dorroll, "Care in the Classroom," *Vocation Matters* (blog), November 10, 2020, https://vocationmatters.org/2020/11/10/care-in-the-classroom/; and Courage of Care Coalition, https://courageofcare.org/.

care and 'walking with' students through their learning journeys and beyond."[81] For those of us who came to an academic career because of our care for students, reflecting upon these vocational inspirations serves to reorient our hearts toward our students.

In a competitive university environment, spaces for collegiality, compassion, and kindness can seem challenging to find. Yet, emerging research describes academics caring for each other with acts of generosity in almost subversive ways, as a direct counter to the dominant narrative of "academic success." Interviews suggest that such acts and interactions are vital to many academics' sense of value and meaning in academic work.[82]

Colleges and universities are well suited to provide models of valuing and supporting compassionate caring.[83] Interdisciplinary research centers drawing from neuroscience, psychology, economics, public health, and contemplative traditions provide evidence of the impacts of compassion training in various settings, including higher education.[84] At the conclusion of a meeting on the "Epidemiology of Compassion and Love," sponsored by the Task Force for Global Health, participants determined that we need rigorous assessment of interventions to foster compassion, particularly at the organizational and community levels. Working across higher education institutions, there are opportunities to consider how to create environments that allow compassion to flourish and to identify characteristics of communities and organizations that support compassion at all levels of the social-ecological model.

Conclusion

This chapter began with my desire to better understand how to support students in sustainable vocational responsiveness. Because my writing coincided with the COVID-19 pandemic, the inquiry was also personal. As an epidemiologist who teaches global public health, I was asked to

---

[81] Martha Caddell and Kimberly Wilder, "Seeking Compassion in the Measured University: Generosity, Collegiality and Competition in Academic Practice," *Journal of Perspectives in Applied Academic Practice* 6, no. 3 (2018): 14–23, https://doi.org/10.14297/jpaap.v6i3.384.

[82] Caddell and Wilder, "Seeking Compassion," 14–23.

[83] See Waddington, *Towards the Compassionate University*.

[84] See the Center for Altruism Research and Education at the Stanford University School of Medicine and the Center for Contemplative Science and Compassion-Based Ethics at Emory University.

contextualize and translate public health guidance for my institution. Loved ones and non–public health colleagues questioned the intensive research, interminable meetings, and little sleep during precious sabbatical time. My response was always quick and easy: "I can't *not* do it." Serving my institution as an epidemiologist during the years of the COVID-19 pandemic has been disorienting, difficult, and rewarding. While I have gained insights into the challenges of applied public health during a crisis, I have also experienced the toll of the responsibility of caring for and protecting the common good. Deliberate study and cultivation of compassion helped me navigate the challenges of pursuing my vocation sustainably in turbulent times.

As protector and promoter of health for all, the field of public health offers a model of caring for the common good that is compassion in action. Those who feel called to care for and protect the common good feel a sense of responsibility to their work while experiencing some of the highest rates of burnout among professions. Educators have an important role in equipping, encouraging, and preparing our students for sustainable vocational responsiveness. Compassionate pedagogy is a framework for preparing whole human beings (body, mind, heart, and soul) to care for the common good. By intentionally designing learning experiences and modeling compassion, we can offer a counterpoint to the individualistic emphasis that is the focus of much of education and vocational exploration, planting seeds for sustainable caring. Our communal responsibility as educators is to minimize burnout and engage in compassionate caring for students, for colleagues, and for ourselves so that we may continue to nurture the common good.

PART FOUR

CALLINGS OF CAMPUS, COMMUNITY, AND BEYOND

The concluding section of this volume explores the shared space, time, and goods of what we call the "commons." The chapters examine how colleges can better serve as common good places and prepare students for lives of contributing to the wider community. Specifically, the authors suggest that higher education has significant opportunities to use its gifts and resources to serve the common good by attending to place and time.

The university should—through its practices and places—invite significant reflection on what it means to be formed by personal and collective experience. Knowing the ways shared space and history shape us is part of vocational exploration. Our campuses offer opportunities to revisit, reimagine, and redesign the structures of campus commons to better facilitate vocational discernment. Furthermore, reflection upon public monuments and historical figures and events allows students to engage with the complexity of history, the challenges of disciplinary learning, and the depth of the liberal arts.

We encourage readers of this section to focus on common places, including the physical, public, and virtual. Key terms for the section include history and memory, freedom and obligation, the campus and community commons, and formation and reformation. What do these terms mean in your classrooms, campus programs, strategic plans, and institutional priorities? How can expanding and reclaiming the role of the campus in cultivating the common good and centering the purpose of a university education to foster vocational reflection through the life course help us foster the flourishing of others?

The questions that follow may be used in professional development, meetings, programming, planning, and teaching. We imagine students and educators alike responding to these in discussion and in writing, in private and public settings. The goal of the questions, and of this section, is to argue for the university's responsibility in fostering the common good, namely through significant attention to formation through place.

How would you describe the campus ecology—the connections between environment and participants—of your institution? How does it form students and educators?

* What are the ways campus and community places invite vocational discernment?

What places on your campus best foster a sense of community and commitment to others?

* What locations in your community can be seen as common good places? How can you strengthen ties between the university and the community through these locations? (Imagine here not only physical locales but also digital and transcendent spaces.)
* What campus spaces are in need of attention so that they better serve the common good of the university? Of the community?

What is the responsibility of the university to your community? In what ways does it contribute to the surrounding community and in what ways could it improve?

* What does the university do well in offering multiple avenues for formation and multiple spaces for connection?
* What are the barriers for students to access the "goods" and "places" of the university?

What practices are used by educators across campus that use the lens of history and place?

* What is the connection between the particularities of our memories within the institution and the relationships beyond the institution?
* How do you think about and activate the history of your campus (and maybe problematic history and legacy) in ways that help students see themselves as obligated to/tethered to that history but also encourage them to see their agency in deciding what to do with it?

* What do we gain by learning about the past that can help us understand our present purpose and responsibility to others? How can that help us look to the future?
* How do educators across campus encourage students to think about their obligations to others? How would this education change if we thought of the university as a place for formation throughout our lives?

11

The University as the (Common) Good Place

Robert J. Pampel

In *The Good Place*, a network comedy that ran on NBC from 2016 to 2020, four recently deceased main characters find themselves in "the good place," where they're all led to believe they've earned entrance by leading exemplary lives. After honest self-assessment and one too many reminders of their moral failings on Earth, they realize they are actually in the "bad place" and are doomed to an eternity of torture. Despite this grim judgment, the central characters do not descend into aggressive self-preservation. Instead, they decide to help one another become better versions of themselves in the afterlife, eventually forming a "soul squad" and expanding their ambitions to assist loved ones still on Earth. In the end, they revolutionize the system by which people are sorted into the "good" and "bad" places so that everyone has a chance for self-improvement and salvation.

Leaving aside the show's well-documented philosophical foundations,[1] *The Good Place* provides a fitting (if unconventional) point of departure for this volume's discussion of vocation and the common good. Four main characters from markedly different backgrounds find themselves in unexpected company with one another, and as unpleasant acquaintance turns into eternal friendship, each character realizes how instrumental the others are to their own development of a best self in the afterlife. These characters form unlikely bonds with one another in "the good place," an intentional community designed to bring different people together. Granted, the original intention is to torment them, but as the neighborhood evolves from a place of emotional and psychological affliction to one of experiment and renewal,

---

[1] Chris Quintana, "Meet the Philosophers Who Give 'The Good Place' Its Scholarly Bona Fides," *Chronicle of Higher Education,* February 6, 2018, https://www.chronicle.com/article/meet-the-philosophers-who-give-the-good-place-its-scholarly-bona-fides/?cid2=gen_login_refresh&cid=gen_sign_in.

Robert J. Pampel, *The University as the (Common) Good Place* In: *Called Beyond Our Selves.*
Edited by: Erin VanLaningham, Oxford University Press. © Oxford University Press 2024.
DOI: 10.1093/oso/9780197691915.003.0012

we realize the importance of common places that shape the character and motivations of their inhabitants. The neighborhood provides the context for relationships built on shared joy, sadness, and intellectual and moral growth.

The show resonated with viewers, even spawning college courses exploring the show's relationship to the good life.[2] One reason for the show's success was the way it represented a desire we often share that the places we inhabit sustain and nurture us (or, at the very least, don't harm us). To the extent these treasured places fall short of their promise, we do not simply abandon them. We work to reform them. Many of us in higher education can relate. A growing share of Americans believe higher education institutions are going in the "wrong direction."[3] Reasons for this assessment vary, but some view these institutions as out of touch ideologically with the needs of their surrounding communities or as bastions of privilege divorced from the needs of the real world.[4] These critiques are valid, but that does not mean we must resign ourselves to our campuses' inevitable decline. Those of us who serve at these institutions might instead work to redeem these places so they achieve their purpose of encouraging deep inquiry, fostering whole-student transformation, and generating knowledge that serves the world. By examining the historical purposes and present realities of the college campus, I aim to identify how and where vocation and dedication to the common good can flourish because of the distinctive context of a college campus. At its best, the modern American academy may be a "common good place" in which students from various backgrounds share in collective intellectual pursuits, discern their vocations in community with one another, and build social networks across ideological and cultural divides.

Historical purposes and present realities

Former Bowdoin College president Joseph McKeen once said, "It ought always to be remembered, that literary institutions are founded and endowed

[2] Lauren Chval, "Of Course *The Good Place* Got Its Own College Seminar," *Vulture*, November 14, 2019, https://www.vulture.com/2019/11/the-good-place-college-class-mike-schur.html.
[3] Anna Brown, "Most Americans Say Higher Ed Is Heading in the Wrong Direction, but Partisans Disagree on Why," *Pew Research Center*, July 26, 2018, https://www.pewresearch.org/fact-tank/2018/07/26/most-americans-say-higher-ed-is-heading-in-wrong-direction-but-partisans-disagree-on-why/.
[4] See Nick Burns, "Elite Universities Are Out of Touch. Blame the Campus," *New York Times*, August 2, 2022, https://www.nytimes.com/2022/08/02/opinion/elite-universities-campus.html.

for the common good" and "owe to God and society the sacred duty of guarding the morals of the youth committed to their care."[5] McKeen's conception of the university in 1802 seems quaint in the twenty-first century. Even before the COVID-19 pandemic, the traditional college experience faced many headwinds, with technological changes and financial pressures challenging the status quo and redefining best practices. The last few years have certainly tested colleges' commitment to a residential way of doing business. The shuttering of on-campus facilities on hundreds of campuses in March 2020, the prohibition of in-person gatherings for many programs once colleges resumed in fall 2020, and the movement of many experiences to an online modality all signaled a vastly changed college landscape in American higher education. In some cases, the pivot to virtual spaces came with many advantages. In other ways, the loss of shared physical public places represented an existential threat to the time-honored tradition of a residential college experience.

In his wide-ranging history of the American college and university, Frederick Rudolph named this tradition "the collegiate way," an ideal "every American college has had or consciously rejected or lost or sought to recapture."[6] By "the collegiate way" Rudolph refers, first and foremost, to the distinctive setting of American colleges and universities. Inspired by English universities like Oxford and Cambridge, many early American college leaders preferred pastoral settings in the countryside where students could "elevate" their "moral character . . . in as great a degree as the natural scenery of their localities would be increased in beauty."[7] Other colleges formed in urban locales maintained "the collegiate way" emphasis on dormitories, commons, and shared experiences among students. Early college leaders believed such shared experiences provided the best and surest way of encouraging students' moral development and their sense of duty to one another. In other words, the distinctive *place* of a college was closely tied to students' intellectual and affective development, as well as their contribution to the common good. As Rudolph admits, the strict adherence to "the collegiate way" brought with it an uncritical belief that students would naturally be

[5] Joseph McKeen, "1802 Inaugural Address," McKeen Center, Bowdoin College, https://www.bowdoin.edu/mckeen-center/about/1802-inaugural-address.html.

[6] Frederick Rudolph, *The American College and University: A History* (Athens: University of Georgia Press, 1991), 87.

[7] Rudolph, *The American College and University*, 93.

made better people by being in a shared setting and under the careful guide of a paternalistic administration.

The reality was far less civil, often unsophisticated, and even brutish. Rudolph recounts "tragedy and misfortune" (e.g., duels in residence halls, student violence) that ensued when "young men on whose time the intellectual purposes of the colleges placed too few demands" were "brought into close proximity, under the harshest of conditions."[8] Even in the early days of American colleges and universities, critics worried about students' frivolity and carelessness as they embraced the seclusion of the college lifestyle. Other critics rightly observe the disparity of opportunities built into the collegiate way. John Thelin describes "the collegiate ideal" as a feature of American higher education that had "serious social implications" by prioritizing opportunities for "talented" White men, who represented a small minority of the population in the early twentieth century.[9] Just as today, the collegiate ideal enticed many students but excluded whole segments of the population and exacerbated existing social divides.

In our contemporary context, we see evidence of the same tension. Perhaps influenced by one too many admissions viewbooks, we often see our campuses at their best, imagining how thought-provoking seminars, late-night discussions in the residence and dining halls, formative clubs and organizations, and impactful service in the community mold students for the better. Along with authors like Sharon Daloz Parks, we think about the richness of a college campus's "hearth, table, and commons" in forming students to pursue "big questions" and "worthy dreams."[10] On my own campus, I see the meticulously landscaped green spaces, the thoughtfully designed residence halls, and even the aged seminar rooms as places of community, renewal, and inspiration. In these common spaces, I imagine students experiencing the freedom to think about their personal and professional goals, to imagine different futures for themselves, and to share in common conversations about meaning and identity.[11]

The reality of a college campus does not always fit with this romantic ideal. A modern college campus can feel more like a richly orchestrated induction

---

[8] Rudolph, *The American College and University*, 97.

[9] John Thelin, *A History of American Higher Education* (Baltimore, MD: Johns Hopkins University Press, 2019).

[10] Sharon Daloz Parks, *Big Questions, Worthy Dreams* (San Francisco, CA: Jossey-Bass, 2000), 154–57.

[11] Charles Mathewes's discussion of the university as a site for formation during the college years and beyond can be found in chapter 13 of this volume.

into privilege with its lavish accommodations, unprecedented autonomy, and (at times) total insulation from the cares of the world. This leads critics to reduce the college experience to little more than "paying for the party" insofar as it indulges students' social growth while exacerbating the divide between the "haves" and "have nots."[12] We also know colleges can produce competition, anxiety, and feelings of isolation among students, especially among members of Generation Z or "iGen."[13] Despite early feelings of camaraderie and shared purpose, the pandemic exacerbated a host of mental health concerns on college campuses.

A few recent examples at my own institution illustrate the dichotomy at play in the common places of a college campus. Students exuded deep gratitude at being in community with one another when we returned to campus in person after the pandemic-induced closure in spring 2020. To be sure, many trappings of a traditional college campus had been curtailed. Students were prohibited from using their residence hall lounges to congregate socially, classrooms were modified for social distancing, and there was a particularly dystopian sign in the library that read, "Eat Silent. Eat Alone." And yet, students engaged fully in class discussions, often with thankfulness for the opportunity to participate and be in proximity to one another. There was a spirit of discovery in the room, especially among first-year students gathered in a place where "they first asked questions about their callings, where they were mentored in their strengths and gifts, and where they contributed to a safe community of supporting peers."[14] They formed bonds of solidarity by being together in the common space of our university's campus, and as an instructor it was among the most gratifying teaching experiences of my career.

These "slower and quieter" venues represent "powerful spaces" where "reflection and discernment can be amplified,"[15] but our campuses also provide other, decidedly louder and often faster-paced places that incite students' vocational awakening in important ways. Indeed, the common spaces of our campuses, often bustling with student activity, can inspire even when (and perhaps especially because) they're crowded, loud, and even disruptive.

---

[12] Elizabeth Armstrong and Laura Hamilton, *Paying for the Party: How College Maintains Inequality* (Cambridge, MA: Harvard University Press, 2015).

[13] Jean Twenge, *iGen: Why Today's Super-Connected Kids Are Growing Up Less Rebellious, More Tolerant, Less Happy—and Completely Unprepared for Adulthood—and What That Means for the Rest of Us* (New York: Astria, 2018).

[14] Paul Burmeister, "Vocation and the Power of Certain Spaces," *Vocation Matters* (blog), April 12, 2022, https://vocationmatters.org/2022/04/12/vocation-and-the-power-of-certain-spaces/.

[15] Burmeister, "Vocation and the Power of Certain Spaces."

When racial protests erupted in St. Louis in the wake of Michael Brown's death in 2014, an outdoor amphitheater on my campus became a locus of activity. As community members poured onto campus, what was normally a place for socializing and studying on warm days transformed into a venue for interrogating the responsibilities of the institution for promoting racial justice. Community members, students, and university administrators met one another in passionate debate, they shared in moments of intense solidarity, and they collectively defined the common goods that bound them together. The result was the university's "Clock Tower Accords," a set of commitments approved by the institutional leaders that have guided diversity and equity efforts ever since.[16]

On the other side of this hopeful picture are troubling trends of student mental health concerns and ingrained privilege on college campuses. In my work with first-year students at a STEM-heavy school, biology and chemistry exam weeks have always been good litmus tests for student stress levels. Students obsess over these exams, often disengaging from a discussion-oriented class for a few sessions as they cling to the facts and equations they've memorized. It is always a bit disconcerting, and a little frightening, to see how students withdraw into themselves in the prelude to major exams. As the pandemic dragged on, these exam weeks produced even more concerning levels of stress and worry. More than ever before, students preemptively asked to be excused from class, and others simply walked out of discussion because of the pressure they felt about an afternoon exam. This situation might be familiar to those of us who work with high-achieving students who internalize an unrealistic narrative of success that suggests that if they're not constantly studying, they're falling short of expectations. In reality, students of all types can struggle in these common places for various reasons, from underdeveloped study habits that fuel negative comparisons to more engaged peers to socioeconomic factors that produce crowded schedules and anxiety around managing yet another on-campus commitment. The bounded system of a college campus can create all sorts of negative conditions that rival the admiration and nostalgia we often associate with our common good places.

---

[16] For more on the racial justice protests at St. Louis University and the "Clock Tower Accords," see Julie Hanlon Rubio and Noelle Janak, "Student Activism Matters: The Parable of Occupy SLU and Its Impact on Racial Justice Dialogue," *Conversations on Jesuit Higher Education* 51, no. 7 (February 2017): 12–15, https://epublications.marquette.edu/conversations/vol51/iss1/7. To see how St. Louis University continues to use the "Clock Tower Accords" for diversity and equity efforts, see Bridjes O'Neil, "SLU's Clock Tower Accords: A Catalyst for Institutional Change," Saint Louis University, February 1, 2022, https://www.slu.edu/news/2022/february/clock-tower-accords.php.

Our colleges and universities are undoubtedly still places of learning, but despite their incredible growth over the last seventy years, they often struggle "to sustain their stated mission and fundamental purpose."[17] Even as college enrollments have soared since World War II, private schools are still overwhelmingly populated by White students,[18] access and affordability remain elusive for large swaths of the population,[19] and, aside from the data that shows higher earning potential for degree holders,[20] it remains to be seen whether colleges can fulfill their larger social functions that relate to the common good, such as developing engaged global citizens or cultivating among students a sense of empathy for others. Moreover, recent data from the pandemic suggests that the student mental health crisis has become an epidemic on college campuses, with depression and suicide (already on the rise in recent decades) reaching heretofore unseen and unsustainable numbers.[21] If our campuses are places where students are supposed to encounter new ideas, build resilience, and form bonds that endure well beyond college, what can be said for a system that ignores or marginalizes diverse voices, one that exacerbates mental health concerns, or one that merely recycles and reinforces privilege for its participants?

And yet, even as "the collegiate way" has fallen short of its lofty aims, it is worth acknowledging how early adherence to this way of life was responsible for "establish[ing] the philosophic and historical foundations for many of the nonintellectual purposes of the American college" that make the experience powerful well beyond the conferral of a degree and serve as a counterweight to the negative outcomes above.[22] Deep connection to a place and context often leads to affinities outside the classroom that build vibrant campus culture and encourage holistic student development. We might consider how participation in shared places and spaces on campus can cultivate among

[17] James Strange and Carney Banning, *Designing for Learning: Creating Campus Environments for Student Success,* 2nd ed. (San Francisco, CA: Jossey-Bass, 2015), 23.

[18] US Department of Education, National Center for Education Statistics, *Characteristics of Postsecondary Students,* May 2022, https://nces.ed.gov/programs/coe/indicator/csb.

[19] Karin Fisher, "The Barriers to Mobility: Why Higher Ed's Promise Remains Unfulfilled," *Chronicle of Higher Education,* December 30, 2019, https://www.chronicle.com/article/why-higher-ed-rsquo-s-promise-remains-unfulfilled.

[20] US Bureau of Labor Statistics, "Learn More, Earn More: Education Leads to Higher Wages, Lower Unemployment," *Career Outlook,* May 2020, https://www.bls.gov/careeroutlook/2020/data-on-display/education-pays.htm.

[21] Anemona Hartocollis, "Another Surge in the Virus Has Colleges Fearing a Mental Health Crisis," *New York Times,* December 22, 2021, https://www.nytimes.com/2021/12/22/us/covid-college-mental-health-suicide.html.

[22] Rudolph, *The American College and University,* 108.

students an openness to exploring vocational identity and concern for the common good, which can complement, extend, and enrich the intellectual pursuits of a college education.

Campus ecology and the commons

Early college leaders took for granted the ways a pastoral campus setting or a tightly controlled residential experience would lead to students' intellectual and moral development. Today, ecological models within student development theories, which explore the connection between students and their environment in promoting or hindering cognitive and affective growth, help us understand the vital importance of context in students' well-being and development.[23] Our campuses, with their distinctive architecture, various artifacts, and behavioral settings, "impress students with a variety of expressed values and tacit images of what it means to be a student on campus."[24] Often these mechanisms are subtle, like curb cuts in public places, elevators in campus buildings, or gender-inclusive bathrooms that make evident an institution's commitment to accessibility. Such changes to the physical design of campus can be done haphazardly (through hastily poured asphalt) or intentionally and thoroughly (with professional concrete molds), sending different messages about the value of accessibility and inclusion in common places on campus. This also extends to the physical design of a campus's support structures, such as the location and accessibility of tutoring services, the diversity and community engagement offices, counseling services, and other informal spaces that encourage gathering or reflective practices that advance the common good. If these spaces are relegated to basements or untrodden corners of the campus, the institution signals a lesser commitment to these ideals. Conversely, if they are centrally located, visible, and well integrated, then the campus confers importance on these "common good places." Campus leaders attentive to the micro- and macro-systems in which students

---

[23] A few foundational theorists in campus ecology are Urie Bronfenbrenner, who used a psychological lens to understand student development within a given environment, and Rudolph Moos, who argued that students' perceptions of the campus environment (e.g., student clubs and organizations, classroom settings) are powerful factors in determining their behavior and their potential to progress along cognitive and affective dimensions while in college. For a full review of these (and other relevant) student development theorists, see Nancy Evans, Deanna Forney, Florence Guido, Lori Patton, and Kristen Renn, *Student Development in College: Theory, Research, and Practice*, 2nd ed. (San Francisco, CA: Jossey-Bass, 2010).

[24] Strange and Banning, *Designing for Learning*, 17.

operate can make thoughtful decisions about campus design that result in a higher sense of belonging and purpose.

We all know students bring in their own distinctive experiences, cultural references, and expectations to a college campus, which influence their behavior and potential to thrive in college.[25] How do our structures and practices meet students in the proper context? Which systems potentially inhibit their growth? Recent debate about public statues and memorials provides some material for reflection. If public memorials carry with them painful legacies of oppression and exclusion, does their place on a college campus hinder students' intellectual and affective growth? A nuanced appreciation for students' human ecology prompts a thoughtful consideration about how environment informs behavior, engagement, and (ultimately) growth. Student responses to the physical environment in which they live and learn, including how and where public spaces advance or hinder student development, are part of vocational discernment that accounts for the common good.[26] While colleges may not completely redesign a space based on student experience or response, such processes can be instrumental in helping students define themselves in concert with or in opposition to these spaces. Examples on my own campus include the removal of offensive memorials depicting Indigenous peoples, construction of new spaces celebrating global identities, more prominent quarters for student identity groups, and even the inclusion of more accessible dining options in new eateries around campus. The commons, configured in multiple ways across a campus, become expressions of the institutional mission that encourage access and celebrate the diversity of the student body.[27]

As we think about how we and our students interact with the common good places on campus, we must not forget the larger commons we inhabit as human beings. Any education oriented toward prioritizing and nurturing common good places must contend with our relationship to the broader ecology of the planet. This issue clearly extends beyond the choices of any

[25] The Marist "Mindset List" (https://www.marist.edu/mindset-list) provides a humbling and eye-opening annual look at the perspectives first-year students bring to campus.

[26] For an extended exploration of the ways public memorials can be avenues for extending compassion to others in history and contemporary life, see Martin Holt Dotterweich's discussion in chapter 12 of this volume.

[27] See Monica M. Smith's discussion of reframing the institutional mission to align with social justice and diversity, equity, and inclusion efforts as a vocational response to the common good in chapter 4 of this volume.

one campus, but there are ways in which our campuses can and should think about what could be termed *the* common good place.[28]

In Jesuit, Catholic higher education, Pope Francis's 2015 *Laudato si'* encyclical provided a forceful articulation of the "urgent challenge to protect our common home" from the ravages of climate change and an admonition to "discover what each of us can do about it."[29] In response, the Society of Jesus identified "caring for our common home" as one of the Jesuits' Universal Apostolic Preferences (UAP).[30] College campuses—as physical and symbolic places—can work toward this important goal as leaders "identify areas where they can make a difference and contribute to a change of mind and heart."[31] Institutions can prioritize environmental stewardship in their campus operations and master planning efforts. How will new buildings be designed to minimize their environmental impact? How can dining services limit the amount of waste, acquire food from local and sustainable sources, and provide attractive plant-based foods to reduce carbon emissions? Can colleges provide discounted public transit passes to encourage sustainable travel in and around their communities?

These questions deserve attention in converting campuses into places that serve the good of the planet.[32] If colleges take environmental concerns seriously, then their campuses must aim for more responsible environment stewardship. Many colleges have embraced the difficult task of pursuing carbon neutrality. The organization Second Nature organized the Presidents' Climate Leadership Commitments in 2007 to encourage college leaders to act on climate leadership; 450 colleges and universities have signed the commitments, though only 10 institutions have achieved this difficult goal to date.[33] As many signatories have observed, such work to achieve carbon neutrality is difficult, and those laboring on the ground may have little say over how and at what pace this work gets done.

[28] See the epilogue of this volume for further discussion of the ecology of the common good, especially the ways interconnectedness fosters individual and collective growth as well as awareness of others' needs.

[29] Francis, *Laudato si'* (Vatican City: Vatican Press, 2015), sec. 13, 19.

[30] "Universal Apostolic Preferences," *Jesuits*, February 19, 2019, https://www.jesuits.global/uap/.

[31] "Universal Apostolic Preferences."

[32] For an extended discussion of the common good within Catholic social teaching, see chapter 1 of this volume by David Mazko McCarthy.

[33] "Carbon Neutral Colleges and Universities," Second Nature, accessed June 1, 2022, https://secondnature.org/climate-action-guidance/carbon-neutral-colleges-and-universities/.

Another, perhaps more actionable, way to work toward changing hearts and minds is through environmental education. If "all education is environmental education,"[34] we need our curricula to treat ideas and progress as inextricably connected to ecological concerns. Curricular ingenuity unites ostensibly disparate disciplines, intertwining economics and history and engineering and stewardship. A full discussion of the "common good place" of the university must account for how our institutions exist in a larger context that our students will inhabit long after they graduate. Our goal must be to frame their education not simply as training for a narrow specialty, or even part of thoughtful discernment of purposeful work in service to others. Instead, we can educate students to develop respect and appreciation for various commons, from the narrowest context of their campus to the broader commons of our planet. Ultimately, we want them to understand their own meaning and purpose as deeply connected to the communities where they heed this call.

Vocation as place

If we grant that colleges create the conditions for great intellectual and affective growth because of their distinctive contexts, then we can begin to understand college campuses as places of great potential for encouraging vocational discernment and care for the common good. David Cunningham rightly orients our thinking toward vocation as something beyond the individual, helping us perceive the calling of the institution itself.[35] What I am suggesting here is a deliberate attention to the places and spaces themselves as integral to vocational development and care for the common good. How do these common good places (along with the people, structures, and practices that populate them) encourage such outcomes? In the sections that follow I offer a few contexts in which ideas like vocation and the common good can find purchase among students as a result of explicit focus on place.

[34] David Orr, *Earth in Mind: On Education, Environment, and the Human Prospect* (Washington, DC: Island Press, 2004), 12.

[35] David Cunningham, "Colleges Have Callings, Too," in *Vocation across the Academy*, ed. David S. Cunningham (New York: Oxford University Press, 2017), 249–71.

Learning communities

At the modern university, the residential living-learning community (LLC) hearkens back to a centuries-old tradition of bringing students together in a common space to ponder life's enduring questions. LLCs are characterized by a shared residential space in which students take similar courses and engage in extracurricular activities together. This joint effort between academic and student affairs has found favor at many institutions since the 1990s, with LLCs in place at over six hundred colleges and universities in the United States today.[36]

At my institution, LLC membership has been a key factor in retention and overall campus satisfaction among first- and second-year students. As an instructor in an LLC for students in the honors program, I have witnessed a qualitative difference in the attitude students bring to the classroom compared to their peers not in the community. They've often discussed (and sometimes commiserated over) shared readings before and after class, leading to richer classroom discussions and a more cohesive classroom culture. The class I teach encourages students to consider aspects of vocation and identity, and at the same time students are enrolled in a philosophy class that addresses the concept of human flourishing. Our students, many of whom enter college with intentions of going to medical school, often report feeling liberated to consider other options while in our classes because they have the time and space to think about why they are in college and what makes a life meaningful.

Our work in the LLC is vitally informed by the Ignatian pedagogical paradigm (IPP), a teaching and learning tool in the Jesuit tradition that encourages deep reflection on meaning and purpose in one's life, making it a helpful tool for vocational discernment. Inspired by the *Spiritual Exercises* of St. Ignatius, which were developed to guide retreatants in reflection on how to live their lives, the IPP offers a dynamic, student-centered, and integrated approach to teaching and learning that promotes deep awareness of and attention to context, experience, reflection, action, and evaluation. These five elements build upon one another, and thoughtful educators can leverage knowledge of students' lives and an appreciation for the environment in which students learn to create distinctive learning situations that

---

[36] Karen Kurotsuchi Inkelas, Joey Jessup-Anger, Mimi Benjamin, and Matthew Wawrynski, *Living-Learning Communities That Work: A Research-Based Model for Design, Delivery, and Assessment* (Sterling, VA: Stylus, 2018).

promote "students' well-rounded growth as persons for others."[37] What is distinctive about an experience in this context is that students do not simply take common courses; they also engage in intentional conversations about what they're learning and how these experiences influence their intended career path. By expanding the scope of a student's learning beyond the class material itself through intentional reflection and cross-disciplinary inquiry, a well-run LLC can reveal how students might feel called not just to a particular career, but to a larger way of life.

The Jesuit mission helps students contextualize these reflections beyond a narrow institutional framework, "[going] beyond a disincarnate spiritualism or a secular social activism, so as to renew the educational apostolate in word and in action at the service of the church in a world of unbelief and injustice."[38] When put into practice, this mission requires attention to education of the whole person (*cura personalis*), which demands direct engagement with the world in which they will live, work, and play. It requires research and scholarship oriented toward the advancement of knowledge, but also toward the advancement of the poor and disadvantaged. By extending course content into these fruitful areas for reflection, LLCs can create vocational moments in which students expand their sense of the commons and see themselves as integrally connected to people beyond the campus community.

If we seek the interplay between vocational discernment and the common good, then this emphasis on place and context is critical. In a sense, what Ignatian pedagogy offers students is an invitation to be thoughtful observers of the context, reflective about their positionality within that context (including place and privilege), and critically evaluative of the choices and actions they make as citizens in their community. Such reflection can be radically transformational for students who begin to see their vocation as something more than a career and instead something deeply connected to the commons they inhabit, both at the institution and beyond. Only by attending to one's personal context and understanding one's place at the institution and in community can students properly understand their own gifts and the way to use them in the world. In other words, a proper understanding of place and context, made possible by a well-designed LLC, is instrumental to both vocational identity and a cultivation of habits to serve the common good.

---

[37] Sharon Korth, "Precis of Ignatian Pedagogy: A Practical Approach," in *A Jesuit Education Reader*, ed. George Traub (Chicago: Loyola University Press, 2008), 218.

[38] Korth, "Precis of Ignatian Pedagogy," 151.

It is important to note that even the most integrative program can fall short of these goals. LLCs often bring students together who share a common intellectual identity or career trajectory. This arrangement can help students feel "at home" at their university by placing them in class and in conversation with students who share their interests. But it can also lead to a highly siloed campus structure. When students classify themselves based largely on major affiliation at the time of their college application, they may get more of what they want in terms of curricular and extracurricular structure, but they might also miss out on the rich insights that flow from students with different perspectives who could introduce them to another "way of knowing" their subject matter.[39] Moreover, LLCs can easily entrench privilege and further marginalize underrepresented groups who are less likely to join these programs, especially when they are housed in expensive facilities or when the curriculum fails to represent diverse views.[40] In these instances, LLCs that perceive themselves as engines of intellectual and social innovation might instead be fortifying structures of exclusion and privilege.

If LLCs are thoughtfully designed to be "social learning spaces," they will exhibit inclusivity, flexibility, and hospitality.[41] These spaces promote both formal and informal learning driven by activities like "focused collaboration, intermittent exchange, serendipitous encounter, and ambient sociality."[42] These activities are often harder to achieve in a formal classroom setting, but when they operate in an LLC they can foster deep social bonds that yield "greater engagement in active and collaborative learning" that extends beyond the classroom.[43] All of this points toward a building up of the common good.

"Placebuilding" and "place as text"

Common spaces on college campuses are central to promoting care for the common good, yet we must also remember that colleges and universities are institutions situated in communities. Strange and Banning use the term "placebuilding" to describe how institutions form intentional relationships

---

[39] Ann Hartman, "Many Ways of Knowing," *Social Work* 35, no. 1 (1990): 3–4, https://doi.org/10.1093/sw/35.1.3.

[40] Inkelas et al., *Living-Learning Communities That Work*, 129–30.

[41] Strange and Banning, *Designing for Learning*, 31.

[42] Strange and Banning, *Designing for Learning*, 31.

[43] Strange and Banning, *Designing for Learning*, 35.

with these local communities, with varying levels of commitment.[44] Institutions that merely exist in a community and monopolize its resources are exploitative and show no concern for the common good. Contributive institutions perceive a distinct relationship with the community and show some support (often financial) for the community. Transformational institutions "see themselves as interdependent change agents within the larger community, who are trying to improve the conditions of both through various partnerships."[45]

There are many positive ways to engage in placebuilding efforts, among them community and experiential learning offices and town-gown committees. At my own institution, a redevelopment office works in tandem with the city's urban planning division to share resources, establish common goals for regional economic growth, and pursue joint projects that will serve the community and the institution. Its efforts have contributed to the construction of a new hospital, development of a sustainable grocery store in the neighborhood, and an attractive new food court and market near campus made up exclusively of local vendors.

These are great initiatives for the institution overall that exhibit a "transformational" approach to placemaking, but in terms of individual students and their understanding of vocational identities and the common good, even these altruistic efforts can feel disconnected from their experiences. Despite the proximity of contributory and transformational community developments, it is not uncommon for students to admit they rarely (if ever) enter the local community.[46] How, then, to help students appreciate their place at the college or university as a series of concentric circles that connects them to broader and more diverse communities? Here, I turn to the world of honors education.

Collegiate honors education may not be the first thing readers think about when considering vocation and the common good.[47] For many reasons (among them biased selection criteria and historically Eurocentric curricula), honors programs are seen as exclusive and exclusionary communities.

---

[44] Strange and Banning, *Designing for Learning*, 39–40.
[45] Strange and Banning, *Designing for Learning*, 40.
[46] For a deeper examination of the transformational power of direct encounter and community-based learning in vocational discernment, see chapter 7 of this volume by Jonathan Golden.
[47] For an overview of the role of vocation in honors education, see Erin VanLaningham, Robert J. Pampel, Jonathan D. Kotinek, Dustin J. Kemp, Aron Reppmann, and Anna Stewart, "Purpose, Meaning, and Exploring Vocation in Honors Education," *Journal of the National Collegiate Honors Council* 641 (2019): 81–118, https://digitalcommons.unl.edu/nchcjournal/641.

While this may be true in some cases, more progressive honors colleges and programs foster an academic culture in which students pursue learning in a spirit of collaboration, humanistic education, and global citizenship. The National Collegiate Honors Council (NCHC) defines honors education as "measurably broader, deeper, or more complex than comparable learning experiences typically found at institutions of higher education."[48] Honors educators often invoke the analogy of an "academic laboratory" to describe a system that is constantly adapting to new challenges and opportunities based on the innate curiosity and diverse interests of students and teachers.[49]

One of the best examples of the honors "living laboratory" is Place as Text,[50] which grew out of the Honors Semesters initiative of the 1970s. Honors Semesters consisted of semester-long, instructor-led explorations of a specific place beyond the campus to learn about local culture, practice active learning, and be critically self-reflective about one's beliefs. Honors Semesters developed more broadly into a Place as Text pedagogy designed to take students into new contexts to promote active learning. Later, the NCHC adopted a City as Text initiative, which invited students to explore "any socially constructed enclave" in which students could follow "structured observations," "laboratory observations," and "formal and informal interviews of people in the community."[51]

Two primary goals of the City as Text methodology are autonomy and community. By inviting students to invest time and attention learning about and from the local community, students are taken "away from the familiar" and encouraged to "create maps of strange and sometimes uncomfortable contexts."[52] In doing so, they gain "confidence in seeking [their] own truth, a truth that is open to critical examination and rational review."[53] But in addition to celebrating a student's burgeoning intellectual and personal autonomy, City as Text charges them with "appreciating the individuality of others" in a "community of support."[54] In other words, students develop the

---

[48] "Definition of Honors Education," National Collegiate Honors Council, accessed June 1, 2022, https://www.nchchonors.org/directors-faculty/definition-of-honors-education.

[49] Marca Wolfensberger, *Teaching for Excellence: Honors Pedagogy Revealed* (Münster, Germany: Waxmann, 2012).

[50] Bernice Braid, "Introduction," in *Place as Text: Approaches to Active Learning*, ed. Bernice Braid and Ada Long (Lincoln, NE: National Collegiate Honors Council, 2000), 5.

[51] Bernice Braid, "Foreword," in *Shatter the Glassy Stare: Implementing Experiential Learning in Higher Education*, ed. Peter Machonis (Lincoln, NE: National Collegiate Honors Council, 2008), 9.

[52] William Daniel, "Honors Semesters: Anatomy of Active Learning," in Braid and Long, eds., *Place as Text*, 10.

[53] Daniel, "Honors Semesters," 12.

[54] Daniel, "Honors Semesters," 12.

capacity to see their own development as inextricably linked to the welfare of others—an objective well suited to vocational exploration in relationship to the common good.

There are many ways to approach the City as Text ideal from a "common good place" perspective, the most obvious of which is to treat the campus and the surrounding community as a place of reverence and exploration. One educator, for instance, encouraged students to develop a personal understanding of the "sacred" in the midst of "profane" imagery like cigarette butts on campus grounds and smokestacks that lurk in the background.[55] At my own institution, several honors courses focus on understanding and living the Jesuit mission in terms of community engagement. One course requires students—many of whom hail from other cities and states—to learn about local government and other issues in the civic discourse, even putting together their own policies to address local concerns and priorities. Another course includes regular conversations with local community leaders as well as walking tours to nearby museums and other cultural venues. A third course on Jesuit and Catholic traditions takes students to local sites (cathedrals, basilicas, even graveyards) to convey the significance of context in understanding local history. In all cases, by emphasizing the importance of common places, these courses demonstrate how personal reflection and discernment can and should accompany appreciation of and concern for community, broadly defined.

City as Text is an active pedagogy that may extend further afield, even to the point of international ventures where students are in decidedly *uncommon* places. Such is the case with a recent study-abroad program at my institution, built on the CASA model of international education. Jesuit colleges and universities have created CASA models of education in places like Nicaragua, El Salvador, the Philippines, and Belize.[56] The idea is not to use a particular country as a launching pad for travel elsewhere, or to promote solutions to problems from a place of privilege and access. Instead, these programs stress community engagement, accompaniment, and solidarity with the host country. As sanguine as it sounds, the CASA model of international immersion is about listening to and learning from hosts, simply being with them in the context of their communities.

---

[55] Mary Lou Pfeiffer, "From Cigarette Butts to the 'Stacks' and Beyond," in Braid and Long, eds., *Place as Text*, 37–44.

[56] CASA is a model of experiential education that stresses community, academics, spirituality, and accompaniment.

In both examples of Place as Text above, the experiences are driven largely by the idea of being persons "for and with others," a foundational principle in Jesuit education.[57] Importantly, Place as Text encourages participants to stress *with* and de-emphasize *for*. Students are accustomed to doing things *for* others. They are eager to use their gifts in service of others, to lean into a vocation of service on behalf of communities in need. This is generally a good thing, as it can spawn rich acts of service for others. But, as Samuel Wells summarizes, " 'For' is a fine word, but it does not dismantle resentment, it does not overcome misunderstanding, it does not deal with alienation, it does not overcome isolation."[58] Instead, Wells invites us to think about the distinction between for and with, or, as he puts it, a distinction between trying to overcome mortality and trying to alleviate isolation. Being with others in common places forces us to sacrifice something of ourselves and to be more thoughtful about the ties that bind us, rather than the gulf that divides us.[59] If our goal is to create connection and to care for our common good, this can be a powerful pivot in our thinking, and the Place as Text pedagogy provides a helpful avenue to this way of thinking.

Digital transcendent space

It would be easy to write off digital spaces as incapable of achieving the almost transcendent quality associated with the "collegiate way," but this impulse to distrust digital spaces is misguided. The pandemic fundamentally altered the physical "common good places" that students knew and accentuated the role of digital spaces. These digital spaces can share qualities with thriving college communities, including a common location, mechanisms for social interaction, and "common ties of purpose and direction."[60] These communities can be recognized "at their fundamental level" by "their distinct and celebrated historical identities, their balance of interdependent roles and relationships, their norms and procedures for functioning, and their linkages to the larger

---

[57] Pedro Arrupe, "Men for Others: Training Agents of Change for the Promotion of Justice," in *Justice with Faith Today: An Anthology of Letters and Addresses*, ed. Jerome Aixala (St. Louis, MO: Institute of Jesuit Sources, 1980), 123–38.

[58] Samuel Wells, "Rethinking Service," *The Cresset* 76, no. 4 (2013): 3–4, http://thecresset.org/2013/Easter/Wells_E2013.html.

[59] See Jonathan Golden's reflections on the power of the direct encounter in chapter 7 of this volume.

[60] Strange and Banning, *Designing for Learning*, 215.

society."[61] While the role of the physical campus space for gathering and community nourishment is significant, the digital experience merits consideration as a "good place."

From a learning design perspective, college students' "everyday experience is much more seamless as they navigate between personal encounters and digital likes."[62] Students are so enmeshed in their digital worlds that they regularly seek and find online communities to accompany their on-campus lives. Recently my institution began inviting newly admitted students to share a picture of themselves and a brief biographical sketch on a class-specific Instagram account. With impressive speed and surprising candor, students who have never physically met form online connections, trade memes and inside jokes, and begin the process of acculturation to the institution before they've even begun classes. In effect, they have found a useful mechanism for interaction in a common place and begun to develop "common ties of purpose and direction." Instagram banter is hardly the substance of deep relationships and care for the common good, but it can be a step toward sincere dialogue and thoughtful engagement.

There's no reason this engagement cannot flourish online. At my institution, we offer a special honors study-abroad online "course" to encourage deliberate and sustained reflection during students' sojourns abroad. Several assignments are submitted for others to see, with the expectation that students read and comment on one another's work. In many ways, the course succeeds precisely because of its online context. The Canvas site where students submit work creates a digital space of hospitality and critical engagement—a small "community of practice"[63]—where students can openly express joys and frustration over international travel, their development as global citizens, and their ongoing discernment about how international experiences influence their personal and professional identity.

Much like the experiences described above, this online course creates a space that transcends national borders, creates threads of continuity across space and time, and invites students to think about both their personal development and their responsibilities to communities new and old.[64] It broadens the common good places where students can create more just communities.

---

[61] Strange and Banning, *Designing for Learning*, 217.

[62] Strange and Banning, *Designing for Learning*, 240.

[63] Lily Arasaratnam-Smith and Maria Northcote, "Communities in Online Higher Education: Challenges and Opportunities," *Electronic Journal of e-Learning* 15, no. 2 (2017): 188–98.

[64] See again chapter 12 by Martin Holt Dotterweich for a discussion of the ways history and memory offer avenues to demonstrate solidarity with others.

The virtues we associate with physical locations in terms of student development and community responsibility can translate to digital spaces that deliver these transcendent outcomes.

Conclusion

Near the end of its four-season run, the main characters in *The Good Place* finally find themselves safely in the true "Good Place," a utopian setting in which all inhabitants can fulfill their desires at a moment's notice. This was the outcome the characters relentlessly pursued since learning of their consignment to eternal torment in "the bad place" seasons earlier. Even after arriving in an ostensibly perfect setting, the characters continue to challenge and critique, ultimately discerning the shortcomings of an afterlife that guarantees perpetual satisfaction. Building on (several) lifetimes of critical reflection, they revolutionize the system, creating a pathway for people who have achieved their ultimate purpose. They can walk through a door and leave, at which point they return their essence to the universe. In the end, the show invites viewers to consider how, even in the best of contexts, we can push ever outward and always seek improvement for ourselves and others.

Throughout this chapter I have suggested that there are places on our campuses, in our communities, in the world at large, and even in digital spaces that are conducive to discerning one's purpose and in serving the world in diverse and significant ways. Instead of seeing vocation as something interior and private, and the common good as simply an ideal that we collectively pursue somewhere "out there," we might instead look to the "common good places" in our midst where these ideas intersect in powerful and transformative ways.

In the context of a college campus, this does not mean embracing some modern version of the "collegiate way" in an uncritical way, as though the place alone is enough to foster intellectual growth, civic virtue, and care for the common good. Indeed, plenty of campus spaces have fallen short of their intended purposes by being exclusionary, transactional, or simply uninspired in design and scope. "Common good places" must be thoughtfully imagined, carefully designed, and critically assessed—meaning they must give voice to students, faculty, and staff of all backgrounds. They must also be attentive to human and environmental ecologies, and inclusive of nontraditional spaces and even digital fora that reimagine what the commons look like for students who enter and exit communities in different ways. This chapter aims to reinforce (and develop appreciation for) the role of context and place as a foundational part of vocational discernment and care for the common good. When designed thoughtfully and with respect for those who inhabit these places, our campuses become places of compassion that foster the prerequisite conditions for realizing the existential goods discussed throughout this volume. We must not lose sight of the potential of "common good places" to promote these important goals.

12

The Yarn in the Tapestry

Weaving Memory into History, Vocation, and Our Common Life

Martin Holt Dotterweich

The bard or the copyist?

The ancient Irish epic *Táin Bó Cúailnge* tells of a war following a cattle raid, but it is also a story about memory. Throughout the tale, events connect to place names, incorporating the memory of a distant past on the land itself. But human memory is also important in the *Táin*. In the twelfth book, in Ciaran Carson's magnificent translation, the warrior Fergus Mac Róich shows off his memory as he identifies the various warriors mustering from Ulster. As each band of fighters is described by the scout Mac Roth, Fergus identifies them and comments on their exploits, showing the breadth of his remembering. As the descriptions finish, Mac Roth sums up, "Wherever I cast my eye, . . . all I could see was men and horses." But with his gift of memory, even though he is relying on the report of another rather than seeing the warriors themselves, Fergus can correct him. "What you saw was a people coming together."[1]

For Fergus, memory provides perspective and connection, and ultimately incorporation: his remembering means that all the warriors named are in some sense part of him. It's a skill that the poets who handed the story down orally valued; in one manuscript, the narrative finishes by pronouncing "a blessing on everyone who shall faithfully memorize the *Táin* as it is written here." It had of course been handed down by word of mouth before, yet still would be memorized by bards from written copies. They could work from descriptions of things they had not seen to find wisdom. However, the copyist of this text, a monk who spoke both Irish and Latin, did not see the value

---

[1] *The Táin: A New Translation of the Táin Bó Cúailnge*, trans. Ciaran Carson (London: Penguin Classics, 2008), 193.

Martin Holt Dotterweich, *The Yarn in the Tapestry* In: *Called Beyond Our Selves*. Edited by: Erin VanLaningham, Oxford University Press. © Oxford University Press 2024. DOI: 10.1093/oso/9780197691915.003.0013

in this exercise. At the end of the text, writing in Latin rather than the Irish of the original, he adds, "I who have written down this story (*historia*) or rather this fable, give no credence to the story, or fable."[2]

What do we make of this stinger in the tail? In the *Táin*, memory is a virtue, weaving us together and offering us wisdom; but in this final note, memory is something other than history, a keeper of falsehood and nostalgia. Should historians find their vocation among the bards or the copyists? Or is it possible that these roles might complement one another? It is my contention here that history teaches us how to remember well, and that historically enriched memory calls us beyond ourselves. If we incorporate the past into memory, we find our place among others, and we find vocation for the common good in the study of history.

Apologists for history

What's the use of history? It's a question we get asked regularly in the profession, and the answers we offer seem to be unsatisfactory, as the question does not go away. Within the university, historians face a struggle to maintain the number of students majoring in history, which leads to questions about maintaining or funding faculty lines, or in some cases the existence of the major itself. This is part of a national trend toward professional degrees that has left most liberal arts subjects struggling. It may be possible to argue the case for history from student satisfaction, from alumni success, from the fact that history costs little. But historians often end up turning to language of the common good when making the case for their discipline.

Whether it is directed to deans or to first-year students, we spend a surprising amount of time explaining why history ought to be required in general education, funded for research, pursued as a major, valued as a department. And that is *at universities*. When we widen our gaze, we find that historians also have to make a case for their field in other contexts: the city council, the school board, the church committee, the cocktail party. Most challenges to the value of history take a pragmatic or utilitarian approach: what use is history for our students? Few choose to study it; if it were more important to them, they'd take the courses. Why would my child major in something so

---

[2] *Táin*, xvii–xviii. Carson notes in his introduction that the copyist "both disparages and privileges the art of memory," xvii.

utterly unconnected to a real-world job? Beyond education, why spend so much public money on something we all disagree about? Won't this just divide us? What good is history?

The case from civics

A reliable rejoinder in such conversations appeals to the common good. In the civic context, partisan sparring should not discourage public funding; rather, it shows just how important the use of the past is and encourages thoughtful civic engagement. With regard to students, we stress the civic virtues that history teaches (e.g., empathy), along with the soft skills (e.g., critical thinking and digital literacy) it demands. History courses that foster humane skills like these, and encourage an appreciation for civic participation, surely contribute to the common good. Such a case can apply both outside and inside the university.

Most texts on history teaching offer versions of the case for history teaching from civic virtue, but for a well-rounded example I offer here the taxonomy provided by Keith Barton and Linda Levstik in their thoughtful and comprehensive volume *Teaching History for the Common Good*.[3] Focused on primary and secondary education, the arguments they identify apply equally well to undergraduate teaching. The study of history, they suggest, inculcates many civic virtues: participation in a pluralist democracy, identification with a communal group, analysis of different sources or points of view, moral development (including remembrance of those who have been oppressed), exhibition of historical material for educational purposes, narrative structure (and its limits), inquiry of evidence, and empathy. While there are, of course, variations on these themes, this is a good precis.[4] Something worth noting is that those who teach in other humanities disciplines may recognize their work here too, and they would be right. In a sense, this is arguing for the

[3] Keith C. Barton and Linda S. Levstik, *Teaching History for the Common Good* (London: Routledge, 2004).

[4] For this chapter, I consulted several volumes, including Alan Booth, *Teaching History at University: Enhancing Learning and Understanding* (London: Routledge, 2003); M. Elaine Davis, *How Students Understand the Past: From Theory to Practice* (Walnut Creek, CA: Altamira, 2005); Peter N. Stearns, "Thinking History," American Historical Association Institutional Services Program (Washington, DC: American Historical Association, 2004); Geoff Timmins, Keith Vernon, and Christine Kinealy, *Teaching & Learning History* (London: Sage, 2005).

value of history teaching not because it is history, but because it is part of wider liberal arts education.

I find these arguments compelling; I have used them many times. Sometimes they work; sometimes they help a student decide to major in history or persuade a dean to approve a course. Sometimes they provide a thoughtful component of conversation outside the university. In many respects, the case from civics is where I should naturally have turned in constructing this chapter. At its best, teaching history encourages understanding and getting along with others, because it shows us that we are all products of particular circumstances, and we owe each other both empathy and attentiveness. In the general education requirements of my institution, we call this *citizenship* in a broad sense, and that surely points to a common good.[5] But for three reasons I'm not focusing my chapter here: first, because this territory has been articulated so well by so many others; second, because it seems to me that this is not a calling to the common good specific to history; and third, because I think that the warrior Fergus was on to something.[6]

In my experience, history teaches us how to remember well, and memory helps us incorporate history; remembered history allows us to see "a people coming together" where otherwise we might see only names and dates. Memory and history are not opposed: memory is the yarn that historians weave into tapestry; and it is also the wall that hangs the tapestry. Remembering is a virtue proper to the vocation of the history teacher and student alike, both its method and goal. This does not mean that students remember all the things that they have been taught in a class, but rather that some of those things will become part of their deepest selves. As history and memory intersect, they can become a point of grace, hospitality, and inclusion, calling us to greater concern and appreciation for ourselves and for each other. Much of my vocation is shaped by remembering, from teaching style to testing to classroom activities, and I am convinced that memory calls me, and my students, to a pursuit of the common good.

---

[5] For an exploration of the aspects of citizenship that range from mutual understanding through dialogue, deliberation, and empathy, see this volume's chapter 7 by Jonathan Golden and chapter 8 by David Timmerman.

[6] There is also a warning sounded by Barton and Levstik: "This is the danger of history that focuses on questions of the common good: Those in positions of authority may think they already know what the common good is and that their role is to reproduce their opinions in students," 39–40. The case from civics may prove uncivil.

History versus memory

The copyist of the *Táin Bó Cúailnge* was not entirely wrong: remembering does differ from history. I am referring here to history as deliberate inquiry into the past, rather than history as past events. That inquiry is conducted with an attempt to discover, as much as possible, what the events and persons of the past were like, how they came to be, what they meant. Most of it comes from words, and it is communicated in words. Using multiple sources—most of them based on the memory of others—history attempts to be fair, understanding motivations and actions in context. Both attention to detail and breadth of knowledge help enrich the understanding of historical context. History looks for patterns, though it eschews rules. Its tendency is to the particular rather than the general, and it always understands contingency; as I tell my survey students on the first day of class, people are complicated.[7] Each history is unique, just as each historian is unique; history is never finished, but always growing.

By memory I refer to the act of memory, of remembering. It can be deliberate and rehearsed, but it is more often involuntary, an "unbroken horse."[8] Memory can explain and give meaning, or it can be unconnected to anything else. It can include words, or it may be primarily about emotion or impression, which sometimes makes it difficult to put memory into words.[9] We think our memories are unbiased at first, yet with time we may question them. Memory sometimes grasps context but often stands starkly against a blank background. Patterns and continuities may be spun from memory, and they may appear to bind the present. Idiosyncratic by nature, memory is utterly individual yet weaves people together. Memory ebbs and flows; it can be gained or lost.

To return to my yarn metaphor earlier, memory is both the source and the goal of history. We begin with the memories of others, whether diaries or

---

[7] I am drawing here on three books I have used regularly in historiography courses: David Bebbington, *Patterns in History: A Christian Perspective on Historical Thought* (Vancouver: Regent College Publishing, 1990); John Fea, *Why Study History? Reflecting on the Importance of the Past* (Grand Rapids, MI: Baker, 2013); and John Lewis Gaddis, *The Landscape of History: How Historians Map the Past* (New York: Oxford University Press, 2004).

[8] Seamus Heaney, *Sweeney Astray: A Version from the Irish* (New York: Farrar, Straus and Giroux, 1985), 48.

[9] For example, one can remember emotional reactions to an event whose details and context are forgotten: Gordon Spencer Shrimpton, *History and Memory in Ancient Greece* (Montreal: McGill-Queen's University Press, 1997), 52ff. Shrimpton believes that ancient history writing is a blend of the empirical and "memorative drama," 58.

letters or books or ledgers. Memory is of course flawed, incomplete, sometimes self-serving or even deceptive. Historians realize this and weave accordingly; memory has to be sifted, compared, evaluated. But without memory, there is simply no history, no tapestry. Nor does the tapestry hang anywhere unless we shape the memory of our students. Somehow memory must be incorporated, becoming part of us, setting historical events and persons beside the things we have personally encountered. If we weave personal and historical memory together, if this tapestry hangs in our view, it affects our view of the world. In this tapestry, the past is not separate from me; I am part of it, and it is part of me. The more my memory develops, the more I see that my place is among others.

The memory boom

The remembered past has been a potent force in historical movements, moments, and persons, even when that memory is not historical: this is the heart of an academic "memory boom." The proliferation of memory studies focuses on the threads of the tapestry, inspecting them critically and opening new dimensions of the past.

The memory boom is also interdisciplinary, reaching into biology, literature, psychology, law, and other fields. There is no single position that has dominated historiographical reflection, but some stand out. French historian Pierre Nora focuses on the problematic ways in which particular memories become national memory ("a common possession and a collective heritage"), especially through places or objects associated with the past, which he calls *lieux de mémoire*.[10] In English, David Lowenthal left a considerable body of work examining the differences between history and memory, particularly in light of the presence of the past in pop culture and in the "heritage industry." These threatened to devour the production of professional, critical history, because "there is now virtually nothing that is not considerably more lively after death than it was before."[11]

Nora and Lowenthal were both attentive to the fact that the memory boom is not confined to the writing of history; the growing importance of

---

[10] Pierre Nora, ed., *Rethinking France: Les Lieux de Mémoire*, vol. 4: *Histories and Memories*, trans. David P. Jordan (Chicago: University of Chicago Press, 2010), xiii.

[11] Quoting George Perkins Marsh, on whom he wrote frequently, in David Lowenthal, *The Past Is a Foreign Country—Revisited* (Cambridge: Cambridge University Press, 2015), 5.

the monument, the historical site, the documentary, the historical drama, the reenactment coincided with the scholarly movement. To some degree, this interest is an encouragement to historians battered down by years of student indifference. But *lieux de mémoire* also threaten critical history because, as Lowenthal says, "wishful thinking plays a major role in public history—a role historians may deplore but cannot afford to ignore."[12] On this account, memory may generate interest in the past, but at the cost of dehistoricizing it; memory is a subject to be analyzed, but also a problem to be addressed.

Memory wars

The memory boom should provide historians with a strong argument for the common good relevance of their discipline, particularly insofar as it can guide discussions on contested public memory. Battles over public memory can be informal, but they also take place in legal proceedings or legislative assemblies. As I was writing this chapter, in nearby Kingsport, Tennessee, a high school history teacher was fired for teaching critical race theory, shortly after the governor had signed a Tennessee General Assembly bill withholding state funding from schools in which inherent privilege is taught. Heated meetings of the school board and city council followed; later a panel upheld the decision, and his appeal for reinstatement was denied.[13] Legislation about memory is more pronounced elsewhere. In Europe especially, interpretations of history are the subject of "memory wars." Beginning in France in the early 2000s, European governments have not simply regulated, but criminalized denial of facts related to the Holocaust, Armenian genocide, the slave trade, and others. According to Nikolay Koposov, this is something new: "The emergence of memory laws in the strict sense shows that in the age of memory, the past has become even more important for cultural identity and political legitimation than it was in the age of history-based political ideologies."[14]

[12] David Lowenthal, "History and Memory," *Public Historian* 19, no. 2 (Spring 1997): 38, https://doi.org/10.2307/3379138.

[13] Hannah Natanson, "A White Teacher Taught White Students about White Privilege. It Cost Him His Job," *Washington Post*, December 6, 2021, https://www.washingtonpost.com/education/2021/12/06/tennessee-teacher-fired-critical-race-theory/; Tennessee HB 0580, SB 0623, https://wapp.capitol.tn.gov/apps/BillInfo/Default.aspx?BillNumber=HB0580.

[14] Nikolay Koposov, *Memory Laws, Memory Wars: The Politics of the Past in Europe and Russia* (Cambridge: Cambridge University Press, 2018), 12.

But memory wars are far more visible in debates about public memorials. These debates surrounded me as I wrote this piece. On a research trip to Charlottesville, Virginia, I saw the places where statues of Robert E. Lee (infamous for the "Unite the Right" rally in 2017), Stonewall Jackson, and Lewis and Clark (with a controversial Sacagawea) had been removed shortly before.[15] Closer to my home, in Abingdon, Virginia, the town council removed a Confederate statue for reasons of construction, though it was relocated to the front of a government building elsewhere in town.[16] Both the removal and relocation of statues were attended with considerable debate and dissent.

Not all the public memory around me was divisive—some encouraged incorporation and the common good. In Charlottesville, I spent time at the recently dedicated *Memorial to Enslaved Laborers*, which honors those who had built and maintained the university in forced servitude.[17] The making of this monument had its detractors but brought far more people together, especially families who had felt separated from the university.[18] Back in Bristol, Tennessee, I attended the unveiling of the first historical markers commemorating African Americans in the town's history.[19] These ways of remembering, informed by history, contribute to the common good.

History enriching memory

To return to the main point of this chapter: I contend that history teaches us how to remember well, and that in doing so, it calls us beyond ourselves. The study of history allows us to weave our personal memory into a tapestry with others, and when we incorporate history into our memory, that tapestry

---

[15] Hawes Spencer and Michael Levenson, "Charlottesville Removes Robert E. Lee Statue at Center of White Nationalist Rally," *New York Times*, July 9, 2021, https://www.nytimes.com/2021/07/09/us/charlottesville-confederate-monuments-lee.html?smid=url-share.

[16] Joe Tennis, "Washington County Board of Supervisors Votes to Relocate Monuments to Green Space," *Bristol Herald-Courier*, December 15, 2021, https://heraldcourier.com/news/local/washington-county-board-of-supervisors-votes-to-relocate-monuments-to-green-space/article_200ab91f-54b1-5c83-a6a8-d5dec3d9c1ca.html.

[17] Caroline Newman, "A Closer Look at the Design and Details of the New Memorial to Enslaved Laborers," University of Virginia, April 7, 2021, https://news.virginia.edu/content/closer-look-design-and-details-new-memorial-enslaved-laborers. The dedication was to have been in 2020 but was postponed owing to COVID-19.

[18] Interview with E. Franklin Dukes, May 20, 2022.

[19] Robert Sorrell, "Two Historical Markers Dedicated in Bristol," *Bristol Herald-Courier*, October 30, 2021, https://heraldcourier.com/news/local/two-historical-markers-dedicated-in-bristol/article_21eafaa5-e8fe-569d-8053-3159ef796158.html.

hangs firmly. The memory boom and memory wars make it possible to argue that history contributes to the common good by teaching us to remember.

I want to use the public memorial as a way of thinking about how history enriches memory and how it helps us to weave the past into our memory to discern our relationships to and empathy for others. For educators, it may be that direct engagement with public memorials, whether through testimony, protest, or correction, is the best expression of this vocation. Within the classroom context, memorials can start conversation about memory and the common good. In guiding these conversations, educators should give themselves and their students sufficient time to account for nuance and complexity. Rather than oversimplify, historians should allow the questions to take on their full difficulty.[20] Annette Gordon-Reed offers an example in her essay "A Different View," suggesting that Harvard Law School not jettison the crest of a slave-owning family who had endowed the school, so that this legacy not be forgotten. One need not agree with Gordon-Reed to appreciate the approach, asking hard questions of historical accountability, the meaning of symbols, and the role of discomfort in memorials. The point of this hard discussion, for Gordon-Reed, is located in the common good: "so that one can be ready to be of service to other people and to purposes outside of (and even more important than) one's personal feelings."[21] Such an approach requires both time and sensitive, respectful dialogue, pointing students toward a vision of historically enriched memory that asks us to consider collective well-being.

Of course, disputed public memorials are only one way to bring history to memory. More generally, historians can help students remember better, and this is true in general education courses as well as major courses. Few general education students will become professional historians, but they are all touched by the need to remember. History courses can help them use their memories well, by encouraging them to consider complexity, context, and contingency, whether in their personal memories or the past events they study. Such practices invite students to incorporate others' experiences into their own, linking individual vocation with a sense of communal life. They weave the past into memory, the self into the other.

[20] For further exploration of the impact of memorials, see Robert J. Pampel's reflections in chapter 11 of this volume.
[21] Annette Gordon-Reed, "A Different View," Harvard Law School, March 2016, https://hls.harvard.edu/wp-content/uploads/2022/08/Shield_Committee-Different_View.pdf.

The Aviator: history incorporating memory

To explore this notion of remembering as a significant aspect of vocational discernment for the common good, I will consider three public memorials. In my accounts of a visit to each memorial, I offer examples of how asking historical questions brings forward a call to empathy, to hospitality, and to grace that fosters a wider sense of communal life.

Every time I went in or out of the Clemons Library at the University of Virginia (UVA) while researching for this chapter, I passed a statue that struck me, at first, as whimsical. A figure stands ready to spring, arms upraised, face upturned. He wears a leather helmet, a loincloth, a belt with a knife, and boots. And wings. I assumed that this statue, *The Aviator*, was a reflection on flight, or perhaps specifically a reference to Icarus. But as I asked historical questions of the statue, I incorporated its subject into my memory.

The Aviator commemorates UVA student James McConnell, who volunteered in 1914 as an ambulance driver for the French army, then joined the Lafayette Escadrille, for which he would fly biplanes in the war. He would not survive, being shot down in 1917. It's a striking statue, raised above head level on its plinth; you have to look up to see it, and on a clear day the wings stand out against a blue sky. If it seems whimsical at first, it expresses a real sadness: this is a modern Icarus, and he too will fall to his death. McConnell's friends wished to commemorate his bravery and zeal for freedom. The statue they commissioned celebrates his flight while mourning his death. An attractive and inoffensive statue at first glance, it offers far more with historical inquiry.[22] McConnell is now incorporated in my memory, his bravery and sacrifice and tragedy woven together with my knowledge of World War I and the history of flight.

But even more could be found here. I discovered that the sculptor had been rising star Gutzon Borglum, who would go on to carve Mount Rushmore. Borglum was as complex as he was gifted. He was the initial sculptor for Stone Mountain, where he was said to form close sympathies with the Ku Klux Klan.[23] But his other work does not fit him into easy categories. Borglum's

---

[22] Brendan Wolfe, "A Flight Forgotten," *Virginia: The UVA Magazine*, Fall 2016, https://uvamagaz ine.org/articles/a_flight_forgotten. I certainly counter the opinion expressed in the article that this is "kind of like the orange ceramic frog your parents got for a wedding present."

[23] Diane Bernard, "The Creator of Mount Rushmore's Forgotten Ties to White Supremacy," *Washington Post*, July 2, 2020, https://www.washingtonpost.com/history/2020/07/03/mount-rushmore-gutzon-borglum-klan-stone-mountain/; Matthew Shaer, "The Sordid History of Mount Rushmore," *Smithsonian Magazine*, October 2016, https://www.smithsonianmag.com/history/sor did-history-mount-rushmore-180960446/.

memorial to Confederate North Carolina troops stands at Gettysburg; on the other hand, his statue of Union General Philip Sheridan stands in Washington, DC, and his massive bust of Abraham Lincoln sits in the US Capitol Crypt. His sculpture of newspaper editor Harvey Scott in Portland, Oregon, was toppled during protests of the death of George Floyd in October 2020, whereas his bas-relief memorial to Sacco and Vanzetti—for which he refused payment—was only finally cast and displayed in 1997, long after the sculptor's death.[24]

Historical inquiry into Borglum makes *The Aviator* more complex and incorporates more into the memory of James McConnell. Expanding on the memory of a young idealist who died for his beliefs takes us in multiple directions: the history of World War I, the history of flight, Greek mythology, the complexities of public art, the nature of public memorials, the history of race in the United States. As history informs memory in the statue of James McConnell, I find that he is part of me, part of a tapestry of history and memory that gives me a strong sense of empathy for the idealists, for the ache of a young life cut short, for the tragedy of war. As I examine Gutzon Borglum historically, his memory leads me to a sharper understanding of the complexities of race in the history of the United States, as well as the complexities of an individual person. History helps me incorporate both the young aviator and the complex sculptor in memory.

Memorial to Enslaved Laborers: weaving a tapestry of memory

The *Memorial to Enslaved Laborers* in Charlottesville weaves history and memory into a striking tapestry. A student-initiated project, this memorial near UVA's best-known building, the Rotunda, commemorates four thousand people whose labor was compelled in the making and life of the university. Working with historian Mabel O. Wilson, designers J. Meejin Yoon and Eric Höweler utilized extensive historical research and thinking and consulted with both students and the community to remember the enslaved workers well. Shaped like the Rotunda, this circular wall recognizes enslaved workers with lines for the names of each of the four thousand enslaved

---

[24] A useful list of these works, with images, may be found at "Gutzon Borglum," Wikipedia, last modified January 2, 2022, https://en.wikipedia.org/wiki/Gutzon_Borglum.

laborers. For the vast majority, the lines are blank, with neither names nor occupations having been noted: history merges with memory for these unknown individuals by telling us their numbers, their location, their plight. Some lines recall people by their tasks, using historical research to provide detail where names have been lost: *cook, wagoner, blacksmith, painter*. A smaller number have names preserved. Names can be added to the blank lines; this is a living memorial that shows the results of continued research. One enslaved worker, Isabella Gibbons, left us words that are engraved on the memorial.

Walking around the memorial, seeing the blank lines, touching the cold stone or the water running inside the semicircle, I found that the history of the enslaved workers wove into my personal memory. Nothing accomplished this more powerfully, though, than when on a return visit I finally saw Isabella Gibbons's eyes. Working from a photograph, sculptor Eto Otitigbe carved her eyes into the wall so that they cannot be seen except at certain angles, in the light of dawn or dusk. My first (failed) attempts to see them were in the afternoon; when I finally saw her eyes, I was stunned and slightly unsettled by the detailed image that had eluded me before. As community facilitator Frank Dukes told me, "You have to look to see her."[25] This moment of revelation, and the historical detail it revealed, is fixed firmly to the wall of my memory.

The *Memorial to Enslaved Laborers* required extensive historical research, into both what is remembered and what is not; those blank lines tell a remarkable story. Historical thinking about the enslaved workers at UVA also introduces complexity, and the memorial does not simplify things; it acknowledges both the deep injustice of slavery and the excellence of the university built upon it. Informed by historical methods and thinking, this memorial honors enslaved workers and ennobles their work, while lamenting the oppression they suffered. As a memorial, it exemplifies how history can weave itself into memory: I now remember people, named or not, in the complex interplay of their oppression and accomplishment. In such remembering, the lives of others are bound up in my own.

[25] Interview with Frank Dukes, May 20, 2022; for credits, see https://mel.virginia.edu/about.

Chamseddine Marzoug's graveyard: history, memory, and a call beyond ourselves

Local graveyards can serve as an image of how memory can encourage students to hear a common good calling. A memorial that generally serves only a generation or two of living relatives, the graveyard is a place of names and dates. They could be only names and dates, rather like Mac Roth's reporting to Fergus Mac Róich. But these are places of calling to remember, and if we use the skills of history, a graveyard can bring a people together.[26]

For several years, I sat on the board of a historic cemetery in Bristol, Tennessee. Most of our meetings were about mowing and maintenance. But one board member, Bud Phillips, went beyond this. He spent time learning about hundreds of those buried here and at board meetings would often expostulate on them. In this act, he brought a historian's skills to a place of remembering, and the combination was potent: it helped us see our work as more than mowing, but rather as a service to the city's residents, living and dead. Bud incorporated these dead into his own memory and ultimately ours, and in doing so served the common good. The cemetery now offers ghost tours as a way of remembering past citizens, and the site—which includes sections for both enslaved persons and Confederate soldiers, all researched by Bud—has become a place of common remembrance and joint endeavor rather than a place of the forgotten.

Historians can bring life to the graveyard in class by transforming names and dates into real persons. We can never research everyone, but we can incorporate some of these individuals into our courses, thus modeling a common good use of memory for students. Not every individual so remembered needs to have played a major role in historical change or continuity; perhaps the most powerful remembering here is of those whose lives are otherwise passed over.

The image of the graveyard also shows us how memory calls us beyond ourselves even when history fails. Chamseddine Marzoug, a Tunisian fisherman who has buried hundreds of bodies of unknown immigrants who died trying to reach Europe, mostly sub-Saharan Africans, embodies this call.[27] With a single exception, the graves he has dug are marked only with

---

[26] For further discussion of the ways the study of place can help discover calls to the common good, see this volume's chapter 11 by Robert J. Pampel.

[27] Sudarsan Raghavan, "A Tunisian Gravedigger Gives Migrants What They Were Deprived of in Life: Dignity," *Washington Post*, September 10, 2018, https://www.washingtonpost.com/world/

numbers, for the persons are not known. Marzoug has served the common good both of his own town and of far-off families who do not know where their dead lie. For historians, this is a call to remember the forgotten, and the tools of history, particularly with regard to context and broader movements, can help students to do so. We may only be able to give these persons numbers individually, but we can remember the types of communities they left, the desperate needs they felt, the dangers they encountered. To remember these forgotten is to incorporate them into ourselves, and this memory calls us to seek those who may be unknown around us.

Hearing a call to the common good in the history classroom

As history weaves into memory in the classroom, and as memory calls us beyond ourselves, this may become a locus for student vocational discernment. By learning skills of historical analysis both applied to memory, and enriched by memory, students can find aspects of their own callings. Deploying historical skills in analyzing memorials, or remembering the forgotten, can serve as firsthand exercises in incorporating others into their own memories, offering guidance or warning or beckoning along the way. Student assignments can also be framed around the interplay of history and memory: describe one of the forgotten, find out about someone for whom you only know a name or a date, dig into the context of a life to see its possibilities and limitations.

Hannah Schell has suggested that part of student vocational discernment is shaped by understanding their various circles of loyalty, to themselves as well as to family and a variety of communities.[28] Such a model is useful for students of history seeking vocational direction from the common good call of memory; it is probable that we conceive this best in a local circle first.[29]

a-tunisian-gravedigger-gives-migrants-what-they-were-deprived-of-in-life-dignity/2018/09/10/ 8b77e72a-a6f5-11e8-ad6f-080770dcddc2_story.html.

[28] Hannah Schell, "Commitment and Community: The Virtue of Loyalty and Vocational Discernment," in *At This Time and In This Place: Vocation and Higher Education*, ed. David S. Cunningham (New York: Oxford University Press, 2016), 235–54.

[29] James K. A. Smith asked theologian Miroslav Volf, "Are there practices of remembering, forgetting, hoping, projecting that the people of God can perhaps offer to the common good?" Volf's answer suggests the same smaller circles of loyalty to begin with. "I'm clear about how we might be able to offer something like that to smaller communities and to individuals. . . . I am less clear that this can be a model of how we deal with 'national' memories." See "Interview with James K.A. Smith" in Miroslav Volf, *The End of Memory: Remembering Rightly in a Violent World*, 2nd ed. (Grand

In a paper assignment for my methods course, I ask students to learn about one of their own ancestors in context. Here, the notion that memory binds us to others is easier to establish: students may not have known their great-grandparents, but they incorporate them genetically. At the end of the assignment, they will have used history to understand their ancestors better; enhancing this close circle of loyalty, they may see through it to the good of incorporating others farther beyond.

In general education courses, I bring history and memory into conversation with a gentle life-writing assignment. I ask students to write a proposal for their life story, breaking it into chapters. As we discuss these, I point out how many historian's skills they are already using: chronological ordering, thematic considerations, periodization, causation, contingency, inquiry. "You already think like historians," I tell them. We then discuss how using those skills has helped organize and enrich their memories—and how reflecting on their own lives in terms of historical context begins to tell them about themselves and their unfolding vocations.

Along with assignments, I try to model how history weaves into my own personal memory, and how the tapestry of memory calls me to the common good. I accomplish this best by simply allowing myself to go on tangents. The tangent shows a connection between material I am teaching and my memory, each contributing to the other. Recently I described the moment in late 406 when Germanic peoples crossed the frozen Rhine, and I wove it into a memory of my own. Several years ago, canoeing with friends in the Boundary Waters in northern Minnesota, I crossed into Canada to see a waterfall. Hence, I too had crossed an international boundary by water, though the boundary was marked only with a metal spike. The story itself finishes with a punchline: we were approached by a couple of Canadian wilderness rangers in a canoe, who hailed us with the phrase (and I am not making this up), "You know you're in Canada, eh?" It's a light story, but I hope that this models how my personal memory incorporates those nameless travelers of long ago, and how this memory calls me to understanding and aid for those I encounter who are moving into new and unfamiliar places.

Rapids, MI: Eerdmans, 2021), 280–81. Two useful reflections on historians serving the common good of particular communities are Robert Tracy McKenzie, "Don't Forget the Church: Reflections on the Forgotten Dimension of Our Dual Calling," and Douglas A. Sweeney, "On the Vocation of Historians to the Priesthood of Believers: A Plea to Christians in the Academy," both in *Confessing History: Explorations in Christian Faith and the Historian's Vocation*, ed. John Fea, Jay Green, and Eric Miller (Notre Dame: University of Notre Dame Press, 2010), 280–98 and 299–315, respectively.

Weaving history and memory in this way does not need to be particularly profound; each connection is a thread in the larger tapestry. Even the addition of an aside can help students incorporate historical material into their own memories. I would suggest that this is the same phenomenon as medieval illuminators adding whimsical illustrations to help guide readers to certain pages in a text. The more students synthesize what they are learning with their own lives, the more they shape memory as a virtue, a tool to tie themselves to persons both dead and living. History and memory can generate more room in them for others, more incorporation of others, a calling to seek the good of others.

Memories of trauma and injustice

I have used the word "incorporation" to suggest that memory is a welcoming exercise, extending grace, hospitality, and inclusion to the dead and the forgotten. Many times, this allows us to honor and ennoble the victims of oppression or injustice. It can offer memory to the nameless in ways that serve the common good. However, this raises the uncomfortable question: when I remember, am I incorporating those guilty of oppression and injustice in that formulation? Does this mean that I am failing properly to apply moral judgment to such individuals, thus betraying the forgotten and oppressed whom I purport to serve? This is a complex question whose dimensions stretch far beyond the scope of this chapter, but it demands consideration.[30]

Whether in well-known events like the Holocaust or slavery or through injustice on a more personal scale, both memory and history lead us to individuals whose actions we may deplore. Remembering such evils and their perpetrators is a vital component of history teaching, just as the public memory of injustice is necessary and significant. In this respect, the history classroom borrows again from public memory: as statues may be torn down, so may we tear down historical figures in our courses. Chipping away at such people may be an important way to show solidarity with the oppressed or forgotten whom we remember.[31] But it requires us to remember the oppressors.

---

[30] For further exploration of the importance of wrestling with institutional and historical systems of injustice and the barriers to communal well-being, see this volume's chapter 4 by Monica M. Smith and chapter 6 by Geoffrey W. Bateman.

[31] In chapter 5 of this volume, Michelle Hayford discusses advocacy in our vocational calls as a step toward solidarity with those on the margins.

Remembering those who have been oppressors helps us keep the memory of the oppressed with greater fidelity; if we did not remember Hitler, we would not remember victims of the Holocaust properly. But history is also complicated, like people are complicated. By adding historical context, detail, and nuance, we discover that persons from the past are as complicated as we are, and that our memory does offer a certain grace to the oppressor. It may remind us too that we are complex individuals, and that may help shape our own vocational discernment.[32] The fact that we, like both the oppressed and the oppressors we remember, are not simply good or bad may temper our self-promotion but may also encourage us to try to follow challenging calls: history humbles and ennobles us simultaneously.

Beth Barton Schweiger offers a helpful window on the problem of remembering people in all their moral complexity. Grounding her study in Christian theology, but with wide applicability,[33] she suggests that the study of persons from the past demands that we *love* them. This is not to ignore their failings, but rather the opposite: love demands truthful knowledge, and "vocation speaks truthfulness in love."[34] Loving persons from the past means that knowledge has certain challenges: first, that we know imperfectly, and second, the "stunning imbalance of power between historian and subject."[35] These challenges can be met with love rather than power. Schweiger suggests that historians exercise what Rowan Williams has called a "pastoral imagination."[36]

Remembering in love does not mean that we forego judgment. Schweiger offers the examples of two Christian slaveowners in her own research. "To see them rightly is not to excuse them or to sentimentalize them or to dismiss them," she says, but it is also not to "strip. . . them down to their perverse core."[37] Following her own categories, Schweiger suggests first that remembering in love means understanding the full moral blindness of both men and allowing ourselves to be addressed by the same question: to whom

---

[32] In the broader sense of vocation, it may call us to be a certain kind of person, in this respect calling us to take on the virtue of prudence, particularly in moral discernment and action. See Thomas Albert Howard, "Virtue Ethics and Historical Inquiry: The Case of Prudence," in Fea et al., eds, *Confessing History*, 83–100.

[33] Toward the end of this chapter (pp. 72–77), Schweiger does sound a note of discord between professional history and Christian assumptions about the priority of love, but I still think that her call to love is more widely applicable. Beth Barton Schweiger, "Seeing Things: Knowledge and Love in History," in Fea et al., eds., *Confessing History*, 60–80.

[34] Schweiger, "Seeing Things," 62.

[35] Schweiger, "Seeing Things," 61–62.

[36] Schweiger, "Seeing Things," 66.

[37] Schweiger, "Seeing Things," 69.

are we blind? Moreover, she suggests remembering each in his own particularity, rather than pushing them into a "universal perspective."[38]

Schweiger's call to "treat knowledge as charity rather than power" and consider persons from the past with a "pastoral imagination" fits my understanding of historically enriched memory as incorporation. The more we remember with historical context and accuracy, the more clearly we will see the evils of which persons are capable and the complexity of each individual. Incorporation does not excuse the wrongs of the past, but neither will it allow us to oversimplify the persons we remember. In this respect, memory contributes to vocation for the common good. By insisting on particularity, such remembering calls us to real persons and real needs beyond ourselves.[39]

Gaps in memory

"Memory is like a dog that lies down where it pleases," says Cees Nooteboom in his novel *Rituals*. The novel's protagonist sometimes remembers things unexpectedly, and at other times "the dog, arrogant beast, let him down."[40] It is impossible to determine what particular historical memories will become incorporated in a student (or educator, for that matter). But the overall content matters less than the discipline.[41] Not everything will be woven into the tapestry, but some strands will be strengthened as they become part of memory. Wherever the dog happens to lie becomes a point of connection between the one remembering and the one remembered. Those connections may be assorted randomly, scattered rather than neatly arranged, but their effect remains.

By giving the time and effort of history to memory, we are not simply assembling a sequence of events from the past. While certain events and persons have an influence that renders them central in most history teaching, we train our remembering just as well when we research the forgotten and the insignificant. We learn to listen, and that listening attunes us to our own

---

[38] Schweiger, "Seeing Things," 70.

[39] As opposed to the opinion expressed by an old man that "the more I love mankind in general, the less I love people in particular, that is, individually, as separate persons" in Fyodor Dostoyevsky's *The Brothers Karamozov*, trans. Richard Pevear and Larissa Volokhonsky (New York: Picador, 2021).

[40] Cees Nooteboom, *Rituals*, trans. Adrienne Dixon (New York: Harcourt Brace & Company, 1983), 1.

[41] On remembering as a discipline, see Margaret Bendroth, *The Spiritual Practice of Remembering* (Grand Rapids, MI: Eerdmans, 2013).

vocation through those to whom we extend the grace of memory. They, in turn, call us to the well-being of others.

Memory and the common good

As the chapters in this volume demonstrate, the notion of the common good can be problematic and difficult to define. But as memory extends grace and incorporation to others, it calls us beyond individual pursuits to the flourishing of others. As a historian, I do not locate my vocation in the technical demands of the guild so much as in the public need to remember well, and I believe that this serves the common good. The power of memory can tear relationships apart, divide societies, even cause violence; when given the context and perspective of history, memory has the power to bind people together. At the end of Wendell Berry's *The Memory of Old Jack*, the "membership" of Port William comes together after Jack's death and comes to realize that "his memory holds them in common knowledge and in common loss."[42] If memory fails for the forgotten dead, history brought to memory can dignify them and turn our attention to the forgotten living. If history can be reduced to names and dates, history brought to memory can add contextual detail, further research, and greater knowledge. As we go beyond statistics and stereotypes to understand individual persons, we hear a call to their good.

These common goods can also help students in the process of vocational discernment. The ability to weave the past into the fabric of our own memory is an act of incorporation, and a grace that we can extend to our neighbors as well. As we incorporate others, through a knowledge based on charity rather than power, we may find our own calling. This includes the knowledge of past oppression and trauma, through which we may find a vocation calibrated to concrete needs and situations. In such practices, we may also find a calling that transforms us by showing us our own frailty and our own nobility, giving us a greater sense of humility and possibility alike.

Memory is at once inescapable and elusive, personal and public, painful and proud, debated and celebrated. We need to remember, and history helps us remember well. Remembering well calls us to serve the forgotten and the oppressed and shapes us into people of grace and charity. Fergus Mac Róich

---

[42] Wendell Berry, *The Memory of Old Jack* (Washington, DC: Counterpoint, 1999), 170.

in the *Táin* models this for us, albeit imperfectly. His naming and description of the warriors of Ulster show the transforming effect of memory; they
are no longer nameless opponents but persons. On the field of battle, he is
twice called to remember: first, that he is himself from Ulster, and second,
a previous agreement he had made to yield. As a result, Fergus does not
persist in the battle, and at what should be his climactic fight with the hero
Cú Chulainn, he simply stomps away. Fergus's memory incorporates his
enemies, and it calls him—again very imperfectly, should you read the tale—
to the common good of the cessation of violence. Indeed, it even transforms
him: in the final moments of the epic, after a battle between two great bulls, it
is Fergus who prevents the killing of the victorious bull. Perhaps in memory
he has found a glimmer of grace. But in any case, he's found in memory a perception of the common good: he's seen a people coming together.

13

What We Are Up Against

Reforming the Vocation of Higher Education for Formation throughout Our Lives

Charles Mathewes

Higher education's future is heavily contested.[1] Critics say it is indulgent, is ingrown, and does not serve the common good. Parents fear it does not help their children get good jobs. Students do not find their studies relevant or engaging. Most defenses of it are reactive and conservative, attempting to secure its traditional scope, early adulthood, and its traditional mode, disciplinary learning, against attacks upon that traditional vision.

I suggest a different route. We "defenders" of higher education should not be defensive, let alone reactionary. I propose to go on the offensive. Our opponents are not superficially but radically mistaken; we must alter the terms of the debate itself. The core challenge facing college education is more daunting, and exhilarating, than anyone has yet appreciated. We need to think *way* bigger than we currently do, expanding the scope of college across the human life course. If we can seize this chance, we may rejuvenate the core of our mission, and expand its scope, in ways few have even partially glimpsed yet.

Much of the fight over higher education today is structured by pressures toward professionalization. This pressure fuels anxieties about the university's purpose. Many people see universities fundamentally as *credentialing* institutions, gateways to a financially secure life. This is understandable. The increase in socioeconomic precarity and the so-called "great risk shift" of the past few decades has made higher education essential for economic security;

---

[1] See especially Steven Brint, *Two Cheers for Higher Education* (Princeton, NJ: Princeton University Press, 2018); Richard Arum and Josipa Roska, *Academically Adrift: Limited Learning on College Campuses* (Chicago: University of Chicago Press, 2010); Andrew Delbanco, *College: What It Was, Is, and Should Be* (Princeton, NJ: Princeton University Press, 2012); Richard Detwiler, *The Evidence Liberal Arts Needs: Lives of Consequence, Inquiry, and Accomplishment* (Boston: MIT Press, 2021).

Charles Mathewes, *What We Are Up Against* In: *Called Beyond Our Selves*. Edited by: Erin VanLaningham,
Oxford University Press. © Oxford University Press 2024. DOI: 10.1093/oso/9780197691915.003.0014

parents are increasingly anxious about equipping their children to compete and succeed in an economic context where failure would be disastrous. For many, education has replaced class as an organizing structure for society.[2]

Nonetheless, a too-narrow focus on credentialing confuses the immediate with the profound. We can always do better at equipping students for their wage-earning careers, and we should always strive to ensure rigor in our disciplinary courses for our students' postcollegiate careers. But training has never been the university's central purpose, and it cannot become so now. College is not fundamentally about developing career skills, nor should it be more seamlessly incorporated into the economic system that is, more or less, the central nervous system of our society. College is about more than our economic lives; at least, it should be.[3]

So far, so predictable, from a humanities professor. But what's next may be more surprising: neither is our core function, as educators, *learning* either. Learning is obviously important, but education is deeper than the acquisition of disciplined ways of knowing. Most basically, education is "drawing out" the person from an earlier stage of their life; our fundamental task, and distinct duty, is to curate, oversee, superintend that process. This task is *formation*: the process of *learning to become an adult*. That process in turn is best understood as one of coming to understand and relate our dual experiences, equally primordial, of freedom and obligation: how should we understand the ways we are called, obligated, and bound, and how also we are yet free, liberated from false ways of life and empowered to become what we are not yet, yet might become?[4] Colleges and universities are uniquely positioned to help us think through what it means to be an adult. And because the process of "becoming an adult" is a process that is never fully or finally completed but unfolds across the whole expanse of one's life, higher education has a potential function for everyone.

Explaining this function, how this practice is partly but crucially constitutive of the common good, and how colleges can help, is my aim here. The chapter argues that higher education—especially in its use of the language of

---

[2] Jacob Hacker, *The Great Risk Shift: The New Economic Insecurity and the Decline of the American Dream* (New York: Oxford University Press, 2006).

[3] Christine Jeske offers an extended argument for replacing the market narrative with more truthful narratives, and higher education's place in shaping these alternative narratives, in chapter 3 of this volume.

[4] In chapter 1 of this volume, David Matzko McCarthy also discusses how an individual's vocation is situated as a responsibility to neighbor, and how our responsiveness within institutions is part of our call to the common good.

vocation in the service of formation—is a privileged site of disciplined reflection and investigation in which these central challenges of the common good are experienced and responses to its problems articulated and explored. As such, it is not a direct but an indirect contributor to the common good, highlighting one profound tension that stands at the center of human life (freedom and obligation), and making that tension the thematic core of its activities, the fundamental focus of "higher education" as a whole.

The challenges and opportunities we confront, as humans and as educators alike, are more fundamental than we typically register. Furthermore, because this is not only true for people in early adulthood—it is true across the whole life course—higher education is far more valuable to all of us than we ordinarily allow. I talk first about the social location of higher education in our society, then about the implications of a focus on formation for higher education, and finally about the implications of this reconceptualization of higher education's vocation in people's lives across adulthood. In sum, the chapter examines what higher education's contribution to the common good is, and what it can be.

The social function of higher education

Critiques of higher education often complain of college's detachment from "regular life." Many of these critiques are offered in bad faith, but not all of them are. In fact, concerns about credentialing and professionalization— too little or too much—are hardly new issues in higher education. There was never an idyllic time "before" careerism. Professionalization is not an alien parasite infecting higher education; the medieval European university was fundamentally an institution for professionalization, a technical school, training for a career in theology, medicine, or law. Only in early modernity did the university become a gateway into adulthood, and then only for sons of the elite; only after World War II in the United States did higher education begin to understand and organize itself around the ideal of the "transition to adulthood" as a path ideally available to all, or at least to all middle-class young people. Certainly, anxieties about professionalization have grown because of larger changes in the institutional ecology of society over the past half-century or so.[5] But those anxieties are best addressed indirectly, by

---

[5] See especially Mitchell L. Stevens, Elizabeth A. Armstrong, and Richard Arum, "Sieve, Incubator, Temple, Hub: Empirical and Theoretical Advances in the Sociology of Higher Education," *Annual Review of Sociology* 34, no. 1 (2008): 127–51, https://doi.org/10.1146/annurev.soc.34.040507.134737.

recalling institutions of higher education to what should be their central task. These critiques hide a recognition worth ruminating over: college's very function demands it be structurally estranged from "everyday life." Here I want to explain that estrangement, and why it means we cannot make higher education's contribution to the common good *too* direct.[6]

To start, consider some basic features of higher education. First, speaking institutionally, it is necessarily "set apart." Most simply, many colleges and some universities are *private*, not part of the formal structures of the "commonwealth," strictly speaking, at all. But whether they are officially or only informally "public," colleges have long thought of themselves as somewhat detached. A "college," after all, is a *collegium*, a gathering together, a *collection*—collected *from* something else and hived off, set apart, inward-facing. As Robert Pampel notes in this volume, most schools have campuses—particular spaces, territories marked by boundaries and walls and gates, signifying and reinforcing a certain self-involvement.[7] College life also has its own temporal structure, partly determined by college students' stage of life: after all, no one else follows an "academic calendar," no other community observes a daily schedule that is politely described as seminocturnal, and no other community has so formally teleological an arc to its inhabitants' time of membership, from "convocation," to maturation, to a culminating "commencement."

Second, speaking explicitly of curriculum, higher education is set apart because of the need for noninterference and concentration on the peculiar work occupying the central energy of the college experience, the work of *disciplinarity*. Colleges are gatherings of multiple self-conscious modes of training to intellectually navigate the world. We call these modes *disciplines*, a word that here has several interlocking senses. The "disciplines" are recognized specializations that cultivate distinct kinds of intellective activity that reveals some dimensions of reality that that specialization claims a particular aptness for exposing and exploring. This "intellective activity" need not be mere cognition, done by an isolated brain; dance, speech, drama, painting and other creative arts, music, architecture, and medicine are somatically anchored activities, practices that require embodiment. They are also disciplined, overseen by a community of educators and experts who develop explicit protocols for training and determine explicit criteria for

---

[6] For an alternative viewpoint, see Michelle Hayford's argument regarding higher education's role in preparing students for advocacy in the "real" world in chapter 5 of this volume.

[7] See chapter 11 entitled "The University as the (Common) Good Place" of this volume.

judging these activities. These "disciplines" invite and enable students to become participants in a tradition of inquiry. Of course these disciplines can be too narrow, and advocates should always beware lest they become overly bureaucratized or rationalized, as opposed to charismatic, or magical, or gracious (all of which may come to the same thing).[8] Colleges and universities are *disciplined* sites for learning and formation, and these disciplines are the main pedagogical structures for forming college students.[9] In encouraging the concentration disciplinarity requires, higher education necessarily courts parochiality; but even when it avoids that trap, it still needs to be set apart from the everyday.

Third, speaking culturally, successful colleges produce quasi-alternative realities that provide "safe spaces" for students' explorations of their possible future selves. Colleges are not only distinct from the "real world" but also worlds unto themselves, with distinct housing options, dining halls, student self-governance, student associations, club sports, and more. Further, each class is a mini-community, and each semester begins with a blank slate—all this goes into the micro-ecology of the college, the nontrivial features of collegiate reality. There is an inescapable "play-nature" to much of the student experience in college. Students are in a way *practicing* for adulthood: they are trying on roles, experimenting, rehearsing for their future lives, not assuming that their intentions, in classrooms, will be the ultimate ones they inhabit. This pretense feature of college is not a bad thing: students are practicing the "common good," and the setting provides space and time for reflecting on the meaning of life.

Of course, colleges are ultimately part of the real world, with real-world effects, both in the short term and in the long. (The current struggles over Title IX and debates about sexual violence on campuses are due to this.) But they are also relatively autonomous, inward-facing spaces, an environment real but revisable (and perhaps revocable, more vividly intimate, and palpably voluntary) than any other that people are likely to experience. This can create a distinct kind of human experience: an artificial mode of life that

---

[8] For example, see Mark McGurl, *The Program Era: Postwar Fiction and the Rise of Creative Writing* (Cambridge, MA: Harvard University Press, 2011); Andrew Abbott, *Chaos of Disciplines* (Chicago: University of Chicago Press, 2001); and Stephen Shapin, *The Scientific Life: A Moral History of a Late Modern Vocation* (Chicago: University of Chicago Press, 2008).

[9] Consider the examples offered in this volume of how disciplinarity can inform vocational exploration rooted in the common good, specifically anthropology (chapter 3 by Christine Jeske), applied theatre (chapter 5 by Michelle Hayford), rhetoric and communications (chapter 8 by David Timmerman), literary studies (chapter 9 by Erin VanLaningham), history (chapter 12 by Martin Holt Dotterweich), and public health (chapter 10 by Meghan M. Slining).

is as much pretense as reality, but with real effects. They can be, in a way, antechambers to adulthood: mini-worlds suitable for people to practice the roles of everyday life.[10]

But this autonomy is only ever partial, for along with being intentional communities, colleges are *liminal* spaces, edge places, transitional zones hived off from the so-called "real world" and the ordinary structures of space and time precisely to enable its members better to inhabit the "real world" when they depart college. Precisely because students are graced with space and time to ask such questions, colleges implicitly demand of their residents a serious accounting of their practices and social norms. The rules and ideals with which students were raised, and to which they may well return after college, must be assessed, and for that assessment to occur, there must be some "distance" from those norms' normal functioning. Colleges thereby function as particularly dense and distinct sites for reflection on the common good. So this distance between "college" and "real life" is also for the purposes of intimacy yet again, of reacquainting us with how we ought to live, un-self-consciously, in our world.[11] Liminality is not finally for critique, but for formation; these institutions give students the space to work on themselves, to begin to become who they will be.[12] In this way, higher education's "distance" from the "real world" is not so much *opposed* to the common good, but functionally central to its continued flourishing.

This language of "formation" is crucial. Higher education is an especially powerful source of both moral formation and ethical and civic deliberation. College's "set apartness" gives students an intense and distinct experience and a depth of reflection they would not easily find elsewhere, including a larger history and background understanding of our culture's dynamics and our place in them. The aim of this dialectic of liminality and intentionality is ultimately formation: to grow adults, citizens, fully "educated adults." College is not simply about *information*, the educational equipping of students by teachers for entry into careers, but more deeply about *formation*, the self-conscious embedding of education in the larger project of moral formation,

---

[10] For further exploration of how campuses reflect the concerns of contemporary society and prepare us to cultivate and live toward the common good, see chapter 4 of this volume by Monica M. Smith.

[11] On intimacy and distance see Georg Simmel, "The Stranger," in *Georg Simmel: On Individuality and Social Forms*, ed. and trans. Donald Levine (Chicago: University of Chicago Press, 1971), 143–50.

[12] See Michelle Hayford's discussion of liminality in chapter 5 of this volume for further exploration of how college can be a site of transformation, allowing students to be agents of transformation.

adult formation. And this formation happens centrally, though not exclusively, through idiosyncratic academic practices like disciplinarity.

The formational function of higher education: a common good

Note: Disciplinary *learning* is not higher *education*. The latter is the overall purpose. Disciplinary learning serves education, and education is sometimes an indirect byproduct, or even a direct consequence, of disciplinary learning, but they are not the same thing. Education is not acquaintance with any disciplinary idiom; education—"leading out"—is formational.

Furthermore, college can be "set apart" for formation not just for young adults but *for all*. The challenges to human life that demand formation do not disappear but in fact mount as we age; hence, throughout our lives, we all need moments of retreat, reflection, and (re)formation. Reforming higher education for the common good, then, centers this formational function, both for our traditional students and for potential nontraditional ones.

Formation

But what exactly is this "formation," and how do we curate it? Formation is a matter of coming to recognize one's entry into adulthood, an entry that is about both agency and responsibility, and the long-term recognition of consequences for one's actions and life projects.

Of course, most human formation happens through direct experience. And college has not always been a site for this transformation. In the first half of the twentieth century, adulthood began with graduation from high school. Even in the United States today, less than 40 percent of adults over twenty-five are college graduates. But now college has become the intentional and circumscribed institutional setting where our culture thinks the transition to adulthood most smoothly happens. College is the paradigmatic formational institution.

This focus on formation asks students to consider anew the received structures of their "home" experience. It demands self-conscious acquaintance with familiar (perhaps unthinking) patterns and ways of life and then requires a critical estrangement from them, both to learn about yourself and to ask whether this is who you want to be. After all, higher education is premised on the wager that we can learn not just through our own experiences but from the experiences of others, sedimented across generations, communicated to us through our education. By educating yourself in the various modes of disciplined perception, you gain perspectives on your life that you would not otherwise possess. Some students, who have had unstable home lives, may already do this, but this hopefully gives them more structured ways to undertake it. Others may find it (initially) existentially wrenching. But whether they find it first disorienting or empowering, it allows all an outsider's perspective on the most intimate and taken-for-granted forms of life that each may have unquestionably inhabited.[13] (This experience of estrangement and reconnection is so common in college as to be a cliché in college memoirs, a kind of synecdoche of the tension between "tradition" and "modernity."[14]) This does not demand that you *reject* those forms of life, only that you come to understand their noninevitability, how it requires investment, commitment, and acceptance, and how it remains always open to revision and transfiguration.

Students can be brought to see formational questions in different ways. One strategy I use employs a simple exercise. In my classes, especially those for first-year students, I occasionally ask, "When did you decide to go to college?" Typically, students understand this question to concern the choice of *which* college they would attend—when, in other words, they decided to choose *this* college. But the question doesn't ask that; it asks them to remember a moment when they decided, "Yeah, I'll get a college education." Most traditional students never made that deliberative decision; it was *assumed*, by all the most important people in their lives, that they would go. Is that a good enough reason to go? Or is it akin to an arranged marriage? They should take responsibility for going to college, as an essential part of what it means to be an adult: to take responsibility for your own life choices. That is what the question urges.

Or consider this: during the fall of 2020, at the height of the COVID-19 pandemic, I taught a class on Business Ethics. Our class was entirely online, though students were in the dorms and the university was, in some way,

---

[13] For examples of how an outsider perspective helps cultivate a critique of self and builds community, see Erin VanLaningham's discussion of "reading with strangers" in chapter 9 of this volume.

[14] For instance, see Richard Rodriguez, *Hunger of Memory: The Education of Richard Rodriguez* (New York: Bantam, 1983), and Tara Westover, *Educated: A Memoir* (New York: Random House, 2018). A (nostalgic) programmatic account is William Deresiewicz, *Excellent Sheep: The Miseducation of the American Elite and the Way to a Meaningful Life* (New York: New Press, 2015).

"open." After several sessions, I realized they were very interested in the question of whether the university should be running at all during the pandemic, or whether it was endangering its employees' and students' lives, and the lives of Charlottesville's residents. So, I proposed an alternative final assignment: they could work in small groups to write a briefing paper, informed by our class readings, concerning whether the University of Virginia should have opened for the pandemic semester. This may sound like a straightforward project, but to answer the question they had to understand what exactly "the university" was, along with the potential costs of closing or staying open. To do that, they had to become acquainted with the scale of an institution with a two-billion-dollar annual budget, a medical center, twenty-eight thousand employees, and twenty-six thousand students; to read carefully the administration's public statements and discern their expressed rationales; to understand the costs and benefits of the options before the administration, none of which were perfect, nor really of their own making; and to offer the best account they could of the various rationales for the various options, *all before* offering a summative judgment themselves about the right course and then defending it. The students, through their own research and interviews, had to confront the ethics of an actual decision, made by actual humans, in a real context, that was directly applicable to their lives—indeed, one that could be construed as a matter of life and death. (We even secured them genuine, off-the-record, conversations with the university provost.) This helped them, I believe, register what it means to reckon with the irrevocable decisions intrinsic to adult responsibility.

Finally, consider a class I teach for graduating seniors, entitled What You're Up Against. The aim of the class is not disciplinary learning, but formation; it seeks to relate and integrate things already known, rather than accrue new information. The course sessions alternate between discussions of books and meetings with "visitors." The books range from Sherwin Nuland's *How We Die* to James Baldwin's *The Fire Next Time* to Virginia Woolf's *A Room of One's Own* to Josef Pieper's *Leisure: The Basis of Culture* (even Richard Arum and Josipa Roska's *Academically Adrift*). But at least as important as the readings are the class visitors, alums of our university, each one a decade older than the last—so one in their twenties, another in their thirties, forties, fifties, sixties, and seventies. We ask each about how they traversed the years from their graduations to the current day. The point of these visits, for the students, is to encounter a later version of themselves—to hear how they think about their college education at different moments in their lives, and to think about the challenges they face today. Class assignments do not aim at mastery of new disciplinary methods, but at integrating the kinds of knowledge students already have in new assemblages and relations, informed by our in-class conversations, about books and with the visitors. This course thus asks, *what does it mean to be an adult*? It means to provoke reflections about agency and responsibility.

College classrooms already reach toward this kind of formation, whether they recognize it or not. Students usually understand college as an uncomplicated extension of previous schooling, but there are important differences. Unlike high school, college classes make you far more responsible for your own learning, granting you vastly more autonomy and agency than you ever had before, to help you develop, or at least enliven, your convictions. After all, *you* are the one who must be reasonably responsible for your life, including determining your values. Not everyone will share those values, and yet you will have to live around and with them, if not in the most intimate modes of community then at least in the kinds of quotidian togetherness that will involve having them as neighbors, coworkers, fellow citizens, participants in projects of realizing various "common goods." This kind of teaching should teach you not to devalue the things you already value but to appreciate better the fragility and contestability of those goods, and the tentativeness of your apprehension of them as well: to "sophisticate" your valuing of the world, your sense of your own sensitivity to that valuing.[15] Students thereby begin to learn of everyday life what Clausewitz said of war, namely, its fundamental, intractable *difficulty*: "Everything in war is very simple, but the simplest thing is difficult."[16] When I speak of "formation," something like this is what I have in mind.

Freedom and obligation, virtue and joy

How does this help us with the common good? Well, perhaps *the* core conundrum is the question of how to understand and relate our dual experiences, equally primordial, of freedom and obligation. One way to imagine the

[15] For an analysis of expanding our notion of "common" to accommodate the uncommon, see Geoffrey W. Bateman's discussion in chapter 6 of this volume.
[16] Carl von Clausewitz, *On War*, ed. and trans. Michael Howard and Peter Paret (Princeton, NJ: Princeton University Press, 1976), 119.

university is as a site for thinking through these languages of freedom and obligation and the tension between them.

Becoming an adult involves accepting responsibility, and what you accept responsibility for is some kind of balance between freedom and obligation.[17] By "freedom" here I mean the capacity to be an agent yourself instead of being perpetually determined by others. You must come to recognize that nobody but you can do the things that you need to get done. Everyone reading this chapter can remember the first time you realized that, while others were there to support you, the living out of your life was *up to you* and no one else. Waking up to that fundamental accountability for one's own choices and one's own life is no simple or easy process. But it is a fundamental one, exhilarating and terrifying in equal parts, and inescapable for us in this world.

And yet, this autonomy is not only about the positive acceptance of agency but also equally about our recognition of obligations. We are each responsible for many things and to many people. Absent truly tragic ruptures, we are all part of larger families and have relations of care and attention and recognition to them; we all live in communities and owe the other members our care and curation, our commitment to our common good. We have duties not only to others but also to our sense of vocation and purpose; we must remain true to ourselves as well. We must also come to grips with the range of commitments, not all of them voluntarily chosen, that constitute the web of relations of common life.[18]

Sometimes freedom and obligation are straightforwardly opposed, but this is simplistic. Consider Martin Luther's famous theological claim: the Christian is the most free *and* the most bound. Parallel claims are made by modern thinkers as diverse as Immanuel Kant to the "ethics of care" theorists. You awaken to your agency, but also to your responsibilities. If we conceive of "maturity" simply as the lonely adventure of our willing self, we miss something important—often our agency is most fully, most authentically experienced in grateful obedience to the demands of love and care that others make upon us. We are caught up in webs of responsibility within which we often, though not always, find real fulfillment; our discovery of obligation is not simply something we experience as a burden; it can be (though, again, is

---

[17] For more on our obligations to community as the source of vocational exploration, see chapter 1 of this volume by David Matzko McCarthy.

[18] In this volume, Christine Jeske extensively explores this web of relations as membership and mutuality in chapter 3, Deanna A. Thompson explores vocations we don't choose in chapter 2, and Jonathan Golden explores the idea of caring for causes that are not our own in chapter 7.

not always) something we find as joy, gift, profoundly meaningful. The radically autonomous subject is not the inevitable human ideal; we often find incomparable sustenance in our commitment to and care for others whom we serve. Our world talks much about freedom and little about service, but both are real, indeed primordial; to understand either properly, we must acknowledge both.

The hybridity of our nature as both agents and patients hence speaks to the kind of capacities we must cultivate. Beyond freedom and obligation, though essential to them, a liberal education ought to cultivate in its participants two distinct capacities: capacities for *virtue* and for *joy*. "Virtue" here means to signify the human's power, as an intentional and dynamic creature, purposively minded, exercising their agency, by and large, to get what they want. But virtue is not merely technological, a matter of determining the passions and then mapping out a plan of action; it is also a dialectical engagement with one's desires, about learning *true* from *counterfeit* passions, about becoming authentically yourself. In this way a training in virtue is also a training in the deepening of self-consciousness and self-awareness, for virtue is not only about capacity but also about responsibility: you always wake up in a world, neither of your making nor likely of your liking. Virtue is about learning how to be a better, more effective, more efficacious agent—one who enacts their life plan, and realizes their vocation, more fully, vibrantly, and powerfully.

Alongside virtue, a liberal education should cultivate in us a deepening capacity for a range of apprehensions, centrally those captured in the term "joy." College should expand your amplitude of soul, give you an apprehension of the world of greater richness than you previously possessed. This is not just about appreciating complicated human artifacts, such as novels or music; it also applies to understanding natural realities, because the exploration of the infinities of mathematics or the intricacies of cells or atoms is as much an inducement to astonishment as any poem. Such "astonishment" and "wonder" are categories closely related to joy, since the amplitude of soul that is cultivated by them shows us, in those sympathetic reverberations between soul and cosmos, how we are connected to others, to that very cosmos, to a sense of the joy beyond the self. And this form of connection is intimately connected to the common good.

Virtue and joy—higher education ought to seek to distinguish, describe, cultivate, and deepen these two foci of the human condition, to help us better understand and enhance both the human condition in general and ourselves. Understanding our task illuminates how the liberal arts do contribute

294 CALLINGS OF CAMPUS, COMMUNITY, AND BEYOND

centrally to the common good, through a discernment of our own vocation vis-à-vis the obligations and empowerments we apprehend. After all, it is in our deepest exploration of ourselves, our interiority, and observing how our interiority resonantly registers its responses to the realities that surround it that we encounter our most fundamental form of attachment with the world and one another.

Liberal arts and vocation

The complex relationship between freedom and obligation manifest in higher education illuminates two potentially distinct ideals, represented by the two most common phrases capturing the education experience in the United States, namely the "liberal arts" and "vocation." These highlight different models of our fundamental moral agency, two basic ways to characterize our being as agents in the world, responding to others while pursuing some assemblage of goals that more or less amount to a self-conscious life plan. The contrast between them can be productive.

The idea of the "liberal arts" is about freedom. It originates in the medieval *artes liberales*, the "arts of being free"—the training that most university students took as preliminary to a professional training in law, medicine, or theology. This was not only about being liberated from the drudgery of natural necessity—growing your own food, for instance, or serving at someone else's pleasure. Along with lessons in not being subjugated by others, it taught students about what ends were *worthy* of their time (as opposed to typical undergraduate diversions like drinking and gambling and wasting their lives). The "liberal arts" are about freeing you *for* an authentic mode of action and way of life, to be sure, but this approach's use of languages of "capacity" and "possibility" reinforce the fact that, here, the accent is on freedom.

On the other hand, the language of "vocation" or "calling" suggests that your agency is constituted by and through the command of another, through obedience. This language does not originate in the university but in the monastery, in the call to another way of life altogether—a way of life withdrawn from the world but still committed to care *for* the world. Vocation is also dialogical, in a way that the "liberal arts" is not: if you hear a call, it must come from *somewhere*, and the somewhere is not the place at which you stand when you hear it. You can understand the call to be from God, or the cosmos, or your own unconscious (or nonconscious, or deepest, or what have you) self, but a *call* implies a *caller*. In vocation, you stand in relation, a relation that can be respected or disrespected, against which you can rebel.[19]

These two accounts of "liberation" and "vocation" may be finally incompatible. They offer two quite different conceptions of freedom, its opposites, and its counterfeits. The language of the "liberal arts" asks, what might *true* freedom look like, beyond its frivolous forgeries? In contrast, the language of vocation questions whether there is another, *deeper* kind of freedom than the one "the world" presumes—whether that "world" is the busy world of the "liberal arts" or simply our everyday "world," with its various spurious substitutes for true freedom. But both are inescapable for us, and we should put them in complicated conversation with one another. Doing so forces us to confront a terrible dilemma: how to understand ourselves as both *called* and *free*?

In our world today, the language of freedom has become simultaneously supremely valued and profoundly counterfeited. We typically confuse it with something like economic or consumeristic *choice*, the shallow selection of prefabricated products presented for our (also prefabricated) transient satisfaction. Focusing on "choice" typically leads to two deformations: one, an economic reductionism, whereby any agency must be (mis)represented in the language of consumerism to be recognized as agency; the other, a moralistic camouflage, wherein all impediments to agency such as inegalitarianism, exploitation, and hierarchical domination are concealed from the self-understanding of the choosing agent. Equating freedom with choice obscures from us the preconditions of our situation and can camouflage the challenges we face in situations of real sociopolitical complexity.[20]

So far so typical; jeremiads against choice are a dime a dozen these days. But "choice" not only ridiculously simplifies our experience of freedom but also obscures how modern life cultivates in us profound senses of obligation alongside, and perhaps within, a deeper sense of agency. Today, we largely all believe that we are all "one humanity," that we *ought* to concern ourselves for everyone's well-being, that we ought to care for all people *equally*, and that it is not charity but obligation to do so—these are astonishing moral beliefs, not often enough recognized. It is a fascinating kind of obligation that has

[19] See David S. Cunningham, "Colleges Have Callings, Too: Vocational Reflection at the Institutional Level," in *Vocation across the Academy: A New Vocabulary for Higher Education*, ed. David S. Cunningham (New York: Oxford University Press, 2017), 249–71.

[20] For a recent analysis of this distorting effect of "choice," see Hartmut Rosa, *Social Acceleration: A New Theory of Modernity* (New York: Columbia University Press, 2015).

taken hold of our collective souls.[21] How are we to relate *this* enormous expansion of our sense of moral obligation to our equally voluble insistence on our moral freedom? In this way, the language of "choice" may itself obscure how our moral projects in the world are more authentically ours when experienced as not liberating but obligating us.

Thus, one central task of college students' lives, central to college's purpose and central to our common life, is to help us understand both how we are *called*, obligated, and bound and how we are also *free*, liberated from false ways of life and empowered to become what we are not yet, empowered in a way involving our own deepest agency. We are asked to live with as rich a sense of purpose, and as little inauthenticity, as possible, and to help others do the same. College should be a site for interrogating that understanding, and a special (but not unique) site for repeated bouts, across the whole life course, of direct and sustained reflection upon those conditions, naming and confronting the various ways they are manifest in our lives.[22] This is no little matter, for your greatest liberation and your deepest obligations are at stake here: in higher education, you are invited to discern *what your obligations are* and you are being taught *how to be free*, and those two tasks are in some radical and interesting tension.[23]

The formation that universities and colleges offer is not for students alone; it can influence society more broadly. The university can "inform public discourse" in part by opening itself as a site for others not entering adulthood but well along its path, to "retreat" from their everyday, reconsider the path they are on, and perhaps reform their character and their aims. This society-wide formation is not a small thing; people across the life course need to think through these challenges—they take different shapes and the pieces bear different relations to one another, at different times. Can higher education help with this task, cultivating a central common good for all adults, not just those in their twenties? I think it can.

---

[21] What Charles Taylor has called "The Drive to Reform" is a good example of this; see *A Secular Age* (Cambridge, MA: Harvard University Press, 2007), 61–63.

[22] On rethinking freedom, I have learned much, recently, from Zadie Smith, *Feel Free* (New York: Penguin, 2018) and Maggie Nelson, *On Freedom: Four Songs of Care and Constraint* (Minneapolis: Graywolf Press, 2021).

[23] See again David Matzko McCarthy's discussion of the claim others have on us as part of vocational calling in chapter 1 of this volume.

The liberal arts and *one* common good: formation across the life course

Understanding higher education as the privileged site for hosting the confrontation between freedom and obligation teaches us that higher education's contribution to the common good need not only be a matter of forming twenty-somethings; it can also help adults across the entire life course confront this tension in their own lives. After all, especially today, vocation is never settled once and for all; we must repeatedly undertake re-formation, reevaluating our freedoms and obligations. By seeing "college education" as a lifelong practice of such reassessment within a community expressly dedicated to this work, we understand the full nature of the challenge before us and the enormously constructive function that the liberal arts provides. "The university" has typically thought about itself as a *nursery*, but perhaps it can also be not a *nursing home* or *retirement community* (as many universities seem to think they can be these days, for financial reasons), but instead a *retreat center*: a liminal space that hosts and curates our repeated processes of (re)formation and the ongoing project of finding meaning and purpose throughout one's life. In this way, universities can uniquely serve the common good of everyone, across the lifespan.

The opening of this function for universities is due to dramatic changes in humanity's conditions, especially our demographics. As humans live longer and birthrates decline, the population shape has changed from a "pyramid" (with each generation larger than the one before) to a "column" at best, with population stability, and perhaps even a shrinking population. This process, happening at different speeds around the globe, is called the "demographic transition."[24] We are moving from being a fundamentally *young* species to a fundamentally *middle-aged* one. Most of the time, higher education thinks about the demographic transition in terms of economic challenges, related to shrinking student populations. That is a real short-term problem. But there are long-term opportunities too, which will reward serious creative reflection. If we expand our understanding of the nature of college as I suggest here, to include different kinds of "student" at our institutions, we will not

---

[24] See Tim Dyson, *Population and Development: The Demographic Transition* (New York: Zed Books, 2010). This global challenge will take different forms in different places; see Kavita Sivaramakrishnan, *As the World Ages: Rethinking a Demographic Crisis* (Cambridge, MA: Harvard University Press, 2018). On the demographic crisis of declining college-age populations in the United States, see Nathan D. Grawe, *Demographics and the Demand for Higher Education* (Baltimore, MD: Johns Hopkins University Press, 2018).

destabilize the central purpose of higher education but enrich and complicate it in potentially transformative ways.

Today, people of all ages seem to need the kind of opportunities for reassessment and reflection that colleges and universities provide. A recent report from Stanford University's Center on Longevity, "The New Map of Life," notes that modern civilization has what it calls a "pacing problem": all "training" is front-loaded in early adulthood, middle age is overstuffed with career concerns, childrearing, and often elder care, while people beyond middle age find that their obligations and hence sense of purpose are increasingly elusive. As Laura Carstensen put it, "Thirty years were added to average life expectancy in the 20th century, and rather than imagine the scores of ways we could use these years to improve quality of life, we tacked them all on at the end. Only old age got longer." In response, the report recommends that education be reconsidered as "a lifelong project rather than a sprint crammed into childhood and early adulthood."[25] It recommends this not to replace the university's formational task for young adults, but to amplify and complement that task by enabling its analogs for people after young adulthood.

So conceived, "formation" would be a continually ongoing project, a matter of repeated practices of reconsidering the shape of one's life commitments. This would have major implications for the future of higher education. First, it would put tremendous pressure on the curricular structures that typically organize higher education today. One might imagine multiple periods of formal, institution-based reconsideration, for a week or a month or a semester or more, scattered throughout one's life. The fixed structure of a four-year curriculum could not contain such a practice; it would require curricular structures simultaneously much more finite and modular and much more open-ended than our typical semester or trimester curricular structure currently allows. What would it mean, for instance, for someone to never be "done" with their college education? Taking that question seriously, and not just as a bit of commencement rhetoric, is likely to have transformative structural consequences for higher education as a whole, and for the liberal arts' relationship to the common good.

---

[25] See Laura Carstensen, "We Need a Major Redesign of Life," *Washington Post*, November 29, 2019, https://www.washingtonpost.com/opinions/we-need-a-major-redesign-of-life/2019/11/29/a63daab2-1086-11ea-9cd7-a1becbc82f5e_story.html. See also "The New Map of Life," Stanford Center on Longevity, April 2022, https://longevity.stanford.edu/the-new-map-of-life-report/. See also Warren C. Sanderson and Sergei Scherbov, *Prospective Longevity: A New Vision of Population Aging* (Cambridge, MA: Harvard University Press, 2019).

Second, such a practice of lifelong formation would alter the *content* of what we think of as teaching and learning. Encountering these "students" would repeatedly reopen the question of an adult relationship to one's values, beliefs, and practices, but it would also ask questions that young adults cannot yet imagine. Indeed, it would likely provoke questions that we educators have not imagined, such as how our teaching might be repurposed or reoriented to help people reconsider the values and practices they have more or less self-consciously held for decades. Unlike the current young adult constituency at the center of our attention, these other potential participants are not readily mistaken simply for younger versions of ourselves; often we will be younger than them, and I suspect we teachers would have to listen in new ways to the questions they bring to us. It would clearly enrich our reconsiderations of the relationship between obligation and freedom, but it asks a great deal of our teaching to manage both constituencies simultaneously. How might their presence press us to redesign our curricular practices, our curricula, our campus cultures?[26]

Third and finally, incorporating this population into our institutions would have an enormously enriching and challenging effect on the young adults around them, and on the faculty attempting to help them on their way. Today, as traditionally constituted, both sides of our current educational system are well established and know their places: there are teachers and there are students. We say that we want to "destabilize" the classroom, make everyone an "active learner," and we talk about the need for teachers always to be students; but while each of these propositions is true, our sincerity only goes so far. The encounter with a new set of participants in higher education, who are their teachers' contemporaries, perhaps their elders and definitely not their children, may shift the educational experience; these participants will be less likely to take for granted the opportunities afforded by the classroom than their younger classmates, and will likely destabilize entrenched pedagogical patterns, which could produce much more interesting learning for all. At other times, it will be useful for the young adults and the life course participants to have separate spaces dedicated to their diverse purposes and for educators to manage their needs and expectations in less intersectional ways.

---

[26] Consider the various discussions throughout the volume about how we might reimagine our campuses, programs, and courses when we situate our vocations in response to a collective call, in particular chapter 1 by David Matzko McCarthy, chapter 7 by Jonathan Golden, and chapter 11 by Robert J. Pampel.

Such a transformation in our student body might also help universities think better about their core mission in a situation where the shape of human life, and the contours of human society, has quite significantly changed from what it ever was before. The main aim of the university would stay stable—it would be a distinct site, set somewhat apart from everyday social life, where people can step out of the flow of the immanent; find the space and time to engage fundamental issues, with expert assistance; and ask basic questions about the shape and nature of their lives, especially the relationship between freedom and obligation within it. But thinking about this challenge will compel college educators to reconsider some basic questions about our vocations and as adults seeking to make sense of our own lives. To imagine a university as a place where such conversations could happen is a way to imagine a future for what the "liberal arts" are and what they teach us about vocation and the common good. Such imagining both is anchored in our received practices of teaching and learning and reaches beyond them toward a vision of higher education that is more profoundly inclusive of the whole human experience, and even of the whole human family—past, present, and even future.

All of this could help transform higher education to address a common, growing, and vital need: the need for human formation and re-formation across the life course. We all need this formation—it is as common a good as humans have. This service to the common good—this work of formation—is what the liberal arts already implicitly do; all I have argued here is that it should be undertaken with a greater degree of self-consciousness than heretofore imagined. Doing so makes us more adept in cultivating virtue and joy and working toward an always-revitalized understanding of the balance of freedom and obligation in each of our lives, individually and communally. In doing so, we help everyone—educators, students, communities, society as a whole—see some aspects of life with greater clarity. We also thereby understand how this calling for formation—the liberal arts' most core vocation—serves the common good in an irreplaceable way.

Epilogue

Toward an Ecology of the Common Good: Vocation in the Gaps

Erin VanLaningham

In the course of writing this book, many of the authors visited George Floyd Square, on the corner of East Thirty-Eighth Street and Chicago Avenue in Minneapolis, Minnesota, where George Floyd was murdered on May 25, 2020. We arrived on an August afternoon and were met upon our approach by Jay Webb, a community leader whose unofficial role as caretaker of the intersection was apparent when he welcomed us and thanked us for coming to "stand in the gap." He invited all of us to plant rescued plants in the garden at the center of the square encircling a sculpture of a "Black Power" fist.[1] After learning that we were educators, he invited us to repeat iterations of this phrase: "It doesn't matter who you are, it matters who you want to be, what kind of professor you want to be, what you want the world to be." He then gifted us with packages of seeds—wildflowers, herbs, sunflowers—to take with us to plant when we returned to our home communities.

This communal experience of encountering a place of injustice, violence, loss, and grief and being met with an invitation to stand in that gap and plant with others was transformative on many levels. As we planted, we knew we were standing in the gap of the sacramental, profound, and symbolic. The makeshift roundabout, built of cinder blocks and fading mulch, necessitated that every approaching car had to pause and consider the square, another invitation to stand in the gap. We saw visitor after visitor welcomed by Jay as they carried plants to the intersection. We hoped for growth not just for that place but for the wider web of relationships and communities that brought us there. We felt again the urgency and necessity of reaching toward a collective purpose.

---

[1] Laurel Bandy and William Domeier, "'This Circle Is about Healing': Gardener Sees Himself as Caretaker of the Energy at George Floyd's Square," Minnesota Public Radio, December 31, 2020, https://www.mprnews.org/story/2020/12/31/gardener-sees-himself-as-caretaker-of-the-energy-at-george-floyds-square.

Erin VanLaningham, *Epilogue* In: *Called Beyond Our Selves.* Edited by: Erin VanLaningham, Oxford University Press.

The contributors to this volume have intentionally emphasized the ecology of the common good throughout their chapters, attending to aspects of place, environment, and connected relationships. In what follows, I develop the ways that ecologies of the common good can help us see with more clarity our interconnectedness. There is a crisis of belief in the common good, made evident by the forces that continually drive us apart—poverty, antisemitism, transphobia, White supremacy, sexism, and any number of other threats to our common human dignity. Yet, we believe that a "we" can still be a "we," and that in our work as educators, we can hold space for our differences and see them as catalysts that strengthen an ecology of the common good.

Sustainable growth

We have used the language of ecology purposefully because referencing communities of interdependent life invites us to widen the aperture of our perspectives. Ecology contains an impulse toward inclusivity and asks us to see the breadth of reality including what is within and beneath and beyond our immediate grasp. Our authors capture ways to amplify, enrich, restore, and rebuild the bonds of our interconnectedness. So too does ecology show us the power of overturning, of decay, of curating, of new life. Ecology has a dynamism to pull us forward into change, into a deep meeting of collective and individual hungers and joys.[2]

The prior chapters provide models and practices for realizing the common good as a context for vocational purpose, paying close attention to injustice and the needs of strangers and neighbors alike. The contributors bring forward specific instances of collective life that highlight our lived ecologies. As emphasized in the introduction to the volume, "the meeting place" of vocation and the common good is a place of flourishing for all, made manifest in how we dwell together. It is in this spirit that we close this volume with a more direct emphasis on the ecological: the principles of "deep ecology," the overlap between economy and ecology, the cultivation of a home place, and the role of community gardens and gardeners. We hope that the authors' attention to the common good in discerning one's callings reveals our relationships within ecosystems and communities.

[2] Frederick Buechner's now iconic definition of vocation—"the place where your deep gladness and the world's deep hunger meet"—is evoked throughout the volume. See *Wishful Thinking: A Seeker's ABC*, rev. ed. (New York: Harper Collins, 1993), 119.

Deepening the ecology of the common good

Many of our authors note that it is interdependence and mutuality that allow us to discern and respond to calls of the common good. Ecologist Rick Landroth highlights the relationships both *among* organisms and *between* organisms and their natural environment, suggesting that "the essence of ecology is the interactions (connections) that run the world." When we stop to consider such ecological interactions—often visually indicated by arrows between organisms—our interconnected purposes as well as disconnections and conflicts emerge.[3] Teaching vocational exploration can and should draw explicitly from these arrows or interactions while attending to what writer Gary Snyder calls "the fundamental questions of who we are, how we exist, and where we belong."[4]

Unpacking the ecology of the common good also identifies crisis, decay, diminishment, death, and even a common "bad." Ecological thinking makes clear that any threat to one component in the life system will invariably affect all members of the community. The fractures across relationships and upon the planet shift and change our collective experience. The power of this interdependence is that it compels us to evolve together, to be more sustainable, to be better fitted for responding to the calls of others.

This observation resonates with the field of "deep" ecology, echoed in the contributors' references to the deep gladness, as well as the deep divides and suffering that bring forward our understanding of vocation in our relationship to the world's deep hungers. Deep ecology sees "the identities of all things—whether at the level of elementary particles, organisms, or galaxies—as logically interconnected: all things are constituted by their relations with other things."[5] Attending to the "deep" reality, experience, and understanding of our interconnectedness, we can help students see their call to be deeply within the world, not beyond, outside of, or disconnected from it.[6] This is a maturation into vocational purpose, a realization of one's "ecological self."[7] Our authors promote the nuanced ways one's individual

---

[3] Rick Landroth, email message shared with the author, September 15, 2022.

[4] Gary Snyder, "Ecology, Place, and the Awakening of Compassion," in *The Deep Ecology Movement: An Introductory Anthology*, ed. Alan Drengson and Yuichi Inoue (Berkeley, CA: North Atlantic Books, 1995), 238–39.

[5] Freya Mathews, "Conservation and Self-Realization: A Deep Ecology Perspective," in Drengson and Inoue, eds., *The Deep Ecology Movement*, 126.

[6] Arne Naess, "Self-Realization: An Ecological Approach to Being in the World," in Drengson and Inoue, eds., *The Deep Ecology Movement*, 27–28.

[7] See the discussion of the ecological self in the introduction of this volume, p. 15.

purpose is constituted within and given shape by a collective purpose that values diversity.

Climate scientist Katharine Hayhoe's suggestions on how to talk about climate change may apply helpfully to a conversation with students about the inherent interconnectedness of vocation and the common good. She suggests we "start with what you like to do" and "talk about what you love" and "bring up what you grow and eat" and show how "we already care" for the environment.[8] In other words, our ecological selves are not different versions of self but authentic selves that are more completely situated within relationships. When we talk about what we do, what we love, what nourishes us, and what we care about, we are talking about our embeddedness within the world. We live within and are dependent upon larger structures that connect us to each other and the environment.

Ecology and economy

Our authors have made regular reference to aspects of ecology through the language of membership, sustainable vocations, responsibility to neighbor, friendship, formation, and placebuilding. It is our hope that we capture what theologian Kiara Jorgenson points to as the "embodied form" of vocation that links our callings to "real-life consequences of relationship."[9] As we close this volume, we wish to emphasize the very real connection between ecology and economy.

Aldo Leopold, author of *A Sand County Almanac*, defines ecology as "animal economics," a study of the "home range" of the living things on his farm.[10] He describes the process of sawing an old oak tree while recounting the land's history, including the political and economic choices that affected the land.[11] More recently, writer and activist Wendell Berry argues that we might intervene in the climate crisis "in ways that are neighborly, convivial, and generous, but also . . . practical and economic."[12] As students explore who they are in relationship to others and what it means to dwell together

---

[8] Katharine Hayhoe, *Saving Us: A Climate Scientist's Case for Hope and Healing in a Divided World* (New York: One Signal/Atria, 2021), 25–27, 33.

[9] Kiara A. Jorgenson, *Ecology of Vocation: Recasting Calling in a New Planetary Era* (New York: Lexington Books, 2020), 130.

[10] Aldo Leopold, *A Sand County Almanac* (New York: Oxford University Press, 1949), 80–81.

[11] Leopold, *Almanac*, 6–18.

[12] Wendell Berry, *Our Only World* (Berkeley, CA: Counterpoint Press, 2015), 63.

in local and global environs, they are engaged in learning about what it means to be a part of a house (*oikos*). Ecology (*oikos logos*) and economy (*oikos nomos*) together direct us to questions of how to manage and steward the house. This overlap between ecology and economy is not hard to tease out from humanity's evident marks on the earth, including even those that are sealed within the rings of an oak. Such vocational discernment is a study of one's situatedness and place in an ecology and economy, considering all aspects of a collective place, from our immediate families to our extended and global networks. Tracing vocational pathways reveals a deeper sense of connection to and responsibility for others.

Choices of economy and ecology involve all of us. Political philosopher Danielle Allen's example is helpful here: "When citizens find themselves newly jobless as a result of collective decisions and accept their losses without violence or rebellion, they grant their fellow citizens stability, a gift of no small account. Are they owed something in return? If so, what? And by whom? Citizens who benefit from the stable polity find themselves, on this view, in debt to the newly jobless."[13] Presenting the lived experiences of economic reality in these terms shows the precarities and the complexities of our interconnectedness. An ecology of the common good includes such economic dimensions of our vocations and mutual dependence, as explored in many of the volume's chapters.

What are we called to do as members of this commons? This volume suggests we are called to intervene to best nurture communal well-being and our common home. Intervention ecology challenges idealistic notions of restoration ecology that try to "preserve or recreate imagined Edens" and privilege historic conditions over present or future possibilities and concerns. Intervention accentuates the relationship between humans and their environment best seen in the identification of certain "leverage points . . . where a small change could lead to a large shift in behavior."[14] The contributors present such leverage points that specifically embrace diversity and the uncommon to shift the environment and, hopefully, shift vocational perspectives. In such mutuality, the chapters resonate with environmental biologist Robin Kimmerer's framework of "reciprocal restoration" in our

---

[13] Danielle S. Allen, *Talking to Strangers: Anxieties of Citizenship since* Brown v. Board of Education (Chicago: University of Chicago Press, 2004), 45.

[14] Richard J. Hobbs, Lauren M. Hallett, Paul R. Ehrlich, and Harold A. Mooney, "Intervention Ecology: Applying Ecological Science in the Twenty-First Century," *Bioscience* 61, no. 6 (2011): 442–50, https://doi.org/10.1525/bio.2011.61.6.6.

emphasis on growth through dialogue and shared spaces.[15] It is the reciprocity between self and other, person and environment, that we highlight in vocational discernment.

By intervening in the dominant narratives of success and fostering collective flourishing, our authors suggest that our institutions are also part of this ecology of the common good, as well as the common bad. Universities are connected to communities, and we have been cognizant throughout the volume of the various forces and realities that our campuses and neighborhoods face daily. These include the rising cost of college along with the perceived lack of value in an undergraduate education by at least half of Americans.[16] The ecology of the common good necessitates that we respond to the very real concerns of students and parents so that we can evolve together, expanding what the value of an education can be. As Jeffrey Selingo suggests in *College (Un)bound*, it is a chance to reframe what education is for—"how rigorously colleges prepare students for the workforce, as well as mature them for life, will play a greater role in the calculation of value."[17] The argument of this volume is that student formation in conjunction with their preparation for contributing to their communities and the workforce is part of vocational discernment for the common good.

Home places

This book proposes greater attention to what it means to expand borders, work toward transformation of self and systems, and extend love and compassion. These themes all point toward creating a sense of belonging, a safe space in which all can thrive. Many of our authors situate vocation within place—campuses, communities, historical landscapes, environments—prompting us to think more expansively and precisely about our shared life in a common home.[18] Theologian Norman Wirzba, drawing from Stan Rowe, suggests replacing "environment" with "home place." He writes, "A home place more clearly communicates that the memberships of life do

---

[15] Quoted in Mari Elise Ewing, "Making a Place for People in Ecological Restoration," *Ecology* 93, no. 8 (2012): 1981–82.

[16] Jeffrey J. Selingo, *College (Un)bound: The Future of Higher Education and What It Means for Students* (Las Vegas, NV: Amazon Publishing, 2013), 71.

[17] Selingo, *College (Un)bound*, 71.

[18] Francis, *Laudato si': On Care for Our Common Home: Encyclical Letter* (Huntington, IN: Our Sunday Visitor, 2015).

not merely surround us . . . but inspire and interpenetrate."[19] In *The Home Place: Memoirs of a Colored Man's Love Affair with Nature*, ornithologist J. Drew Lanham describes his family's land and his childhood experiences on it as "ghosts I conjure up from time to time to help me understand who I am and perhaps recapture who I need to be."[20] A home place can be both individual and collective, allowing us to connect, or reconnect, with self and others and affording us ways to think differently about the practices and paradigms that govern our choices.

Bringing the idea of vocational discernment "home" in this context is not a way to separate it from the world but to extend our notion of care and obligation outward while also prioritizing an engagement with vocation in our local environment. As ecologist William Cronon argues, our fascination with the concept of the "wilderness" at times teaches us to disregard the complexity within our home environments, to the detriment of our valuing of the diversity of all environments.[21] This is particularly helpful when we talk with students about vocation, allowing dreams and possibilities to touch down in our backyards, classrooms, and campuses, prompting us to see that a connection to the here and now is part of our call to collective life.

Prioritizing the local includes political, agricultural, and social movements in communities and on our campuses. Breaking open idealized notions of home to allow for an ecological understanding of our relationships within these places and our calls to care for and contribute to them means that we see ourselves as pieces of a whole rather than singular forces. As theologian Kiara Jorgenson suggests, "Part of what it means to be human is to partner with pollinators. That is, the moral nature of our anthropologies must adopt an adaptive ethic beginning with local experience while not being limited to it. To live out vocation, we must hear what our place has to say and respond in the most considerate and conserving manner."[22]

The issues of land management as well as land acknowledgments, invasive species as well as endangered species, cause us to consider what it means to be violating or contributing to, threatened or nourished by, our environments.

---

[19] Norman Wirzba, *Food and Faith: A Theology of Eating* (Cambridge: Cambridge University Press, 2011), 60.

[20] J. Drew Lanham, *The Home Place: Memoirs of a Colored Man's Love Affair with Nature* (Minneapolis, MN: Milkweed, 2016), 33.

[21] William Cronon, "The Trouble with Wilderness; or, Getting Back to the Wrong Nature," in *Uncommon Ground: Rethinking the Human Place in Nature*, ed. William Cronon (New York: W. W. Norton, 1995), 69–90.

[22] Kiara A. Jorgenson, *Ecology of Vocation: Recasting Calling in a New Planetary Era* (New York: Lexington Books, 2020), 145.

The language of an ecosystem, rather than an ecology, can suggest a resistance to "outsiders." The complexities of adaptation in the context of the common good are important to emphasize here, embracing the stranger and the uncommon as part of our ecology. Thus, the ways we seek to uplift and promote an ecology of the common good can emphasize the connections within our common home, and the possibility for all to grow and develop within this interdependence.

Furthermore, as we consider the call to the common good within a framework of home, we acknowledge that home can be fraught and fragmented, evocative of belonging, fear, or estrangement. For example, race scholar Imani Perry captures the many layers of calling a place "home" in her exploration of Birmingham, Alabama, explaining that "home for the Southerner eases into the cracked places like Alaga, thick and dark sugarcane syrup."[23] Within the cracks, within the "warmth and charm" of the South rest the realities of trauma: "Murderous home, sweet home, old home week, home."[24]

As curators and caretakers of a common home, reckoning with the systems and histories upon which we have built our common life and recognizing our bonds to others, means seeing the deep vulnerability and strengths of our common ecology. Inviting students to investigate the home place in its many forms is a way to draw forth vocations for the common good, connecting our purpose with that of others, seeing that collective purpose embedded in a place.

Gardens and gardeners

The campus of an urban university just three miles from George Floyd Square features a vibrant neighborhood garden with over sixty plots, farmed by gardeners from the upper Midwest alongside those from Ethiopia, Somalia, Mexico, and Vietnam. The garden serves as a meeting point for anyone seeking green space in the city and shares a larger plot of campus land with the modern academic building that houses religion, business, and science (a center of ecology and economy).[25] Many college campuses, local neighborhoods, and urban rooftops have shared gardens, working

---

[23] Imani Perry, *South to America: A Journey below the Mason Dixon to Understand the Soul of a Nation* (New York: Ecco, 2022), 155

[24] Perry, *South to America*, 155.

[25] Augsburg University is home to the Medtronic Foundation Community Garden, which provides "a space for the community to come and learn together; beautify the neighborhood and campus; provide growing space for those without it; and to assist gardeners in providing themselves a healthy

in collaboration with local communities to grow food for the college, for neighbors, and for food banks, while simultaneously building ties to the neighborhood. Many colleges work with local farmers to source food for their dining halls and teach and practice sustainable agriculture. Gardens can be literal embodiments of collective well-being, places to meet and dwell with others.

Of course, anyone who has ever put their hands in the ground or tended to a plot understands that gardening is also that exercise in failure, facing "our own fragility, vulnerability, and ignorance."[26] Gardening, in the real and not ideal sense, asks us to "turn one's life into various forms of service that will strengthen and maintain the many memberships that make up the garden. It is to give up the much-trumpeted goal of modern and post-modern life— individual autonomy—and instead live the life of care and responsible inter-dependence."[27] Within our local ecologies we can see that living vocations within the common good is living into both a radical and everyday practice. It is also a practice that invites the reflective pause and patient waiting, the reverence for forces beyond and beneath, the hope and space for growth. As we tend the vocations of others in our homes and communities, we realize our own embodied vocations.

The contributors of this volume have made apparent in their various chapters that nurturing vocation for the common good is an active response to others. As authors and collaborators on this volume, we have felt acutely that our embodiment as writers—as individuals and a collective—has been purposefully situated in this time and place. We have gathered through the COVID-19 pandemic, in moments and locations of significant trauma and loss, and responded to our local campus and community needs and to the common work of this project.

The ecology of the common good invites a deep responsibility and care for others that we ought to emphasize again and again with students. The work, the science, the symbol, the fruits, and the failures of gardening can aid in our attempts to illustrate such membership. As we think about what it means to tend, to plant, to weed, to cultivate, to harvest, to let lie fallow, we can imagine our vocational purpose in action.

---

diet." The campus also features the Hagfor Center for Science, Business, and Religion building. See https://www.augsburg.edu/green/2017/11/13/big-changes-at-the-augsburg-community-garden.

[26] Wirzba, *Food and Faith*, 51.
[27] Wirzba, *Food and Faith*, 51.

At the intersections and in the gaps: vocation and
the common good

The intersection of George Floyd Square is just a few blocks from an empty city lot that has been made into a memorial cemetery for Black lives claimed by police violence. In that public space, at the time of our visit, there was an empty folding chair, with George Floyd's name spray painted upon it, as well as a fence with multiple hanging signs and fabric murals calling for defunding the police and prayers for healing a broken city, and one large one that read "the 8ᵗʰ wonder of the world is Us." That intersection of anger and sadness, prayers for the world, and a call to action crystallized for our group and countless others what it means to stand at the intersections and in the gaps of the common good, invited to respond to the call of place and neighbor. In the gaps, we might realize our vocations for collective healing and well-being.

The invitation into the work of planting, bearing witness, and pausing together was an experience of the meeting of individual and collective calls. And while many have seen the work of educators as the work of cultivating hope and empowering others, it is important for all of us engaged in talking with students about vocational purpose to draw forward examples, experiences, and images of what it means to make collective well-being a priority. We can listen to the noise of the meeting place and intersection of suffering and possibility. We can heed the messages of murals on urban walls in communities signaling a call for justice.[28] We can literally get our hands dirty in the work of the world. The ecology of a common good, then, means, as Martin Luther King Jr. suggests, to live creatively in "the world house."[29] This house as home place and garden, reflecting the deep sense of hope and purpose, calls us beyond our selves to each other in our common life.

[28] For more about the impact of murals and urban street art see the "George Floyd and Anti-Racist Street Art Archive" and the Urban Art Mapping project based at the University of St. Thomas in St. Paul, Minnesota: https://www.urbanartmapping.org/.
[29] See the final chapter of Martin Luther King Jr.'s *Where Do We Go from Here: Chaos or Community?* (New York: Harper & Row, 1967), 166–91.

Index of Names

For the benefit of digital users, indexed terms that span two pages (e.g., 52–53) may, on occasion, appear on only one of those pages.

Index of Subjects

For the benefit of digital users, indexed terms that span two pages (e.g., 52–53) may, on occasion, appear on only one of those pages.

Figures are indicated by *f* following the page number